T0238695

Communications in Computer and Information Science 812

Commenced Publication in 2007
Founding and Former Series Editors:
Alfredo Cuzzocrea, Xiaoyong Du, Orhun Kara, Ting Liu, Dominik Ślęzak,
and Xiaokang Yang

More information about this series at http://www.springer.com/series/7899

Jianzhong Li · Huadong Ma
Keqiu Li · Li Cui
Limin Sun · Zenghua Zhao
Xiaofei Wang (Eds.)

Wireless Sensor Networks

11th China Wireless Sensor Network
Conference, CWSN 2017
Tianjin, China, October 12–14, 2017
Revised Selected Papers

 Springer

Editors

Jianzhong Li
Harbin Institute of Technology
Harbin
China

Huadong Ma
Beijing University of Posts
  and Telecommunications
Beijing
China

Keqiu Li
Tianjin University
Tianjin, Tianjin
China

Li Cui
Chinese Academy of Sciences
Beijing
China

Limin Sun
Chinese Academy of Sciences
Beijing
China

Zenghua Zhao
Tianjin University
Tianjin
China

Xiaofei Wang
Tianjin University
Tianjin
China

ISSN 1865-0929   ISSN 1865-0937   (electronic)
Communications in Computer and Information Science
ISBN 978-981-10-8122-4   ISBN 978-981-10-8123-1   (eBook)
https://doi.org/10.1007/978-981-10-8123-1

Library of Congress Control Number: 2018934338

Printed on acid-free paper

This Springer imprint is published by the registered company Springer Nature
Singapore Pte Ltd. part of Springer Nature
The registered company address is: 152 Beach Road, #21-01/04 Gateway East, Singapore 189721, Singapore

Preface

The China Wireless Sensor Network Conference (CWSN) is an annual conference sponsored by the China Computer Federation (CCF). The 11th China Wireless Sensor Network Conference (CWSN2017) was cosponsored by the China Computer Federation Technical Committee on Internet of Things and took place at Tianjin University, China. The theme of CWSN2017 was "The Era of the Internet of Things: State of the Art, Opportunities, and Challenges." CWSN is a premier event that aims to provide a high-level forum to bring together academic researchers, engineering professionals, and industry experts to exchange information, share achievements, and discuss future developments on various topics related to wireless sensor networks, which will promote the research and technical innovation in these fields.

The papers contained in these proceedings address challenging issues in energy-efficient network infrastructure, network architecture, wireless communication systems and protocols, power control and management, resource management, positioning and location-based services, new models of sensor usage, sensor data storage, retrieval, processing and management, quality of service, fault tolerance and reliability, experience with real-world applications, security and privacy, software development, testing and debugging tools as well as simulation environments, sensor data quality, integrity and trustworthiness, performance modeling and analysis, cyber-physical systems (CPS), as well as Internet of Things.

This book constitutes the refereed proceedings of the 11th China Wireless Sensor Network Conference (CWSN 2017), held in Tianjin, China, during October 12–14, 2017. The 29 revised full papers were carefully reviewed and selected from 213 submissions. Each submission received around three reviews, and for those recommended for CCIS, we further improved the technical quality and the language with one more careful review round. In these proceedings, papers are organized in topical sections on wireless sensor networks, energy efficiency and harvesting, privacy and security, cloud computing and virtualization, and mobile computing and services.

November 2017

Jianzhong Li
Huadong Ma
Keqiu Li
Li Cui
Limin Sun
Zenghua Zhao
Xiaofei Wang

Organization

CWSN 2017 (the 11th China Wireless Sensor Network Conference) was sponsored by CCF, cosponsored by the China Computer Federation Technical Committee on Internet of Things, and organized by Tianjin University, China.

Conference Chairs

Jianzhong Li   Harbin Institute of Technology, China
Keqiu Li   Tianjin University, China

Honorary Chair

Hao Dai   Chinese Academy of Engineering, China

Technical Program Committee Chairs

Huadong Ma   Beijing University of Posts and Telecommunications
Li Cui   Chinese Academy of Sciences
Bin Wu   Tianjin University, China

Technical Program Committee Co-chair

Xiaofei Wang   Tianjin University, China

Best Paper Award Chair

Xue Wang   Tsinghua University, China

Outstanding Young Research Workshop Chair

Limin Sun   Chinese Academy of Sciences, China

University Education of IoT Workshop Chairs

Huadong Ma   Beijing University of Posts and Telecommunications, China
Ming Bao   Chinese Academy of Sciences, China

Local Organization Chairs

Zenghua Zhao   Tianjin University, China
Wenyuan Tao   Tianjin University, China

Technical Program Committee

Gaotao Shi	Tianjin University, China
Chunfeng Liu	Tianjin University, China
Xiaobo Zhou	Tianjin University, China
Lei Zhang	Tianjin University, China
Yajun Yang	Tianjin University, China
Chung-Ming Own	Tianjin University, China

Program Committee

Guangwei Bai	Nanjing Technology University, China
Ming Bao	The Institute of Acoustics of the Chinese Academy of Sciences, China
Shaobin Cai	Harbin Engineering University, China
Qingsong Cai	Beijing Technology and Business University, China
Bin Cao	Harbin Institute of Technology, China
Canfeng Chen	Nokia Research Center, China
Xi Chen	State Grid Information & Telecommunication Company Ltd., China
Xiaojiang Chen	Northwest University, China
Zhikui Chen	Dalian University of Technology, China
Wei Chen	Beijing Jiaotong University, China
Guihai Chen	Nanjing University, China
Hong Chen	Renmin University of China, China
Jiaxing Chen	Hebei Normal University, China
Yongle Chen	Taiyuan University of Technology, China
Li Cui	Institute of Computing Technology, Chinese Academy of Sciences, China
Xunxue Cui	New Star Research Institute of Applied Technology in Hefei, China
Siyao Cheng	Harbin Institute of Technology, China
Xiaochao Dang	Northwest Normal University, China
Zhidong Deng	Tsinghua University, China
Rong Ding	Beihang University, China
Hongwei Du	Harbin Institute of Technology Shenzhen Graduate School, China
Yong Fan	Beijing Timeloit Technology Co., Ltd, China
Dingyi Fang	Northwest University, China
Xiufang Feng	Taiyuan University of Technology, China
Deyun Gao	Beijing Jiaotong University, China
Hong Gao	Harbin Institute of Technology, China
Jibing Gong	Yanshan University, China
Zhongwen Guo	Ocean University of China, China
Zhanjun Hao	Northwest Normal University, China
Guangjie Han	Hohai University, China

Yanbo Han	North China University of Technology, China
Daojing He	East China Normal University, China
Shibo He	Zhejiang University, China
Chengquan Hu	Jilin University, China
Yanjun Hu	Anhui University, China
Qiangsheng Hua	Huazhong University of Science and Technology, China
He Huang	Soochow University, China
Liusheng Huang	University of Science and Technology of China, China
Qi Jing	School of Software & Microelectronics, Peking University, China
Jie Jia	Northeastern University, China
Hongbo Jiang	Huazhong University of Science and Technology, China
Bo Jing	Air Force Engineering University, China
Deying Li	Renmin University of China, China
Fangmin Li	Wuhan University of Technology, China
Guanghui Li	Jiangnan University, China
Guorui Li	Northeastern University at Qinhuangdao, China
Hongwei Li	University of Electronic Science and Technology of China, China
Jianbo Li	Qingdao University, China
Jianzhong Li	Harbin Institute of Technology, China
Jie Li	Northeastern University, China
Jinbao Li	Heilongjiang University, China
Shining Li	Northwestern Polytechnical University, China
Renfa Li	Hunan University, China
Xiangyang Li	University of Science and Technology of China, China
Zhetao Li	Xiangtan University, China
Feng Li	Shandong University, China
Hongbin Liang	Southwest Jiaotong University, China
Jiuzhen Liang	Changzhou University, China
Wei Liang	Shenyang Institute of Automation, Chinese Academy of Sciences, China
Yaping Lin	Hunan University, China
Chunfeng Liu	Tianjin University, China
Jiajia Liu	Xidian University, China
Liang Liu	Beijing University of Posts and Telecommunications, China
Min Liu	Institute of Computing Technology, Chinese Academy of Sciences, China
Xingcheng Liu	Sun Yat-sen University, China
Yunhao Liu	Tsinghua University, China
Xiang Liu	Peking University, China
Zhaohua Long	Chongqing University of Posts and Telecommunications, China
Juan Luo	Hunan University, China
Huadong Ma	Beijing University of Posts and Telecommunications, China
Li Ma	North China University of Technology, China

Jian Ma	North Institute of Technology Nanjing Institute of Technology, China
Jianwei Niu	Beihang University, China
Xiaoguang Niu	Wuhan University, China
Jian Peng	Sichuan University, China
Li Peng	Jiangnan University, China
Shaoliang Peng	National University of Defense Technology, China
Wangdong Qi	PLA University of Science and Technology, China
Tie Qiu	Dalian University of Technology, China
Fengyuan Ren	Tsinghua University, China
Shikai Shen	Kunming University, China
Yulong Shen	Xidian University, China
Jian Shu	Nanchang Hangkong University, China
Lijuan Sun	Nanjing University of Posts and Telecommunications, China
Limin Sun	Institute of Information Engineering, Chinese Academy of Sciences, China
Liqin Tian	North China Institute of Science and Technology, China
Xiaohua Tian	Shanghai Jiao Tong University, China
Dan Tao	Beijing Jiaotong University, China
Haisheng Tan	University of Science and Technology of China, China
Yang Tang	University of Science and Technology of China, China
Liangmin Wang	Jiangsu University, China
Ping Wang	Chongqing University of Posts and Telecommunications, China
Ruchuan Wang	Nanjing University of Posts and Telecommunications, China
Xiaodong Wang	National University of Defense Technology, China
Yiding Wang	North China University of Technology, China
Yuexuan Wang	Tsinghua University, China
Zhi Wang	Zhejiang University, China
Zhu Wang	Harbin Institute of Technology at Weihai, China
Kun Wang	Nanjing University of Posts and Telecommunications, China
Xiaoming Wang	Shaanxi Normal University, China
Xinbing Wang	Shanghai Jiao Tong University, China
Xue Wang	Tsinghua University, China
Zhibo Wang	Wuhan University, China
Xiaofei Wang	Tianjin University, China
Hui Wen	Institute of Information Engineering, China
Xiaojun Wu	Shaanxi Normal University, China
Xingjun Wu	Institute of Microelectronics, Tsinghua University, China
Deqin Xiao	South China Agriculture University, China
Fu Xiao	Nanjing University of Posts and Telecommunications, China
Qingjun Xiao	Southeast University of China, China
Yongping Xiong	Beijing University of Posts and Telecommunications, China
Guangtao Xue	Shanghai Jiao Tong University, China
Kun Xie	Hunan University, China
Lei Xie	Nanjing University, China

Contents

Wireless Sensor Networks

Wireless Mote Middleware for Flexible Resource Allocation Validation.   3
   Yanhong Yang, Shaozhong Cao, and Zhongxiang Ding

Improving the Lifetime of Scale-Free Fault Tolerant Topology
for Wireless Sensor Networks.   12
   Rongrong Yin, Haoran Liu, Yinhan Xu, and Xueliang Yin

Target Detection in Sea Clutter Based on ELM.   22
   Wei Jing, Guangrong Ji, Shiyong Liu, Xi Wang, and Ying Tian

Fuzzy-Assisted Event-Based kNN Query Processing in Sensor Networks. . . .   33
   Yinglong Li and Mingqi Lv

A Hierarchical Identity-Based Signcryption Scheme
in Underwater Wireless Sensor Network   44
   Chi Yuan, Wenping Chen, and Deying Li

A Weighted Fuzzy c-Means Clustering Algorithm for Incomplete
Big Sensor Data.   55
   Peng Li, Zhikui Chen, Yueming Hu, Yonglin Leng, and Qiucen Li

Energy Efficiency and Harvesting

Mobile Sink Data Collection Mechanism for Throughput Maximization
with RF Energy Harvesting in WSNs   67
   Yulong Han, Qiuling Tang, Xian Li, and Jiahao Shi

Improved Energy Efficient Adaptive Clustering Routing
Algorithm for WSN.   74
   Guozhi Song, Guoliang Qu, Qing Ma, and Xin Zhang

Energy-Efficient Routing Protocol Based on Probability in DTSN.   86
   Xiong Tang, Dan Sha, Yixiong Bian, Hai-ping Huang, and Min Wu

An Efficient Energy-Hole Alleviating Algorithm for Wireless Sensor
Network Based on Energy-Balanced Clustering Protocol   103
   Weiwei Zhou and Bin Yu

The Maximum and Minimum Ant Colony Optimization Waking Strategy
Based on Multi-Principle and Reprocessing   117
   Wang Pengcheng and Lin Tao

Improved Asynchronous Energy Saving Mechanism with Mesh-Based
Routing for Digital Media Over IEEE 802.15.5-Based Mesh Networks   127
    Li-yong Yuan, Gen-mei Pan, Xing-Ze Xu, Zhen Cheng, and Yi-hua Zhu

Understanding Sensor Data Using Deep Learning Methods
on Resource-Constrained Edge Devices   139
    Junzhao Du, Sicong Liu, Yuheng Wei, Hui Liu, Xin Wang,
    and Kaiming Nan

Data Fusion

The Improved Genetic Algorithms for Multiple Maximum Scatter
Traveling Salesperson Problems   155
    Wenyong Dong, Xueshi Dong, and Yufeng Wang

Online Multi-label Feature Selection on Imbalanced Data Sets   165
    Jing Liu, Zhongwen Guo, Zhongwei Sun, Shiyong Liu,
    and Xupeng Wang

A Clustering Density Weighted Algorithm of KNN Fingerprint Location
Based on Voronoi Diagram   175
    Xiaochao Dang, Yili Hei, and Zhanjun Hao

Detecting Bogus Messages in Vehicular Ad-Hoc Networks: An Information
Fusion Approach.   191
    Jizhao Liu, Heng Pan, Junbao Zhang, Qian Zhang, and Qiusheng Zheng

A Synchronization Detection and Time Delay Estimation Algorithm Based
on Fractional Fourier Transform   201
    Yu Deng, Fei Yuan, En Cheng, Jinwang Yi, and Ye Li

Segment Clustering Based Privacy Preserving Algorithm for Trajectory
Data Publishing   211
    Li Fengyun, Xue Junchao, Sun Dawei, and Gao Yanfang

Direction-of-Arrival Estimation of Near-Field Sources Based
on Two Symmetric Nested Arrays with Enhanced Degrees of Freedom   222
    Shuang Li, Shunren Hu, Wei Liu, Xiaoxiao Jiang, and Wei He

Finding the Minimal Sufficient Set in Causal Graph Under Interventions:
A Dimension Reduction Method for Data Analysis   234
    Mengjiao Pan and Qingsong Cai

Mobile Computing and Social Services

LDA-TIM: An Approach for Individual Sentiment Prediction
in Social Networks 247
   Wenxin Kuang and Ming Zhao

Real-Time Road Traffic State Prediction Based on SVM
and Kalman Filter 262
   Peng Qin, Zhenqiang Xu, Weidong Yang, and Gang Liu

An Efficient Routing Algorithm Based on Interest Similarity
and Trust Relationship Between Users in Opportunistic Networks 273
   Xueyang Qin, Xiaoming Wang, Yaguang Lin, Liang Wang,
   and Lichen Zhang

A Routing Algorithm Based on the Prediction of Node Meeting Location
in Opportunistic Networks 285
   Xinyan Wang, Xiaoming Wang, Lichen Zhang, Yaguang Lin,
   and Ruonan Zhao

A Cooperative Optimization Method for Mobile User Data Offloading 296
   Guangsheng Feng, Dongdong Su, Junyu Lin, Fumin Xia, Hongwu Lv,
   and Huiqiang Wang

Inferring the Most Popular Route Based on Ant Colony Optimization
with Trajectory Data 307
   Hong Zhang, Wei Huangfu, and Xiaoyan Hu

Trust Model Based Uncertainty Analysis Between Multi-path Routes
in MANET Using Subjective Logic 319
   Sohail Muhammad, Liangmin Wang, and Bushra Yamin

SA-Min: An Efficient Algorithm for Minimizing the Spread of Influence
in a Social Network 333
   Yong Liu, Zhe Han, Shengshu Shi, Wei Zhang, and Ping Xuan

Author Index 345

Wireless Sensor Networks

Wireless Mote Middleware for Flexible Resource Allocation Validation

Yanhong Yang[✉], Shaozhong Cao, and Zhongxiang Ding

School of Information Engineering, Beijing Institute of Graphic Communication,
Beijing 102600, China
yangyanhong@bigc.edu.cn

Abstract. The heterogeneity of the available protocols and hardware platforms makes validation in resource allocation a time-consuming and complex work. It needs to involve the hardware platforms, link layer and network layer to verify algorithms. To minimize the unnecessary and repetitive implementation of similar functionalities for different platforms, we present our resource allocation validation (RAV) middleware which supports the discovery of sensor networks and provides flexible resource allocation. RAV enables the user to specify XML-based deployment descriptor which can easily modify from link layer to network layer and customize the configuration of sensors. In the demonstration, three different resource allocation algorithms are tested to deploy a network, to dynamically reconfigure and to monitor the changes.

Keywords: Middleware · Wireless sensor network · Validation

1 Introduction

The different software and hardware platforms in the sensor network create complex work when sensor networks are being deployed and applications being developed. At the same time, developers have to transplant their original design for each platform. For protocol designers and algorithms proposers, it is impossible to test validation for variable platforms. All above is a time-consuming and tedious task which admittedly more stable domains has been addressed by abstracting from the physical view of a system to a logical model and implementing this logical model in terms of a middleware. The general purpose of middleware systems is to provide powerful abstractions providing flexible configuration means for applying it to the real physical environment. The middleware speeds up deployment and standardized APIs.

In the sensor network research, to hide the underlying platform differences middleware is proposed for different WSNs in terms of hardware platforms and Operating System (OS) that runs on all these platforms. However, as the price of wireless sensors decreases rapidly, large numbers of heterogeneous sensors are deployed in different locations around the global. Then, a major challenge is to minimize the deployment effort which is a key cost factor. Global Sensor Networks (GSN) middle-ware [1] provides a uniform platform for fast and flexible integration and deployment of heterogeneous sensor networks. Their work encapsulates protocol implementation, data processing, and web-based management tools. There have been numerous works on

© Springer Nature Singapore Pte Ltd. 2018
J. Li et al. (Eds.): CWSN 2017, CCIS 812, pp. 3–11, 2018.
https://doi.org/10.1007/978-981-10-8123-1_1

middleware for handheld devices. Most of those handheld devices use operating systems like Windows CE, Palm OS, Symbian OS, Tiny Linux, etc. But here we propose middleware for sensors which are smaller than those devices. Especially, our work provides open access to every protocol layers which can easily configure sensor running.

This paper provides a framework for simulations of different platforms. Our work is making the simulations easy for users. Just need to define some configurations in layers for simulation which release developer's burden to transplant their design to different platforms. RAV provides TDMA and CSMA two MAC methods which are very useful for large-scale sensor networks. Our RAV middleware not only cuts cost for deploying sensors but also provide reliable and flexible resource allocation validation platform. Researchers can easily transfer their simulation work into practice and omit the specific details of hardware and protocol stack program implementation. The design of RAV accords the following goals: simplicity, scalability and lightweight implementation.

The rest of this paper is organized as follows. In Sect. 2 discusses some related work in middleware. Then, in Sect. 3 introduces our architecture. Section 4 describes the interfaces of each layer. Section 5 states implementation and discusses demonstration in Sect. 6. Section 7 is dedicated to conclusions.

2   Related Work

The existence of the sensor middleware is to support the connection of the sensor network. Sgroi et al. [2] suggest basic abstractions, a standard set of services, and an API to free application developers from the details of the underlying sensor networks. However, the focus is on definition and classification of abstractions and services, while RAV not only takes a more general view but also provides APIs and complete management infrastructure. Etherios [3] is a machine-to-machine (M2M) platform service that manages different connected devices from one user interface. It works with 3G, Wifi, Zigbee, and 4G networks. The platform is not free and offers its services based on different pricing packs. The WSO2 [4] platform is a middleware platform that is 100% open source. Users can explore and experiment this platform with no licensing costs. Most importantly, users can download and play with the same version that runs in production at no cost. WSO2 not only uses an open source license but also follows an open development process, which customers can observe and provide input into. The WSO2 platform is made up of over 25 products covering all major categories from integration and API management to identity and mobile. All products are built using a single code base; therefore, they work seamlessly with each other so less engineering resources are needed when integrating them.

Hourglass [5] provides an infrastructure for connecting sensor networks to applications and offers topic-based discovery and data processing services. IrisNet [6] proposes a two-tier architecture consisting of sensing agents (SA) which collect and pre-process sensor data and organizing agents (OA) which store sensor data in a hierarchical, distributed XML database modelled after the Internet DNS and supporting XPath queries. Archises [7] supports mechanisms for self-organization, networking and energy optimization to build higher-level service structures in wireless sensor networks.

All above middleware platforms have not provided access to protocol layers, which are very important for resource allocation researchers. In contrast to above middleware, RAV provide TDMA and CSMA two MAC methods which are very useful for large scale networks.

3 Architecture

RVA supports two hardware platforms Mica-Z and OpenMote which are most popular testbed. RVA implements SPI configuration, led configuration, radio configuration, radio timer, RTC timer and serial ports. Mica-Z and OpenMote both adopt IEEE 802.15.4, but the implementations are quite different. For researchers, this is quite a complex and time consuming work. In wireless sensor networks, the layers are quite similar in the following.

RVA adopts WIA-PA protocol architecture and time sequence diagram, which is illustrated in Figs. 1 and 2, is based on ISO/IEC 7498 OSI Basic Reference Model. The protocol architecture defines the Data Link Sub-Layer (DLSL), Network Layer (NL) and Application Layer (AL), while its PHYsical (PHY) and Medium Access Control sub-layer (MAC) are based on IEEE STD 802.15.4-2006.

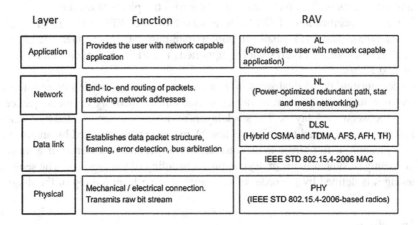

Layer	Function	RAV
Application	Provides the user with network capable application	AL (Provides the user with network capable application)
Network	End- to- end routing of packets. resolving network addresses	NL (Power-optimized redundant path, star and mesh networking)
Data link	Establishes data packet structure, framing, error detection, bus arbitration	DLSL (Hybrid CSMA and TDMA, AFS, AFH, TH) / IEEE STD 802.15.4-2006 MAC
Physical	Mechanical / electrical connection. Transmits raw bit stream	PHY (IEEE STD 802.15.4-2006-based radios)

Fig. 1. Architecture

The DLSL provides a service interface between the NL and the MAC. The DLSL conceptually includes a Data Link Sub-Layer Data Entity (DLDE) and a Data Link Sub-Layer Management Entity (DLME). The DLDE provides data service interfaces. The DLME provides the layer management services such as configuring the parameters of DLSL and monitoring the operation status of DLSL.

The network layer (NL) receives and transports packets over networks, provides interfaces to the below layer, and carries out network layer management, configuration and control.

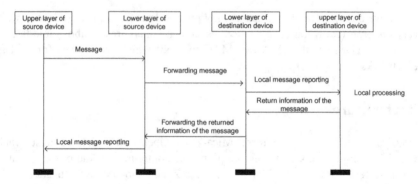

Fig. 2. Time sequence diagram

The AL is composed of the UAP and the ASL. The AL defines application objects that interact with the industrial processes. It defines communication services to support the communications between multiple objects for the distributed applications in the industry field environment.

The PHY is responsible for activation and deactivation of the radio transceiver, energy detection, link quality indicator, channel selection, clear channel assessment, and transmitting as well as receiving packets across the physical medium.

The PHY specification of WIA-PA is based on the IEEE STD 802.15.4-2006 compliant radio. The PHY shall support a minimum of 16 channels. IEEE STD 802.15.4-2006 channels 11–26 shall be supported. The PHY shall support a basic data rate of 250 Kbit/s.

To demonstrate the logical steps in data stream processing inside this architecture, we use time sequence diagram to depict interaction by focusing on the sequence of messages between stack layers. The stack layers of devices are represented by rectangle block. Time is represented by a vertical line. A message is represented by an arrow. In this specification, a full arrow is used to depict the general occurrence of a message independently of synchronous or asynchronous handling of the message. The sequence of messages is defined by the order of messages starting from the top of the diagram.

4   Interfaces

RAV contains a small set of powerful and easily combinable abstractions. The key is to define the sensors abstraction from accessing sensor data to management. RAV provide flexible access to Link Layer and network Layer. In the following, all the detailed interfaces will be described. The specification provides all necessary information required for deploying and using.

4.1   Sensor Configuration

For different applications, it is needed to declare sensor properties which are provided in deployment descriptor. Figure 3 shows an example which defines a sensor that

```
1   <sensor name="temperature node" priority="11">
2       <sensor-type name="temperature" />
3       <radio>
4           <radio-chip name="CC2420" type="cc2420"/>
5           <radio-strength value="3"/>
6           <radio-frequency>
7               <init-freq>13</init-freq>
8               <frequency change="true" change-duration="10s"
9                   type="Increment"/>
10          </radio-frequency>
11      </radio>
12      <life-cycle pool-size="10" />
13      <connection>
14          <send-buffer size="375000"/>
15          <recive-buffer size="750000"/>
16      </connection>
17      <output-structure>
18          <field name="temp" type="int" />
19          <storage permanent="true" history-size="10h" />
20      </output-structure>
21      <input-stream>
22          <stream-source alias="temperature" storage-size="1m"
23              disconnect-buffer-size="10">
24              <address wrapper="">
25                  <predicate key="type">temperature</predicate>
26              </address>
27                  <query>select temp as T2 from WRAPPER</query>
28          </stream-source>
29      </input-stream>
30  </sensor>
```

Fig. 3. Configuration for a temperature sensor.

reading temperature sensor, single strength, battery, id, hardware code, etc. Next, the detailed configuration will be specified.

In line 1 sensor has a unique name and has priority 11 which means low priority. The type of sensor is defined as temperature in line 2. The example describes basic radio information lines 3–11 which contains radio chip, strength and frequency. The frequency can set as unchangeable or changeable. In line 8 and 9, the frequency can change to another frequency and the type is increment. For example, if the node initial works in channel 13 but failed to join in network, and after 10 s the node will use channel 14 to work. Line 12 gives the estimate lifetime cycle.

At the same time, it needs to specify connection buffer size in line 13–16.

The structure of the data stream produces is encoded in XML as shown in lines 17–20. The structure of the input streams in line 21–29 produce the output stream. We use SQL queries which refer to the input streams by the reserved keyword WRAPPER.

4.2 Link Layer Configuration

Link layer refers to DLSL in Protocol architecture. RAV provides CSMA and TDMA two MAC methods. By default the node uses CSMA if there is no link layer configuration. However in link layer configuration, if the slot is assigned as transmit or receive, then the slot use TDMA.

Figure 4 shows the configuration of link layer. Line 1 defines the name of layer. The common constants are described in Line 2–Line 7. Line 8–line 27 specifies the structure of link which shows two whole links. Neighbor Id refers to a neighbor table entry. Link type should follow the requirements: Bit 7 represents the link type:0 = Unicast; 1 = Broadcast; Bit 5 and bit 6 represent the character of a link: 00 = Transmitting; 01 = Transmit-shared; 10 = Receiving; Bit 4 represents the type of a timeslot: 0 = Data timeslot; 1 = Management timeslot. Bit 3 represents the aggregation character: 0 = Non-aggregation; 1 = Aggregation slot; others are reserved. RelativeSlotNumber means the number of slots after beacon. Active Flag indicates that if a link is being used: 0 = Not used; 1 = Being used.

```
1    <layer name="link" >
2        <enable-constant>
3            <filed name="bitmap" type="int" value="1"/>
4            <filed name ="EtoEACKTimeOut"  time="1s" )/>
5            <filed name ="TimeSlotDuration" time="30ms"/>
6        </enable-constant>
7        <structure>
8            <link id="1" property="DLSL">
9
10               <filed name="NeighborID" value="1"/>
11               <filed name="LinkType" value="00100000"/>
12               <filed name="RelativeSlotNumber" value="15"/>
13               <filed name="ActiveFlag" value="true"/>
14               <filed name="ChannelIndex" value="1"/>
15               <filed name="SuperframeID" value="1"/>
16           </link>
17           <link id="2" property="DLSL">
18               <filed name="NeighborID" value="1"/>
19               <filed name="LinkType" value="0100000"/>
20               <filed name="RelativeSlotNumber" value="16"/>
21               <filed name="ActiveFlag" value="true"/>
22               <filed name="ChannelIndex" value="1"/>
23               <filed name="SuperframeID" value="1"/>
24           </link>
25       </structure>
26   </layer>
```

Fig. 4. Configuration for link layer.

Channel index is the channel used. SuperFrame Id relates which superframe will be used, usually network will use the same superframe.

4.3 Network Layer Configuration

Network layer refers to DLL in Protocol architecture. The structure contains two parts: neighbor and route. The configuration of network layer refers Fig. 5. Line 1 defines the name of layer. Line 3–line 10 specifies the first neighbor. Line 11–line 18 specifies the second neighbor. NeighborAddr is the short address of neighbour device. NeighborStatus is a byte in which bit 7 represents whether this neighbour device is a time source; bit 6 represents the status of neighbor device; others are reserved. The time source is 1 that represents the device is time source. BackoffCounter is the time when last communicated with the neighbour device. BackoffExponent is the exponent of back off. LastTimeCommunicated is the last time communicated with the neighbor. AveRSL represents the average of signal strength. Line 19–line 30 specifies the route structure. Line 19–line 24 specifies the first route. Line 25–line 30 specifies the second route. RouteID is an unique routing identifier. SourceAddress is the short address of source device. DestinationAddress is the short address of destination device. NextHop is the short address of next-hop device. RetryCounter is used as a counter to record end-to-end retries.

```
 1   <layer name="network" >
 2     <structure>
 3       <neighbor id="1" property="DLL">
 4         <filed name="NeighborAddr" value="1"/>
 5         <filed name="NeighborStatus" value="128"/>
 6         <filed name="BackoffCounter" value="0"/>
 7         <filed name="BackoffExponent" value="0"/>
 8         <filed name="LastTime-Communicated" value="0"/>
 9         <filed name="AveRSL" value="128"/>
10       </neighbor>
11       <neighbor id="2" property="DLL">
12         <filed name="NeighborAddr" value="2"/>
13         <filed name="NeighborStatus" value="0"/>
14         <filed name="BackoffCounter" value="6"/>
15         <filed name="BackoffExponent" value="0"/>
16         <filed name="LastTime-Communicated" value="0"/>
17         <filed name="AveRSL" value="100"/>
18       </neighbor>
19       <route id="1" >
20         <filed name="SourceAddress" value="0"/>
21         <filed name="DestinationAddress" value="1"/>
22         <filed name="NextHop" value="1"/>
23         <filed name="RetryCounter" value="2"/>
24       </route>
25       <route id="2" >
26         <filed name="SourceAddress" value="0"/>
27         <filed name="DestinationAddress" value="2"/>
28         <filed name="NextHop" value="2"/>
29         <filed name="RetryCounter" value="0"/>
30       </route>
31     </structure>
32   </layer>
```

Fig. 5. Configuration for network layer.

5 Implementation

The RAV implementation consists of the RAV-CORE, implemented in C++, and the platform specific RAV-WRAPPERS, implemented in C++. The implementation currently has approximately 30,000 lines of code. RAV is implemented to be highly modular in order to be deployable on various hardware platforms. RAV includes visualization systems for sensing data and visualizing the net-work structure. Currently RAV includes already wrappers for the TinyOS family of motes and USB.

6 Demonstration

The key advantages of RAV are its scalability and low effort are required for integrating new sensors, and the flexibility in supporting fast and simple deployment. In the demonstration we focus on the TDMA deployment which are regarded as time consuming work in applications. In the demo we will set up network topology as shown in Fig. 6. The motes equipped with temperature and pressure sensors. It is extensive to add new sensors through SPI interface.

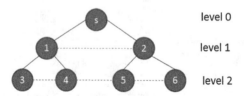

Fig. 6. An example of network topology.

Three different assignment algorithms are joint frequency time slot scheduling (JFTSS), receiver-based channel assignment (RBCA), and tree-based multichannel protocol (TMCP), which are aimed at reducing the data collection time from the perspectives of the communication links, the receivers, and the clusters, respectively. In such topology, those algorithms include sensor description, link layer configuration and network layer configuration decide three different assignments. RAV implements the algorithms according our previous work [8]. The middleware RAV is not limited to the only three assignment algorithms. It can be applied to other algorithms, but we suggest to follow the configuration requirements or may need more time to transfer the result.

We also provide a Graphic User Interface to help users to complete XML-based configuration, and checking the correctness before download to the real sensor mote. The specific configuration has been shown in Figs. 3, 4 and 5.

Then, put the sensor motes into their positions and turned on. The auto networking is controlled by the finding network program which is also provided by our design. This process contains finding neighbor and building connections. Actually, this process is more serial than parallel because the network is hierarchal layer by layer. The time to connect the whole network subjects to the number of sensor motes. The processes of data collecting and networking are separated. When the sensor is added to the network, it can produce the temperature data and submit the gateway. Three algorithms can successful be deployed to the sensor mote. And the time to configure all the sensor motes for each algorithm is less than 1 h. Eventually, all sensor motes can work normally.

After this initial configuration with RAV, we next test the scalability of RAV. The users are invited to add, remove, and reconfigure virtual sensors while the system is running and processing queries. Without any programming effort, through the GUI detects the exceptional situation, then just by providing a simple XML configuration then the network recover to run normally. The recovery time is related to the layer of sensors and also effected by influenced by the number of neighbors.

During the whole demonstration, users are able to monitor the effective status of all parts of the system and how it reacts to changes in the configuration through a GUI and various plots and networks connection configures.

7   Conclusion

RAV provides a flexible middleware for fast deployment of sensor networks meeting the challenges that arise in real-world environments.

The RAV provides the abstract interface from implementation details of access to sensor data and corresponds either to data streams received directly from sensors or to data streams. Thus RAV hides complex data sources and provides simple and uniform access to the host of heterogeneous technologies. RAV enables the user to specify XML-based deployment descriptor which can easily modify from link layer to network layer and customize the configuration of sensors.

Acknowledgments. This paper was supported by major project of science and technology plan of Beijing education commission (No. KZ201110015017), National Natural Science Foundation (61472461) and Initial Funding for the Doctoral Program of BIGC (27170115005/008).

References

1. Aberer, K., Hauswirth, M., Salehi, A.: The Global Sensor Networks middleware for efficient and flexible deployment and interconnection of sensor networks. Technical report EPFL
2. Sgroi, M., Wolisz, A., Sangiovanni-Vincentelli, A., Rabaey, J.: A service-based universal application interface for ad hoc wireless sensor and actuator networks. In: Weber, W., Rabaey, J.M., Aarts, E. (eds.) Ambient Intelligence, pp. 149–172. Springer, Heidelberg (2005). https://doi.org/10.1007/3-540-27139-2_8
3. Etherios (2014). http://www.idigi.com/
4. WSO2. http://wso2.com/.2014
5. Shneidman, J., Pietzuch, P., Ledlie, J., Roussopoulos, M.: Hourglass: an infrastructure for connecting sensor networks and applications. Technical report TR - 21-04, Harvard University, EECS (2004)
6. Gibbons, P., Karp, B., Ke, Y., Nath, S.: IrisNet: an architecture for a world-wide sensor web. IEEE Pervasive Comput. 2(4), 22–33 (2003)
7. Nguyen, T., Jamalipour, A., Pujolle, G.: Archises - middleware architecture for service creation in wireless sensor networks. In: IEEE International Conference on Wireless and Mobile Computing, Networking and Communications, vol. 4, pp. 165–168. IEEE (2017)
8. Yanhong, Y., Huan, Y., Liang, C., Zhang, X.: Optimal time and channel assignment for data collection in wireless sensor networks. In: IEEE, International Conference on Mobile Ad Hoc and Sensor Systems, pp. 456–457. IEEE (2015)

Improving the Lifetime of Scale-Free Fault Tolerant Topology for Wireless Sensor Networks

Rongrong Yin[1,2(✉)], Haoran Liu[1,2], Yinhan Xu[1], and Xueliang Yin[1]

[1] Yanshan University, Qinhuangdao 066004, China
yrr@ysu.edu.cn
[2] Key Laboratory for Special Fiber and Fiber Sensor of Hebei Province,
Qinhuangdao 066004, China

Abstract. In order to ensure adequate fault-tolerance and lifetime for network, this paper obtains an optimal degree distribution. The optimal degree distribution is used as a target to help design the best network topology, and then the scale-free fault tolerant topology control algorithm with adjustable parameters is proposed. Based on the analysis of the relationship between the algorithm parameters and its degree distribution, the algorithm parameters are also derived accurately. Simulation results show that the scale-free fault tolerant topology generated by proposed algorithm with the certain parameters outperforms the other, it achieves stronger fault-tolerance while prolonging lifetime.

Keywords: Wireless sensor networks · Fault-tolerance · Scale-free topology
Lifetime · Degree distribution

1 Introduction

Wireless Sensor Networks (WSNs) are usually deployed in harsh environments to accomplish certain specific missions over a period of time [1]. Node failure often occurs in WSNs due to several factors such as environmental hazards, energy depletion and device faults. This can lead to the interruption of services and then affect the network operates. So it is essential that the network continues to operate, even if some of its nodes fail. It is also important that the network is able to support the mission for a minimum specified period of time [2].

It is well known that sensor nodes are vulnerable to failures. Therefore, it is extremely important to have sufficient degree of redundancy. This can contribute in prolonging the network lifetime since faults do not cause a significant impact into the connection view of nodes. Many energy-efficient fault tolerant topology control algorithms have been proposed for WSNs. These algorithms are based on the redundancy of the nodes. It ensures that every node in the initial design has one available path to the sink after the failure of up to $k - 1$ nodes. However, on the one hand, in presence of more faults, providing nodes with limited number of available paths is not sufficient to ensure fault-tolerance. On the other hand, by adding more nodes or more links, they lead to bad utilization of the resources to transmit data to the sink, which

© Springer Nature Singapore Pte Ltd. 2018
J. Li et al. (Eds.): CWSN 2017, CCIS 812, pp. 12–21, 2018.
https://doi.org/10.1007/978-981-10-8123-1_2

increases the communication overheads and costs. Thus, the redundancy algorithms are not adequate to large scale WSNs.

To deal with these limitations, the scale-free fault tolerant topology control algorithm is desirable to enhance the network fault-tolerance while maximizing the network lifetime. The most important result for the scale-free fault tolerant topology is the high fault-tolerance against random faults without extra consumption of resources [3]. In this paper, we address the problem of maximizing the lifetime of the scale-free fault tolerant topology for WSNs. We present a new lifetime model for prolonging the lifetime of the scale-free fault tolerant topology, and obtain the optimal degree distribution which has the characteristic of maximizing the lifetime. Then the scale-free fault tolerant topology control algorithm is put forward. And the optimal degree distribution is applied to determine the algorithm parameters, it makes the scale-free fault tolerant topology generated by the proposed algorithm meet the requirement of maximizing the lifetime.

2 Related Works

Scale-free fault tolerant topology exhibits a power-law degree distribution, in which the probability that a given node is connected to k other nodes is described by $p(k) \propto k^{-\lambda}$ where λ is the power-law exponent. The research found that the power-law degree distribution is effective for fault-tolerance against random faults [4]. In order to make the network possess the power-law degree distribution, and to make the proposed network suitable for energy-constrained WSNs, numerous researches have been done to design the scale-free fault tolerant topology which has the characteristics of saving energy.

In [5], the authors proposed the scale-free fault tolerant topology with small-world feature for WSNs. It combined more characteristics of nodes, including the maximum communication radius and the residual energy. In [6], the authors proposed the efficient algorithm EAEM which regarded the node current energy as the judgment basis for establishing the links. Finally, the scale-free fault tolerant topology having the characteristics of saving energy was obtained. In [7, 8], the authors proposed the algorithms TEBAS and AGEM. The two algorithms considered respectively the nodes fitness, node saturation, node communication range and the network self-healing ability based on node residual energy to establish the scale-free fault tolerant topology. Results showed that the topologies generated by the two algorithms have a good fault-tolerance, and can prolong the network lifetime. In [9, 10], the evolutions of scale-free fault tolerant topology were finished in which the parents of node joined newly were chosen according to the node residual energy too.

Although the scale-free fault tolerant topologies generated by above algorithms can prolong the network lifetime by increasing the possibility of the interconnection among the nodes with higher energy reserve, the above algorithms implicitly assume that the low-energy nodes and the high-energy nodes are allowed in network. This means that the above algorithms cannot be directly applied to the homogeneous sensor network. Moreover, the above algorithms improve the network lifetime from the perspective of critical nodes. However, this definition of the network lifetime may not stand in real scenarios where the scale-free fault tolerant topology, there are a large number of nodes, is still working even if few critical nodes fail. Here, the network lifetime should have been redefined and reconsidered [11].

Our proposed algorithm has the following advantages over the existing ones. First it takes care of the homogeneous sensor network where the node has the same initial energy reserve. Then in order to prolong the lifetime of scales-free fault tolerant topology, it not only considers the lifetime of the minimal number of critical nodes, but also takes care of the other nodes. Third, it provides a scale-free fault tolerant topology whose power-law degree distribution satisfies the lifetime requirement by adjusting the algorithm parameters for WSNs.

3 Optimal Degree Distribution of Scale-Free Fault Tolerant Topology for Improving the Lifetime

In this section, through studying the lifetime model, we will get the relationship between the topological degree distribution and the network lifetime. Then the optimal degree distribution satisfying the requirements of maximizing lifetime will be obtained.

3.1 Criterion I

For the scale-free fault tolerant topology with power-law degree distribution $p(n) = Cn^{-\lambda}(C > 0, \lambda > 0)$, the structure data of node i can be measured by n_i^α [12]. Here, n_i is the degree of node i. Thus the data l transmitted by node i can be expressed as follows

$$l = l' + l'' = l' + n_i^\alpha l' \tag{1}$$

where l is the sum of data including both the owned data l' and the forwarded data l'', α is the coefficient of data.

According to the radio communication energy consuming model [13], the sending energy consumption E_{tx} is dissipated by two portions that the sending circuit cost $E_{elec}l$ and the power amplifier cost $\varepsilon_{fs}d^2l$, where d represents the communication distance of node i. Considering that the receiving energy consumption E_{rx} of node i in the process of receiving data $n_i^\alpha l'$ depends on the receive circuit cost $E_{elec}n_i^\alpha l'$. The total energy consumption E_i can be defined as

$$E_i = E_{tx} + E_{rx} = \mu(1 + n_i^\alpha) + \psi \tag{2}$$

where $\mu = (2E_{elec} + \varepsilon_{fs}d^2)l'$, $\psi = -E_{elec}l'$.

Now combining the initial energy E_0 with the energy consumption E_i, because the network lifetime is usually defined as the survival time of the critical node whose energy is going to be first depleted [14], the first lifetime criterion of scale-free fault tolerant topology can be expressed as follows

$$Life = \frac{E_0}{\max\{E_i | i \in V\}} = \frac{E_0}{\mu(1 + n_{max}^\alpha) + \psi} \tag{3}$$

where V is the set of nodes, n_{max} is the maximum degree of nodes.

Note that when N nodes are placed evenly in the monitoring area G whose size is A, according to the node-position's probability density function $f(x, y) = \begin{cases} \frac{1}{A}, (x, y) \in G \\ 0, otherswise \end{cases}$, the relationship between the degree n_i and the communication distance d accords with the constraint $n_{max} \leq \frac{N\pi d^2}{A}$. Therefore, in the Eq. (3), when the monitoring parameters N, A, d and energy consumption parameters E_0, E_{elec}, ε_{fs}, l', α are defined, $\mu = (2E_{elec} + \varepsilon_{fs}d^2)l'$ and $\psi = -E_{elec}l'$ will be defined, the lifetime of scale-free fault tolerant topology only relies on the maximum degree n_{max} of nodes in the network.

3.2 Criterion II

In the above criterion, we can find that the lifetime of node is inversely proportional to its degree, and the network lifetime has been defined as the time when a specific fraction of critical nodes (their degree is all n_{max}) remains alive in the network. But this criterion may not stand in large scale network [15]. Considering the lifetime of the other nodes in the network, we take the average degree of network as the second lifetime criterion to measure the scale-free fault tolerant topology.

For the scale-free fault tolerant topology with power-law degree distribution $p(n) = Cn^{-\lambda}(C > 0, \lambda > 0)$, the minimized degree is marked as $n_{min}(n_{min} \leq n_{max})$, thus the average degree $\hat{n}$ of scale-free fault tolerant topology can be calculated as follows

$$\hat{n} = \int np(n)dn = \begin{cases} \frac{C(n_{max}^{2-\lambda} - n_{min}^{2-\lambda})}{2-\lambda}, \lambda \neq 2 \\ C(\ln n_{max} - \ln n_{min}), \lambda = 2 \end{cases} \tag{4}$$

According to this condition $\int_{n_{min}}^{n_{max}} p(n)dn = 1$, the coefficient C is obtained by Eq. (5).

$$C = \begin{cases} \frac{1-\lambda}{n_{max}^{1-\lambda} - n_{min}^{1-\lambda}}, \lambda \neq 1 \\ \frac{1}{\ln n_{max} - \ln n_{min}}, \lambda = 1 \end{cases} \tag{5}$$

Furthermore, the maximum degree n_{max} of scale-free fault tolerant topology can be obtained based on the condition $\int_{n_{max}}^\infty p(n)dn = \frac{1}{N}$, i.e., $n_{max} = \left(\frac{\lambda-1}{CN}\right)^{\frac{1}{1-\lambda}}, \lambda > 1$. When $n_{min} \geq 1$, the relationship between the minimum degree n_{min} and the maximum degree n_{max} can be expressed by $n_{min} = n_{max}(N+1)^{\frac{1}{1-\lambda}}, \lambda \geq 1 + \frac{\ln(N+1)}{\ln n_{max}}$. Now the average degree $\hat{n}$ of scale-free fault tolerant topology is expressed as follows

$$\hat{n} = \frac{n_{\max}(1 - \lambda)\left(1 - (N+1)^{\frac{2-\lambda}{1-\lambda}}\right)}{N(\lambda - 2)}, \lambda \geq 1 + \frac{\ln(N+1)}{\ln n_{\max}} \tag{6}$$

In the Eq. (6), when monitoring parameter N is defined, the average degree $\hat{n}$ of scale-free fault tolerant topology only depends on the maximum degree $n_{\max}$ and the power-law exponent λ.

3.3 Maximizing Lifetime Model

According to the Sects. 3.1 and 3.2, we model the maximizing lifetime problem of scale-free fault tolerant topology as a linear program and obtain the optimal solution. Below the relationship between the lifetime and the parameters that $n_{\max}$ and λ is discussed.

Because λ is an estimate parameter of degree distribution and it usually ranges from 2 to 3, by combining Eqs. (3) and (6), the optimal degree distribution of scale-free fault tolerant topology which meets the requirement of maximizing lifetime can be modeled by Eq. (7).

$$\min f(n_{\max}, \lambda) = \frac{\min\{\hat{n}\}}{\max\{Life\}} = \frac{n_{\max}(1 - \lambda)\left(1 - (N+1)^{\frac{2-\lambda}{1-\lambda}}\right)}{N(\lambda - 2)} \cdot \frac{\mu(1 + n_{\max}^{\alpha}) + \psi}{E_0}$$

$$s.t. \quad 3 \geq \lambda \geq 1 + \frac{\ln(N+1)}{\ln n_{\max}} \tag{7}$$

$$n_{\max} \leq \frac{N\pi d^2}{A}, n_{\max} \in Z^+$$

According to Eq. (7), the degree distribution parameters $n_{\max}$ and λ meeting $\min f(n_{\max}, \lambda)$ could be got, and be marked as $n_{\max}^*$ and λ^* respectively. Then the optimal degree distribution $p(n)^* = C^* n^{-\lambda^*}$ which satisfies the requirement of maximizing lifetime could be calculated.

4 Scale-Free Fault Tolerant Topology Control Algorithm on the Basis of the Optimal Degree Distribution

The nature of the scale-free fault tolerant topology control algorithm for maximizing lifetime (named MNL algorithm) is that its degree distribution follows the optimal degree distribution $p(n)^* = C^* n^{-\lambda^*}$. Because the optimal degree distribution $p(n)^*$ varies with application scenarios, the degree distribution of MNL algorithm should be adjustable. The algorithm MNL includes the following two construction processes:

(i) **Nonlinear growth rule**——The initial network has m_0 nodes, at time t there are $r[N(t)]^{\theta}$ nodes joint the network based on the Poisson process in which the arrival rate is ζ, and each new node independently connects with m old nodes. Here parameters $r > 0$, $\theta \geq 0$, $N(t)$ represents the total number of nodes joined newly.

(ii) **_Local preferential connection rule_**——The probability $\prod_{local-area}(n_k)$ of a new node which will be connected to node k in its transmission range depends on the degree n_k. And the probability $\prod_{local-area}(n_k)$ has the following expression.

$$\prod_{local-area}(n_k) = \frac{M}{S(t)} \frac{n_k}{\sum_{k \in local-area} n_k} \qquad (8)$$

where $S(t)$ is the number of all nodes existing in the network, M represents the number of neighbors of the new node, $\frac{M}{S(t)}$ represents the probability that M nodes chosen from the network compose the local world of the new node.

In the MNL algorithm, the process that the new node joins the network obeys the Poisson process which has power law relation with θ, and each new node connects with m old nodes. So the validity of the generated degree distribution $p(n)$ can be achieved by controlling the parameters θ and m.

t_i represents the time of the i batch of nodes joining network, $n_{ij}(t)$ is the degree of the j node which belongs to the i batch of nodes at time t. Assuming that n_{ij} is continuous, the probability $p(n_{ij})$ can be interpreted as rate of change of n_{ij}.

$$\frac{\partial n_{ij}}{\partial t} = mr[N(t)]^{\theta}\zeta \prod_{local-area}(n_{ij}) = mr[N(t)]^{\theta}\zeta \frac{M}{S(t)} \frac{n_{ij}}{\sum_{ij \in local-area} n_{ij}} \qquad (9)$$

According to the Poisson process, we have the average batch of nodes $E[N(t)] = \zeta t$ within the scope of $[0, t)$. Considering the total number of degrees for all nodes appeared in the network is $L(t) = \int_0^t 2mr(N(t))^{\theta}\zeta dt$ and the average degree of a node at time t is $\frac{L(t)}{S(t)}$, then the sum of degrees for all nodes appeared in the local world of the new node is calculated by $\sum_{ij \in local-area} n_{ij} = M\frac{L(t)}{S(t)}$. Based on the derivation of n_{ij} and the limited t, we can obtain $n_{ij}(t) = m\left(\frac{t}{t_i}\right)^{\frac{1+\theta}{2}}$ by using the initial condition of $n_{ij}(t_i) = m$. Since t_i obeys the Γ-distribution, we have

$$p\{n_{ij}(t) \leq n\} = 1 - p\left\{t_i < t\left(\frac{m}{n}\right)^{\frac{2}{1+\theta}}\right\} = e^{-\zeta t\left(\frac{m}{n}\right)^{\frac{2}{1+\theta}}} \sum_{x=0}^{i-1} \frac{\left(\zeta t\left(\frac{m}{n}\right)^{\frac{2}{1+\theta}}\right)^x}{x!} \qquad (10)$$

Because the probability $n_{ij}(t)$ can be expressed as $p(n_{ij}(t) = n) = \frac{\partial p(n_{ij}(t) \leq n)}{\partial n}$, let t tend to infinity, we can obtain the degree distribution $p(n)$ generated by MNL.

$$p(n) = \lim_{t \to \infty} \frac{1}{E[N(t)]} \sum_{i=1}^{\infty} \frac{1}{r[N(t)]^{\theta}} \cdot \sum_{j=1}^{r[N(t)]^{\theta}} p(n_{ij}(t) = n) = \frac{2m^{\frac{2}{1+\theta}}}{(1+\theta)n^{1+\frac{2}{1+\theta}}} \qquad (11)$$

In order to ensure $p(n) = Cn^{-\lambda}$ could equal to the optimal degree distribution $p(n)^*$, when $p(n) = p(n)^*$, we can obtain the parameter values of θ and m in MNL.

$$\begin{cases} \theta = \frac{2}{\lambda^*-1} - 1 \\ m = \left(\frac{C^*}{\lambda^*-1}\right)^{\frac{1}{\lambda^*-1}} \end{cases} \tag{12}$$

We can see that, the degree distribution evolved by MNL based on θ and m in Eq. (12) can reach the optimal degree distribution $p(n)^*$, that is, it can maximize the network lifetime.

5 Simulation and Analysis

In this section, we will compare the MNL algorithm with typical EAEM algorithm. The main goal of EAEM is to enhance fault-tolerance and to save network energy by taking different values of m which has the same meaning as in MNL, and consider $m = 1, 2$ as the comparative types. We conduct simulation experiments. The value of parameters used in the simulation experiments is defined in Table 1.

Table 1. Experiment parameters.

Scenario parameters	Value	Model parameters	Value	Algorithm parameters	Value
Network scale N	$100 \sim 300$	Initial energy E_0(J)	1	Initial network scale m_0	3
Monitoring area A(m²)	500×500	Sending/Receiving circuit loss E_{elec}(J/bit)	50×10^{-9}	Arrival rate ζ	0.7
		Power amplifier loss ε_{fs}(J/bit/m²)	100×10^{-12}		
Maximum communication distance d(m)	150	Data length l'(bits)	100	Parameter r	1
		Coefficient of data α	2		

Experiment 1. *Calculates the parameters θ and m of MNL algorithm based on the monitoring scenario.*

Based on the monitoring scenario (shown in Table 1), we give an example $N = 100$ to illustrate the process for computing parameters θ and m of MNL. By setting $N = 100$, based on the constraint of Eq. (7), we can obtain the range of n_{max} from 11 to 28. We get the $\min f(\lambda)$ and λ for different n_{max}, thus the parameters $\{n_{max}^*, \lambda^*\}$ are obtained by comparing different $\min f(\lambda)$, i.e., $n_{max}^* = 11$, $\lambda^* = 2.92$. And then we can get $n_{min}^* = 1$ and degree distribution coefficient $C^* = 1.94$. Finally, the degree distribution of scale-free fault tolerant topology for maximizing lifetime can be expressed by $p(n)^* = C^* n^{-\lambda^*} = 1.94 n^{-2.92}$. Therefore, the parameters of MNL are $\theta = \frac{2}{\lambda^*-1} - 1 = 0.0391$ and $m = \left(\frac{C^*}{\lambda^*-1}\right)^{\frac{1}{\lambda^*-1}} = 1.0052$ respectively.

Experiment 2. *Compares the comprehensive properties between MNL algorithm and EAEM algorithm.*

In this part, we will measure the network properties such as fault-tolerance and lifetime when $N = 300$. In order to simulate the fault-tolerance to random faults of nodes, we will assume that each node has the same removal probability. Figure 1 reflects the fault-tolerance of the algorithms.

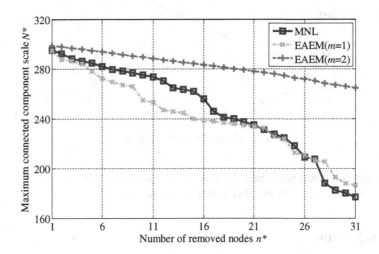

Fig. 1. Comparing network fault-tolerance

We found that removing random nodes has little impact on the topologies generated based on the EAEM($m = 1,2$) and MNL. When 10% nodes have been removed, almost two-thirds of nodes are available in the maximum connected component. The main reason is that the two algorithms above both build a scale-free fault-tolerant topology. Since the topology is not uniform, the removal for the less important nodes has less impact on the network topology. Moreover, Fig. 1 also shows that the EAEM($m = 2$) has better fault-tolerance, due to the fact that the EAEM($m = 2$) makes the number of network links increase multiply. These redundancy links can further enhance the fault-tolerance of the network but also shorten the other performances, such as network lifetime.

Furthermore, we will compare the lifetime of the topologies generated based on the above algorithms. It is assumed that data gathering is periodic, i.e., one such period of data gathering is referred to as one "round". The lifetime is defined as the number of rounds. Figure 2 shows the lifetime changes of topologies generated respectively based on the MNL and the EAEM($m = 1,2$) under the different number of failed nodes.

It can be seen that until the first node fails, there is little difference on lifetime between EAEM($m = 1,2$) and MNL. When the percentage of node failures reached 10%, 30%, 50%, 70%, 90% respectively, the lifetime of MNL is 13%, 47%, 73%, 118%, 176% better compared with the EAEM($m = 1$), and 14%, 49%, 77%, 113%,

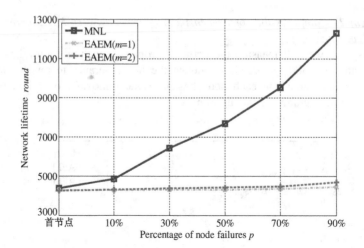

Fig. 2. Comparing network lifetime

162% better compared with the EAEM($m = 2$). It is mainly because the MNL maximizes the lifetime property of other nodes in the network.

6   Conclusions

This paper presents an energy efficient scale-free fault tolerant topology control algorithm MNL in WSNs. The theory analysis of MNL algorithm shows that the degree distribution of topology obtained by MNL has the optimal distribution which could satisfy the requirement for maximizing the lifetime. Moreover the comprehensive performance in the simulation shows that the generated topology has strong fault-tolerance to the random node failures. And it can optimize effectively the network lifetime.

References

1. Li, S., Kim, J.G.: Maximizing the lifetime of wireless sensor networks with random forwarding. Int. J. Electron. Commun. **69**, 455–457 (2015)
2. Azharuddin, M., Kuila, P., Jana, P.K.: Energy efficient tolerant clustering and routing algorithms for wireless sensor networks. Comput. Electr. Eng. **41**, 177–190 (2015)
3. Ghamry, W.K., Elsayed, K.M.F.: Network design methods for mitigation of intentional attacks in scale-free networks. Telecommun. Syst. **49**, 313–327 (2012)
4. Chen, I.R., Speer, A.P., Eltoweissy, M.: Adaptive fault-tolerant QoS control algorithms for maximizing system lifetime of query-based wireless sensor networks. IEEE Trans. Dependable Secure Comput. **8**(2), 161–176 (2011)
5. Liu, L.F., Qi, X.G., Xue, J.L., et al.: A topology construct and control model with small-world and scale-free concepts for heterogeneous sensor networks. Int. J. Distrib. Sens. Netw. **1**, 1–8 (2014)

6. Zhu, H.L., Luo, H., Peng, H.P., et al.: Complex networks-based energy-efficient evolution model for wireless sensor networks. Chaos Solitons Fractals **41**(4), 1828–1835 (2009)
7. Qi, X.G., Ma, S.Q., Zheng, G.Z.: Topology evolution of wireless sensor networks based on adaptive free-scale networks. J. Inf. Comput. Sci. **8**(3), 467–475 (2011)
8. Zheng, G.Z., Liu, S.Y., Qi, X.G.: Scale-free topology evolution for wireless sensor networks with reconstruction mechanism. Comput. Electr. Eng. **38**(3), 643–651 (2012)
9. Telcs, A., Csernai, M., Gulyas, A.: Load balanced diffusive capture process on homophilic scale-free networks. Physica A **392**(3), 510–519 (2013)
10. Zheng, G.Z., Liu, Q.M.: Scale-free topology evolution for wireless sensor networks. Comput. Electr. Eng. **20**(2), 1–10 (2013)
11. Xu, K.J., Zhou, M.: Energy balanced chain in IEEE 802.15.4 low rate WPAN. In: International Conference on Computing, Networking and Communications, vol. 1, pp. 1010–1015 (2013)
12. Wang, J.W.: Mitigation strategies on scale-free networks against cascading failure. Physica A **392**(3), 2257–2264 (2013)
13. Kumar, D., Aseri, T.C., Patel, R.B.: EECDA: energy efficient clustering and data aggregation protocol for heterogeneous wireless sensor networks. Int. J. Comput. Commun. Control **6**(1), 113–124 (2011)
14. Xu, N., Huang, A.P., Hou, T.W., et al.: Coverage and connectivity guaranteed topology control algorithm for c luster-based wireless sensor networks. Wirel. Commun. Mob. Comput. **34**(12), 23–32 (2012)
15. Dong, Q.: Maximizing system lifetime in wireless sensor networks. In: International Symposium on Information Processing in Sensor Networks, pp. 13–19 (2013)

Target Detection in Sea Clutter Based on ELM

Wei Jing[✉], Guangrong Ji, Shiyong Liu, Xi Wang, and Ying Tian

Department of Computer Science and Technology, Ocean University of China,
Qingdao, China
jingw_1103@foxmail.com

Abstract. Target detection is a hot topic in the research of sea clutter. The solution of this problem can be divided into two aspects. Firstly, find out the different characteristics between the target and sea clutter. Secondly, take advantage of the classifier to realize the feature classification. Thus, we study the characteristics of sea clutter. As a result, the decorrelation time, the K distribution fitting parameters and the Hurst exponent in the FRFT domain are proved to be three feature vectors that can better distinguish the target from sea clutter. Finally, we bring the Extreme Learning Machine (ELM) in the feature classification. Experiment results demonstrate that the chosen feature vectors are effective. Moreover, the ELM is also effective by comparison with SVM.

Keywords: Target detection · Sea clutter · Feature vectors
Extreme Learning Machine

1 Introduction

The research of sea clutter has received more and more attention in the study of all aspects of the oceans. On the one hand, sea clutter contains much important and useful information, and we can have a better understanding of the ocean situation by this information. On the other hand, the research of sea clutter can be used to detect targets in the military field and civilian areas [1].

Sea clutter refers to the backscattering echo which is reflected back when the radar detects the sea. There is a significant impact on the performance of the radar's target detection. Thus, the extraction of the target echo from sea clutter is the requirement that we use to detect the sea objects. Therefore, in this paper, we focus on the characteristics of sea clutter to find out the difference between the target signal and sea clutter signal. Finally, we demonstrate that three feature vectors are effective and ELM is qualified for the classification. The Sects. 2, 3 and 4 introduce three characteristics that can be used. In Sect. 5, we apply an effective method to realize the classification. Moreover, we make a conclusion in Sect. 6.

In the following sections, there are many experiments based on the actual measured sea clutter data, and these actual measured data are IPIX radar (Ice Multiparameter Imaging X-Band Radar) data which was published in 1993 [2]. The information of the data files is listed in Table 1. It can be seen that the information includes the location of the target and the Douglas sea state level.

© Springer Nature Singapore Pte Ltd. 2018
J. Li et al. (Eds.): CWSN 2017, CCIS 812, pp. 22–32, 2018.
https://doi.org/10.1007/978-981-10-8123-1_3

Table 1. Information of IPIX radar data

No.	Douglas level	Main target unit	Sub-target unit
17	1	9	8:11
54	2	8	7:10
283	1	10	8:12
310	4	7	6:9
320	3	7	6:9

2 The Correlation Characteristics of Sea Clutter

The statistical characteristics of sea clutter are mainly divided into two aspects; the first is the correlation characteristics of sea clutter, the second is the amplitude characteristics of sea clutter. Moreover, the correlation characteristics are divided into temporal correlation and spatial correlation. In this section, we mainly introduce the temporal correlation as the feature vector in target detection.

2.1 Temporal Correlation Characteristics

Temporal correlation reflects the fluctuation characteristics of clutter, which refers to the correlation characteristics of clutter on time measurement in the same resolution unit. The temporal correlation coefficient of the clutter sequence on the same unit of IPIX radar data is calculated as follows

$$ACF_k = \frac{\sum\limits_{n-0}^{N-1} x_n x^* n + k}{\sum\limits_{n-0}^{N-1} x_n x_n^*} \tag{1}$$

In this formula, $x_n = a_n exp(j\theta_n)$; $a_n = \sqrt{x_{cn}^2 + x_{sn}^2}$, $\theta_n = arctan\left(\frac{x_{sn}}{x_{cn}}\right)$, a_n is amplitude information; θ_n is phase information; x_{cn} is same direction signal; x_{sn} is orthogonal signal.

We have learned relevance in mathematics, and now for the need to discuss the temporal correlation of sea clutter. The function we used to solve the problem is

$$r(m) = \sum\limits_{n=-\infty}^{+\infty} x(n) x(n+m) \tag{2}$$

Among them, X is the discrete time signal with limited energy; m is the displacement, that is, delay time. Equation (2) is normalized to a coherence function. The coherence coefficient is defined as each value on the coherence function. Moreover, the decorrelation time is the time which the coherence coefficient reduces from 1 to $1/e$.

2.2   Temporal Correlation of Measured Sea Clutter

In order to reflect the temporal correlation characteristics of sea clutter in target detection. The decorrelation time of 14 range gates echoes is obtained by taking data file #310 as an example. The results are shown in Fig. 1. It can be found that the decorrelation time of the seventh range gate echo is much larger than the other range gates. So it can be inferred that the target object is very likely in the seventh range gate. With the influence of environment, the target object will be displaced on the sea surface because of the action of the wind and the sea. As a result, there are sub-target units around the main target unit, so the decorrelation time of the sixth and eighth range gate is slightly higher than that of pure sea clutter.

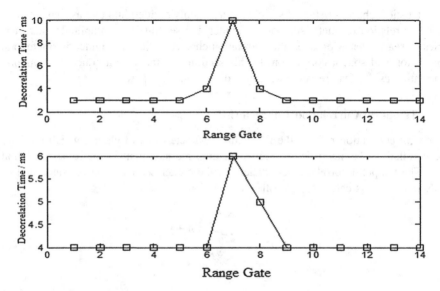

Fig. 1.   HH & VV polarization of file #310

3   The Amplitude Characteristics of Sea Clutter

There is a large number of scatterers distribute in the resolution unit of the radar randomly. The scatterers themselves have the characteristics of random transformation. At the same time, the echoes also change because of the motion of the radar. Finally, the amplitude distribution of the clutter is random. The amplitude probability density function can be approximated for this randomness. Sea clutter amplitude characteristics are an important part of the statistical characteristics of sea clutter, and it has far-reaching effects on radar detection and performance evaluation.

3.1   Common Amplitude Statistical Models of Sea Clutter

There are four common amplitude statistical models of sea clutter: Rayleigh distribution, Log-Normal distribution, Weibull distribution and K distribution.

Rayleigh distribution used to describe the amplitude characteristics of sea clutter when the radar technology is not developed. With the continuous improvement of radar performance and the use of high-frequency radar, sea clutter echo began to show a long trailing phenomenon, a non-Gaussian feature [3]. So the Rayleigh model cannot describe the amplitude distribution of sea clutter accurately. Log-Normal distribution and Weibull distribution can be better to simulate the long trailing phenomenon of sea clutter. However, all of the three distributions are based on a single point statistics instead of correlation characteristics of sea clutter.

3.2   K Distribution

The sea surface is mainly composed of two types of waves: the tension wave and the gravity wave. The K distribution model describes sea clutter as speckle component and texture component. The speckle component conforms to the Rayleigh distribution, and the texture component conforms to the Gamma distribution. The K distribution can be obtained by modulating Rayleigh distribution to Gamma distribution:

$$Z = \sqrt{r}G = hG \tag{3}$$

Among them, G conforms to Rayleigh distribution and it corresponds to the speckle component. r conforms to Gamma distribution. h conforms to the χ distribution, and it corresponds to the texture component.

The function of G is

$$f(g \mid x) = \frac{g\pi}{2x^2} \exp\left(-\frac{g^2\pi}{4x^2}\right) \tag{4}$$

The function of h is

$$f(x) = \frac{2d^{2v}x^{2v-1}}{\Gamma(v)} \exp(-d^2x^2) \tag{5}$$

Finally, the form of the K distribution function can be summarized as follows

$$f(x) = \frac{2}{\alpha\Gamma(v)} \left(\frac{x}{2\alpha}\right)^v \bullet K_{v-1}\left(\frac{x}{\alpha}\right), x > 0, v > 0 \tag{6}$$

Among them, K_v is the second type of modified Bessel function, α is the scale parameter, v is the shape parameter. The range of v is $(0.1, +\infty)$ for most clutter. What's more, the clutter distribution will be close to the Rayleigh distribution when v is approaching infinity. The image of the K distribution is shown in Fig. 2. It can be found that the "tail" of K distribution is mainly determined by shape parameter. The "tail" becomes longer with the increase of v when α unchanged. And the waveform becomes flat with the increase of α when v unchanged.

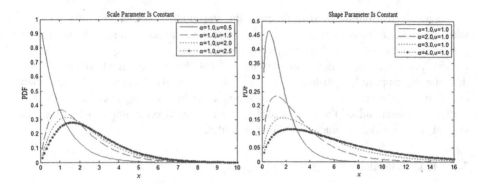

Fig. 2. K distribution charts with different parameters

K distribution can simulate the actual clutter from the perspective of the scattering mechanism of the clutter. It is the best and the widest used method in amplitude statistical models of sea clutter.

3.3   K Distribution of Measured Sea Clutter

We used HH polarization of file #54 as the actual measured data. In order to prove that the K distribution is better than the others, we get the 14 range gates' fitting parameters of four common amplitude statistical models. The results are shown in Fig. 3. It can be found that the four distributions can distinguish between the target echo and the pure sea clutter. However, K distribution has the most extensive range of fitting parameters, and the main target unit and the sub-target unit can be effectively separated.

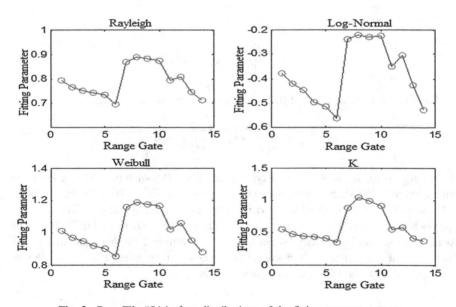

Fig. 3. Data File #54 in four distributions of the fitting parameter curve

In another experiment, the data comes from VV polarization of file #310. The experimental results are shown in Fig. 4. It can be found that the fitting parameter of the main target unit range gate i the minimum. Based on the two cases, the K distribution is the most significant method of target detection. So the fitting parameter of K distribution will be used as a feature vector in target detection.

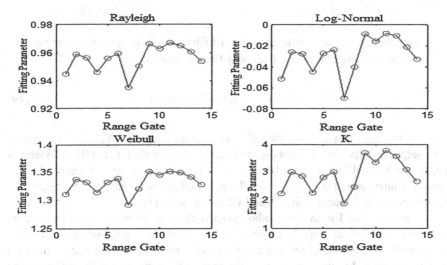

Fig. 4. Data File #310 in four distributions of the fitting parameter curve

4   Fractal Characteristics in FRFT Domain of Sea Clutter

The nature of sea clutter is a typical non-stationary and non-linear signal [4], then one of the research directions of sea clutter is the non-stationary and non-linear. It is well known that the time-frequency joint analysis is to analyze the non-stationary signal and fractal characteristics are used in the non-linear signal. So the study of sea clutter in both directions has been a long time [5].

4.1   Sea Clutter in Fractional Fourier Transform Domain

The echo signal of the target with constant velocity or constant acceleration can be regarded as linear frequency modulation (LFM) signal in some circumstances of radar monitoring system. Fractional Fourier Transform (FRFT) is a generalized extension of the traditional Fourier transform. V. Namias first published the new method of fractional Fourier transform in 1980. L. B. Almeida gave a definite definition of fractional Fourier transform: a rotation by an angle in the time-frequency plane [6]. It is defined by means of the transformation kernel $K_a(t, u)$, and expressed as

$$X_a(u) = \int_{-\infty}^{+\infty} x(t)K_a(t, u)dt \tag{7}$$

Where a is the transform order. Then the integral kernel function is

$$
K_a(t, u) = \begin{cases} \sqrt{\dfrac{1 - j \cot \alpha}{2\pi}} e^{j\frac{t^2 + u^2}{2} \cot \alpha - jut \csc \alpha} & , \alpha \neq n\pi; \\ \delta(t - u), & , \alpha = 2n\pi; \\ \delta(t + u), & , \alpha = (2n + 1)\pi; \end{cases} \tag{8}
$$

Among them, a is the transform order of FRFT, $\alpha = \frac{a\pi}{2}$ is the rotation angle. The inverse transformation of fractional Fourier transform is

$$
x(t) = \int_{-\infty}^{+\infty} X_a(u) K_{-a}(t, u) du \tag{9}
$$

It can be found that $x(t)$ is obtained by computing integral of $X_a * K_{-a}(t, u)$ which is the negative exponential function. The energy of sea clutter in FRFT domain is mainly distributed around order $a = 1$, i.e. in frequency domain. Hence, signal-to-clutter ratio of the signal is finally increased and sea clutter can be regarded as the sum of single frequency signals and Gaussian noise [7].

In summary, FRFT is another method to solve the non-stationary signal problem by combining time domain with frequency domain, which has a good energy concentration property of LFM signal without cross-terms interference [8]. The energy of target can be accumulated to the full extent in the best FRFT domain, and the detection and parameter estimation for a target in low signal-to-clutter ratio environment are then applicable without extra prior knowledge of sea clutter.

4.2 Fractal Characteristics of Sea Clutter

B. Mandelbrot first proposed the concept of fractal in 1975. Sea clutter is also considered to have fractal properties. The fractal characteristics of the target echo will be different from those of the pure sea clutter, which also provide another method for the target detection of sea clutter.

The fractional Brownian motion (FBM) model is a commonly used fractal model of sea clutter. FBM is a nonstationary stochastic fractal process, which is a generalization of general Brownian motion, and the most important parameter of FBM is Hurst exponent. The representation of FBM is

$$
B_H(t) = B_H(0) + \frac{1}{\Gamma(H + 1/2)} \int_{-\infty}^{t} K(t - s) dB(s) \tag{10}
$$

Hurst exponent not only determines the FBM characteristics but also indirectly affect the characteristics of the sea clutter fractal model. The sea clutter signal has fractal characteristics only over a period. So the Hurst exponent can be derived by wavelet transform and expressed as

$$log_2\Gamma(j) = (2H+1)j + c_i \tag{11}$$

Where $\Gamma(.)$ is Gamma function. So the Hurst exponent is determined by the slope of $j \sim log_2\Gamma(j)$. Figure 5 shows the Hurst exponent of 14 range gates with HH and VV polarization. It can be found that Hurst exponent is able to distinguish between the target echo and the pure sea clutter. What's more, it can achieve the target detection effectively when the signal-to-clutter ratio is relatively high.

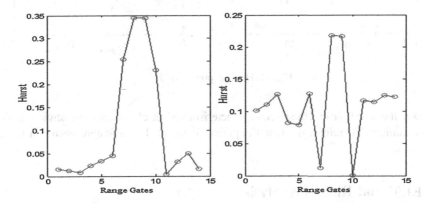

Fig. 5. HH & VV polarization of file #54

4.3 Fractal Characteristics in FRFT Domain

It is difficult to meet the requirements of target detection when the signal-to-clutter ratio is relatively low. The FRFT is exactly the method that can increase the signal-to-clutter ratio of the signal. So FRFT and fractal characteristics can be combined to realize the detection of sea target.

The experiments use #17 and #54 data files. The results are shown in Figs. 6 and 7. "—⊖—" is original fractal characteristics, "—✳—" is fractal characteristics in the FRFT

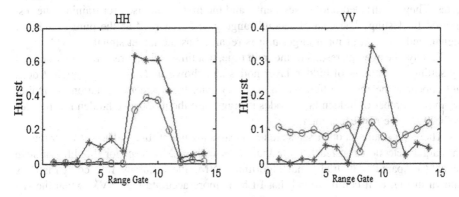

Fig. 6. Hurst exponent of #17

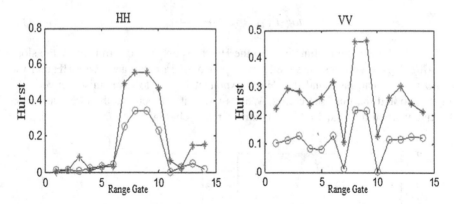

Fig. 7. Hurst exponent of #54

domain. It can be seen that the fractal characteristics of sea clutter are more obvious in the FRFT domain. Therefore, the Hurst exponent is selected as a feature vector in target detection.

5   ELM and Results Analysis

Extreme learning machine (ELM) [9] is a new type of single-hidden-layer feedback neural network (SLFN) proposed by Associate Professor Huang of Nanyang Technological University in 2004. Compared with the traditional gradient descent algorithm, the ELM algorithm has the advantages of fast learning ability and strong generalization ability, which can avoid the drawbacks of the gradient descent algorithm. It is flexible in selecting the activation function and avoids the limitation of the traditional neural network in this field.

Through the previous sections, the decorrelation time, the fitting parameter of K distribution amplitude and Hurst exponent have been proven to be three feature vectors that can better distinguish target echo from sea clutter.

The experiments are also used IPIX radar data. There are 131072 data in each range gates. They are divided into 64 segments, and the first 32 are used for training, the rest is used for testing. The data of second range gate is regarded as the pure sea clutter signal, and the data of main target unit is regarded as the target signal.

Finally, the average results of the train time, test time and accuracy rate are obtained by setting the number of hidden layer nodes and shown in Table 2. Although it does not appear to be much difference in accuracy rate, the standard deviation is smaller when the number of hidden layer nodes is bigger. So the number of hidden layer nodes is 20000 in the rest experiments.

Then, the results of other sea state levels are shown in Table 3. The accuracy rate of the target detection can reach more than 96% with ELM except for the 4th sea state level. Compared with traditional algorithm SVM, the accuracy rate comparison is shown in Fig. 8. It can be found that ELM is more accurate than SVM when the sea

Table 2. The results of different hidden nodes with #283

Hidden nodes	Polarization	Train time (s)	Test time (s)	Accuracy (%)
5000	HH	0.0967	0.0374	97.19
	VV	0.0936	0.0530	71.25
20000	HH	0.3931	0.1404	97.81
	VV	0.3912	0.1310	72.19

Table 3. The results of other sea state level

Sea level/File	Polarization	Train time (s)	Test time (s)	Accuracy
2/#54	HH	0.3775	0.1154	98.44
	VV	0.3962	0.1372	98.44
3/#320	HH	0.3962	0.1466	100
	VV	0.4118	0.1435	96.88
4/#310	HH	0.3868	0.1435	79.06
	VV	0.4118	0.1373	57.81

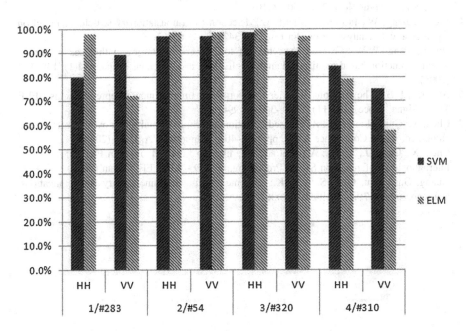

Fig. 8. The accuracy comparison of SVM and ELM

state level is lower. ELM also has a very high efficiency with the train time less than 0.45 s and the test time less than 0.15 s.

6 Conclusions

We have analyzed temporal correlation characteristics, amplitude characteristics and fractal characteristics in the FRFT domain of Sea Clutter. All of these characteristics are proven to be effective as the feature vectors in target detection. Moreover, Extreme Learning Machine is used as the classifier to realize pattern classification. After the comparison with SVM, we demonstrate that ELM can distinguish target echo from pure sea clutter effectively. In future research, we will do more research in sea clutter and devote to looking for new characteristics which have a better detection perform. Then we consider improving the ELM so that it will have high accuracy rate and low computation time in target detection of sea clutter.

References

1. Watts, S., Baker, C.J., Ward, K.D.: Maritime surveillance radar. II. Detection performance prediction in sea clutter. IEE Proc. F Radar Signal Process. **137**(2), 63–72 (1990)
2. IPIX radar sea clutter database (2001). http://soma.ece.mcmaster.ca/ipix/index.html
3. Greco, M., Stinco, P., Gini, F.: Identification and analysis of sea radar clutter spikes. IET Radar Sonar Navig. **4**(2), 239–250 (2010)
4. Nie, L., Jiang, W., Fu, Q.: Marine target detection from nonstationary sea-clutter based on topological data analysis. Procedia Eng. **29**, 3429–3433 (2012)
5. Hu, J., Tung, W.W., Gao, J.: Detection of low observable targets within sea clutter by structure function based multifractal analysis. IEEE Trans. Antennas Propag. **54**(1), 136–143 (2006)
6. Almeida, L.B.: The fractional Fourier transform and time-frequency representations. IEEE Trans. Signal Process. **42**(11), 3084–3091 (1994)
7. Chen, X., Guan, J.: A fast FRFT based detection algorithm of multiple moving targets in sea clutter. In: Radar Conference IEEE, pp. 402–406, Arlington, VA, USA (2010)
8. Chen, X., Guan, J., Yu, S.: A novel adaptive filtering for LFM signal in FRFT domain. In: International Conference on Signal Processing,pp. 239–242. IEEE, Dalian (2010)
9. Huang, G.B., Zhu, Q.Y., Siew, C.K.: Extreme learning machine: theory and applications. Neurocomputing **70**(1), 489–501 (2006)

Fuzzy-Assisted Event-Based kNN Query Processing in Sensor Networks

Yinglong Li[✉] and Mingqi Lv

College of Computer Science and Technology,
Zhejiang University of Technology, Hangzhou 310023, China
liyinglong@ruc.edu.cn

Abstract. This paper proposes a novel event-based k-Nearest Neighbor (kNN) query processing framework using fuzzy sets for distributed sensor systems. Our key technique is that linguistic e-kNN event information instead of raw sensory data is used for e-kNN information storage and in-networks kNN query processing, which is very beneficial to energy efficiency. In addition, event confidence based grid storage method and e-kNN query processing algorithm are devised for e-kNN information storage and retrieval respectively. The experimental evaluation based on real data set show promising results when compared with other methods in the literature.

Keywords: k Nearest Neighbors (kNN) · Event detection · Fuzzy sets
Energy efficiency · Privacy protection · Sensor network

1 Introduction

Tiny sensor devices have limited computing ability, memory, and energy resources. For these limited-resource sensor nodes, handling massive raw sensory data (relatively big data) is an unaffordable task. Therefore, a significant challenge is to design reliable, energy-efficient data processing algorithms to reduce the data transmission.

k Nearest Neighbors (kNN) query is a common required service in distributed sensor systems, such as event monitoring [1, 2] and object tracking [3, 4]. There are location-dependent kNN queries [5, 6] and location-independent kNN queries [7, 8]. The former one is to find k nearest neighbors to the specified geographical location, while the latter is to search k nearest neighbors with respect to the given value or event. Whatever the types of kNN queries, their strategies might rely on using raw sensor readings, which resulting in large data transmission in in-network processing, as well as long response time. Besides, using raw sensor data is likely to cause data leakage and is harmful to the data privacy protection.

In addition, the existing kNN query methods in sensor networks always require large data transfer or flooding, which is time-consuming and energy-wasting.

Based on the observations above, this paper aims to address the problem of event-based kNN query and proposes an novel event-based kNN query scheme using fuzzy sets. The main contributions are summarized as follows:

© Springer Nature Singapore Pte Ltd. 2018
J. Li et al. (Eds.): CWSN 2017, CCIS 812, pp. 33–43, 2018.
https://doi.org/10.1007/978-981-10-8123-1_4

- Linguistic e-kNN event information instead of raw sensory data is used for e-kNN query processing, which is very beneficial to the energy efficiency and data privacy protection.
- Fuzzy-assisted kNN event information storage and fusion algorithm are proposed respectively. And extensive experimental evaluations based on real-life data set are performed to validate our motivation.

The rest of this paper proceeds as follows: Sect. 2 presents the e-kNN problem and examples. Section 3 details the e-kNN event information description using fuzzy sets. Section 4 proposes e-kNN information storage and query processing algorithm. Section 5 presents experimental results. Finally, Sect. 6 concludes this paper.

2 Problem Statement

Definition 1 (fuzzy assisted event-based kNN query, e-kNN): Given a set of sensor nodes S (where $|S| = N$) and a given event e, find a subset S' of k nodes ($S' \subseteq S, k \le N$) such that $\forall i \in S'$ and $\forall j \in S - S'$, $eConf(eDist(R_i, eT(e))) \le eConf(eDist(R_j, eT(e)))$.

Where R_i is i's sensory readings, $R_i = (D_i[1], D_i[2], \dots, D_i[m])$, and m is the number of sensor attributes. $eConf(R_i)$ is a fuzzy assisted membership degree function that measure the event confidence of node S_i to be the e-kNN result. How to define the $eConf$ function will be discussed in later Subsect. 3.1. $eT(e)$ is the *event Threshold* of e. $eDist(R_i, eT(e))$ represents the *event distance* (e.g., *Euclidean* distance) of R_i and $eT(e)$, and an example of $eDist$ function is shown as (1).

$$dist(R_i, eT(e)) = \sqrt{\omega_1(D_i[1] - eT[1])^2 + \omega_2(D_i[2] - eT[2])^2 + \dots + \omega_m(D_i[m] - eT[m])^2}$$
(1)

Where $\omega_i (i = 1, \dots m)$ is a tunable weight value, which determines how much these attributes influence the *event distance* respectively, and $\omega_1 + \omega_2 + \dots + \omega_m = 1$. $D_i[m]$ and $eT[m]$ are the sensory data and event threshold value of attribute m in node i respectively.

Example 1. In a sensor based aquaculture surveillance application, sensors are used to collect PH values of monitored water area. There is a pre-defined event "*suitable for the growth of certain aquatic organism* (e.g., a fixed PH value)". When users want to find the nearest neighbor with respect to this *event*, the query result is the node with shortest *event distance*, which makes it with largest *event confidence* to be the result of e-1NN query. Another exmaple, in a sensor based farm automatic watering system, sensors are used for collecting the environmental data (*temperature, soil moisture*, etc.). When there is an event "*in need of watering locations*", users can find the global e-kNN with respect to this *event*.

3 Description of e-kNN Event Information

In this section, we introduce a fuzzy sets based approach to describe the event information for e-kNN query processing.

3.1 Event Confidence Measurement

Fuzzy sets [9] which was first introduced by Lotfi A. Zadeh in 1965 provides a good idea for analyzing and processing the imprecise and uncertain data of complex systems in a robust and understandable way [10, 11].

Definition 2. Fuzzy set $\tilde{F}$ over a universe of discourse X is a set characterized by membership function, and the membership function is mapping function from X to $[0, 1]$, namely:

$$\tilde{F} : X \rightarrow [0, 1], x \mapsto \tilde{\mu}(x) \tag{2}$$

In this paper, the e-kNN based *event confidence* can be viewed as a fuzzy set $\tilde{E}$. x is the *event distance* (*eDist*) of a node S_i in a sampling time window, and $eConf(x)$ is the event confidence mapping function of *eDist* x to the fuzzy set $\tilde{E}$. When $eConf(x)$ is 0, it indicates that node S_i is by no means a result of e-kNN query in the sampling time window; Due to the inverse relationships between *event distance* and *event confidence*, a desirable event confidence function $eConf(x)$ can be defined according to the lower semi-trapezoid distribution [12].

Definition 3. The α–cut set of fuzzy set $\tilde{E}$ ($\tilde{E} \in \wp(X)$), denoted by $\tilde{E}_\alpha$, complies with: $\tilde{E}_\alpha = \{x \in X | eConf(x) \geq \alpha\}$, where α is usually 0.5, which indicates the maximum uncertainty.

Definition 4. The *event distance* (*eDist*) that makes the *eConf*(*eDist*) within α–cut set of $\tilde{E}$ is called Noteworthy Event Distance, denoted as NED. Namely, The *event confidence* of NED (*eConf*(NED)) is above α, and the value range of *eConf*(NED) is usually [0.5, 1). The definition is intended to filter those sensor data far away from given event, which can reduce the total in-network data transmission.

3.2 Linguistic e-kNN Event Information

Non-uniform Discretization of *eConf*(NED). We divide *eConf*(NED) range non-uniformly into several sub-ranges *sub*$\Re$, and all the values in the same sub-range represents the same kind of e-kNN event information. This non-uniform partition can be based on a mathematical model (such as arithmetic sequence), as well as the guidance of domain experts. And a guiding principle of such non-uniform division is that the larger of an *event confidence* value, its interval size is smaller.

Example 2. The *eConf*(NED) range is [0.5, 1), and it is divided into five sub-ranges, as is shown in the 3rd column of Table 1. The interval of [0.95, 1.00) is 0.05, which is the smallest. The interval of [0. 50, 0.70) is 0.2, which is the largest. Each sub-range corresponds to a linguistic e-kNN event information.

Table 1. Example of e-kNN event information description

LEC	Interpretation	$sub\Re(eConf)$
A	Impending happen	[0.95, 1.00)
B	Close to event	[0.85, 0.95)
C	Alert	[0.70, 0.85)
D	Noteworthy	[0.50, 0.70)

e-kNN Event Information Description. As discussed above, there are several non-uniform sub-ranges, then we define the same number of *Linguistic Event Confidences* (LEC) corresponding to these sub-ranges to describe the node-level semantic event information. Each LEC has a semantic interpretation and describes a class of NEDs with similar e-kNN event confidences. The sub-range with larger event confidence and smaller interval is used to describe the events closer to given event, such as [0.95, 1.00) is used to describe the *impending happen* events shown in Table 1.

Example 3. There are four sub-ranges in Table 1, which results in four corresponding LECs ('*A*', '*B*', '*C*', '*D*'), as is shown in the 1st column of Table 1. And their corresponding semantic interpretations are shown in the 2nd column.

LECs instead of raw sensor data is not only helpful to reduce the data transmission, but also beneficial to the data privacy protection.

4 e-kNN Query Processing

4.1 LEC Based Grid Storage of e-kNN Information

We consider N nodes ($\{S_1, S_2, ..., S_N\}$) in a square sensing area, where the area is divided into several grids logically. Every node S_i is equipped with a GPS device, thus has its own two-dimensional geographic coordinates ($S_i \cdot x$ and $S_i \cdot y$). The global information such as sensing area boundary (*width*) and grid size (*G·width* and *G·height*) are broadcast by the sink after the network deployment, and then every node can obtain its Grid ID (GID) via following method.

$$GID(S_i) = \left\lfloor \frac{S_i \cdot y}{G \cdot height} \right\rfloor \times \left\lceil \frac{width}{G \cdot width} \right\rceil + \left\lceil \frac{S_i \cdot x}{G \cdot width} \right\rceil$$

Where $\lceil a \rceil$ and $\lfloor a \rfloor$ demonstrate the CEILING and FLOOR of number a respectively. There is a Grid Manager (GM) in each grid, which the GM manages the e-kNN event information of the local grid. An example of grid based network is shown as Fig. 1 in later Subsect. 4.3.

LEC Based Grid Storage of e-kNN Information. After every sensor node getting its LEC, its node ID (nodeID) is transmitted and stored to a corresponding grid

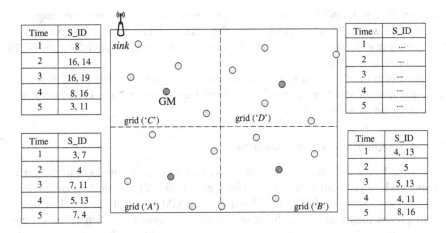

Fig. 1. An example of e-kNN storage and query processing.

(GM actually) via a specified **hash function**. Hash function should be devised in an energy-efficient and real-time way. As discussed earlier, the grid number is equal to the number of LECs, therefore, each nodeID with noteworthy LECs can be stored in a hash mapped grid, and the stored nodeID values in GMs are the required e-kNN event information.

Example 4. In a sensor system, the e-kNN event information stored in a GM (e.g., LEC is 'A') in recent n sampling periods are shown in above Table 2.

Table 2. An example of e-kNN event information storage in a GM

Time	nodeID
Sampling period 1	8, 12, 13
Sampling period 2	1, 4, 8, 12
...	...
Sampling period n	7, 8, 13

From Table 2, we know that only nodeID are transmitted during the storage process, which is energy-efficient without sensor data leakage, thus has good privacy protection performance.

4.2 Comparison Operator of LCE

According to Subsect. 3.2, our e-kNN query problem becomes to find the event nodes with top k largest LECs in recent sampling time windows. Therefore, before introducing the e-kNN query processing algorithm, comparison operator of LCE should be defined. We define LCE comparison operator based on the *s-norm* operator of fuzzy sets.

Definition 5. Let X and Y be two LECs, and their event confidence sub-ranges be $sub\Re(X)$ and $sub\Re(Y)$, if $sub\Re(X) < sub\Re(Y)$, then define function $\Theta(X, Y) = Y$, which means that the function Θ returns the LEC with larger event confidence. $\Theta(X, Y)$ can also be written as $X \Theta Y$.

Comparison operator Θ is s-norm according to fuzzy sets [9]. The proof is omitted due to the limited space. Θ is the LEC comparison operator for e-kNN query processing later on in Subsect. 4.3.

4.3   e-kNN Query Processing Algorithm

Due to LEC based grid storage, sink only needs to send query message to the corresponding GM. Firstly, sink sends query messages to grid ('A'), and the GM of grid ('A') calculates the *count* of nodeID stored locally. Then GM takes all the nodeIDs whose *count* is greater than 1 as the candidate query results (*candidates*). If there are enough *candidates* for e-kNN query, GM returns k *candidates* with top largest *counts* as the final e-kNN results; else, the GM forwards the query message as well as the left nodeIDs in grid ('A') to the grid ('B') for further e-kNN query process, until sink gets k nearest neighbors to the given event. More details of e-kNN query processing are shown as Algorithm 1 and Example 5.

Algorithm 1. e-kNN query processing

Input: Query Message (QM) with *given event* and k
Output: k nearest neighbors to the *given event*
1: sink sends QM to grid ('A') firstly;
2: **Do**
3:    The GM who receives the QM calculates the *count* of each nodeID that stored locally as well as the ones brought by QM;
4:    GM takes all the nodeIDs whose *count* is greater than 1 as the candidate query results (*candidates*);
5:    **if** #(*candidates*) $\geq k$ **then** //# means "number of"
6:       return the top k largest *count* of *candidates* as the final e-kNN results;
7:    **else**
8:       return all the *candidates* as part of the e-kNN query results;
9:       $k \leftarrow k - \#(candidates)$;
10:      GM forwards QM with those nodeIDs (whose *count* is 1) to the grid with lower LEC (using LEC comparison operator Θ) to find the left k e-kNN results;
11:   **endif**
12: **while** (sink gets k nearest neighbors to the given *event*) // initial k value here

---

Example 5. There were four LECs in a sensor system, which results in four grids ('A', 'B', 'C' and 'D'), as shown in Fig. 1. The sensor data collected in recent five sampling periods are used for e-kNN query processing. All the noteworthy event information is stored in corresponding grids. In Algorithm 1, sink sends query message to the grid ('A') firstly, and there are two nodes (nodeIDs are 7 and 4) whose *counts* are larger than 1. According to Algorithm 1, we can know that e-1NN result is node 7, since *count* (node 7) is three (biggest one) and the result set of e-2NN is {node 7, node 4}. When user-specified k is bigger than 2, there are not enough *candidates* for e-kNN query results. Therefore, the GM in grid ('A') forwards the query message to grid ('B'), and also transmitted the left nodes in grid ('A') (nodeIDs are 3, 5, 11, 13) to the GM in grid ('B'). When the GM in grid ('B') receives the message packet from grid ('A'), it calculates the *count* of each nodeID that stored locally as well as the ones come from grid ('A'). The *count* of node 5 and node 13 are both three, therefore, the result set of e-3NN is {node 7, node 4, node 13} or {node 7, node 4, node 5}, which is randomly chosen by Algorithm 1, therefore, the result of Algorithm 1 is not absolutely accurate. However, this kind of inaccuracy is fully acceptable because both node 13 and node 5 are very close to the specified event. The result set of e-4NN is {node 3, node 19, node 13, node 15}, and the result set of e-5NN query is {node 3, node 19, node 13, node 15, node 11}. When k is larger than 5, grid ('C') joins the e-kNN query processing similarly.

Accuracy Analysis of e-kNN Query Scheme. There might be a small number of false positives due to the random choice in Algorithm 1 when there are two nodes with same *count* in a grid. However, these false positives are also highly accurate query results event their actual event distances are a little different. For instance, in Example 5, the result set of e-3NN is {node 7, node 4, node 13} or {node 7, node 4, node 5}, which either of them is highly accurate. There is almost no false negative in e-kNN because our storage method and Algorithm 1 do not miss any noteworthy event information. In addition, in Algorithm 1, LECs instead of raw sensor data are used in in-network fusion, which improves the data privacy protection.

Overhead Analysis e-kNN Query Scheme. Our e-kNN storage approach only needs to store noteworthy nodeID to corresponding grids, which reduces the data transmission dramatically. In addition, the time overhead on large-scale data transfer is greatly reduced. In addition, e-kNN does not need to flood query message, but to send query message to corresponding GM. Therefore, e-kNN can reduce most of the time overhead of query message flooding.

5   Performance Evaluations

We use OMNET++ [12] to evaluate our e-kNN scheme as well as make comparison with other methods based on real-life data set from LUCE [13], which we had downloaded before. The real-life data set consists of location information and sensory data (node ID, Surface Temperature, Relative Humidity, Solar Radiation, etc.) of 88 valid sensor nodes. We used two attributes (Surface Temperature and Relative Humidity) to describe a *required watering* event. We set up a grid topology over the network deployment of the data set, and these 88 nodes were deployed in a rectangular region of 450×300 m^2 with four grids partition.

To the best of our knowledge, there is no similar related work in literature. Therefore, we compared our e-kNN scheme with following two conventional methods in a fair manner.

– *Local data storage based approach* (Local). In Local, sink floods query message to the whole network, and then each node calculates the average *event distance* based on its local measurements in recent sampling periods. If the *event distance* of a node S_i is noteworthy, then S_i sends a message packet including its nodeID and *event distance* to sink directly.

- *Data-centric storage based approach* (Data-centric). Each node stores its sensor data to other place using a specified *hash function* [7], and then sink sends query message to the corresponding storage locations to get the k nearest neighbors to the given event in a distributed way.

Evaluation Metrics

(1) **Data transmission.** In wireless communication, data transmission accounts for most of the total energy consumption [14]. In addition, small amount of data transmission also contributes quick response time. Therefore, the data transmission can be an important evaluation metric.

(2) **Response time.** In wireless communication, the number of relay hops after query starting directly influence the response time. We take distribution communication of Local and Data-centric into consideration.

5.1   Comparison of Data Transmission

In the sensor data storage process of Data-centric and e-kNN, the main data structures of message packet are "nodeID, Temperature, Humidity" and "nodeID" respectively. Where both Temperature and Humidity were FLOAT number, which required 32bits space (due to the 32-bit simulation platform). nodeID was INTERGER (8 bits). The main data structure of message packet of e-kNN is "nodeID". When sink sends query message in Data-centric and e-kNN, "nodeID" of destination GM should be added. In the query result return phase of ekNN and Data-centric, the main data packet structure is "nodeID" (8 its), due to the hash function based storage process. And the main data packet structure of Local in result return phase is "nodeID, *event distance*", which requires 48 bits. The e-kNN query message was 10 bits, and we did not consider other information in message packet, e.g., HEAD.

Among Local, Data-centric and e-kNN, the data transmission of Data-centric was the largest, and one of e-kNN was the smallest. The average data transmission of e-kNN was 9.83% of the one of Data-centric, and 89.8% of the one of Local with different k (2, 5, 8 and 13), as is shown in Fig. 2(a). The massive raw sensory data transfer in Data-centric as well as linguistic e-kNN event information instead of raw sensory data used in e-kNN mainly contributed to this phenomenon. With the increase of k, the data transmission of e-kNN grew slightly, while the one of Local and Data-centric remained unchanged, as is shown in Fig. 2(a). This is because the information or data storage accounts for most of the total data transmission in the above three approaches, which is almost independent of k. In e-kNN, more GMs might join the in-network fusion when k increases, which results in a slight growth of data transmission in e-kNN. Although the data transmission of Local is also small, its response time performance is not satisfactory (discussed in Subsect. 5.2).

We studied the data transmission comparison when n (number of sampling periods) varied with fixed k (here 8). The data transmission and its growth of Data-centric were both the largest, due to the massive sensor data transfer in the storage stage. The data transmission of e-kNN was the smallest when n was a smaller number (i.e., 1, 2 and 5), but it exceeded slightly the one of Local when n became larger number (i.e., 8), as shown in Fig. 2(b). The average data transmission of e-kNN was almost 9.7% of the one of Data-centric, while the data transmission of Local was 70.9% of the one of e-kNN, as is shown in Fig. 2(b). This is because that bigger n value means larger information or data transfer was considered in storage process of e-kNN and Data-centric.

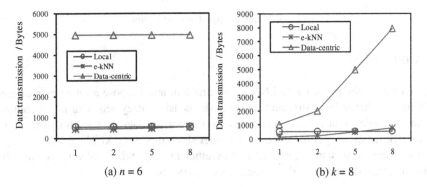

Fig. 2. Comparison of data transmission.

5.2   Comparison of Response Time

The response time is another critical metric to evaluate these three approaches. As discussed above, we take the number of relay hops as the response time metric under the consideration of distributed transmission cases in Data-centric and Local.

When sink was at location (250, 200), the number of relay hops of Local was the biggest. The relay hops of Data-centric was 53.3% of the one of Local, and the average relay hops of e-kNN was 36.7% of the one of Local, as shown in Fig. 3(a). Though the data transmission of Local is the smallest, the relay hop number of Local is much bigger than the one of e-kNN. Therefore, Local is not suitable for delay-sensitive sensor systems.

When sink moved to location (100, 180), the number of relay hops of Local is still the biggest. With k increasing, the total relay hops grew a little, while the one of Local and Data-centric was unchanged. This is because that the bigger the k is, sink should turn to more grids for e-kNN query, while both Local and Data-centric are k-independent due to their centralized query processing manager. The relay hops of Data-centric was 62.5% of the one of Local, and the average relay hops of e-kNN was approximate 34.4% of the one of Local. The average relay hops of e-kNN were approximate 55% of the one of Data-centric, as shown in Fig. 3(b).

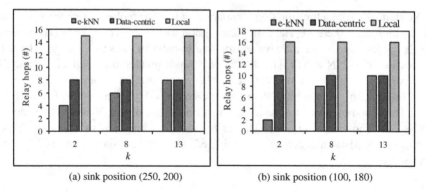

(a) sink position (250, 200)   (b) sink position (100, 180)

Fig. 3. Comparison of response time

6   Conclusions

We investigate the event-based kNN query problem and propose a novel event-based kNN query scheme for distributed sensor systems using fuzzy sets. Our key technique is that linguistic event information instead of raw sensor data are used for storage and in-network fusion. Experimental results further show that our e-kNN approach can get reliable query results in a fast and energy-efficient way, which is very suitable for real-time event detection in distributed sensor systems.

Acknowledgements. This work was funded by the Zhejiang Provincial Natural Science Foundation of China (No. LY15F020026, No. LY15F020025), as well as the National Natural Science Foundation of China (No. 61502421).

References

1. Chirici, G., Mura, M., McInerney, D., et al.: A meta-analysis and review of the literature on the k-Nearest Neighbors technique for forestry applications that use remotely sensed data. Remote Sens. Environ. **176**(1), 282–294 (2016)
2. Islam, R.U.I., Hossain, M.S., Andersson, K.: A novel anomaly detection algorithm for sensor data under uncertainty. Soft Comput. (2016). https://doi.org/10.1007/s00500-016-2425-2
3. Liu, Y., Fu, J.S., Zhang, Z.: k-Nearest Neighbors tracking in wireless sensor networks with coverage holes. Pers. Ubiquit. Comput. **20**(3), 431–446 (2016)
4. Sharma, G., Busch, C.: Optimal nearest neighbor queries in sensor networks. Theor. Comput. Sci. **608**(pt. 2), 146–165 (2015)
5. Komai, Y., Sasaki, Y., Hara, T., Nishio, S.: k Nearest Neighbor search for location-dependent sensor data in MANETs. Ind. Sens. Netw. Adv. Data Manag. Design Secur. **3**(1), 942–954 (2015)
6. Li, Y.Y., Parker, L.E.: Nearest neighbor imputation using spatial–temporal correlations in wireless sensor networks. Inf. Fusion **15**(1), 64–79 (2014)
7. Lai, Y., Chen, H., Li, C.: Processing the v-kNN queries in wireless sensor networks. In: International Conference on Parallel Processing, pp. 1–6. IEEE, New York (2007)

8. Zhao, Z., Yu, G., Li, B., Yao, L., Yang, X.: An algorithm for optimizing multidimensional k-NN queries in wireless sensor networks. J. Software **18**(5), 1186–1197 (2007). (in Chinese)
9. Galindo, J.: Handbook of Research on Fuzzy Information Processing in Databases. IGI Global, Hershey (2008)
10. Zheng, Y., Ling, H., Chen, S., Xue, J.: A hybrid neuro-fuzzy network based on differential biogeography-based optimization for online population classification in earthquakes. IEEE Trans. Fuzzy Syst. **23**(4), 1070–1083 (2015)
11. Rodger, J.A.: A fuzzy nearest neighbor neural network statistical model for predicting demand for natural gas and energy cost savings in public buildings. Expert Syst. Appl. **41**(1), 1813–1829 (2014)
12. http://www.omnetpp.org
13. http://sensorscope.epfl.ch/index.php/Environmental_Data
14. Anastasi, G., Conti, M., Francesco, M.D., Passarella, A.: Energy conservation in wireless sensor networks: a survey. Ad Hoc Netw. **7**(3), 537–568 (2009)

A Hierarchical Identity-Based Signcryption Scheme in Underwater Wireless Sensor Network

Chi Yuan⑩, Wenping Chen$^{(\boxtimes)}$⑩, and Deying Li⑩

School of Information, Renmin University, Beijing, China
{Chiyuan, Chenwenping, deyingli}@ruc.edu.cn

Abstract. The sensors in UWSN are vulnerable to malicious attack due to the transmission nature of wireless media under the water. Secure message delivery with low energy consumption is one of major aims in UWSN. In this paper, a Hierarchical Identity-based Signcryption (HIS) scheme is proposed for UWSN. Signcryption mechanism, which completes the signature and encryption in a single logical step, is adopted in the HIS scheme to decrease the communication and computation cost. The private keys of nodes are generated based on the node's identity to decrease the communication cost. Two-layer architecture, cluster head layer and intra-cluster layer, is employed in the HIS scheme. Taking the difference on capacity between the cluster heads and ordinary nodes into account, we perform encrypting operations with different computation complexity in the two layers. The simulation results show that the HIS scheme outperforms ECC-CA, GLKM and AVM algorithm on energy consumption and time cost.

Keywords: Identity-Based Encryption · Signcryption · Vandermonde Matrix
Wireless Sensor Network

1 Introduction

Underwater Wireless Sensor Network (UWSN) is an ad hoc network comprised mainly of small sensor nodes with limited resources and one or more base stations (BSs). UWSN is deployed under water and is suitable for monitoring some possible hash environment. UWSN can be utilized to oceanographic data collection, pollution monitoring, mine detection, disaster prevention, assisted navigation, and so on [1–4].

Due to the transmission nature of wireless media under the water, the communication channel is public and it is not difficult for an adversary to manipulate the sensors of an unprotected UWSN. That is to say, the sensors in UWSNs are vulnerable to malicious attack. Therefore, security is one of the principal concerns while designing protocols and mechanisms for UWSN [5, 6]. Compared with radio frequency waves in

This work is partly supported by National Natural Science Foundation of China under grant 11671400.

J. Li et al. (Eds.): CWSN 2017, CCIS 812, pp. 44–54, 2018.
https://doi.org/10.1007/978-981-10-8123-1_5

ground WSN, underwater acoustic channel features large-latency and low-bandwidth, which consumes more energy and time. Thus the energy and time consumption are important factors when we design security protocol for UWSN.

Cryptographic plays a very important role in security. In the traditional Public Key Cryptography (PKC) schemes, Public Key Infrastructure (PKI) based method needs the Certificate Authority (CA) to manage the certificate, which result high communication and computation cost and is not affordable for UWSN [7–9]. In Identity-Based Encryption (IBE) scheme, the PKI is not required and the public keys are computed according to the users' identifier (e.g., node IDs) instead. Since IBE scheme avoids the resource cost for storing and granting certificate, it is regarded as a practical mean of public key encryption for WSNs [6]. However, the communication cost led by PKG issuing private key is a burden for the resource-limited UWSN. In traditional public key schemes, it is common to digitally sign a message then encrypt. Another public key scheme, named signcryption, is first proposed by Zheng [10], achieves digital signature and encryption in a single logical step, and can effectively decrease the computational costs and communication overheads compared with the traditional signature-then-encryption public key schemes. Therefore, signcryption schemes have advantages to apply in UWSN.

In this paper, we propose a Hierarchical Identity-based Signcryption (HIS) scheme. Different from the traditional IBE scheme that requires the PKG to issue users' private keys, the private key in HIS scheme is computed by node itself. In the HIS scheme, we employ the signcryption method to accomplish the digital signature and encryption in a single logical step, which decreases the computation and communication overhead in comparison with the traditional signature-then-encryption schemes.

To decrease the communication overhead of data aggregation, cluster architecture is often employed in UWSN. Thus, we adopt cluster-based hierarchy security scheme. There are two layers, cluster head layer and intra-cluster layer. The whole UWSN consists of a few clusters and a BS. The nodes with stronger capacity are set as cluster head. Each cluster head is responsible for managing a number of ordinary sensor nodes. We perform encrypting operations with different computation complexity in the two layers. In the cluster head layer, the BS, as the KGC, assigns a Vandermonde matrix-based identifier for cluster heads to generate the public key, which achieves quite high security and low communication cost. In intra-cluster layer, the cluster head computes the public key for each sensor node by hash function, which is a low complexity operation. The simulation results show that the HIS scheme outperforms ECC-CA and AVM scheme on energy and time consumption.

2 Related Work

PKI-based cryptographic solutions are common public key schemes. However, they usually require tens of seconds and up to minutes to perform encryption and decryption operations on resource constrained wireless nodes in UWSN, which exposes vulnerability to malicious attacks. Moreover, the communication overhead is unaffordable for the nodes in UWSN [11, 12].

Shamir first proposed an identity-based cryptosystem and signature scheme [13]. Without issued public key by PKI, the users choose their names or network addresses that uniquely identify them as their public keys, such that they cannot later deny. The corresponding secret keys are computed by PKG and issued to the users when they first join the network. In [10], the authors argued that Identity-Based Encryption (IBE) is the ideal encryption scheme for WSNs. By using Elliptic Curve Cryptography (ECC), the identity-based public key encryption scheme is feasible in WSNs, since it consumes considerably less resources than conventional public key encryption algorithms, for a given security level. However, the communication overhead for issuing private key in UWSN is still a problem that needs to resolve. Yang et al. proposed an identity-based symmetric key authentication protocol for sensor network. In this protocol, a pair of nodes computes a secret pairwise key by each other's identity [14]. Thus, PKG is not needed to generate the private key.

In order to decrease the communication overhead of data collection and balance the resource difference among the nodes, cluster-based architecture is often employed in WSN. Li et al. employed layered identity-based encryption method to accomplish the authentication and key negotiation [15]. In a cluster, a shared key is established between the cluster member and cluster head when they communicate. However, the computation overhead brought by bilinear pairing on elliptic curve is a problem for the nodes in UWSN.

Combing the advantages of IBE, signcryption and cluster-based architecture, the HIS scheme is proposed in this paper.

3   Hierarchical Signcryption Scheme

In UWSN, cluster-based hierarchical architecture can decrease the communication overhead when collecting and aggregating data from sensor nodes. Moreover, it is helpful to extend the lifetime if nodes are assigned to different tasks according to their resources. As shown in Fig. 1, there are two layers in the HIS scheme, cluster head

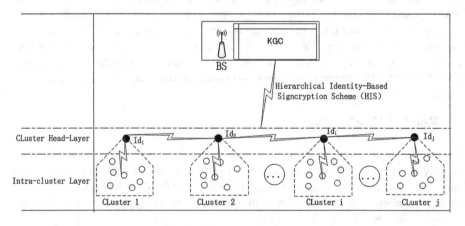

Fig. 1. System architecture

layer and intra-cluster layer. We will present the signcryption scheme of the two layers respectively. Some notations in the HIS scheme are described in Table 1.

Table 1. Deployed notations

Notations guide	
ID	Identity matrix of cluster head
E	Elliptic curve on finite field $GF(r)$
C_i	Cluster i
CH_i	Cluster head of Cluster C_i
Id_{ij}	The identifier of node N_{ij} in cluster C_i
Gq	Cyclic group of order q
$Zq*$	Nonzero multiplicative group based on prime number q
$H_0: \{0,1\}* \to Gq$	Hash function that maps a string consisting of 0 or 1 to a finite group
$H_1: \{0,1\}$ $* \times Gq \to Zq$	Hash function that maps a Cartesian product to a multiplicative group
S_i/P_i	Secret/Public key of cluster head CH_i
S_{ij}/P_{ij}	Secret/Public key of node j in cluster C_i

3.1 Signcryption Scheme in Cluster Head Layer

In cluster head layer, the communication happens between cluster heads and the BS. The security scheme consists of three phases: initialization, signcryption and unsigncryption. In the initialization phase, the corresponding parameters are set and the private/public keys are computed. In signcryption phase, a sender signcrypts its message and sends it to a receiver. The receiver unsigncrypt and recover the signcrypted text and verify the signature in unsigncryption phase.

Initialization. In cluster head layer, the BS is trustable to generate keys for cluster heads. As a KGC, the BS first needs to select adequate parameters, including a large prime number q, the corresponding cyclic group Gq, elliptic curve E, base point $G \in E(Gq)$, hash function $H_0: \{0,1\}* \to Gq$, $H_1: \{0,1\}* \times Gq \to Zq$ and a secret D, which is $n \times n$ symmetric matrix.

$$
D = \begin{bmatrix} d_{0,0} & \cdots & d_{0,n-1} \\ \vdots & \ddots & \vdots \\ d_{0,n-1} & \cdots & d_{n-1,n-1} \end{bmatrix} \tag{1}
$$

The steps of generating keys are described as follows.

1. Supposing there are n cluster heads, the BS, as the KGC, sets the identifiers $\{Id0, Id1, Id2, \cdots, Idn - 1\}$ for each cluster head. Then, according to the identifiers, a Vandermonde Matrix I, which used to represent the identity of cluster heads,

is constructed as follows. The character of Vandermonde Matrix is beneficial to decrease the communication cost without sacrificing the security level.

$$
\text{ID} =
\begin{bmatrix}
Id_0^0 & Id_1^0 & \cdots & Id_{n-1}^0 \\
Id_0^1 & Id_1^1 & \cdots & Id_{n-1}^1 \\
\vdots & \vdots & & \vdots \\
Id_0^{n-1} & Id_1^{n-1} & \cdots & Id_{n-1}^{n-1}
\end{bmatrix}
\tag{2}
$$

2. The KGC generates a one-way function according to the identifiers of cluster head as follows, which is used to compute a fake secret matrix.

$$
y = f(x, p) = \left(Id_1 \cdot x^{n-1} + Id_2 \cdot x^{n-2} + \cdots + Id_{n-1} \cdot x^0\right) Mod\, p
\tag{3}
$$

3. The BS selects and broadcasts the parameters, including the cyclic group Gq, the elliptic curve E, the base point G and hash function H_0, H_1.

Key Generation. Once the parameters for generating keys are set by KGC, the keys for cluster head can be generated. The steps are described as follows.

1. Cluster head CH_i selects a point $P(x_i, y_i)$ on E as its secret key, that is, $S_i = <x_i, y_i>$, then selects a random number $z_i \in Z$ and stores its value to signcrypt message in its own cluster.
2. Cluster head CHi computes the verification parameter $Vi = ziSi = (Vx, Vy)$, then sends the verification information (Vi, Idi) to KGC.
3. After receiving the verification information (V_i, Id_i), the KGC computes the fake secret matrix D' by the one-way function $y = f(x, p)$ and secret matrix D. To ensure the security, each cluster head should have its own fake matrix, so the verification parameter is adopted as the parameter p of the one-way function.

$$
y = f\left(d_{ij}, V_x\right) = \left(Id_1 \cdot d_{ij}^{n-1} + Id_2 \cdot d_{ij}^{n-2} + \cdots + Id_{n-1} \cdot d_{ij}^0\right) Mod\, Vx
\tag{4}
$$

The fake secret matrix is shown as follows

$$
D' =
\begin{bmatrix}
d_{0,0}' & \cdots & d_{0,n-1}' \\
\vdots & \ddots & \vdots \\
d_{n-1,0}' & \cdots & d_{n-1,n-1}'
\end{bmatrix}
\tag{5}
$$

4. KGC randomly selects a column, such as column j, from the Vandermonde Matrix to compute vector $B_j = \{b_{j0}, b_{j1}, ..b_{j(n-1)}\}$ and $B_i = \{b_{i0}, b_{i1}, ..b_{i(n-1)}\}$, where

$$
b_{jk} = \sum_{p=0}^{n-1} d_{kp} \cdot Id_j^p \, (0 \le k \le n-1)
\tag{6}
$$

$$
b_{jk} = \sum_{p=0}^{n-1} d_{kp}' \cdot Id_j^p \, (0 \le k \le n-1)
\tag{7}
$$

then the public key of cluster head CH_i is computed by $P_i = G \cdot V_i$, and the corresponding verification parameter K_{ij} for KGC is

$$k_{ij} = \sum_{p=0}^{n-1} b_{ip} \cdot Id_j^p \tag{8}$$

5. The KGC sends (P_i, B_j, K_{ij}) to the cluster head CH_i, CH_i verify the KGC by computing

$$k_{ji} = \sum_{q=0}^{n-1} b_{iq} \cdot Id_i^q \tag{9}$$

if $K_{ij} = K_{ji}$, then accepts the public key P_i and stores the corresponding secret key, otherwise, returns error for key generating.

Signcryption. Supposing cluster head CH_i sends a message to CH_j, the communication process is described as follows.

1. CH_i computes $K = z_iG = (k_1, k_2)$, where z_i is the random number selected by CH_i in initialize phase and G is the base point on E. Then generates the verification parameter $U = k_1P_j = (u, v)$, where u is employed to encrypt the message and v is the cluster secret which is used to signcrypt in intra-cluster layer. Then, CH_i computes the cipher text as $c = Eu(m)$, where m is the plaintext of the message.

2. CH_i calculates the parameters, M, N, O' and O as follows:

$$M = H_1(k_1 C) \tag{10}$$

$$N = H_0(k_1M)G \tag{11}$$

$$O' = S_i - H_0(k_1M) \text{ MOD } q \tag{12}$$

$$O = M + O' \tag{13}$$

3. CH_i sends the signcrypted text $\sigma(K, c, N, O\ z_i)$ to cluster head CH_j.

Unsigncryption. When CH_j receives the message from CH_i, CH_j performs the following operations.

1. Extracts the parameter k_1 from the received parameter K, computes the verification parameter $U' = k_1z_jS_jG = k_1V_jG$. If $U' = k_1P_j$, then the identity of CH_i is verified.
2. Computes $M = H_1(k_1||C)$, $O' = O - M$.
3. Decrypts the received cipher text C as $m = D_u(C)$.
4. Computes $P' = N + O'G$, and compares the value of $zi \cdot P'$ with P_i, if they are equal, then accepts the message m and the session key u between CH_i and CH_j, otherwise, returns error.

Thus, the communication process in cluster head layer is finished.

3.2   Signcryption in Intra-cluster Layer

In intra-cluster layer, the security scheme consists of four phases: initialization, sign-cryption, unsigncryption and key updating.

Initialization. Since the resource of ordinary nodes in a cluster is often less than that of cluster head and they are not as important as cluster head, we replace the matrix operation in cluster head layer with simple hash operation to generate the keys. Thus, the energy overhead of ordinary nodes for encryption is decreased. The detail steps are described as follows.

1. *Node N_{ij} selects a random number r_j and stores the value.*
2. *CH_i sends the secret v to N_{ij}.*
3. *N_{ij} computes $S_j = r_j\,v$, then sends $(S_i||Id_{ij})$ to CH_i.*
4. *CH_i selects random number r_n and computes two parameters*

$$K_1 = r_n S_j - H_0\left(Id_{ij}\right) \ and \ K_2 = r_n + H_0(Id_i)H_0\left(K_1 Id_{ij}\right)$$

5. *CH_i computes the public key $P_{ij} = G \cdot S_j$ for N_{ij}, then sends the ciphertext $\sigma = (K_1, K_2, H_0(Id_i))$ to Node N_{ij}.*
6. *Node N_{ij} verifies the identity of CH_i by comparing the values of $K_2 S_j$ and $K_1 + H_0(Id_{ij}) + r_j\,H_0(Id_i)\,H_0(K_1)$, if they are equal, then accepts the public key P_{ij} and stores the secret key S_j, otherwise, reports the error.*

Signcryption and Unsigncryption. The process of signcryption and unsigncryption in intra-cluster layer is similar to that in cluster head layer. Therefore, we omit the detail description here.

Key Updating. The key updating happens periodically in each cluster to ensure the security. The following shows the update process in cluster C_i.

1. *CH_i generates the new cluster secret v'.*
2. *CH_i signcrypts $m = E_V(S_i||Id_i||Clock||v')$ with the old cluster secrect v, then broadcast m in cluster C_i. Si is the secret key of CH_i.*
3. *When other ordinary nodes in the cluster receive the message m, they unsigncrypt the message with old cluster secrect v. Then they verify the message with the public key of CH_i to decide whether accept the new cluster secret v'. If the verification fails, then discards the message. Otherwise, accepts the new cluster secret v'.*

4   Simulation Experiments

4.1   Experiments Setup

According to the energy consumption model in literature [18], we simulate the HIS scheme and compare its energy and time consumption with other cryptographic solutions, including AVM [5], GLKM [17] and ECC-CA [16] scheme by Network Simulator 2. The computation complexity of the HIS scheme and other schemes is listed in Table 2, where M is the power of polynomial, L is the vector length in Vandermonde Matrix, P is the bilinear pairings operation, X is the computation complexity of exclusive OR operation and N is the length of module that decides the security level. The main operation of the HIS scheme includes the scalar multiplication on elliptic curve (ECCmu) as well as Matrix multiplication and addition (MAop).

Table 2. Computation complexity

Scheme	Computation complexity
AVM	$(M + 8) * L^{2.5}$
GLKM	$2P + nX$
ECC-CA	$0.8 * N^3$
HIS	$ECC_{mu} + 7nMA_{op}$

To guarantee the security, we select several classical configurations for AVM and ECC-CA scheme as shown in Table 3 to represent different scenarios, denoted as S1–S6.

Table 3. Setting of the experiments (S1–S6)

	N	L	M
S1	1024	64	256
S2	1024	128	256
S3	1024	64	512
S4	2048	256	256
S5	2048	256	1024
S6	2048	128	2048

4.2   Consumption of Energy and Time

As shown in Fig. 2, the energy and time consumption of the HIS scheme outperforms the ECC-CA, AVM and GLKM schemes. One reason is that hierarchical architecture is adopted in the HIS scheme, which decreases the storage overhead and improves the communication efficiency. Another reason is that employing Vandermonde Matrix-based identity not only improves the security, but also decreases the computation complexity and save the storage cost. Moreover, the HIS scheme adopts the signcryption method, which accomplish the signature and encryption in one step, such that the communication time is decreased greatly.

It is also observed that the HIS scheme is very stable. From scenario S1 to S6, the energy and time consumption of the HIS changes very slowly, which span is no more than 0.9 mJ. However, the ECC-CA scheme changes greatly in S3 and S4.

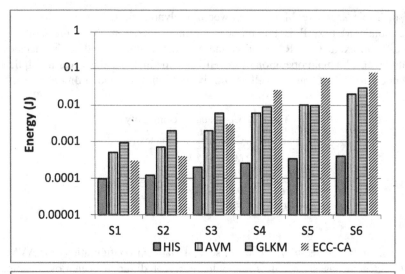

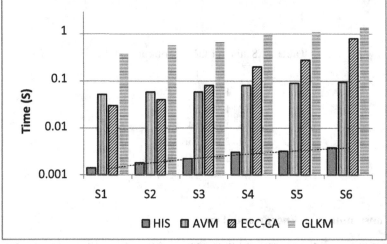

Fig. 2. Energy & time consumption

5   Conclusion

UWSN could be utilized to monitor underwater environment, especially some hash underwater environment. Since the wireless transmission media is public, the sensors in UWSNs are vulnerable to malicious attack. Secure message delivery is one of the main concerns in UWSN. Taking the character of UWSN into account, we should design low energy and time consumption security scheme. In this paper, we proposed a hierarchical identity-based signcryption (HIS) scheme to guarantee the secure message delivery. Cluster-based hierarchical architecture is often employed for data collection and aggregation to decrease the communication overhead. There are two layers, cluster heads and intra-cluster layer, in the HIS scheme. We adopt matrix-based identifier to generate key in cluster head layer, which provides higher security level than in intra-cluster layer. Different from traditional identity-based encryption scheme, the private key is generated by node itself in the HIS scheme, which avoids the risk of the PKG disclosing the private keys. Signcryption mechanism, which completes the signature and encryption in a single step, is adopted in the HIS scheme to decrease the communication and computation overhead. The experiment results demonstrate the HIS scheme has low energy overhead and time consumption. In the future, we will research the encryption scheme with dynamical topology in UWSN.

References

1. Tran, K., Oh, S.H.: UWSNs: a round-based clustering scheme for data redundancy resolve. Int. J. Distrib. Sens. Netw. **2**(2014), 1–6 (2014)
2. Coutinho, R., Lourei, V., Roaaf, R.: Depth-controlled routing protocol for underwater sensor networks. In: 18th IEEE Symposium on Computers and Communications. IEEE Press, Split (2013)
3. Zhong, H., Zhang, Q., Tian, L., Wang, L.: Distributed key sharing based scheme for security clustering in unattended wireless sensor network. J. Commun. **5**(36), 31–39 (2015)
4. Ajalakshmi, P., Logeshwa, R.: Performance analysis of cluster head selection routing protocol in underwater acoustic wireless sensor network. In: Internet Conference on Electronics and Communication Systems (ICECS), Coimbatore, pp. 1005–1011 (2015)
5. Yuan, C., Chen, W., Zhu, Y., Li, D.: A low computational complexity authentication scheme in underwater wireless sensor network. In: International Conference on Mobile Ad-hoc & Sensor Networks, Shenzhen, China, pp. 116–123 (2015)
6. Oliveira, L.B., Dahab, R., Lopez, J.: Identity-based encryption for sensor networks. In: The 5th Annual IEEE International Conference on Pervasive Computing and Communications Workshops, White Plains, New York, USA (2007)
7. RSA Homepage. https://en.wikipedia.org/wiki/RSA_(cryptosystem)
8. Zhang, B., Wang, X.: ECC-based security clustering algorithm for wireless sensor network. J. Lanzhou Jiaotong Univ. **1**(35), 20–24 (2016)
9. Li, F., Zhong, D.: A survey of digital signcryption. Netinfo Secur. **12**, 1–8 (2011)
10. Zheng, Y.: Digital signcryption or how to achieve cost (signature & encryption) ≪ cost (signature) + cost (encryption). In: Kaliski, B.S. (ed.) CRYPTO 1997. LNCS, vol. 1294, pp. 165–179. Springer, Heidelberg (1997). https://doi.org/10.1007/BFb0052234
11. Wang, H., Sheng, B., Li, Q.: Elliptic curve cryptography-based access control in sensor networks. Int. J. Secur. Netw. **1**(3/4), 127–137 (2006)
12. Katz, J., Yung, M.: Scalable protocols for authenticated group key exchange. J. Cryptol. **1**(20), 85–113 (2007)
13. Shamir, A.: Identity-based cryptosystems and signature schemes. In: Blakley, G.R., Chaum, D. (eds.) CRYPTO 1984. LNCS, vol. 196, pp. 47–53. Springer, Heidelberg (1985). https://doi.org/10.1007/3-540-39568-7_5
14. Yang, M., AI-Anbuky, A., Liu, W.: An identity-based authentication protocol for sensor networks. In: 9th International Conference on Intelligent Sensors, Sensor Networks and Information Processing (ISSNIP), pp. 1–6. IEEE Press, Salvador (2014)
15. Wei, R., Zhao, D.: Key-management scheme based on identity and cluster layer for wireless sensor network. Eng. J. Wuhan Univ. **4**(48), 580–583 (2015)

16. Guo, P., Zhang, H., Fu, D., Zhou, M.: Hybrid and lightweight cryptography for WSN. Comput. Sci. **1**(39), 69–78 (2012)
17. Deng, S., Wang, Y.: Grouping and layered key management strategy in WSN based on EBS. Comput. Eng. **9**(39), 64–68 (2013)
18. Sozer, E., Stojanovic, M., Proakis, J.: Underwater acoustic networks. IEEE J. Oceanic Eng. **1** (25), 72–83 (2000)

A Weighted Fuzzy c-Means Clustering Algorithm for Incomplete Big Sensor Data

Peng Li[1], Zhikui Chen[1(✉)], Yueming Hu[2], Yonglin Leng[1],
and Qiucen Li[1]

[1] School of Software Technology, Dalian University of Technology,
Dalian 116620, China
zkchen@dlut.edu.cn
[2] College of Natural Resources and Environment,
South China Agricultural University, Guangzhou 510642, China

Abstract. Sensor data processing plays an important role on the development of the wireless sensor networks in the big data era. Owning to the existence of a large number of incomplete data in wireless sensor networks, fuzzy c-means clustering algorithm (FCM) finds it difficult to produce an appropriate cluster result. The paper proposes a distributed weighted fuzzy c-means algorithm based on incomplete data imputation for big sensor data (DWFCM). DWFCM improves Affinity Propagation (AP) clustering algorithm by designing a new similarity metrics for imputing incomplete sensor data, and then proposes a weighted FCM (wFCM) by assigning a lower weighted value to the incomplete data object for improving the cluster accuracy. Finally, we validate the proposed weighted FCM algorithm on the dataset collected from the smart WSN lab. Experiments demonstrate that the weighted FCM algorithm could fill the missing values very accurately and improve the clustering results effectively.

Keywords: Wireless sensor network · Big sensor data
Fuzzy c-means algorithm

1 Introduction

In the past decades, wireless sensor networks (WSNs) have made a numerous advance for many applications such as Internet of Things (IoT) [1–3], buildings health monitoring [4], and smart world [5–8]. With the further development of WSNs, data generated by various sensors and mobile devices is increasing exponentially, which has gradually become a major concern in academia and information industry, that is, big sensor data [9–11].

Big data analytics have a great effect on supporting the development of WSNs. As one important data mining tool, the fuzzy c-means clustering algorithm (FCM) can be extensively used. However, in big sensor data, many data sets are of incompleteness, i.e. a data set X can contain some objects with missing attribute values. FCM could not succeed completely in clustering such incomplete data sets in real time. On the one hand, FCM is easily corrupted by incomplete objects. On the other hand, FCM is

© Springer Nature Singapore Pte Ltd. 2018
J. Li et al. (Eds.): CWSN 2017, CCIS 812, pp. 55–63, 2018.
https://doi.org/10.1007/978-981-10-8123-1_6

difficult to meet real-time requirements of clustering incomplete big sensor data due to the huge amount of data.

The paper proposes a distributed weighted fuzzy c-means algorithm (DWFCM) based on incomplete data imputation for clustering incomplete big sensor data. The paper imputes the incomplete data and then clusters the dataset using FCM.

First, the paper improves Affinity Propagation (AP) clustering algorithm, published in Science magazine proposed by Frey [13], by designing a new similarity metrics for clustering incomplete sensor data directly and then fills the missing values according to the cluster results.

Second, the paper presents a weighted FCM algorithm (wFCM) by assigning a lower weighted value into incomplete data objects to develop the strength against missing values.

Third, we validate the proposed weighted FCM algorithm on the dataset collected from the smart WSN lab. Experiments demonstrate that the weighted FCM algorithm could fill the missing values very accurately and improve the clustering results effectively.

2 Preliminaries and Related Works

2.1 AP Clustering Algorithm

Affinity propagation (AP) inputs the similarity matrix with each item $s(i, k)$ indicating the difference between objects k and i.

One appealing advantage of AP is to discover the number of clusters and AP determines clustering centroids by conveying messages between objects, that is, iteratively calculating the responsibility matrix $R = [r(i, k)]$ and the availability matrix $A = [a(i, k)]$ as follows.

$$r(i, k) = s(i, k) - \max_{k' \neq k}\{a(i, k') + s(i, k')\} \tag{1}$$

$$a(i, k) = \min\{0, r(k, k) + \sum_{i' \notin \{i, k\}} \max\{0, r(i', k)\}\} \tag{2a}$$

$$a(k, k) = \sum_{i' \neq k} \max\{0, r(i', k)\} \tag{2b}$$

2.2 FCM Algorithm

FCM divides a m-dimensional dataset $X = \{x_1, x_2, \ldots, x_n\}$ into several groups to illustrate the data distribution structure. Specially, a fuzzy clustering is determined by a $c \times n$ matrix $U = \{u_{ij}\}$, where u_{ij} represents the membership value of x_j assigned into the i th group, c and n represent the number of clusters and objects, respectively. FCM is determined by [10]

$$M_{fcm} = \{U \in R^{c \times n} | u_{ij} \in [0,1] \quad \forall j,i; \quad 0 < \sum_{j=1}^{n} u_{ij} \leq n, \forall i; \quad \sum_{i=1}^{c} u_{ij} = 1, \forall j\} \quad (3)$$

The objective function of FCM is Eq. (4).

$$J_m(U,V) = \sum_{i=1}^{c} \sum_{k=1}^{n} u_{ij}^m \|x_k - v_i\|^2 \quad (4)$$

for the membership matrix u_{ik} and the i th clustering centroid-c_i, $m \, (1 \leq m < \infty)$.
FCM updates the matrix and the clustering centroid as:

$$u_{ik} = \left[\sum_{j=1}^{c} \left(\frac{\|x_k - v_i\|}{\|x_k - v_j\|} \right)^{\frac{2}{m-1}} \right]^{-1} \quad (5)$$

$$v_i = \sum_{k=1}^{n} u_{ik}^m x_k \bigg/ \sum_{k=1}^{n} u_{ik}^m \quad (6)$$

Repeat Eqs. (5) and (6) until the convergence condition is satisfied, i.e.
$\varepsilon \leq \|v_{k,new} - v_{k,old}\|^2$.

Since the original FCM algorithm was proposed, many FCM variants were presented for improving the performance of FCM.

To improve the cluster accuracy of FCM, a weighted FCM algorithm has been proposed by Urso et al. [14] to find homogeneous groups. Yang et al. [15] presented a robust FCM algorithm to avoid noisy corruption, which can determine the cluster number automatically. Besides, some kernel FCM algorithms are proposed to improve the accuracy by using rows to for a c-means scheme. Other improved FCM algorithms can be found in. Improved FCM algorithms usually works well, However, they are corrupted by missing values easily. To develop the strength against missing values, the paper presents a wFCM algorithm to improve the standard FCM algorithm by assigning a lower weighted value into each incomplete data object.

3 Incomplete Data Imputation Algorithm

3.1 Improved AP Algorithm for Clustering Incomplete Data

In this subsection, an improved AP algorithm is proposed to cluster incomplete data directly.

Assume that there are n objects in the dataset O, $O = \{o_1, o_2, \ldots, o_n\}$, where every object is depicted by m numerical features that have the form $O = \{o_1, o_2, \ldots, o_n\}$. To produce a good result for clustering incomplete data, the algorithm first divides the dataset O into two disjoint subsets, C and U. In the subset C, there are no data objects with missing values and in the set I, each data object has one or more missing values. Next, k-means is used to cluster the objects in the subset C. Finally, each object in the subset I is assigned to the nearest cluster according to the similarity metrics proposed by the paper.

Suppose the j-th feature, a_j, of the object in the i-th cluster, C_i, is belonging to $[x, y]$. Its value can be denoted as a_{ij}, $a_{ij} \in [x, y]$. α and β, can be denoted by: $\alpha = min\{|x - aij|, |y - aij|\}$, $\beta = max\{|x - aij|, |y - aij|\}$.

For each object b in a subset I, let a_j^b denote the j-th feature $P_{aj}(b, c_i)$, indicating the value of b and c_i on feature a_j, is defined as follows.

(1) $1,\ \left|a_j^b - a_j^i\right| \leq \alpha$;

(2) $1/|V|, \alpha < \left|a_j^b - a_j^i\right| \leq \beta$;

(3) $1/|V|^2, a_j^b = *$;

(4) $0, \left|a_j^b - a_j^i\right| > \beta$

From Eqs. (1), (2a), (2b), (3) and (4), calculating the difference between object b of I and the i-th clustering center can be determined by

$$Similar(b, c_i) = \sum_{j=1}^{m} Pa_j(b, c_i) \tag{7}$$

Consequently, the main steps of the improved AP algorithm for clustering incomplete big data are outlined as follows.

Step 1. Divide the objective dataset O to two different subsets, C and U.

Step 2. Calculate the distance matrix S between each two objects of C.

Step 3. Calculate $R = [r(i, k)]$ and $A = [a(i, k)]$.

Step 4. Repeat step 3 till convergence condition is satisfied.

Step 5. For every object with $a(k, k) + r(k, k) > 0$ indicating a clustering center. Divide rest objects to a distinct cluster, and for the data object i, the center with max $a(i, k) + r(i, k)$ is its clustering representative.

Step 7. Calculate coefficients, α and β, of each group.

Step 8. Assign rest objects in the subset I into the representative clusters depend on Eq. (7).

3.2 Missing Values Filling Algorithm Based on Clustering and Mahalanobis Distance

To improve the estimation accuracy of the target object, the paper uses the Mahalanobis distance between the target object and each object in the same cluster with the target object to determine the weighted value of the object. Afterwards, the weighted sum of all the objects in the same cluster with the target object is used as the predicted value.

Consider the objects in the subset C, $o_1, o_2, \ldots, o_m$, which are in the same cluster with the target object g. The main steps of the filling algorithm are outlined as follows.

Step 1. Calculate the Mahalanobis distance between the target object g and the object $o_1, o_2, \ldots, o_m$ respectively, denoted as $d_1, d_2, \ldots, d_m$.

$$d_i = \sqrt{(g - o_i)\, \Sigma^{-1}(g - o_i)^T} \tag{8}$$

Step 2. Normalize all of the distances $d_1, d_2, \ldots, d_m$.

$$p_i = d_i \bigg/ \sum_{i=1}^{m} d_i, \ i = 1, 2, \ldots, m \tag{9}$$

Step 3. Calculate the entropy of each data object according to the Eq. (10).

$$h_i = -(Inm)^{-1} \ln(p_i + \frac{1}{m}), i = 1, 2, \ldots, m \tag{10}$$

Step 4. Calculate the weighted value of each data object according to the Eq. (11).

$$\omega_i = \frac{1}{m-1}\left(1 - \frac{1 - h_i}{\sum_{i=1}^{m}(1 - h_i)}\right), i = 1, 2, \ldots, m \tag{11}$$

Step 5. Calculate the predicted value of the missing data according to the Eq. (12).

$$g' = \sum_{i=1}^{m} w_i \times o_i, \ i = 1, 2, \ldots, m \tag{12}$$

4   A Weighted FCM Algorithm

Even though missing values have been filled in the Sect. 3, the filled values are not exactly equal to the original values, which will reduce the accuracy of the standard FCM algorithm. To produce a good cluster result, the paper improves the FCM algorithm by assigning a lower weighted value into each object with missing values, which aims at reducing the corruption caused by missing values.

For the dataset $O = \{o_1, o_2, \ldots, o_n\}$, the weighted value of each data object is determined by the following rule:

$$w_i = 1 - l/m \tag{13}$$

Where m is the number of the features of the data object and l is the number of missing feature values of the data object o_i. Hence, the weighted FCM algorithm (wFCM) is defined as the constrained optimization of:

$$J_m(U, V) = \sum_{i=1}^{c} \sum_{k=1}^{n} w_k u_{ij}^m \|x_k - v_i\|^2 \tag{14}$$

where w_k is the weighted value of the k-th object, which is determined by Eq. (13). The steps of the wFCM algorithm are outlined as follows.

Step 1: Fix $m > 1$ and $\varepsilon > 0$ for some positive constant;
Step 2: Initialize the parameters, c and V(0);
Step 3: Calculate the degree of membership u_{ij} according to Eq. (5);
Step 4: Calculate the cluster centers according to Eq. (15).

$$v_i = \sum_{k=1}^{n} w_k u_{ik}^m x_k \bigg/ \sum_{k=1}^{n} w_k u_{ik}^m \tag{15}$$

Step 5: If $\varepsilon > \max\{\|vk, \text{new-}vk, \text{old}\|\}$, stop; else repeat step 3.

5 Experiments

Some experiments are run to validate the proposed algorithms in this section. The setup is on the computer with a 3.2 GHz core, 4 GB memory and 1 TB desk. In this section, the experimental dataset is collected from the smart WSN lab.

5.1 Experiment Results of the Missing Values Filling Algorithm

To validate the efficiency of our algorithm for filling missing values, select different number of objects from the primitive dataset randomly and remove several features to simulate the incomplete dataset O.

Assume that the number of objects of O is N with the data missing rate a, the execution times are n, and the number of objects which are filled right is C. The filling accuracy, called IA, is defined in the Eq. (16).

$$IA = (C/n)/(N \times a) \tag{16}$$

The proposed method called FBIAP is evaluated by comparing its effectiveness with two of most representative algorithms, MIBOI and Nevile. The result is shown as in Fig. 1.

From Fig. 1, the filling accuracy decreases with the growth of the missing rate. The filling accuracy of the presented algorithm is highest because it effectively avoids the interference of the unrelated objects with the target object. At the data missing rate > 20%, contrary to MIBOI and Nevile whose filling accuracy decreases sharply, the presented algorithm get a stable filling accuracy, about 80% or more, validating our scheme to fill missing values.

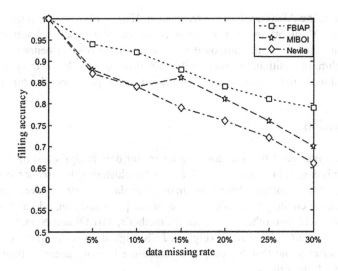

Fig. 1. Filling accuracy of three algorithms.

5.2 Experiment Results of the WFCM Algorithm

To demonstrate the performance of the proposed wFCM algorithm, an evaluation criterion called ARI is introduced. ARI(U, U'), adjusted Rand Index, is a bias-adjusted formulation of the Rand index developed by Hubert and Arabie.

The standard FCM algorithm is used to cluster the primitive dataset to obtain the fuzzy partition U,which represents the ground truth labels for the objects in the dataset. Next, the standard FCM algorithm and the proposed wFCM algorithm are used to cluster the dataset mentioned in Sect. 5.1, which will obtain fuzzy partitions FU and wFU respectively. To compute the ARI, we first harden the fuzzy partitions by setting the maximum element in each column of U to 1, and all else to 0. The result is depicted in Table 1.

Table 1. Results of FCM algorithm and wFCM algorithm.

Data missing rate	FCM algorithm		wFCM algorithm	
	ARI I(U, FU)	Iteration times	ARI(U, wFU)	Iteration times
5%	0.9561	14	0.9893	9
10%	0.9317	21	0.9754	8
15%	0.9021	17	0.9556	10
20%	0.8249	19	0.9331	6
25%	0.8249	20	0.9092	9
30%	0.7627	15	0.8861	7

From Table 1, with the increasing rate of missing data, the ARI(U, FU) and ARI(U, wFU) decrease because the accuracy of the two algorithms are corrupted by missing data. However, the ARI(U, wFU) is greater than ARI(U, FU), which indicates that the proposed wFCM algorithm is performed better on incomplete dataset than FCM algorithm. In other word, the proposed wFCM algorithm obtains better partition than FCM algorithm. In addition, the average iteration times of wFCM are fewer than that of FCM algorithm, which demonstrates the efficient of the proposed algorithm.

6 Conclusion

The paper has presented two technologies for sensor data analysis and mining, FBIAP for filling missing values and WFCM for fuzzy clustering big sensor data. In the FBIAP algorithm, a method based on incomplete data cluster is investigated to fill missing values accurately. The effectiveness of the proposed method has been proved by comparison with two other representative methods, MIBOI and Nevile. To produce a good cluster result efficiently, a weighted FCM algorithm is designed. Experiments on a real dataset show that the proposed technique is more accurate than the other improved FCM algorithms.

In the future research work, we will investigate a further improvement of WFCM to improve the effectiveness and efficiency of clustering big sensor data with many missing values. Additionally, for many semi-structured and unstructured data in big sensor data, our future research plans will modify WFCM to cluster the two types of incomplete data into appropriate groups.

Acknowledgement. This work was supported in part by the National Natural Science Foundation of China under Grants No. 61602083, 61672123 and U1301253, in part by the Fundamental Research Funds for the Central Universities under Grant No. DUT2017TB02, and the Dalian University of Technology Fundamental Research Fund under Grant No. DUT15 RC(3)100.

References

1. Al-Fuqaha, A., et al.: Internet of Things: a survey on enabling technologies, protocols, and applications. IEEE Commun. Surv. Tutor. **17**(4), 2347–2376 (2015)
2. Gao, J., et al.: Approximate event detection over multi-modal sensing data. J. Combinatorial Optim. https://doi.org/10.1007/s10878-015-9847-0
3. Li, P., et al.: A privacy-preserving high-order neuro-fuzzy c-means algorithm with cloud computing. Neurocomputing **256**, 82–89 (2017)
4. Zhang, Q., et al.: An incremental CFS algorithm for clustering large data in industrial Internet of Things. IEEE Trans. Industr. Inform. (2017). https://doi.org/10.1109/tii.2017.2684807
5. Bose, A.: Smart transmission grid applications and their supporting infrastructure. IEEE Trans. Smart Grid **1**(1), 11–19 (2010)
6. Gao, J., et al.: Composite event coverage in wireless sensor networks with heterogeneous sensors. In: Proceedings of 2015 IEEE Conference on Computer Communications (INFOCOM), pp. 217–225 (2015)

7. Zhang, Q., et al.: A node scheduling model based on markov chain prediction for big data. Int. J. Commun. Syst. **28**(9), 1610–1619 (2015)

8. Gungor, V.C., Sahin, D., Kocak, T., et al.: Smart grid technologies: communication technologies and standards. IEEE Trans. Industr. Inform. **7**(4), 529–539 (2011)

9. Musolesi, M.: Big mobile data mining: good or evil. IEEE Internet Comput. **18**(1), 78–81 (2014)

10. Bergelt, R., Vodel, M., Hardt, W.: Energy efficient handling of big data in embedded, wireless sensor networks. In: 2014 IEEE Sensors Applications Symposium (SAS), pp. 53–58. IEEE (2014)

11. Takaishi, D., Nishiyama, H., Kato, N., Miura, R.: Towards energy efficient big data gathering in densely distributed sensor networks. IEEE Trans. Emerg. Topics Comput. **2**, 388–397 (2014)

12. Diaz-Valenzuela, T., et al.: On the use of fuzzy constraints in semisupervised clustering. IEEE Trans. Fuzzy Syst. **24**(4), 992–999 (2016)

13. Frey, B., et al.: Clustering by passing messages between data points. Science **315**(5814), 972–976 (2007)

14. Zhang, Q., et al.: Distributed fuzzy c-means algorithms for big sensor data based on cloud computing. Int. J. Sensor Netw. **18**(1), 32–39 (2015)

15. Yang, X., et al.: A robust deterministic annealing algorithm for data clustering. IEEE Trans. Data Knowl. Eng. **62**(1), 84–100 (2007)

Energy Efficiency and Harvesting

Mobile Sink Data Collection Mechanism for Throughput Maximization with RF Energy Harvesting in WSNs

Yulong Han, Qiuling Tang$^{(\boxtimes)}$, Xian Li, and Jiahao Shi

School of Computer, Electronics and Communication,
Guangxi University, Nanning 530004, People's Republic of China
qiulingtang@gxu.edu.cn

Abstract. Recent years have witnessed the studies of mobile vehicle scheduling to recharge sensor nodes via wireless energy transfer technologies. However, most of them just overlook radio frequency (RF) energy harvesting methods and few applications are mentioned. This paper presents a novel mobile sink data collection mechanism (MSDCM) for clustered wireless sensor networks (WSNs), where RF energy harvesting technology is put use into recharging cluster head nodes for maximizing the network throughput while prolonging the network lifetime. In this scheme, the mobile sink visits every cluster head in turn. At each cluster head, the mobile sink stops, collects data from the cluster head, then charges the cluster head by RF (in other words, the cluster head harvests energy from the mobile sink). The network throughput is investigated and maximized by optimizing the tradeoff between data collecting time and energy harvesting time in Matlab.

Keywords: Energy harvesting · Data collecting · Mobile sink
Throughput

1 Introduction

Energy limitation is a crucial issue in WSNs, where nodes are genernally powered by tethered batteries and the batteries can't be replaced in some extreme circumstances so that the lifetime of the WSNs is greatly limited [1,2].

For solving the energy bottleneck problem and improving the performance of WSNs, these years emerge a large number of researches on energy harvesting from natural sources, such as solar and wind. In [3–6], solar energy is used to charge sensor nodes, where the research led by PengShuai and Chor Ping Low in [5] proposes ENR (Energy Neutral Routing) algorithm which makes sensor nodes not be energy exhausted and the energy of each node is relatively balanced. Meantime, surrounding RF energy is also investigated to be harvested as an important energy resource for sensor nodes. In [7], authors successfully realizes the RF energy harvesting in urban and semi-urban environment. In [8], a control

© Springer Nature Singapore Pte Ltd. 2018
J. Li et al. (Eds.): CWSN 2017, CCIS 812, pp. 67–73, 2018.
https://doi.org/10.1007/978-981-10-8123-1_7

scheme about recharge cycle is presented in WSNs and further upgraded to be adaptive control. Recent breakthrough in RF energy harvesting technology is owed to Rui Zhang et al., who provide a RF energy harvesting general model for WSNs [9,10].

With regard to data collection technology in WSNs, static sink and the related multi-hop routing are traditional used. The energy of sensor nodes around the static sink are generally over-depleted due to frequent data communication and the resulting energy black hole appears. To solve the problem, some researchers introduce mobile sink to collect data [11–13], where Yuanyuan Yang and Miao Zhao [14] present a model that joints mobile energy harvesting and data collecting. And a selection algorithm to search dwell point for the mobile sink tour is suggested in [14,15], but the RF energy harvesting technology is not applied. In this paper, a mobile sink data collection scheme is put forward, where the mobile sink is introduced to collect sensed data from cluster head and charge these heads on demands through RF for maximizing the network throughput and prolonging the network lifetime.

The rest of the paper is organized as following: the system model is discussed in Sect. 2. The network maximum throughput performance is analyzed in Sect. 3. Section 4 presents the numerical results and simulations about maximum throughput performance. Finally, Sect. 5 summarizes the paper.

2   System Model

Figure 1 depicts a mobile sink collection data system, which is mainly composed of a mobile sink and clusters of sensor nodes. There are a cluster head node and a number of cluster member nodes in each cluster. The mobile sink periodically visits each cluster head according to a regular order and track. And the mobile

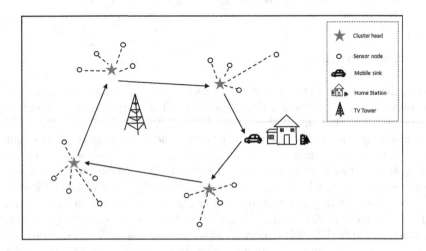

Fig. 1. System model for mobile sink data collecting and energy charging.

sink can recover its power capacity when it returns to its home station at every period. When the mobile sink visits and stops at each cluster head, it has to complete the same two operations–collects data from the cluster head, then charges the cluster head. Or the demanded energy of the cluster head can be supplied by other power sources, such as TV tower.

In this model, the distance between mobile sink and cluster head is very close so that some energy loss can be ignored, such as circuit energy loss and data fusion energy loss. And only the data transmission energy consumption for each cluster head is considered as the cluster head energy consumption E_{con} and

$$E_{coni} \leq E_{0i} + E_{ci} - E_{Ti}, \tag{1}$$

where E_{0i} is the current energy of cluster head, E_{ci} is the energy harvested from the mobile sink and E_{Ti} is the minimal energy threshold with which the clust head can keep working normally.

3   Mobile Sink Data Collection Scheme (MSDCS)

Based on the system model, an operation machinism, namely mobile sink data collection scheme (MSDCS), is designed for maximizing the network throughput and prolonging the network lifetime. In this scheme, RF energy harvesting technology is introduced and the cluster heads can harvest the RF signal energy from mobile sink or from other RF signal sources (such as TV Tower). For simplifying the scheme, only RF signal energy from the mobile sink is harvested and each cluster head can harvest enough energy on demands to keep the network work sustainably or permanently.

At each cluster head, the mobile sink stops for a period of time, called the dwell time T_i at the cluster head, to complete data collection during the data collection time T_{si} and power supply for the cluster head during the energy harvesting time T_{ci}, as depicted in Fig. 2.

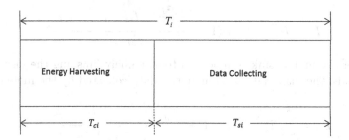

Fig. 2. Block time for data collecting and energy harvesting.

During T_{ci}, the mobile sink charges a cluster head by RF energy, in other words, the cluster head harvests the RF signal energy transmitted by the mobile sink as its power supplyment. Considering a Rayleigh distribution channel, the power harvested by the cluster head P_r is given by [9] and

$$P_{ri} = \frac{\xi |h_i|^2 P_{ti}}{d_i^{-m}} \tag{2}$$

where P_t is the RF signal power transmitted by the mobile sink, d is the distance between the mobile sink and the cluster head, ξ is the battery energy conversion efficiency with $0 < \xi < 1$, h is channel gain, and m is the path loss exponent of the channel.

Because the distance between the mobile sink and the cluster head is very small, the energy loss of transmitting circuit and receiving circuiting can be ignored. Then the energy harvested by the cluster head is

$$E_{ci} = P_{ri} \cdot T_{ci} = \frac{\xi |h_i|^2 P_{ti}}{d_i^{-m}} \cdot T_{ci}. \tag{3}$$

Accordingly, the maximum information rate between the mobile sink and the cluster head is

$$C_i = B \cdot log_2(1 + \frac{P_{Si}}{P_{Ni}}), \tag{4}$$

where P_S is the signal power and P_N is the noise power received by the cluster head, and

$$P_{Si} = \frac{E_{ci} + E_{0i} - E_{Ti}}{T_{si}}. \tag{5}$$

Substituting (3) and (5) into (4), C is obtained as

$$C_i = B \cdot log_2(1 + \frac{\frac{\xi |h_i|^2 P_{ti}}{d_i^{-m}} \cdot T_{ci} + E_{0i} - E_{Ti}}{T_{si} \cdot N_i}), \tag{6}$$

then, the maximal total amount of data which is able to be sent by the cluster head can be derived as

$$L_i = T_{si} \cdot B \cdot log_2(1 + \frac{\frac{\xi |h_i|^2 P_{ti}}{d_i^{-m}} \cdot T_{ci} + E_{0i} - E_{Ti}}{T_{si} \cdot N_i}). \tag{7}$$

Then, after the mobile sink completes a tour, namely finishing the visit to all k cluster heads, the maximal total amount of data collected by the mobile sink is

$$L_A = \sum_{i=1}^{k} T_{si} \cdot B \cdot log_2(1 + \frac{\frac{\xi |h_i|^2 P_t}{d_i^{-m}} \cdot T_{ci} + E_{0i} - E_{Ti}}{T_{si} \cdot N_i}). \tag{8}$$

When T_i is specified, the network throughput is followed to be

$$R_A = \frac{1}{T} \cdot \sum_{i=1}^{k} T_{si} \cdot B \cdot log_2(1 + \frac{\frac{\xi |h_i|^2 P_{ti}}{d_i^{-m}} \cdot T_{ci} + E_{0i} - E_{Ti}}{T_{si} \cdot N_i}), \tag{9}$$

where $T = \sum_{i=1}^{k} T_i + T_{vac}$ is the period for the mobile sink complete a tour.

The network throughput can be attracted to be maximal by optimizing the data collecting time T_{si} and the maximization problems can be modeled as follows,

$$max\ R_A$$
$$s.t.\quad T_i = A\ ,$$
$$T_i = T_{si} + T_{ci} \tag{10}$$
$$T = \sum_{i=1}^{k} T_i + T_{vac},\ i = 1, \cdots, k$$

where A is a constant.

4   Numerical Results

Numerical simulation in Matlab is used to solve the maximization problems. The initial energy of all cluster head are set the same value to be 0.1 J. Other related parameters are respectively set to be: Conversion efficiency $\xi = 1$, the channel power gain $|h_i|^2 = 1$, the mobile sink charging power $P_{ti} = 3\,$W, path attenuation exponent $m = 2.7$, the distance between mobile sink and cluster head $d_i = 1M(i = 1, \ldots, k)$, the minimum energy threshold $E_{Ti} = 0.05\,$J, the signal noise power $N_i = 0.00001\,$W, the wireless channel bandwidth $B = 300\,$Mbps.

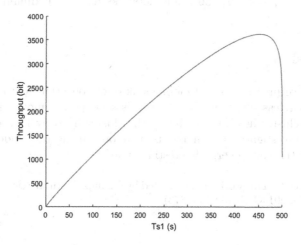

Fig. 3. The relationship between T_s and throughput when i = 1.

Figure 3 depict the relationship between data collecting time T_s and networks throughput. There exists an optimal T_s to achieve the maximum throughput. In order to verify the maximum throughput expressed in (9), we assume the dwell

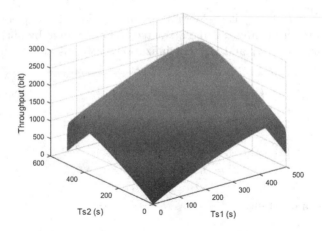

Fig. 4. The relationship between T_s and throughput when i = 2.

time $T_i = 500$ s. Figure 3 shows variation of throughput with time when there are only one cluster head. As shown in the Fig. 4, we simulate the variation of throughput with time when there are two cluster heads. We can see that the maximum throughput is related to the data collecting time. In addition, we also simulate the case of multiple cluster heads. In first 450 s, throughput increases rapidly with time. In the last 50 s, throughput sudden drops to zero. It can be seen from Figs. 3 and 4 that: When data collecting time and energy harvesting time satisfy $T_s : T_c = 9 : 1$, the whole networks have a maximum throughput value.

5   Conclusion

In this paper, we present a novel mobile sink data collection scheme (MSDCS) for clustered wireless sensor networks. In this scheme, the mobile sink collects data from the cluster head, then charges the cluster head by RF. The network throughput is investigated and maximized by optimizing the tradeoff between data collecting time and energy harvesting time.

Acknowledgment. This work was supported by Guangxi Natural Science Foundation under Grant (No. 2014GXNSFAA118373).

References

1. Tan, Q., An, W., et al.: Energy harvesting aware topology control with power adaptation in wireless sensor networks. Ad Hoc Netw. **27**, 44–56 (2015)
2. Li, X., Tang, Q., Sun, C.: Energy efficient dispatch strategy for the mobile sink in wireless rechargeable sensor networks with mobile data gathering. Wirel. Netw. (2016)

3. Peng, S., Low, C.P.: Energy neutral directed diffusion for energy harvesting wireless sensor networks. Comput. Commun. **63**, 40–52 (2015)

4. Peng, S., Low, C.P.: Prediction free energy neutral power management for energy harvesting wireless sensor nodes. Ad Hoc Netw. **13**, 351–367 (2014)

5. Peng, S., Low, C.P.: Energy neutral routing for energy harvesting wireless sensor networks. In: 2013 IEEE Wireless Communication and Networking Conference (WCNC), Networks, pp. 2063–2067 (2013)

6. Martinez, G., Li, S., Zhou, C.: Wastage-aware routing in energy-harvesting wireless sensor networks. IEEE Sens. J. **13**, 2967–2974 (2014)

7. Pinuela, M., Mitcheson, P.D., Lucyszyn, S.: Ambient RF energy harvesting in urban and semi urban environments. IEEE Trans. Microw. **61**, 2715–2726 (2013)

8. Shigeta, R., Sasaki, T., Quan, D.M., et al.: Ambient RF energy harvesting sensor device with capacitor-leakage-aware duty cycle control. IEEE Sens. **13**, 2973–2983 (2013)

9. Zhou, X., Zhang, R., Ho, C.K.: Wireless information and power transfer: architecture design and rate-energy tradeoff. IEEE Globecom (2012). https://doi.org/10.1109/GLOCOM

10. Ju, H., Zhang, R.: Throughput maximization in wireless powered communication networks. IEEE Trans. Wirel. Commun. **13**(1), 418–428 (2013)

11. Liang, W., Xu, W., Ren, X., et al.: Maintaining sensor networks perpetually via wireless recharging mobile vehicles. In: IEEE 39th Conference on Local Computer Networks (LCN), Edmonton, AB, 8–11 September (2014)

12. Xie, L., Shi, Y., Yi, H., et al.: Making sensor networks immortal: an energy-renewal approach with wireless power transfer. IEEE/ACM Trans. Network. **6**(20), 1748–1761 (2012)

13. Keskin, M.E.: A column generation heuristic for optimal wireless sensor network design with mobile sinks. Europ. J. Oper. Res. **260**(1), 291–304 (2017)

14. Guo, S., Wang, C.: Joint mobile data gathering and energy provisioning in wireless rechargeable sensor networks. IEEE Trans. Mob. Comput. **12**(13), 2836–2852 (2014)

15. Zhao, M., Li, J., Yang, Y.: A framework of joint mobile energy replenishment and data gathering in wireless rechargeable sensor networks. IEEE Trans. Mob. Comput. **12**(13), 2689–2705 (2014)

16. Chen, H., Li, Y., Rebelatto, J.L., Uchoa-Filhoand, B.F., Vucetic, B.: Harvest-then-cooperate: wireless-powered cooperative communications. IEEE Trans. Sig. Process **63**(7), 1700–1711 (2015)

Improved Energy Efficient Adaptive Clustering Routing Algorithm for WSN

Guozhi Song[✉], Guoliang Qu, Qing Ma, and Xin Zhang

School of Computer Science and Software Engineering,
Tianjin Polytechnic University, Tianjin 300387, China
songguozhi@tjpu.edu.cn, quguoliang718@gmail.com,
qing.mapub@gmail.com

Abstract. Routing algorithm is the key to prolong the lifetime of the overall wireless sensor network. At present, clustering routing algorithm is more widely used in wireless sensor networks. But this way of transmitting information through the cluster can lead to uneven energy consumption in the network, which is known as the "hot zone" problem. However, the uneven clusters, the way of multi-hop transmission between clusters can solve this problem. According to the characteristics of routing in wireless sensor network, this paper analyzes the defects and disadvantages of the current routing algorithm. This paper proposes a series of improvement measures for the current uneven clustering routing algorithm. This paper proposes a new algorithm which has a longer network life and better stability compared with the existing routing algorithm through experimental results and analysis.

Keywords: Wireless sensor networks · Routing algorithm
Uneven clustering routing

1 Introduction

Wireless sensor network (WSN) [1] is a widely used distributed sensing network. WSN is able to connect a large number of wireless sensor nodes through wireless connection. It builds the network through self organization, which makes the WSN flexible and changeable. Therefore, WSNs are widely used in various fields, such as medical, commercial and military et al.

At present, the research on WSNs mainly focuses on localization, routing, storage and trustworthiness, but routing is the key to prolong the overall network lifetime. From the aspect of network topology, routing algorithms for WSNs are mainly divided into plane routing algorithm and clustering routing algorithm.

As matters stand, cluster routing is more widely used in WSNs. The nodes are divided into clusters and each cluster head is responsible for the collection and integration of data within the cluster. The information of one cluster will be transmitted to the sink node by the cluster head. It thus can effectively reduce the overall energy consumption of the network nodes. However, transmitting information through cluster heads can make the energy consumption of cluster head nodes too large which will lead to uneven energy consumption of the network, also known as the "hot zone" problem.

© Springer Nature Singapore Pte Ltd. 2018
J. Li et al. (Eds.): CWSN 2017, CCIS 812, pp. 74–85, 2018.
https://doi.org/10.1007/978-981-10-8123-1_8

Furthermore, multi-hop transmission between clusters, the uneven clusters, can improve this problem. In order to extend the overall network lifetime and increase the average energy of the whole network, an improved algorithm is designed in this paper when analyzes the defects and shortcomings of the current routing algorithm according to the characteristics of routing in wireless sensor network routing and make a series of improvement on the current uneven clustering routing algorithm.

There are several drawbacks in EEUC and BEERA algorithm and problems such as the energy consumption asymmetric of nodes. The routing algorithm is designed on the basis of the features of the problems which need to be resolved: this paper puts forward an Improved Energy-Efficient Adaptive Clustering Routing Algorithm, IEACRA.

The innovation of this paper is that the cluster head election considers more about the current network state, simultaneously, applying different competition radius calculation methods according to different state of network. So that the nodes within the scope can join the cluster and finally through the inter cluster multi-hop data transmission. Finally, we successfully balanced the energy load and prolonged the network life time.

The rest of the paper is organized as follows. Section 2 describes the related work for clustering routing in WSN. In Sect. 3, models used in the IEACRA algorithm of the WSNs are introduced. Section 4 explains the proposed improved energy-efficient adaptive clustering routing algorithm. In Sect. 5, simulation results are discussed and Sect. 6 concludes the major findings of the whole paper.

2　Related Work

In recent years, researchers have been pushing forward the research of clustering routing for wireless sensor networks. The most typical and the first hierarchical routing algorithm, i.e., LEACH (Low Energy Adaptive Clustering Hierarchy) [2], proposed by Heinzelman et al. The algorithm can balance the energy of nodes in the whole network by cluster head rotation, so that the lifetime of the whole network is extended by 15% compared with the static clustering routing algorithm.

EEUC [3] (Energy-Efficient Uneven Clustering) was proposed by the Li from Nanjing University, which selects cluster heads through competitions mainly based on the residual energy of nodes. Taking into account the node energy while reselecting the cluster head node and also setting the node density for the nodes, Wang proposed the NCHS-Leach [4] (Novel Cluster Head Selecting Leach) algorithm. LBMC [5] (Layer Based Multi-hop Clustering routing algorithm for wireless sensor networks) was proposed by Zhou et al. based on the communication cost as a benchmark for hierarchical network. Jiang et al. proposed DEBUC [6] (Distributed Energy-balanced Unequal Clustering Routing Protocol), which controls the competition radius based on the time cluster head competition algorithm and the residual energy of nodes.

Feng focus on the "hot zone" problem, through improving the LEACH algorithm and the optimal threshold competition radius to improve the energy of cluster head load balancing, proposed BEERA [7] (Balanced Energy Efficient Clustering Routing Algorithm). Li proposed UAUC [8] (uneven clustering routing algorithm). The algorithm through divided non equal partition of the network and according to the energy factor, distance factor and intensity factor in each region to select the appropriate cluster head node.

PEGASIS [9] proposed by Lindsey et al. on the basis of knowing the location information of each node, it organizes the network node into chains, then data fused on the chain and transmitted to the sink. Younis et al. have studied a hybrid clustering algorithm, HEED [10], which present the idea of backup cluster head.

DECAR [11] algorithm was proposed by Tarach and Amgoth of India, and it balances the load of the whole network by taking into account the coverage area of the cluster head. Martins et al. combine Dijkstra algorithm with BBE-C [12] routing algorithm to reduce the energy used in computing route, and develop a routing algorithm called MBBEC [13]. The ElhamRezaei team from Iran proposed the MMRCE [14] algorithm to select the optimal cluster head by adding residual energy and distance factors to further prolong network lifetime.

3   Analysis of the Problem

We make a description about the network model and the energy model before elaborating the core algorithm design of this paper.

3.1   Network Model

This paper uses a network model similar to paper [3]. In a square region A, N wireless sensor nodes are randomly distributed among them. The application scenario is a periodic WSN for data collection. The i sensor nodes are represented using s_i, and eventually the sensor nodes in the network are represented as:

$$S\{s_1, s_2, s_3, s_4, \ldots\ldots, s_N\}, |S| = N. \tag{1}$$

We assume that the WSN model has the following characteristics:

(1) The sink node of WSN is outside the WSN, and after the network is randomly arranged, the location of the sink node and all the sensor nodes is not changing.
(2) All sensor nodes have the same data processing capability and network communication function, and all nodes have the opportunity to become cluster head nodes, and each node has their unique ID.
(3) The communication power of the sensor nodes can be adjusted automatically, that is, the nodes can automatically adjust the transmit power of their signals according to the current communication distance, thus further reducing the energy consumption.
(4) The overall link is symmetric. If the transmitted power of the other node is known, then the node that receives the information can estimate the distance between them based on the strength of the signal received at this time.
(5) All nodes of the network are not installed with GPS modules, and could not know their detailed location through GPS.

3.2   Energy Model

The energy model is the same as the wireless communication energy consumption model used by the Leach algorithm. If the WSN node sends k bit data, the distance from the receiving data node is d, total energy consumption at this time is the sum of emission circuit consumption and power amplification losses, as follows:

$$E_{Tx}(k, d) = \begin{cases} k \times E_{elec} + k \times \varepsilon_{fs} \times d^2, d < d_0 \\ k \times E_{elec} + k \times \varepsilon_{mp} \times d^4, d \geq d_0 \end{cases} \qquad (2)$$

Among them, $E_{Tx}(k, d)$ represents the overall energy consumption. k indicates the size of the data to be sent. d stands for the distances between the nodes. The E_{elec} represents the emission circuit consumption. In the free space model, the energy required for power amplification is ε_{fs}. In multipath fading model, the energy needed for power amplification is ε_{mp}. $d_0 = \sqrt{\frac{\varepsilon_{fs}}{\varepsilon_{mp}}}$ is a decision threshold that represents the transmission distance. When the transmission distance is less than it, the loss of power amplification calculation using the free space model. Otherwise, multipath fading model is adopted.

Thus, when the data received by the node is k bit, the total amount of energy consumed at this time is

$$E_{Rx}(k) = k \times E_{elec} \qquad (3)$$

If the data is fused at the cluster head node, the energy consumption of the data fusion is also generated, and at this point the E_{Rx} is used to represent the energy consumed when fusing 1 bit data. At the same time, assuming that the data collected by nodes is more redundant, the cluster head nodes can fuse the data collected from the nodes in the cluster into fixed length packets, and finally send them to the sink node.

4   IEACRA Algorithm Design

When the network initializes, all sensor nodes need to receive a signal, whose transmission power is known, broadcast by sink node. Then the sensor node calculates the approximate distance between it and the sink node by the received RSSI signal strength.

Next, the IEACRA algorithm uses a recursive method with two stages in each round including the cluster formation phase and the data transfer phase. The cluster formation stage includes the election of cluster head nodes and the establishment of clusters, and the data transfer stage includes inter cluster routing and cluster head data transmission.

4.1   Cluster Formation Stage

At the beginning of the algorithm, cluster-headed elections are required. In the beginning of the network, the cluster head election is still random. Therefore, in this paper we refer to paper [15] to improve the threshold calculation formula for controlling cluster head election in LEACH [2].

$$T(n) = \begin{cases} \frac{p}{1-p\times[r\times mod(\frac{1}{p})]} \times \frac{E_{res}}{E_o}, & n \in G \\ 0, & n \notin G \end{cases} \tag{4}$$

Where $T(n)$ represents the threshold of the node at this point. p is the proportion of all nodes that need to be selected for cluster heads. r is the current number of rounds. E_{res} is the residual energy of the current node. E_o is the initial energy of the node.

But this way of calculating the threshold is too one-sided. The overall choice of thresholds should take into account the average energy of the current network. In this way, it is possible to increase the chances that the nodes with large remaining energy are selected as cluster heads. Therefore, the following threshold selection formulae are proposed.

$$T(n) = \begin{cases} \frac{p}{1-p\times[r\times mod(\frac{1}{p})]} \times \frac{E_{res}}{E_{avg}}, & n \in G, \frac{E_{res}}{E_{avg}} \leq 0.7 \\ 1 & n \in G, \frac{E_{res}}{E_{avg}} > 0.7 \\ 0, & n \notin G \end{cases} \tag{5}$$

Among them, E_{avg} is the average node energy of the current network, taking into account the existence of residual energy is greater than the average energy. Therefore, when the value of $\frac{E_{res}}{E_{avg}}$ is greater than 0.7, the node becomes a candidate cluster head directly, thus ensuring that the nodes with large energy have the opportunity to become cluster heads. A large number of factors needs to be considered in choosing the threshold of the election cluster head, so there is no definite way to determine the threshold. A threshold range of 0.3–0.9 is tested in this paper. The selection of the ratio is the optimal value selected by many experiments.

After the candidate cluster heads are generated, the candidate cluster heads need to broadcast their competition messages to the nodes within their competition radius. The competition information includes the ID of the node, the competition radius, the distance between the sink node, and the current residual energy of the candidate cluster head. Previous studies have used a fixed radius calculation formula of competition in order to implement the uneven clustering, but in the initialization of the network should not rush to realize uneven clustering. We should let the nodes of the network consider the problem of energy consumption after the node becomes the cluster head. It means we need to select the cluster head, and then proceed to realize uneven clustering. Therefore, this paper refers to the paper [3] and paper [8] for the study of the radius of competition, and obtains the following formula for the calculation of the competition radius.

$$R_c = \begin{cases} \sqrt{4\frac{2\varepsilon_{mp}}{\pi\rho\varepsilon_{fs}}}, & r = 1 \\ \left(1 - c\frac{d_{max}-d(s_i,DS)}{d_{max}-d_{min}}\right)R_c^0, & r > 1 \end{cases} \tag{6}$$

Among them, R_c is the competition radius. ε_{mp} and ε_{fs} are radio signal propagation parameters used by cluster members and cluster heads for communication, and wireless model propagation parameters for cluster heads to communicate with sink nodes. ρ is the current network node density. d_{max} and d_{min} represent the maximum and minimum values of the distance between nodes in the network to the sink node, respectively. $d(s_i, DS)$ represents the distance from node s_i to the sink node. R_c^0 is the maximum value of the competition radius of cluster heads. c takes $\frac{1}{3}$.

When $r = 1$, the formula is derived from BEERA proposed by Jiang [8]. It has been found that the excellence of the formula adopted in this algorithm lies in the time of network initialization. That is because the energy of the nodes is the same in the start, however, as the network continues to process, the nodes will die and the energy varies. As a result, the decisive factor is the path from the node to the sink node. Therefore, when $r > 1$ is used, an algorithm based on the competition radius algorithm of EEUC [3], which focus on uneven clustering of WSNs, should be used. At the same time, the value of the important parameter c is also determined according to the analysis in this paper [3].

In order to verify the most appropriate use of time for different formulae, all cases are divided into three categories. These three different situations are the initial time of node, the initial stage of node operation, and the later stage of node operation. At the same time, each case is set with 9 different thresholds. Finally, after research and experimental verification, we can get the conclusion that it is appropriate only at the node initialization.

Figure 1 is the schematic diagram of network initialization, at which time the network belongs to even clustering stage.

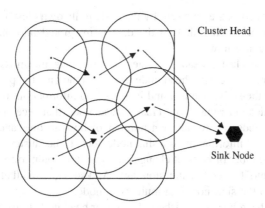

Fig. 1. Schematic diagram of cluster routing in network initialization

Then, with the continuous operation of the network, clustering routing starts from the original even clustering to the current uneven clustering. It is easy to see that the closer to the sink node, the smaller the candidate cluster head will be and the number of cluster heads will increase, thus alleviating the "hot zone" problem in WSNs. As shown in Fig. 2.

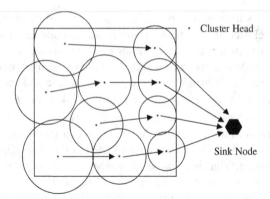

Fig. 2. Schematic diagram of uneven clustering routing in network operation

After all nodes have successfully broadcast their own campaign information, each cluster head begins to compete with other cluster heads. Among the candidate cluster heads in the same range of competition, the most remaining energy node can eventually become cluster heads. At the same time, successful candidates for the cluster head send a "succeed" information to other nodes within the radius, and the other candidate nodes will also send a "unsucceed" information. After that, each common node joins the nearest cluster according to the accepted message. At this point, each cluster is successfully created.

4.2 Data Transfer Stage

Each cluster head receives the data sent by the node in its own cluster, simultaneously, the data is fused which means that all the data is integrated into one packets. Each packet has the same size now.

At this point, the cluster head generates its own data transmission path by the minimum hop count. Each cluster head node initializes the direct hop value of 500. The initial hop value of the sink node is 0 and it sends hop information to all cluster heads within its communication range. The cluster head node that receives the hop information of the sink node can set its own number of hops to one, and simultaneously send its own hop count information as a sink node does. If the cluster head receives less hops than its own number of hops, it changes its own hop count to this new hop count plus 1 and adding into its own transmission path. And so on, until all cluster head nodes can transmit data to the sink node via multi hop mode.

When all paths have been established, the cluster head node transmits its integrated packets to the sink node through a multi-hop way.

Flow chart of IEACRA algorithm is given as follows (Fig. 3).

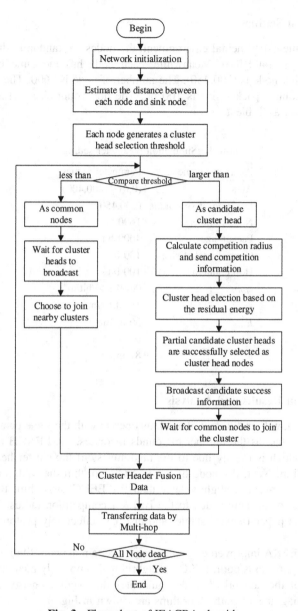

Fig. 3. Flow chart of IEACRA algorithm

5   Simulations and Analysis

This paper uses Matlab to build network models. The LEACH, EEUC, BEERA and IEACRA algorithms described in this paper are all simulated. The performance of the algorithm is compared from two aspects, the network lifetime and the network state.

5.1   Simulation Settings

For simulating the experimental environment, the nodes are randomly distributed in a region of (0,0) ~ (400,400). Meanwhile, each node has the same initial energy. Coordinate of sink node is (200,450). The number of node is 1600. The packet size is 4000 bit. The control packet size is 100 bit. The hop count size is 100 bit. All the parameters are set as Table 1.

Table 1. Simulation parameter setting

Parameter name	Parameter values
Area	(0,0) ~ (400,400)
Location of sink node	(200,450)
Node number	1600
Packet size	4000 bit
Control packet size	100 bit
Hop count size	100 bit
ε_{mp}	0.0013 pJ/bit/m^4
ε_{fs}	10 pJ/bit/m^2
E_{elec}	50 nJ/bit
E_0	0.3 J
d_0	87 m

5.2   Simulation Results and Analysis

Figure 4 shows how four different algorithms operate with the same parameter setting. It is easy to see that, as the number of rounds increases, the LEACH algorithm first begins to die, which is mainly due to the randomness of the cluster head election in LEACH algorithm. Next, the node of the EEUC algorithm dies. Although the death node of BEERA appeared slightly later than the EEUC algorithm, the BEERA is always in a state of instability due to the BEERA competition radius. The IEACRA algorithm in this paper is more stable, and also can effectively prolong the network lifetime.

Although BEERA improvements can extend a certain network lifetime, the average energy of the algorithm is poor. IEACRA algorithm can not only guarantee the overall life extension of the network, but also guarantee the average energy of nodes. The network state diagrams of both algorithms are shown in Fig. 5.

By comparing the two best selected algorithms, you can see that a small jump occurs around 430 round because the overall energy consumption of the BEERA is unstable. This is mainly due to a large number of node deaths, leaving only some nodes with great energy. It is obvious that the average energy of IEACRA algorithm is better than that of BEERA algorithm and the curve of which is also smoother.

The reason why the algorithm improves the network lifetime is the following two points. Firstly, as shown in formula (4), we propose a threshold selection method that

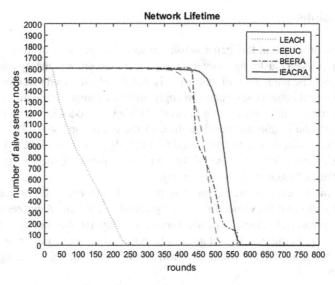

Fig. 4. Network lifetime comparison

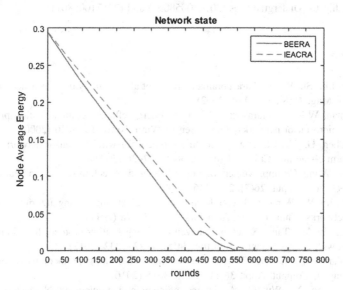

Fig. 5. Network state diagram

takes more into account the average energy of the current network. Secondly, as shown in formula (5), we modify the selection formula of competition radius according to different network states.

6 Conclusions

The algorithm proposed in this paper is used to solve the problem of the insufficiency of the current uneven clustering routing algorithm and the uneven energy consumption of WSN nodes. The innovation of this paper is that the cluster head election takes into account the current network state and can apply different competitive radius calculation method according to different state of network. So that the nodes in the range can join the cluster and finally transmit the data through the multi-hop mode. The simulation results show that compared with EEUC and BEERA algorithm, the IEACRA algorithm achieves the effective improvement of the "hot zone" problem, the energy load balancing and the extension of network life time.

Because of the experimental error, this paper had not been able to make a reasonable explanation for the value of threshold parameter selection. A further analysis of the threshold parameter values in the algorithm and comparison of network parameters and environments in more ways still need to be done. At the same time more excellent scheme can be considered in routing transmissions, thus further reducing the "hot zone" problem.

Acknowledgements. This work is supported by National Training Program of Innovation and Entrepreneurship for Undergraduates (201610058096) and (201710058071).

References

1. Akyildiz, I.F., Su, W., Sankarasubramaniam, Y., et al.: A survey on sensor networks. IEEE Commun. Mag. **40**(8), 102–114 (2002)
2. Heinzelman, W.R., Chandrakasan, A., et al.: Energy-efficient communication protocol for wireless microsensor networks. Adhoc Sensor Wirel. Netw. **18**, 8020 (2000)
3. Li, C., Chen, G., Ye, M., et al.: A routing protocol for wireless sensor networks based on nonuniform clustering. Chin. J. Comput. **30**(1), 27–36 (2007)
4. Wang, G., Wang, C.: Improvement of cluster head node selection strategy in Leach protocol. Microelectron. Comput. **26**(7), 254–256 (2009)
5. Zhou, D., Jin, W., Rong, Z.: Hierarchical multi hop clustering routing algorithm for wireless sensor networks. Chin. J. Sens. Actuators **24**(1), 73–78 (2011)
6. Jiang, C., Shi, W., Tang, X., et al.: Uneven clustering routing protocol for wireless sensor networks with energy balance. J. Softw. **34**(5), 1222–1232 (2012)
7. Li, S., Yang, W., Wu, X.: Wireless sensor network routing protocol based on unequal partitioning. J. Comput. Appl. **36**(11), 3010–3015 (2016)
8. Feng, J., Mao, X., Wu, C.: An energy efficient and efficient WSN clustering routing algorithm. Comput. Eng. **38**(23), 88–91 (2012)
9. Lindsey, S., Raghavendra, C., Sivalingam, K.M.: Data gathering algorithms in sensor networks using energy metrics. IEEE Trans. Parallel Distrib. Syst. **13**(13), 924–935 (2002)
10. Younis, O., Fahmy, S.: HEED: a hybrid, energy-efficient, distributed clustering approach for ad hoc sensor networks. IEEE Trans. Mob. Comput. **3**(4), 366–379 (2004)
11. Amgoth, T.: Energy and coverage-aware routing algorithm for wireless sensor networks. In: International Conference on Distributed Computing and Internet Technology, pp. 111–121. Springer, New York (2014)

12. da Silva Rego, A., Celestino, J., Dos Santos, A., et al.: BEE-C: a bio-inspired energy efficient cluster-based algorithm for data continuous dissemination in wireless sensor networks. In: IEEE International Conference on Networks, pp. 405–410. IEEE (2012)

13. Martins, F.L.J., Celestino, J.J., da Silva Rego, A., et al.: MBEEC: a bio-inspired routing protocol with multihop between cluster-heads for energy saving in WSN. In: Wireless Communications and Mobile Computing Conference, pp. 349–354. IEEE (2015)

14. Rezaei, E., Baradaran, A.A., Heydariyan, A.: Multi-hop routing algorithm using Steiner points for reducing energy consumption in wireless sensor networks. Wirel. Pers. Commun. **86**(3), 1557–1570 (2016)

15. Yue, L., Dai, Y., Wu, D.: An energy optimization of WSNs non uniform clustering routing protocol. Comput. Eng. Appl. **51**(15), 80–85 (2015)

Energy-Efficient Routing Protocol Based on Probability in DTSN

Xiong Tang[1,2], Dan Sha[1,2], Yixiong Bian[1], Hai-ping Huang[1,2,3(✉)] ⓘ,
and Min Wu[1,2]

[1] College of Computer, Nanjing University of Posts and Telecommunications,
Nanjing 210003, China
hhp@njupt.edu.cn
[2] Jiangsu High Technology Research Key Laboratory
for Wireless Sensor Networks, Nanjing 210003, China
[3] College of Computer Science and Technology,
Nanjing University of Aeronautics and Astronautics, Nanjing 210016, China

Abstract. Energy supply of nodes in a Delay Tolerant Sensor Network (DTSN) usually relies on batteries, and the energy consumption unbalance caused by complicated topology and intermittent communication links has been becoming an issue for routing protocol design. DTSN achieves opportunistic communications using the mobility of nodes, where nodes deliver messages by the mechanism of Storage-Carry-Forward. This paper proposes an Energy-Efficient Routing Protocol based on Probability in DTSN (a.b. EERPP), where each sensor node takes a number of neighbors as the node list of its potential receiver set. A node makes its routing decision according to the metric of the average energy consumption for a message arriving at the destination node, which is modeled based on the probability of a message successfully delivered from the source node to the destination node or dropped before arriving at the destination node. Simulation results and discussions show that EERPP algorithm achieves satisfactory energy efficiency, as well as acceptable delay in a large scale network, compared with some traditional protocols.

Keywords: Energy-efficient · DTSN · Routing protocol · Probability routing
Opportunistic routing

1 Introduction

The traditional sensor network is composed of a large number of densely deployed sensor nodes with short range radio and several sink nodes, and sensors in the network collaborate together to collect the target data and transmit them to the sink nodes. Delay Tolerant Sensor Network (DTSN) is a new network architecture in recent years, and the rise of DTSN is to address the problem that data cannot be transmitted from the source to the destination because of fast sensor network topology changes and frequent disconnections caused by the sparse network density, obstacles, sensor node mobility or sensor energy exhaustion and so on [1]. These restricted networks exist in interstellar

© Springer Nature Singapore Pte Ltd. 2018
J. Li et al. (Eds.): CWSN 2017, CCIS 812, pp. 86–102, 2018.
https://doi.org/10.1007/978-981-10-8123-1_9

network, deep-sea exploration and wildlife tracking [2]. The difference between DTSN and the traditional Internet is that there may not be a complete end-to-end network path in DTSN. Therefore, traditional routing algorithms cannot be applied to such a sensor network environment and meanwhile a new protocol layer, called bundle layer in DTSN, is defined between the transport layer and the application layer. The buddle layer achieves the goal that bundles, also known as messages, are successfully delivered from the source node to the destination node by the mechanism of Storage-Carry-Forwarding.

The delay tolerant sensor networks will incur delays that can be serious and unpredictable. A DTSN is characterized by sensor nodes' intermittent connectivity. That is, it is difficult to form a well-connected end-to-end path for all the sensor nodes to transmit data in the network. The existing DTSN routing protocols mainly focus on the methods to increase the likelihood of finding opportunistic paths [3]. Some protocols achieve high delivery success radio by adding plentiful duplicates of one message however lead to the considerable sensor energy exhaustion. Others just permit one duplicate of message in DTSN to reduce the overhead while they fail in the hop by hop transmission. Consequently, how to ensure the desirable delivery success rate with the minimum duplicates and energy exhaustion is the concern of this paper. And meanwhile, for the convenience of modeling, the probability model is introduced to measure the delivery rate of data transmission and calculate the optimal copies of message. Furthermore, due to the limited energy supply for each mobile sink node, energy consumption in DTSN is a salient problem and the energy-saving becomes a key design criterion for the proposed routing protocol in DTSN.

In view of the metrics described above, the main contributions of our proposal include:

(1) Taking the average energy consumption into account, an Energy-Efficient Routing Protocol based on Probability (EERPP) is proposed, which makes routing decision on the basis of the metric of the average energy formatted in terms of the probability of a message successfully delivered from the source node to the destination node or dropped before arriving at the destination node. Moreover, EERPP achieves the tradeoff between the efficiency and routing availability.
(2) Theoretical analysis and experimental evaluation show that EERPP has higher energy efficiency and acceptable delay and delivery success rate, when comparing with the Spray-And-Wait (SAW) protocol and ProPhet (PP) protocol.

The rest of this paper is organized as follows. Section 2 gives a brief review on the related work. Section 3 presents our system model, including the network model and energy model. In Sect. 4, we present the proposed routing protocol EERPP, consisting of protocol description and algorithm design. The simulation parameters and results are illustrated in Sect. 5, while essential discussion is shown in Sect. 6. Finally, Sect. 7 provides our conclusions.

2 Related Work

With the increasing focus on DTSN, its routing algorithm is also becoming a wide-spread concern for researchers. An energy-efficient routing protocol can provide a message store-and-forward service and meanwhile enable low-power sensor nodes to conserve energy. At present, existing routing strategies in DTSN can be classified into two categories: the routing based on replication and that based on forwarding, in which some routing protocols that work in DTN can also be deployed effectively in DTSN and achieve desirable performance.

The replication routing strategy tries to improve the data delivery ratio for data transmission from the source node to the destination node through adding the copies of a message [4]. Epidemic routing protocol [5] is the earliest one among all replication routing algorithms, where every node sends all messages in its buffer to all neighboring nodes within its communication range. Epidemic routing achieves very high data delivery ratio, but it also wastes energy resources and degrades the sensor network performance. Spray-and-Wait/Focus routing [6, 7] constrains the number of copies to reduce the energy consumption and improve the sensor network performance. Taking the energy, the movement speed of nodes and the social relations into consideration, Zhang et al. [8] proposed an Energy-Aware Sociality-Based Spray and Search Routing algorithm (a.b. ESR). To avoid random and blindfold forwarding in Spray-and-Wait routing, Liu et al. [9] suggested a Relay-probability-based Adaptive Spay and Wait algorithm (a.b. R-ASW) using the performance of receiver nodes to determine whether to forward message to the encountering node and meanwhile calculate the number of message copies to be forwarded.

Forwarding routing strategy refers to forwarding a message hop by hop from the source node to the destination node, and there is only one copy of the message in the network during the whole forwarding process. ProPhet [10] routing protocol (Proba-bilistic Routing Protocol using History of Encounters and Transitivity) takes advantage of the historical information and the delivery probability to reduce network overhead, but it is still insufficient in the calculation of transmission expectation and the handling of congestion. Bulut et al. [11] used conditional intermeeting time as the metric to propose a conditional shortest path routing scheme. Ahmed et al. [12] proposed a Bayesian classifier based on DTSN routing framework to optimize the performance of routing algorithm.

Besides, some novel routing algorithms of DTSN are put forward. Taking delay, buffer and congestion into consideration, Zeng [13] et al. put forward a Directional Routing and Scheduling Scheme (a.b. DRSS) for green vehicle DTSNs by means of Nash Q-learning to optimize the energy efficiency. Papastergiou et al. [14] highlighted the benefits of an additional layer protocol of application-independent which offers transparent data to control end-to-end services, and meanwhile they proposed a Delay Tolerant Payload Conditioning protocol (a.b. DTPC) to realize this layer. Vardalis et al. [15] designed a novel rendezvous mechanism and showed experimentally that the DTSN overlay can shape network traffic and allow wireless interfaces of mobile devices to switch to the state of sleep during idle intervals without degrading performance. Tournoux et al. [16] proposed RECOR, a centralized resource-constrained oracle-based DTSN routing mechanism, which spreads the demand across multiple storage-carry-forward paths to yield to the node storage and link transport constraints observed in intervention situations. Furthermore, Bulut et al. [17] analyze the temporal correlation between the meeting of two mobile sink nodes, and design a new metric called conditional intermeeting time (CIT), which calculates the average intermeeting time between two mobile sink nodes. Prior knowledge about the probability of future presence of a node near the destination eases this process significantly. Ganguly et al. [18] put forward a location based mobility prediction scheme that facilitating the appropriate forwarder selection by predicting the mobility status of nodes. Johari et al. [19] propose a hybrid routing algorithm POSOP which is persistent, on-demand, scheduled, opportunistic, and predicted to provide health services that exploits various types of contacts existing in a partitioned, hybrid, and sparse network.

Compared with existing approaches, w e propose an Energy-Efficient Routing Protocol based on Probability in DTSN (a.b. EERPP). The relay nodes from the source to the destination are selected deliberately in terms of the link with the minimum energy consumption in EERPP, So EERPP minimizes the average energy consumption in each relay. Because of taking the average energy consumption into consideration in the process of relay nodes selection, the death speed of EERPP is the slowest and the death rate of EERPP is the smallest. Moreover, EERPP has higher energy efficiency and acceptable delay and delivery success rate, when compared with the Spray-And-Wait (SAW) protocol and ProPhet (PP) protocol.

3   System Model

In this section, some assumptions about the system model are considered, including the network model and the energy model.

3.1   Sensor Network Model

We construct a DTSN network model with the following properties:

(1) DTSN network is on the basis of the model of Shortest Path Map Based Movement.
(2) Each node is assigned a unique identifier (ID).
(3) All nodes in any node's neighbor list belong to this node's potential receiver set S_r.
(4) Nodes are distributed sparsely and randomly in DTSN with the given average density.

3.2   Energy Model

The energy consumption E of one node in DTSN can be calculated as (1), where e_s denotes the scan energy consumed per slot time, e_r denotes the scan response energy consumed per slot time, e_t denotes the transmission energy consumed per slot time and t_0 represents the duration of a slot time.

$$E = (e_s + e_r + e_t)t_0. \tag{1}$$

4 Protocol Implementation

In this section, theoretical scheme and specific algorithm are given in detail.

4.1 Theoretical Scheme

For the sake of clarity, we introduce the following notations:

(1) s: the source node
(2) d: the destination node
(3) n_i: the i-th relay node
(4) N_0: the maximum number of retransmissions
(5) t_0: the duration of a slot time
(6) $p_{a,b}$: the probability of a message being successfully delivered from the node a to the node b
(7) $\mathbf{U}$: the delay probabilities vector when a message is successfully delivered from the source node s to the destination node d
(8) $\mathbf{V}$: the delay probabilities vector when a message is dropped before arriving at the destination node d
(9) E_t: the total energy consumed
(10) E_a: the average energy consumed

In the traditional Internet, there is a stable end-to-end connection. So, traditional routing algorithm always transmits messages along the specific pre-selected path until the path is broken, and then reselects a new one. However, a stable end-to-end connection doesn't exist in DTSN. Therefore, the DTSN routing algorithm must make a real-time choice based on the current network conditions.

A two-hop network shown in Fig. 1 has a single source node s, K relay nodes n_1, n_2 ... n_{K-1}, n_K, and a single destination node d. Wherein, the set of $\{n_1, n_2 \dots n_{K-1}, n_K\}$ are the intersection between the neighbor list of s and that of d.

For the convenience of measuring the energy consumption from s to d, we may tentatively assume the K relay nodes aren't capable of communicating with each other.

The energy $M_{a,b}$ required for the successful message transmission from node a to node b and $N_{a,b}$ required for the failed message transmission from node a to node b are respectively given by (2) and (3),

$$M_{a,b} = \sum_{i=1}^{N_0} (1 - p_{a,b})^{i-1} p_{a,b} iE. \tag{2}$$

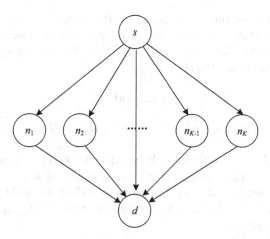

Fig. 1. A two-hop network with a single source node s, K relay nodes and a single destination node d

$$N_{a,b} = (1 - p_{a,b})^{N_0} N_0 E. \tag{3}$$

where E is calculated by (1).

The average time $B_{a,b}$ required for the successful message transmission and $C_{a,b}$ required for the failed message transmission from node a to node b in the one-hop network are respectively given by (4) and (5).

$$B_{a,b} = \sum_{i=1}^{N_0} (1 - p_{a,b})^{i-1} p_{a,b} i t_0. \tag{4}$$

$$C_{a,b} = (1 - p_{a,b})^{N_0} N_0 t_0. \tag{5}$$

After n retransmission, the probability of a message successfully delivered from the source node s to the destination node d, denoted by $p_{s,d(n)}$, and via the k-th relay node n_k ($k = 1, 2, ..., K-1, K$) to d, denoted by $p_{s,n_k(n)}$, are respectively described by (6) and (7),

$$p_{s,d(n)} = A^{n-1} p_{s,d}. \tag{6}$$

$$p_{s,n_k(n)} = A^{n-1} (1 - p_{s,d}) \prod_{i=1}^{k-1} (1 - p_{s,n_i}) p_{s,n_k}. \tag{7}$$

Where

$$A = (1 - p_{s,d}) \prod_{k=1}^{K} (1 - p_{s,n_k}) \tag{8}$$

In the above process, after n retransmission, the energy consumption of a message successfully delivered from the source node s to the destination node d, denoted by $E_{s,d(n)}$, and via the k-th relay node n_k ($k = 1, 2, ..., K-1, K$) to d, denoted by $E_{s,n_k(n)}$, are respectively deduced from (9) and (10),

$$E_{s,d(n)} = nE. \tag{9}$$

$$E_{s,n_k(n)} = nE + E_{n_k,d} = nE + M_{n_k,d} + N_{n_k,d}. \tag{10}$$

where E, $M_{n_k,d}$ and $N_{n_k,d}$ can respectively be calculated by (1), (2) and (3).

Similarly after n retransmission, the average delays of a message successfully delivered from the source node s to the destination node d, denoted by $D_{s,d(n)}$, and via the k-th relay node n_k ($k = 1, 2, ..., K-1, K$) to d, denoted by $D_{s,n_k(n)}$, are respectively described by (11) and (12),

$$D_{s,d(n)} = nt_0. \tag{11}$$

$$D_{s,n_k(n)} = nt_0 + D_{n_k,d} = nt_0 + B_{n_k,d} + C_{n_k,d}. \tag{12}$$

where $B_{n_k,d}$ and $C_{n_k,d}$ are respectively given by (4) and (5).

Therefore, taking all the possible conditions into consideration, the total energy consumption of a message transmitted from the source node s to the destination node d, denoted by E_t, is

$$E_t = \sum_{n=1}^{N_0} p_{s,d(n)} E_{s,d(n)} + \sum_{n=1}^{N_0} \sum_{k=1}^{K} p_{s,n_k(n)} E_{s,n_k,d(n)} + A^{N_0} N_0 E. \tag{13}$$

And the total delay of a message transmitted from the source node s to the destination node d, denoted by D_t, is

$$D_t = \sum_{n=1}^{N_0} p_{s,d(n)} D_{s,d(n)} + \sum_{n=1}^{N_0} \sum_{k=1}^{K} p_{s,n_k(n)} D_{s,n_k(n)} + A^{N_0} N_0 t_0. \tag{14}$$

Meanwhile, the probabilities of a message dropped from s to d, from s to n_k, from n_k to d, denoted by $q_{s,d}$, q_{s,n_k} and $q_{n_k,d}$ are shown as (15), (16) and (17) separately.

$$q_{s,d} = A^{N_0}. \tag{15}$$

$$q_{s,n_k} = A^{N_0}, \ k = 1, 2, ..., K. \tag{16}$$

$$q_{n_k,d} = \sum_{n=1}^{N_0} \sum_{k=1}^{K} A^{n-1} (1 - p_{s,d}) \prod_{i=1}^{k,i\neq k} (1 - p_{s,n_i}) p_{s,n_k} (1 - p_{n_k,d}), \tag{17}$$

$$k = 1, 2, 3, ..., K$$

Therefore, the end-to-end failed probability q is deduced by (18),

$$q = q_{s,d} + \sum_{k=1}^{K} q_{s,n_k} + \sum_{k=1}^{K} q_{n_k,d}. \tag{18}$$

Substituting the expression of (15), (16) and (17) successively for the values of $q_{s,d}$, q_{s,n_k} and $q_{n_k,d}$ in (18), we deduce (19).

$$q = (K+1)A^{N_0} + K \sum_{n=1}^{N0} \sum_{k=1}^{K} A^{n-1}(1 - p_{s,d}) \prod_{i=1}^{K, i \neq k} (1 - p_{s,n_i}) p_{s,n_k}(1 - p_{n_k,d}) \tag{19}$$

Finally, we figure out the average energy consumption E_a as

$$E_a = E_t/(1 - q). \tag{20}$$

And the end-to-end delay D is given by

$$D = \sum_{n=1}^{N_0} p_{s,d(n)} D_{s,d(n)} + \sum_{n=1}^{N_0} \sum_{k=1}^{K} p_{s,n_k(n)} D_{s,n_k(n)}. \tag{21}$$

In this section, we mainly analyze a two-hop network. However, our analysis will be extended to a multi-hop network consisting of numerous two-hop sub-networks in the following section.

4.2 Algorithm Design

To extend the previous theoretical analysis to a larger scale network, we just need to apply the EERPP algorithm for each step of multi-hop communication. To implement EERPP algorithm, we have to make initialization. Firstly, in order to minimize the average energy consumption, we suppose every node's initial average energy consumption E_v is larger than its initial energy in terms of the characteristics of the EERPP algorithm. And the node v belongs to the vertex set S_v of the whole network. Secondly, let the destination node d become the element of the potential receiver set S_r. Thirdly, let the elements of the delay probabilities vector $\mathbf{U}$ and $\mathbf{V}$ be "1" no matter whether a message is successfully delivered from the source node s to the destination node d or dropped before arriving at the destination node d. And then, the specific algorithm steps are shown in Table 1.

Wherein, $\mathbf{U}_u$ and $\mathbf{U}_{v,d}$ represents the probability vector of a message successfully delivered from the node v to d; $\mathbf{V}_u$ and $\mathbf{V}_{v,d}$ represents the probability vector of a message dropped before arriving at the destination node d; $\mathbf{U}_{v,d;(n)}$ represents the delay probabilities vector of a message which is successfully delivered from the node v to the destination node d when the number of retransmissions is n; $\mathbf{V}_{v,d;(n)}$ represents the delay probabilities vector of a message which is dropped before arriving at the destination node d when the number of retransmissions is n.

Table 1. EERPP algorithm.

EERPP Algorithm:

1: Initialization:

$E_v=x$, $S_r=\{d\}$, $\mathbf{U}=[1]$, $\mathbf{V}=[1]$.   /* where x is larger than the initial energy, and $v \in S_v$. */

2: Calculation:

while $S_r\ != S_v$, do

$E'=x$.   /*E' is a temporary variable*/

for every node $v \notin S_r$,   do Calculating the average energy consumption

$E_{v,d}$ according to Eq. (20);   /* a message transmission from the node v to the destination node d */

Searching the minimum $E_{v,d}$;

Calculating $q_{v,d}$ according to Eq. (19);   /* a message dropped before arriving at the destination node d */

$p_{v,d}=1-q_{v,d}$.   /* a message successfully delivered from the node v to the destination node d */

Set $\mathbf{U}_{v,d}=[0]$, $\mathbf{V}_{v,d}=[0]$.

/*Let the elements of the delay probabilities vector be zero no matter whether a message is successfully delivered from the node v to the destination node d or dropped before arriving at the destination node d. */

for every node $u \in S$ ($S=S_v-S_r$) and u is the k-th element, do $n=1$

while $n \leq N_0$, do

if the node u is not the destination node d, then

$$\mathbf{U}_{v,d;(n)} = (1-p_{v,u})^{n-1}\prod_{i=1}^{K,i\neq k}(1-p_{v,n_i})p_{v,n_i}\mathbf{U}_u \, , \, \mathbf{V}_{v,d;(n)} = (1-p_{v,u})^{n-1}\prod_{i=1}^{K,i\neq k}(1-p_{v,n_i})p_{v,n_i}\mathbf{V}_u \, .$$

Let the elements of the delay probabilities vectors $\mathbf{U}_{v,d;(n)}$ and $\mathbf{V}_{v,d;(n)}$ both be shifted to the right by n positions and the left positions be filled with zeros.

else

$$\mathbf{U}_{v,d;(n)} = (1-p_{v,u})^{n-1}p_{v,d}\mathbf{U}_u$$

Let the elements of the delay probabilities vector $\mathbf{U}_{v,d;(n)}$ be shifted to the right by n positions and the left positions be filled with zeros.

end if

$n=n+1$.

end while

$$\mathbf{U}_{v,d} = \mathbf{U}_{v,d} + \sum_{n=1}^{N_0}\mathbf{U}_{v,d;(n)} \, , \, \mathbf{V}_{v,d} = \mathbf{V}_{v,d} + \sum_{n=1}^{N_0}\mathbf{V}_{v,d;(n)} \, .$$

end for

if $E_{v,d}<E_v$, then

$$E_v = E_{v,d} \, , \, \mathbf{U}_v = \mathbf{U}_{v,d} \, , \, \mathbf{V}_v = \mathbf{V}_{v,d} \, , \, q_v = q_{v,d} \, .$$

end if

if $E_v<E'$, then $E'=E_v$, $v'=v$.

end if

end for

$$S_r = S_r \cup \{v'\} \, .$$

end while

We take advantage of Fig. 2 to show a simple example. According to the preceding definitions, we know that $S_v = \{s, d, n_1, n_2, n_3\}$ and $S_r = \{d\}$ in Fig. 2. And then we follow the steps below to make the routing choice.

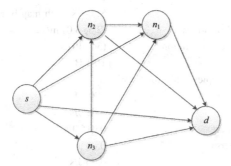

Fig. 2. A network topology having one source node, one destination node and 3 relay nodes

At first, according to Eq. (20), nodes s, n_1, n_2, n_3 calculate their respective average energy consumption $E_{s,d}, E_{n_1,d}, E_{n_2,d}, E_{n_3,d}$ for a message transmission to the destination node d. And then we can find the value of minimize average energy consumption. For example, if $E_{n_1,d}$ is the lowest of all four, the set S_r is updated to $\{d, n_1\}$. Taking $\{d, n_1\}$ as the forwarder set into account, nodes s, n_2, n_3 recalculate their respective average energy consumption $E_{s,d}, E_{n_2,d}$ and $E_{n_3,d}$. Suppose that $E_{n_2,d}$ is the lowest of all three, the set S_r is updated to $\{d, n_1, n_2\}$. Furthermore, considering $\{d, n_1, n_2\}$ as the forwarder set, if the new $E_{n_3,d}$ is less than the new $E_{s,d}$, the set S_r is updated to $\{d, n_1, n_2, n_3\}$. Finally the source node s minimizes average energy consumption considering $\{d, n_1, n_2, n_3\}$ as its forwarder set. This algorithm is similar with the shortest path algorithm, which always selects the link with the minimum energy consumption in the forwarder set.

5 Simulation Evaluation

In this section, we conduct some simulation experiments to evaluate the performance of EERPP algorithm comparing with the Spray-And-Wait (SAW) and ProPhet (PP) protocols by ONE simulator [20].

5.1 Simulation Parameters

The key parameters of simulation scenarios are summarized in Table 2.

Table 2. Simulation parameters.

Sample	Value
Network size	5000 m * 4000 m
Simulation time	12 h
Mobility model	Shortest path map based movement
Interval of speed of nodes	(2.5, 3.0) m/s
Interval of message generation	(30, 40) s
Message size	10 KB
Initial number of copies (only for SAW)	6
Initial energy	2000 J
Scan energy	0.02 J/s
Scan response energy	0.015 J/s
Transmission energy	0.03 J/s
Moving energy	0.05 J/s

5.2   Performance Metrics

We consider the following metrics:

1. The Average Energy Consumption:

$$AEC = \sum_{i=1}^{N} E_i/N. \tag{22}$$

where N is the number of nodes in the network, and E_i denotes the energy consumed by the i-th node, i.e., "initial energy - current energy".

2. The Message End-to-end Delay:

$$MED = \sum_{i=1}^{N} (t_2 - t_1)/N. \tag{23}$$

where t_1 represents the time of a message when is created, t_2 represents the time of a message when is delivered.

3. The Message Delivery Ratio:

$$MDR = (m_1 - m_2)/m_1. \tag{24}$$

where m_1 represents the number of messages which are created, m_2 represents the number of messages which successfully arrive at the destination node.

5.3   Simulation Results

In Fig. 3(a) and (b), it can be seen that EERPP consumes less energy than SAW and PP no matter with the same nodes or the same transmission range. The reason is that the relay nodes from the source to the destination are selected deliberately in terms of the link with the minimum energy consumption in EERPP, however it is done blindly in the other two routing protocols. So EERPP minimizes the average energy consumption in each relay. When the number of nodes increases, it takes more time and hops to deliver messages, and then the average energy consumption increases. By contrast, the average energy consumption decreases as the transmission range increases in Fig. 3(b), and meanwhile a message can be delivered farther.

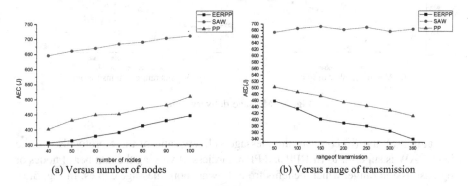

(a) Versus number of nodes   (b) Versus range of transmission

Fig. 3. Average energy consumption

Figure 4(a) and (b) show the message end-to-end delay of the three routing protocols when varying the number of nodes and the transmission range respectively. In Fig. 4(a), it is found that the message end-to-end delay of all the protocols increases as the number of nodes increases. However, the message end-to-end delay of EERPP is almost little longer than that of other two protocols. This is because in the process of a message transmission, EERPP haven't considered the influence on delay, originated from the number of copies and the historical information. Nevertheless, such delay is acceptable. In Fig. 4(b), especially, when the transmission range exceeds 200 m, EERPP achieves the best performance for the reason that it can ensure the more selective paths based on the increase of nodes which can be connected in forwarder set. There is no sharply impact on SAW because of the initial advantage of the message duplicates.

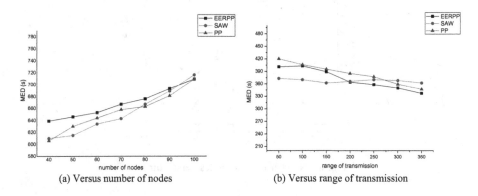

(a) Versus number of nodes   (b) Versus range of transmission

Fig. 4. Message end-to-end delay

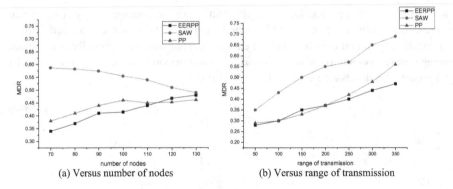

(a) Versus number of nodes   (b) Versus range of transmission

Fig. 5. Message delivery ratio

Figure 5(a) and (b) compare the message delivery ratio of three protocols. On the whole, SAW is superior to EERPP and PP regardless of varying the number of nodes or the transmission range, which benefits from it owns more message copies. In Fig. 5(a), it is found that the message delivery ratio of EERPP and PP increase as the number of nodes increases while SAW decreases. This is because when the number of nodes increases, relay nodes in SAW increase with the fixed number of message copies, and the message delivery ratio of SAW decreases. As shown in Fig. 5(b), the message delivery ratio of all three increases as the range of transmission increases. When the range of transmission increases, it is easier to meet more relay nodes.

Finally, Fig. 6 depicts the number of dead nodes of three protocols. When the residual energy of nodes is less than zero, we consider it to be dead. It is obvious that since we take the average energy consumption into consideration in the process of relay nodes selection, the death speed of EERPP is the slowest and the death rate of EERPP is the smallest.

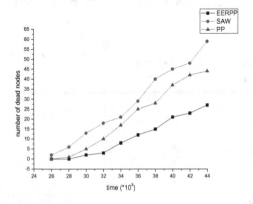

Fig. 6. Number of dead nodes versus time

6   Discussions

Some problems on our simulations need further exploration. As previously mentioned, Fig. 5(a) and (b) show that the message delivery ratio of EERPP is the lowest of all three. As we all know, during the process of a message transmitting from the source to the destination, in the SAW protocol there are more than one copy in the sensor network while in the PP protocol the historical information is taken into account. So the SAW and PP protocols' message delivery ratios are higher than that of EERPP protocol which hasn't considered the number of copies and the historical information.

Additional experiments on the above-mentioned problem are conducted, where except initial number of copies, other key parameters of simulation scenarios are summarized in Table 2.

Figure 7(a) and (b) respectively illustrate the change of the message delivery ratio and the average energy consumption with the change of the number of copies. In Fig. 7(a), it can be found that with the increase of copies in EERPP, the message delivery ratio of both EERPP and SAW becomes similar with each other. But it can be seen in Fig. 7(b) that the average energy consumption in EERPP is far less than that in SAW because EERPP minimizes the average energy consumption during the process of a message transmission.

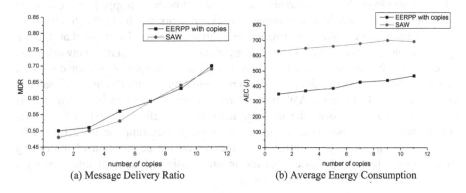

(a) Message Delivery Ratio   (b) Average Energy Consumption

Fig. 7. MDR/AEC versus number of copies

Figure 8(a) and (b) illustrate the change of the message delivery ratio and the average energy consumption with the change of nodes' number. Comparing Fig. 8(a) with (b), it is found that taking the historic information [21] into consideration the message delivery ratio of EERPP cannot be improved obviously, but MDR also increases as the number of nodes increases. On the contrary, the average energy consumption of EERPP with the historic information increases to some extent. This is because the historic information has little effect on the metric of routing decision, but it increases the energy consumption owing to the extra computation and communication cost.

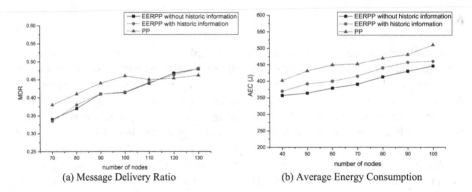

(a) Message Delivery Ratio   (b) Average Energy Consumption

Fig. 8. MDR/AEC versus number of nodes

7   Conclusions

In this paper, we propose an Energy-Efficient Routing Protocol in Delay Tolerant Sensor Network, called EERPP, which makes routing decision in line with the metric of the average energy E_a formatted in terms of the probability of a message successfully delivered from the source node to the destination node or dropped before arriving at the destination node. We also implement experiments on the ONE simulator for DTSN network and make performance evaluation. The results show that EERPP algorithm can effectively improve the energy efficiency, and the sensor network delay is acceptable when the scale of sensor network is large. Some problems related with the message delivery ratio and the average energy consumption are discussed in order to investigate EERPP, PP and SAW more objectively and comprehensively. The results show that EERPP improves the message delivery ratio efficiently when the copies increase in the sensor network, and the average energy consumption in EERPP is far less than that in SAW. Our further work focuses on the degradation of the energy consumption when the historic information are considered through integrating the success experience of PP into our proposal.

Acknowledgment. The authors would like to thank the anonymous reviewers of this paper for his/her objective comments and helpful suggestions while at the same time helping us to improve the English spelling and grammar throughout the manuscript.

And meanwhile, the subject was sponsored by the National Natural Science Foundation of P. R. China (Nos. 61373138 & 61672297), Postdoctoral Foundation (Nos. 2015M570468 & 2016T90485), the Key Research and Development Program of Jiangsu Province (Social Development Program, No. BE2017742), Jiangsu Natural Science Foundation for Excellent Young Scholar (No. BK20160089), and the Sixth Talent Peaks Project of Jiangsu Province (No. DZXX-017).

References

1. Gupta, S.: An adaptive and efficient data delivery scheme for DFT-MSNs (delay and disruption tolerant mobile sensor networks). In: International Conference on Advances in Engineering, pp. 99–104 (2012)
2. Zhang, F.P., Liu, Y.A., Wu, F., Tang, B.: A data delivery scheme based on sink centrality for delay tolerant mobile sensor networks. In: International Conference on Cyber-Enabled Distributed Computing & Knowledge Discovery, pp. 217–222 (2014)
3. Zhu, K., Li, W., Fu, X.: SMART: a social- and mobile-aware routing strategy for disruption-tolerant networks. IEEE Trans. Veh. Technol. **63**(7), 3423–3434 (2014)
4. Balasubramanian, A., Levine, B.N., Venkataramani, A.: Replication routing in DTNs: a resource allocation approach. IEEE/ACM Trans. Netw. **18**(2), 596–609 (2010)
5. Zhang, F., Wang, X.M., Lin, Y.G.: Adaptive adjustments of n-epidemic routing protocol for opportunistic networks. In: IEEE International Conference on Progress in Informatics & Computing, pp. 487–491 (2016)
6. Spyropoulos, T., Psounis, K., Raghavendra, C.S.: Spray and wait: an efficient routing scheme for intermittently connected mobile networks. In: Proceedings of the 2005 ACM SIGCOMM Workshop on Delay-Tolerant Networking, 22–26 August, pp. 252–259 (2005)
7. Spyropoulos, T., Psounis, K., Raghavendra, C.S.: Spray and focus: efficient mobility-assisted routing for heterogeneous and correlated mobility. In: Workshops of the Fifth Annual IEEE International Conference on Pervasive Computing and Communications (PerCom Workshops 2007), 19–23 March, pp. 79–85 (2007)
8. Linjuan, G.S.: Energy-aware multi-replica routing in delay tolerant mobile sensor network. China Commun. **8**(8), 87–97 (2011)
9. Liu, J., Tang, M., Yu, G.: Adaptive spray and wait routing based on relay-probability of node in DTN. In: Proceedings of the 2012 International Conference on Computer Science & Service System (CSSS 2012), 11–13 August, pp. 1138–1141 (2012)
10. Conan, V., Leguay, J., Friedman, T.: Routing method intended for intermittently connected networks. WO (2014)
11. Bulut, E., Geyik, S.C., Szymanski, B.K.: Conditional shortest path routing in delay tolerant networks. In: The 2010 IEEE International Symposium on World of Wireless Mobile and Multimedia Networks (WoWMoM 2010), 14–17 June, pp. 1–6 (2010)
12. Ahmed, S., Kanhere, S.S.: A bayesian routing framework for delay tolerant networks. In: Proceedings of the 2010 IEEE Wireless Communications and Networking Conference (WCNC 2010), 18–21 April, pp. 1–6 (2010)
13. Zeng, Y., Xiang, K., Li, D., et al.: Directional routing and scheduling for green vehicular delay tolerant networks. Wirel. Netw. **19**(2), 161–173 (2013)
14. Papastergiou, G., Alexiadis, I., Burleigh, S., et al.: Delay tolerant payload conditioning protocol. Comput. Netw. **59**(11), 244–263 (2014)
15. Vardalis, D., Tsaoussidis, V.: Exploiting the potential of DTN for energy-efficient internetworking. J. Syst. Softw. **90**(2), 91–103 (2014)
16. Tournoux, P., Conan, V., Crowcroft, J., et al.: Wardrop equilibrium formulation of resource-constrained DTN routing in public safety networks. In: Proceedings of the 8th IEEE International Conference on Mobile Ad hoc and Sensor Systems (MASS 2011), 17–22 October, pp. 968–974 (2011)
17. Bulut, E., Geyik, S.C., Szymanski, B.K.: Utilizing correlated node mobility for efficient DTN routing. Pervasive Mobile Comput. **13**(4), 150–163 (2014)

18. Ganguly, S., Basu, S., Roy, S., et al.: A location based mobility prediction scheme for post disaster communication network using DTN. In: The 2015 International Conference on Applications and Innovations in Mobile Computing, 12–14 February, pp. 25–28 (2015)

19. Johari, R.: POSOP routing algorithm: a DTN routing scheme for information connectivity of health centres in Hilly State of North India. Int. J. Distrib. Sensor Netw. **2015**, 1–9 (2015)

20. Cuka, M., Shinko, I., Spaho, E., Oda, T., Ikeda, M.: A simulation system based on ONE and SUMO simulators: performance evaluation of different vehicular DTN routing protocols. J. High Speed Netw. **23**(1), 59–66 (2017)

21. Penurkar, M.R., Deshpande, U.A.: "Max-Util: A Utility-Based Routing Algorithm for a Vehicular Delay Tolerant Network Using Historical Information, pp. 587–598. Springer, New Delhi (2016). https://doi.org/10.1007/978-81-322-2529-4_61

An Efficient Energy-Hole Alleviating Algorithm for Wireless Sensor Network Based on Energy-Balanced Clustering Protocol

Weiwei Zhou$^{(\boxtimes)}$ and Bin Yu

Zhengzhou Institute of Information Science and Technology,
Zhengzhou 450001, China
zww15238060801@163.com

Abstract. Illegal nodes can send malicious data to WSN continuously, which will accelerate the energy consumption rate. Even if the cluster heads in the inner regions have been exhausted simultaneously, the ones in the outer regions may still hold sufficient energy resource. This situation is defined as energy-hole problem in WSN. To investigate the principle of such problem and design corresponding defense strategies, it is critical to analyze the configuration and distribution of cluster heads. According to the balance conditions of energy consumption, a novel mathematical model is formulated to accurately estimate the communication radius of cluster heads in network deployment. Then mobile sinks are introduced to gather the data transmitted by malicious nodes in circular regions. Considering the uniformity principle in collecting data and shortest path routing, the migration path of mobile sinks is calculated. An energy-hole alleviating algorithm is ultimately proposed based on the energy analysis in WSN. Finally, experimental results validate the efficiency and effectiveness of the proposed algorithm in energy-hole detection and mitigation.

Keywords: Wireless sensor network (WSN) · Energy-hole problem
Communication radius · Node distribution · Cluster-head lifetime

1 Introduction

A classical wireless sensor network (WSN) is composed principally of central sink, cluster heads and sensor nodes with high reliability and low-power consumption. Central sink is responsible for data collection in the network. Cluster heads and sensor nodes can be deployed to transmit and relay the message to central sink by using the 802.15.4 protocol [1–5]. The characteristics of WSN, such as large scale, high capacity and fast deployment, make it extraordinarily potential to monitor large amounts of data in specific scenarios. These scenarios typically include intelligent transportation, battlefield-environment monitoring, situational awareness, etc. However, cluster heads are equipped with constrained resources in terms of storage space, battery power, arithmetic capability, transmission bandwidth, etc. Traditionally, the cluster is composed of multiple sensor nodes and one cluster head, and the WSN follow the many to one data collecting topology. Thus, the cluster heads that are deployed near the central sink would exhaust their energy much faster than the ones which are deployed far away

© Springer Nature Singapore Pte Ltd. 2018
J. Li et al. (Eds.): CWSN 2017, CCIS 812, pp. 103–116, 2018.
https://doi.org/10.1007/978-981-10-8123-1_10

from the central sink. Worse still, malicious nodes can transmit invalid data to accelerate the energy consumption of cluster heads, and the lifetime of the network ends prematurely. This unbalanced energy consumption causes energy-hole problem in WSN. Low-power integrated chips and batteries with high reliability have been adopted to extend the lifetime of cluster heads. At the same time, the modified routing algorithms and protocols for ultra-low power dissipation are also under research [6–8]. However, the constrained resource and complicated topology of WSN are not taken into consideration in these approaches.

Considering the routing path, the network topology can be divided into two patterns, which are defined as hierarchical and distributed structures respectively. In a distributed WSN, the data collected by sensor nodes is transmitted to multiple cluster heads. Then large numbers of data will be forwarded to central sink respectively for further processing. In other words, traffic flows from cluster heads to central sink directly in a distributed WSN. Thus, distributed WSN is a single-hop network. In a hierarchical WSN, the system chooses the optimal path for data gathering, which indicates hierarchical WSN is a multi-hop network. Compared with distributed WSN, cluster heads in hierarchical WSN are more vulnerable to energy-hole problem. In recent years, hierarchical WSN has been widely used in many fields, such as military reconnaissance, meteorological monitoring, situation awareness, etc. [9–12]. The main objective of this paper is focused on the solution to energy-hole problem in clustered WSN with hierarchical topology.

Due to multi-hop topology in hierarchical WSN, the energy consumption of cluster heads around central sink is much faster than that in exterior regions. Thus, it may lead to uneven energy consumption and dysfunction of the entire network, even if most of the cluster heads have sufficient energy. This phenomenon can be defined as the fundamental energy-hole problem (FEHP). The open channel brings convenience to construct the optimal communication link in WSN. However, malicious nodes can easily break into the network and relay the traffic to critical cluster heads. The energy resource of these cluster heads will be rapidly exhausted by invalid data. Then the entire network is dysfunctional in WSN. The hostile attack in this pattern is marked as energy-hole attack (EHA). Consequently, the energy-hole problem in clustered WSN is composed principally of FEHP and EHA.

Currently, there have been several existing works studying the restraining methods of energy-hole problem in clustered WSN, which are typically divided into two patterns, namely, static FEHP suppression and mobile EHA suppression. The suppression methods against static FEHP can be generally categorized into three types. The first one is focused on reasonable deployment of cluster heads and data aggregation in hierarchical structure. Depending on the multi-hop topology in WSN, Villas et al. [13] proposed an analytical model for FEHP and adopted data redundancy and spatial correlation to define the aggregation details of data. In this algorithm, it is assumed that central sink can provide real-time reconfiguration to cluster heads in case of data congestion [14, 15]. However, the routing information and timestamps can be easily collected by malicious nodes and then the critical routing path is particularly vulnerable to attack. Although the secure authentication and encrypted-key-exchange mechanisms are proposed [16], these methods only can be used in the case where the nodes are deployed with unlimited resources. More importantly, with the increasing number of malicious nodes, data processing efficiency declines sharply in these schemes. To address the problem above, Salarian et al. [17] introduced a mobile-sink based security framework with three-tier topology. Unfortunately, the parameters related to node deployment are still not calculated. The second one is to investigate the relationship between circular-region radius and cluster-head lifetime. Considering the complexity of calculation, Abd et al. [18] applied self-correlation model to the solution of nonlinear equations of the network suffered from FEHP. O. Assuming that communication radius of cluster heads in each circular region is adjustable, Cheng et al. [19] further extended the nonlinear equations and analyze the traffic flow to compute the communication radius of cluster heads under the constant density of sensor nodes. However, those studies are lack of approaches to quantitative analysis. Taking into consideration the single-hop and multi-hop routing strategies, the third one transforms the balance of cluster-head lifetime into dynamic energy allocation and emphasizes the importance of robustness, complexity, and constrained resource. Depending on the assumption of non-uniform density in the network, Liu [20] put forward a multi-weight based scheme to configure the density of sensor nodes in each circular region. In their work, the density decreases with the distances from the central sink. Thus the energy consumption of cluster heads is balanced. But it's proved that those strategies of privilege distribution are unsuitable for clustered WSN.

Compared with static FEHP suppression algorithms, the mobile sinks are introduced in the EHA algorithms according to the real-time traffic flow influenced by malicious nodes. Therefore, it can update data forwarding strategy depending on the number of circular regions infected by malicious nodes. Based on the throughput and energy consumption rate of cluster heads, Lin and Uster [21] have tried to employ a heuristic method with dynamic position of central sink. During the design of energy-hole alleviating mechanisms, the existing algorithms are still obviously defective and vulnerable to hierarchical WSN since they do not take cluster-head layout and redundant traffic flow into account.

Contribution. In this paper, an energy-balanced model against FEHP and strategy for EHA suppression are proposed respectively. In order to ensure the balance of energy consumption, the solution of circular-radius equations is formulated and calculated. Then the feasibility of solution to the equation group is analyzed. Depending on the energy-balanced model, the corresponding traffic flow in each circular region is estimated for further detection of the EHA. It can be proved that the transmitting distance of malicious nodes is equivalent to constant length by using the integro-differential equation. With the assumption of constant transmitter amplifier, path-loss exponent, and electronics energy, the optimal migration path of mobile sinks in circular regions is acquired. On this base, an energy-hole alleviating algorithm against FEHP and EHA is proposed with the adoption of mobile-sink strategy to collect and transmit redundant data. Numerical analysis and experimental simulation show the efficiency and effectiveness of the proposed algorithm in energy-hole detection and mitigation.

Organization. The rest of the paper is organized as follows. Section 2 presents the energy-hole principles and definitions. Then the suppression model against FEHP and corresponding equations are constructed for quantitative analysis in Sect. 3 respectively. In Sect. 4, the optimal strategy for EHA suppression is given depending on the parameter analysis. An algorithm against FEHP and EHA is proposed in Sect. 5.

Performance evaluation is given in Sect. 6. Finally, the conclusion and direction for future research are presented in Sect. 7.

2 Preliminaries

2.1 Network Model

Sensor nodes are responsible for information collection and then forward the data to cluster heads. Cluster heads transmit the data it received to the central sink depending on the routing algorithm. Moreover, all cluster heads and sensor nodes are distributed uniformly in a circular region with the radius R. Furthermore, the energy resource of central sink is infinite. The energy consumption of cluster heads is negligible if they are dormant. Compared with cluster heads, the energy resource of sensor nodes is relatively sufficient. Consequently, the quantitative model is analyzed depending on the energy consumption of cluster heads and mobile sinks in the process of data transmission, mobility, and reception respectively.

If $1 < i \leq n$, the data collected by sensor nodes in c_i will be transmitted to cluster heads and then forwarded to c_{i-1} immediately. Cluster heads in c_{i-1} will deliver it to the next circular region continually. The network structure is shown in Fig. 1.

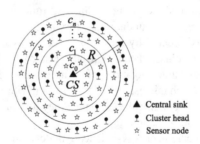

Fig. 1. Network model

Network nodes are typically made up of data transceiver unit, message processing units and clock control unit. The nodes keep in the sleep state before it executes data forwarding tasks. The energy consumption in the sleep state can be ignored. Sensor nodes are only responsible for data collection and transmission.

2.2 Energy Consumption Model

According to [22, 23], the energy consumptions of data transmission and reception with the length of k bits over a distance d are calculated as follows respectively.

$$E_{tr}(d) = k(\varepsilon d^a + E_{elec}),$$
$$E_{rec} = kE_{elec}.$$

Correspondingly, the total energy consumption when k bits data are transmitted from mobile sink to central sink over a distance d can be given by

$$E_{total}^{move} = k(\varepsilon d^a + 2E_{elec}) + e_{move}d_{move},$$

where e_{move} is the energy consumption in each unit, and d_{move} is the distance mobile sink has moved.

3 New Proposal for FEHP Suppression

3.1 Suppression Model

Figure 2 depicts the structure of node distribution in clustered WSN. All the nodes are deployed in a circular area with a radius of R. In order to simplify the calculation, it is assumed that the communication radius of cluster head in each circular region is equal to half of the width of corresponding circular region. Assume that radius of the first circular region is defined as R_0. Then the remaining radiuses of circular regions can be denoted as $R_1, R_2, \cdots, R_n$, respectively.

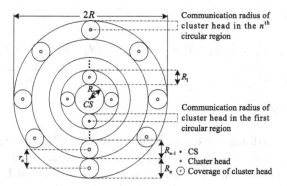

Fig. 2. Structure of node distribution

Cluster heads are uniformly distributed in the circular area. Thus, we have $R_0 = R_1$ and the communication radius of cluster heads in the first circular region is calculated as $R_1/2$. Thus, the coverage of cluster head in the first circular region is $\pi R_1^2/4$.

The number of cluster heads in the outer annular region can be calculated as

$$N_n = \frac{\pi(R_0 + R_1 + \cdots + R_n)^2 - \pi(R_0 + R_1 + \cdots + R_{n-1})^2}{\pi R_n^2/4}. \tag{1}$$

Assume that the total number of cluster heads in circular area is N. Correspondingly, N_i denotes the number of cluster heads in the ith circular region.

Let λ_i denote the data volume collected by sensor nodes in unit area of the ith circular region. Then the data volume collected by sensor nodes in the ith circular region is given by

$$\sum_{j=i+1}^{n} \lambda_j \left\{ \pi (R_0 + R_1 + \cdots + R_j)^2 - \pi (R_0 + R_1 + \cdots + R_{j-1})^2 \right\} \qquad (2)$$

Ideally, cluster heads in the $(i + 1)^{th}$ circular region transmit the data to the ith circular region according to the routing algorithm. Hence, depending on the formula (1) and (2), the average data volume received by cluster head in the ith circular region from outer circular regions can be denoted as

$$d_o^i = \frac{\sum_{j=i+1}^{n} \lambda_j \left\{ \pi (R_0 + R_1 + \cdots + R_j)^2 - \pi (R_0 + R_1 + \cdots + R_{j-1})^2 \right\}}{N_i} \qquad (3)$$

The average data volume transmitted from sensor nodes to each cluster head in the ith circular region is given by $d_i^i = \lambda_i \pi R_i^2$. Thus, the total data volume received by cluster head in the ith circular region is calculated as

$$
\begin{aligned}
d_{total}^i &= d_o^i + d_i^i \\
&= \frac{\pi R_i^2 \sum_{j=i+1}^{n} \lambda_j \left\{ (R_0 + R_1 + \cdots + R_j)^2 - (R_0 + R_1 + \cdots + R_{j-1})^2 \right\}}{4\left[(R_0 + R_1 + \cdots + R_i)^2 - (R_0 + R_1 + \cdots + R_{i-1})^2 \right]} \\
&\quad + \lambda_i \pi R_i^2
\end{aligned} \qquad (4)
$$

The transmission distance of cluster heads between the ith circular region and the $(i-1)^{th}$ circular region is given by $r_i = (R_i + R_{i-1})/2, i \in \{1, 2, \cdots, n\}$.

With no consideration of the malicious node, it is assumed that $E_{total}^{static}(r_i)$ denotes the average energy consumption of cluster head in the ith circular region. T_{min} and E respectively denote the minimum lifetime of cluster head to work normally and initial energy in each cluster head. Therefore, the problem to inhibit FEHP is converted to maximize the lifetime of the cluster heads in clustered WSNs. Thus, the suppression model against energy-hole problem can be calculated as

$$
\begin{cases}
\max(T) = \min_{0 < i \leq n} (E_i), d_{size}^{move} = d_{size}^{attack}, \min(N) \\
N = N_1 + N_2 + \cdots + N_n \\
R = R_0 + R_1 + \cdots + R_n \\
E_{total}^{static}(r_1) = E_{total}^{static}(r_2) = \cdots = E_{total}^{static}(r_n) \\
T \geq T_{min} \\
T = \frac{E}{E_{total}^{static}(r_1)}
\end{cases} \qquad (5)
$$

3.2   Solution Analysis

Assume that the radius of cluster heads is finite in WSN. Thus, the set of values that radius of cluster heads can have is defined as $\{1, 2, \cdots, l\}$.

Based on the analysis above, the solution of $R_1, R_2, \cdots, R_n$, T and N is acquired in two cases as follows.

(1) If the transmission distance between adjacent circular regions is under the threshold φ, then we have $a = 2$. In order to simplify the solution of equations, assume that data volume is uniform in each unit area. Consequently, it can be indicated that $\lambda_1 = \lambda_2 = \cdots = \lambda_n = A$. If $\eta = R_0 + R_1 + \cdots + R_{i-1}$, the energy consumption of cluster head in the ith circular region can be calculated as

$$E_{total}^{static}(r_i) = Am\pi R_i^2 \left\{ \frac{R^2 - (\eta + R_i)^2}{4R_i^2 + 8\eta R_i} + \frac{1}{4} \right\} \cdot \left\{ \varepsilon (\frac{R_i + R_{i-1}}{2})^2 + 2E_{elec} \right\} \tag{6}$$

Since the parameter R_0 is a fixed value in WSN, the energy consumption of cluster head in the region c_0 can be given by:

$$E_{total}^{static}(r_1) = Am\pi \left(\frac{R^2 - 4R_0^2}{12R_0^2} + \frac{R_0^2}{4} \right) \cdot \left[2E_{elec} + \varepsilon \left(\frac{3}{2} R_0 \right)^a \right] = B \tag{7}$$

According to the assumption, the energy consumption of each cluster head is uniform. Thus, depending on the formula (6) and (7), the equation is given by

$$Am\pi R_i^2 \left\{ \frac{R^2 - (\eta + R_i)^2}{4R_i^2 + 8\eta R_i} + \frac{1}{4} \right\} \cdot \left\{ \varepsilon \left(\frac{R_i + R_{i-1}}{2} \right)^2 + 2E_{elec} \right\} = B \tag{8}$$

After substituting the parameter $E_{total}^{static}(r_i)$ given by formula (6), the formula (8) can be simplified as below.

$$
\begin{aligned}
& Am\pi\varepsilon (R^2 - \eta^2) R_i^3 + 2Am\pi\varepsilon R_{i-1} R_i^2 - 8B\eta \\
& + \left[2Am\pi E_{elec} (R^2 - \eta^2) + Am\pi\varepsilon (R^2 - \eta^2) R_{i-1}^2 - 16B \right] R_i = 0
\end{aligned}
\tag{9}
$$

Formula (9) is a cubic equation associated with one uncertain parameter R_i. The solution of the equation can be calculated.

Knowing that R_0 is a determined value, R_1 can be computed depending on the formula (9). By that analogy, the remaining radiuses of circular regions can be calculated respectively. Correspondingly, the optimal T and N can be obtained.

(2) If the transmission distance between adjacent circular regions is out of the threshold φ, then we have $a = 4$. The energy consumption of cluster head in the ith circular region can be given by

$$E_{total}^{static}(r_i) = Am\pi R_i^2 \left\{ \frac{R^2 - (\eta + R_i)^2}{4R_i^2 + 8\eta R_i} + \frac{1}{4} \right\} \cdot \left\{ \varepsilon \left(\frac{R_i + R_{i-1}}{2} \right)^4 + 2E_{elec} \right\} \qquad (10)$$

After substituting the parameter B given by formula (7), the formula (10) can be simplified as

$$Am\varepsilon\pi(R^2 - \eta^2)R_i(R_i + R_{i-1})^4 - 64BR_i \\ + 32Am\pi(R^2 - \eta^2)E_{elec}R_i - 128B\eta = 0 \qquad (11)$$

Similarly, All the radiuses of circular regions can be calculated. Simultaneously, the optimal parameters $R_1, R_2, \cdots, R_n$, T and N can be computed precisely.

4   Analysis for EHA Suppression

4.1   Parameter Analysis

The optimal trajectory of mobile sink should collect the data uniformly in the circular region where malicious nodes exist.

Theorem 1 [16]. If $\beta = R_0 + R_1 + \cdots + R_{i-1}$, the optimal radius of a trajectory to mobile sink in the ith circular region is computed as $\delta = \frac{1}{2}\sqrt{4\beta^2 + 2R_i^2 + 4R_i\beta}$.

Theorem 2 [19]. In the EHA-suppression model, the equivalent Euclidean distance, $d_{avg,i,1}$, between mobile sink and region $c_{i,1}$ whose width is x, can be calculated as $d_{avg,i,1} = \frac{1}{3}x$. Similarly, the equivalent Euclidean distance in region $c_{i,2}$ is computed as $d_{avg,i,2} = \frac{1}{3}(R_i - x)$.

4.2   Optimal Strategy for EHA Suppression

If there is single circular region suffered from the EHA, execute 1-1 mobile-sink suppression strategy. The trajectory of the single mobile sink is shown in Fig. 3.

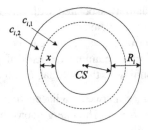

Fig. 3. The optimal trajectory of mobile sink

Hence, the energy consumption introduced by malicious nodes can be given by (Fig. 4)

$$
\begin{aligned}
E_{avg,i}(x) &= E_{avg,i,1}(x) + E_{avg,i,2}(x) \\
&= \frac{2\beta x + x^2}{2\beta R_i + R_i^2} d_{size}^{attack} [\varepsilon(x/3)^a + 2E_{elec}] \\
&\quad + \frac{R_i^2 + 2\beta R_i - 2\beta x - x^2}{2\beta R_i + R_i^2} d_{size}^{attack} [\varepsilon(x/3)^a + 2E_{elec}]
\end{aligned}
\tag{12}
$$

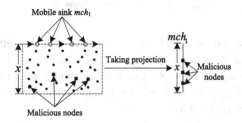

Fig. 4. The location of mobile sinks for suppression

As is shown in Fig. 3, mch_1 moves along the trajectory whose radius is $(\beta + x)$. The energy consumption in moving the circle with radius $(\beta + x)$ is calculated as

$$
E_{move,i}(x) = e_{move} \cdot 2\pi \cdot (\beta + x)
\tag{13}
$$

Similarly, the energy consumption in moving from mch_1 to central sink is given by

$$
E_{move,i,1}(x) = e_{move}(\beta + x)
\tag{14}
$$

Then, the energy consumption introduced by malicious nodes is calculated as

$$
E_{avg}^{total}(x) = E_{avg,i}(x) + E_{move,i}(x) + E_{move,i,1}(x)
\tag{15}
$$

As is shown in Fig. 5, assume that there are n circular regions in the network. If malicious nodes exist in more than one circular region, execute 1−m mobile-sink suppression strategy.

The network area is divided into m sectors, whose central angle is computed as $2\pi/m$. Thus, the redundant data collection requires m mobile sinks, namely mch_1, mch_2, ..., mch_1, mch_m. As is shown in Fig. 5, sector ∇_j has the intersections with mobile sink mch_j which are named as l_n, p_n, p_{n-1} and q_{n-1} respectively.

mch_j moves along the trajectory in sector ∇_j, which is computed in theorem 1. It follows the $arc(l_n, p_n)$ and then turns to segment $[p_n, p_{n-1}]$, $arc(p_{n-1}, q_{n-1})$, $[q_{n-1}, q_{n-2}]$, etc.

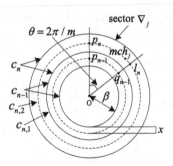

Fig. 5. 1-m sector area zoning map

$c_i(\nabla_j)$ denotes the iterative area between c_i and ∇_j. It is divided into two segments by trajectory analyzed in theorem 1, namely $c_{i,1}(\nabla_j)$ and $c_{i,2}(\nabla_j)$.

Thus, the total energy consumption of data transmission and reception in region $c_i(\nabla_j)$ is denoted by $E_{avg,i,\nabla_j}(\beta, R_i, x, m)$. The energy consumption of data transmission and reception in ∇_j is denoted as

$$E_{avg,\nabla_j}(\beta, R_i, x, m) = \sum_{i=1}^{n} E_{avg,i,\nabla_j}(\beta, R_i, x, m) \tag{16}$$

The migration path of mobile sink mch_j includes arcs and radius $(R - R_n + x)$. Obviously, the length of $arc(p_i, q_i)$ can be denoted as $\overline{(p_i, q_i)} = \frac{2\pi(\beta+x)}{m}$. Thus, the energy consumption of mobile sink mch_j due to the migration is given by

$$E_{move,n,\nabla_j}(R_i, x, n) = e_{move}\left[\sum_{i=1}^{n} \frac{2\pi(\beta+x)}{m} + R - R_n + x\right] \tag{17}$$

Combining the formula (16) and (17), the energy consumption in ∇_j introduced by malicious nodes is calculated as

$$E_{avg,\nabla_j}^{total}(R_i, x, n) = E_{move,n,\nabla_j}(R_i, x, n) + E_{avg,\nabla_j}(\beta, R_i, x, m) \tag{18}$$

Thus, the total energy consumption introduced by malicious nodes in 1-m mobile-sink suppression strategy is given by

$$E_{avg}^{total}(x) = m E_{avg,\nabla_j}^{total}(R_i, x, n) \tag{19}$$

5 Algorithm Against FEHP and EHA

In this section, the detailed algorithm descriptions against FEHP and EHA are introduced in the following.

Suppression algorithm against FEHP and EHA

Input: network radius R, minimum network lifetime $T_{\min}$, constrained condition $T \geq T_{\min}$, network parameters and $E_{total}^{static}(r_1) = E_{total}^{static}(r_2) = \cdots = E_{total}^{static}(r_n)$.

Output: configuration parameters $R_1, R_2, \cdots, R_n$, T, N, $d_{size}^{move} = d_{size}^{attack}$, $\max(T) = \min_{0<i\leq n}(E_i)$, and $\min(N)$.

Step 1. Set up the initial value R_0 and corresponding network parameters, and then calculate the parameters $R_1, R_2, \cdots, R_n$, T and N depending on the constrained conditions and equations in formula (5).

Step 2. Deploy the cluster heads in each circular region according to the parameters $R_1, R_2, \cdots, R_n$, T, N calculated in Step1. Then the imbalance of energy consumption in each cluster head due to the FEHP is solved in clustered WSN.

Step 3. Calculate the theoretical value of data traffic in the ith circular region, which is denoted as v_i^0. Similarly, the practical data traffic monitored by cluster heads in the ith circular region is computed as v_i^1. If $v_i^1 - v_i^0 \leq 0.1v_i^0$, it is considered that energy consumption in WSN is balanced. On the contrary, if $v_i^1 - v_i^0 > 0.1v_i^0$, it can be concluded that the network is attacked by EHA. Detect every circular region to confirm the number of the regions attacked by EHA.

Step 4. If $Q = 1$, execute 1-1 mobile-sink suppression strategy. If $Q > 1$, execute 1-m mobile sink path-optimal strategy. According to the suppression strategy against EHA, the redundant data introduced by malicious node is delivered to central sink directly.

Step 5. Monitor and compare the data traffic of each circular region in cycle T_0. If the EHA is detected, turn to step 3.

Step 6. End.

6 Performance Evaluation

6.1 Simulation Environment

The custom simulators of OPNET and NS2 is adopted to simulate the experiment. The initial energy resources that sensor node and cluster hold are 3 J and 5 J respectively. The communication parameters and are introduced based on the energy consumption model in [22]. Thus, we have $E_{elec} = e_{move} = 50 \times 10^{-9}$ J/bit, $\varepsilon = 10^{-11}$ for $\alpha = 2$ and $\varepsilon = 13 \times 10^{-16}$ for $\alpha = 4$. The length of data frame is 1024 bits. The number of sensor nodes and cluster heads are 2000 and 400, respectively. The number of circular regions is set to 10. The communication radius of sensor nodes is 70 m and the sensor nodes are uniformly distributed in the network. The radius of the experimental region is 500 m.

6.2 Simulation Results

In the simulation environment, 2000 sensor nodes are deployed with 10 circular regions. Figure 6 shows the performance of the network with different energy-hole algorithms. The network is attacked by EHA in this situation. Figure 6(a) depicts the remaining energy of cluster head in different circular regions when the network lifetime ends. Sequence number i denotes the cluster head in the ith circular region in Fig. 6(a). The number of data frames cluster head received is shown in Fig. 6(b) with different distances between cluster head and CS.

No matter which sequence number the cluster head belongs to, the remaining energy of cluster head is approximately constant. However, the remaining energy of cluster head in [4, 14] increases rapidly with the sequence number of circular region, which indicates the EHA still has a large amount of influence on the energy consumption of cluster head in the inner circular regions. With the increase of distance between cluster head and CS, the amplitude of variation of the number of data frames cluster head received is 50, while it can be 110 and 280 in [4, 14] respectively. Compared with the algorithm in [4, 14], it can be inferred that the algorithm against EHA proposed in this paper can balance the energy consumption and inhibit the EHA effectively.

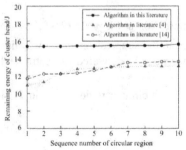

(a) Average residual energy of cluster head in different circular regions

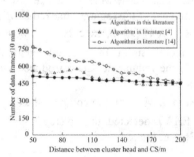

(b) Number of frames cluster head received with different distances between cluster head and CS

Fig. 6. Performance of the network with different energy-hole algorithms

7   Conclusion

In this paper, the theoretical aspects of the energy-balanced protocol are explored, which addresses the energy-hole problem in WSN. According to network model, the energy-hole problem is divided into two parts, namely FEHP and EHA. First, the network model and energy consumption model in clustered WSN are constructed. On this base, a new proposal for FEHP suppression is introduced based on the energy-balanced conditions. Then, the parameter analysis and optimal strategy for EHA suppression is presented later. Also, the optimum trajectory of the mobile sinks is computed in proposed algorithm. Besides, depending on the number of circular regions attacked by EHA, two strategies are designed to collect redundant data generated by malicious nodes. Combining the proposal for FEHP suppression and strategy against EHA, the algorithm against FEHP and EHA is proposed. Numerical analysis and experimental results validate the improved performance in the suppression of energy-hole problem in clustered WSN.

References

1. Nayak, P., Devulapalli, A.: A fuzzy logic-based clustering algorithm for WSN to extend the network lifetime. IEEE Sensors J. **16**(1), 137–144 (2016)
2. Sun, J., Zou, J., Huang, L.: Distributed optimization of lifetime and throughput with power consumption balance opportunistic routing in dynamic wireless sensor networks. Int. J. Distrib. Sensor Netw. **12**(10), 1–15 (2016)
3. Yu, X., Chang, X., Zhong, S., et al.: An efficient energy hole alleviating algorithm for wireless sensor networks. IEEE Trans. Consum. Electron. **60**(3), 347–355 (2014)
4. Zhang, D., Li, G., Zheng, K., et al.: An energy-balanced routing method based on forward-aware factor for wireless sensor networks. IEEE Trans. Industr. Inform. **10**(1), 766–773 (2014)
5. Pak, J.M., Ahn, C.K., Shi, P., et al.: Distributed hybrid particle/FIR filtering for mitigating NLOS effects in TOA-based localization using wireless sensor networks. IEEE Trans. Industr. Electron. **64**(6), 5182–5191 (2017)
6. Liu, Y., Dong, M., Ota, K., et al.: ActiveTrust: secure and trustable routing in wireless sensor networks. IEEE Trans. Inf. Forensics Secur. **11**(9), 2013–2027 (2016)
7. Dong, M., Ota, K., Liu, A.: RMER: reliable and energy-efficient data collection for large-scale wireless sensor networks. IEEE Internet Things J. **3**(4), 511–519 (2016)
8. Han, G., Liu, L., Jiang, J., et al.: Analysis of energy-efficient connected target coverage algorithms for industrial wireless sensor networks. IEEE Trans. Industr. Inform. **13**(1), 135–143 (2017)
9. Kurt, S., Yildiz, H.U., Yigit, M., et al.: Packet size optimization in wireless sensor networks for smart grid applications. IEEE Trans. Industr. Electron. **64**(3), 2392–2401 (2017)
10. Kuo, T.W., Lin, K.C., Tsai, M.J.: On the construction of data aggregation tree with minimum energy cost in wireless sensor networks: NP-completeness and approximation algorithms. IEEE Trans. Comput. **65**(10), 3109–3121 (2016)
11. Zhang, H., Xing, H., Cheng, J., et al.: Secure resource allocation for OFDMA two-way relay wireless sensor networks without and with cooperative jamming. IEEE Trans. Industr. Inform. **12**(5), 1714–1725 (2016)
12. Gu, Y., Ren, F., Ji, Y., et al.: The evolution of sink mobility management in wireless sensor networks: a survey. IEEE Commun. Surv. Tutor. **18**(1), 507–524 (2016)
13. Villas, L.A., Boukerche, A., Ramos, H.S., et al.: DRINA: a lightweight and reliable routing approach for in-network aggregation in wireless sensor networks. IEEE Trans. Comput. **62**(4), 676–689 (2013)

14. Ren, J., Zhang, Y., Zhang, K., et al.: Lifetime and energy hole evolution analysis in data-gathering wireless sensor networks. IEEE Trans. Industr. Inform. **12**(2), 788–800 (2016)
15. Keskin, M.E., Altınel, İ.K., Aras, N., et al.: Wireless sensor network lifetime maximization by optimal sensor deployment, activity scheduling, data routing and sink mobility. Ad Hoc Netw. **17**, 18–36 (2014)
16. Farash, M.S., Turkanović, M., Kumari, S., et al.: An efficient user authentication and key agreement scheme for heterogeneous wireless sensor network tailored for the Internet of Things environment. Ad Hoc Netw. **36**, 152–176 (2016)
17. Salarian, H., Chin, K.W., Naghdy, F.: An energy-efficient mobile-sink path selection strategy for wireless sensor networks. IEEE Trans. Veh. Technol. **63**(5), 2407–2419 (2014)
18. Abd, M.A., Al-Rubeaai, S.F., Singh, B.K., et al.: Extending wireless sensor network lifetime with global energy balance. IEEE Sensors J. **15**(9), 5053–5063 (2015)
19. Cheng, H., Su, Z., Xiong, N., et al.: Energy-efficient node scheduling algorithms for wireless sensor networks using Markov random field model. Inf. Sci. **329**, 461–477 (2016)
20. Liu, X.: A novel transmission range adjustment strategy for energy hole avoiding in wireless sensor networks. J. Netw. Comput. Appl. **67**, 43–52 (2016)
21. Lin, H., Uster, H.: Exact and heuristic algorithms for data-gathering cluster-based wireless sensor network design problem. IEEE/ACM Trans. Netw. **22**(3), 903–916 (2014)
22. Han, Z., Wu, J., Zhang, J., et al.: A general self-organized tree-based energy-balance routing protocol for wireless sensor network. IEEE Trans. Nuclear Sci. **61**(2), 732–740 (2014)
23. Yao, Y., Cao, Q., Vasilakos, A.V.: EDAL: an energy-efficient, delay-aware, and lifetime-balancing data collection protocol for heterogeneous wireless sensor networks. IEEE/ACM Trans. Netw. (TON) **23**(3), 810–823 (2015)

The Maximum and Minimum Ant Colony Optimization Waking Strategy Based on Multi-Principle and Reprocessing

Wang Pengcheng$^{(\boxtimes)}$ and Lin Tao

School of Computer Science and Software, Hebei University of Technology,
Tianjin 300401, China
muyexueshang@foxmail.com

Abstract. The sensor's waking strategy is critical to the sensor network. The basic mathematical model of waking strategy is TSP problem. Some typical intelligent algorithms for TSP problem model include ant colony algorithm, genetic algorithm and so on. On the basis of the maximum and minimum ant colony algorithm, this paper improves the following disadvantages: According to the principle of choosing the city based on the pheromone principle, the non-contract principle is added, The principle of city selection and make it in the process of selecting the city, the priority to follow the principle of non-contract; in a single path after the help of the enumeration algorithm with the special advantages, refer to the enumeration algorithm part of the results of the re-processing of the path, The path can cover the search space. The improved algorithm avoids the occurrence of stagnation to a certain extent, weakening the blindness of search. The possibility of the results is increased by 25%, single results of the calculation time is reduced by 89.79%.

Keywords: Maximum and minimum ant colony algorithm
Optimization algorithm · Enumeration algorithm · Traveling salesman problem
Intelligent algorithm · Waking strategy

1 Algorithm's Introduction and Analysis

Internet of things penetrates into the various industries gradually, wisdom campus as a typical representative of the Internet of things in the campus, more and more concerned by the education sector. Wisdom campus makes data collection and processing as the key point, with a large number of sensors to form a huge sensor network; it Implements the data foundation data base and then is applied to the wisdom of the campus construction. In the process of building intelligent, it is unavoidable to maintenance of the sensor network, load balancing, and ensures system security. Sensor network is the cornerstone of the entire system, load balancing is an intermediate building, and the system security is the future direction. The sensor has a wide distribution area, large density and close to its own power supply characteristics lead to the sensor cannot work for a long time, so the working state of the sensor is essential for its use cycle, its working state needs an effective network wake-up strategy to ensure switching efficiency and power consumption from normal work to hibernation. The inspection strategy

© Springer Nature Singapore Pte Ltd. 2018
J. Li et al. (Eds.): CWSN 2017, CCIS 812, pp. 117–126, 2018.
https://doi.org/10.1007/978-981-10-8123-1_11

necessarily requires traversing all the sensors in the network, and traversing the sensor is actually a patrol problem, looking for a route that passes through all the sensors only once in the entire sensor network, which can make the network load the smallest and the lowest energy consumption of the sensor. This only one-time path can be attributed to the Hamiltonian problem in the undirected complete graph. The most classic representative of the Hamilton loop problem is the traveler's problem, which is not covered here because the traveler's problem is described in many places. There are many ways to solve traveler's problem, such as particle swarm optimization algorithm, simulated annealing algorithm, ant colony algorithm, neural network algorithm and so on in intelligent algorithm. These algorithms have their own advantages and disadvantages for different problems in their respective fields. So far, there have been many corresponding optimization algorithms, such as elite ant colony algorithm, maximum and minimum ant colony algorithm, chaotic particle swarm optimization algorithm, positive feedback BP neural network algorithm, negative feedback BP neural network algorithm.

1.1 Ant Colony Algorithm

Ant colony algorithm (ACO) is a natural group intelligence algorithm, proposed in 1992, because ACO has a strong randomness, its search is too aimless and makes the search stagnant and time-consuming; it is very likely trapped into the local optimal solution. Our work mainly follows the pheromone principle etc., specific formula as follows:

The Volatile Formula of Pheromone is as follows:

$$T_{ij} = (1 - \rho) * T_{ij} \tag{1}$$

while ρ called volatile rate, it is a customize parameter with the range of (0,1). Its update formula is as follows:

$$\Delta T_{ij}^k = \begin{cases} \frac{E}{D^k} & in\ use \\ 0 & others \end{cases} \tag{2}$$

$$T_{ij} = T_{ij} + \sum_{k=1}^{n} \Delta T_{ij}^k \tag{3}$$

(2) represents update Pheromone according to the length of path, (3) represents self-update according to accumulating Pheromone. In which ΔT_{ij}^k is pheromone concentration of k-th ant in i-th city to j-th city, D^k is the total through length of k-th ant. E is the experience parameter and verify according to different person, it's defaults is set as 1. Max-min Ant colony algorithm(MMAS) is an improved ACO, it mainly constrain the original pheromone concentration to a certain range, and update the pheromone of global optimal ant and current optimal ant. The formula of Pheromone concentration is as follows:

$$T_{ij}(t+1) = \rho * T_{ij}(t) + \Delta T_{ij}^{best} \tag{4}$$

$$\Delta T_{ij}^{best} = \frac{1}{D_{best}}. \tag{5}$$

The formula of Pheromone range is as follows:

$$T_{max} = \frac{1}{(1 - \rho) * D_{best}}. \tag{6}$$

$$T_{min} = \frac{T_{max} * (1 - \sqrt[N]{\rho_{best}})}{(\frac{N}{2} - 1) \sqrt[N]{\rho_{best}}}. \tag{7}$$

While T_{min}. and T_{max} are the lower and upper bound of pheromone, respectively, and D_{best}. is the global optimal path. ρ is Pheromone residual parameter, and ρ_{best}. is the probability of each a search for the optimal solution in one search process, and N is the number of cities. The smooth strategy formula of Pheromone is as follows:

$$T_{ij}^*(t) = T_{ij}(t) + \delta(T_{max}(t) - T_{ij}(t)), \ (0 < \delta < 1). \tag{8}$$

MMAS mainly improve the range of Pheromone, however, these improvements constrained the search ability of algorithm in some extent. What's more, it isn't amending the experience parameter and search space of original ACO, and it still exists the uncertainty of the algorithm results.

ACO's Validation and summary
In our experiment, the typical TSP problem is taken as an example, and TSPLIB51 is used as the experimental object, and the optimal path length is 426 obtained by other algorithms. The number of experimental nodes in this experiment is 20, and the operation time of a single node is 100 h, experiment environment is Intel(R) Core(TM) i7-6700 K CPU @4.00 GHz, 16 GRAM, 64 bit, experiment results is shown as follows:

As shown in Fig. 1, 20 nodes only obtained 15 set results in a certain time; computing success rate is 75.00%, and Fig. 2 shows that the algorithm is very unstable. As to the experiment time, average computing time is 36.45 time step, and the fastest computing time step is 20.76 around, the time step in our experiment is 107 ms $\approx$ 2.78 h. So the shortest computing time is about 60 h, and experiment time of single node is 100 h. Theoretically, one node should obtain at least 1 set of result, but some nodes obtained no result in Fig. 1, it demonstrates that most nodes trapped into the local optimal solution. So the basic ACO has poor practicality.

1.2 Enumeration Algorithm

Comparison of enumeration algorithms with others
The enumeration algorithm is the exhaustive method, which enumerates the required computing objects one by one. It can be seen as the realization of the combination algorithm and the full permutation algorithm. It is equivalent to use the combination

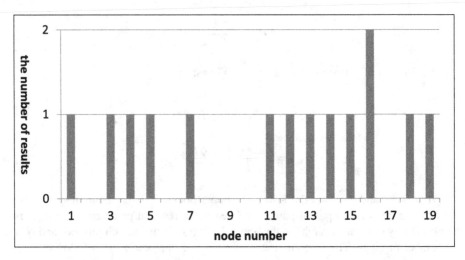

Fig. 1. ACO's calculated results

algorithm for the object, and then using the full permutation for the single combination algorithm, which makes the enumeration algorithm very high complexity. The characteristics of an ideal enumeration algorithm: for one set, extract a subset of it to achieve a subset of the exhaustive. Especially extracting subset is just the advantage of the combination algorithm, and enumerating the subset is only completed by full permutation. The shortcomings of the enumeration algorithm are as follows:

(1) Because of the uncertainty of the result, for the concrete, it must compute in the whole process which leads to low efficiency.
(2) The independence of result is very poor, and the calculation of each length depends on the calculation of the previous length, once an error occurs, it must start from scratch. Although it can record the breakpoint, the time to find the breakpoint is far more than the recalculated time.

The advantages are as follows:

(1) Disposable calculation, that is, all the results can be calculated once, the results are applicable for the selective issues, it does not need to be calculated when the problem changed.
(2) After the calculation is completed, the corresponding selectivity problems of length can be resolved. Only each of the results of the calculation and the actual problem can be one-to-one, and it has the benefits of once and for all.
(3) The results of the calculation have been fully covered for all the possibilities, and there is no local optimal solution to the problem except the most appropriate solution, which is unmatched by other algorithms.

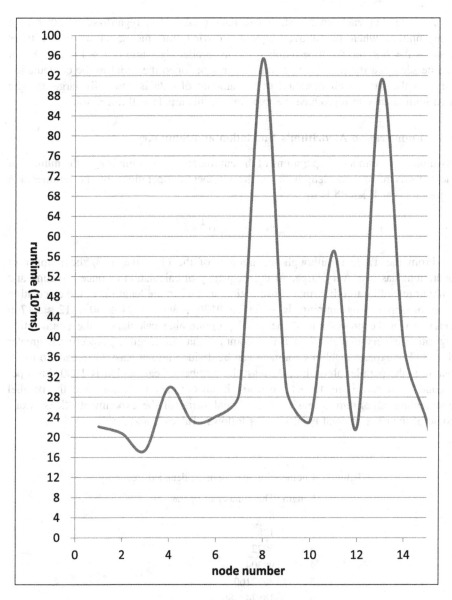

Fig. 2. ACO's calculated runtime

1.3   Serial and Parallel Enumeration Algorithm

Making enumerate A, B two nodes as an example, the steps are as follows:

(1) Enumeration of all possible cases of a single node as A, B;
(2) On the basis of A, enumerating all the combinations of them with B is: AB, BA;
(3) On the basis of B, enumerating all the combinations of them with A: BA, AB;

Assume that each enumeration calculation takes 1 s, regardless of other time consumption: when the above steps are carried out, the serial algorithm takes $2 + 2 + 2 = 6$ s, but the time required in the parallel algorithm is $1 + 1 = 2$ s. And it can be seen that the parallel algorithm is far superior to the serial in the computation time; as the parallel enumeration of the amount of data is unusually large and the algorithm is easy to reproduce the experiment, this article will not repeat.

1.4   Enumeration Algorithm's Validation and Summary

Assuming the number of operations of the enumeration algorithm is e_c, the number of elements is n, and the length is m, the number of operations of the enumeration algorithm which length is m:

$$e\_c = \sum\nolimits_{k=1}^{m} \left(n^k * k! \right) \tag{9}$$

From the Table 1: although the number of the objective is 8, the number of operations has been very large. At the frequency of calculation as once a second and without regarding to other time consumption, and when the length is 8, the calculating time of serial programming is $676457349120 \div 3600 \div 24 \div 30 \div 12 \approx 21749$ years. So in the procession of the serial programming calculation, the enumeration algorithm is very unrealistic, and it is common that the length of objective is greater than 8. The experimental environment can be divided into at least 24 threads to run if one uses the parallel algorithm, At least the number of calculation is 1000 times per second, so it can easily to get the result in an ordinary laboratory and the parallel enumeration algorithm is feasible. The initial string of the experiment: "!qzs9wxa", some of the experimental results are as follows (Tables 2 and 3):

Table 1. Enumeration algorithm's calculated frequency

Length	The number of operations
1	8
2	128
3	3072
4	98304
5	3932160
6	188743680
7	10569646080
8	676457349120

Table 2. Results of the parallel enumeration with one length

!	q	z	s	9	w	x	a

Table 3. Results of the parallel enumeration with one length

q!	w!	!z	wz	!9	!w	xw	qa	wa	xx
!q	!w	z!	zw	9!	w!	wx	aq	aw	xx
z!	zq	qz	xz	q9	zw	!!	ax	aa	q!
!z	qz	zq	zx	9q	wz	!!	xa	aa	s!
s!	sq	zz	zs	z9	qw	qx	!a	xa	qa
!s	qs	zz	sz	9z	wq	xq	a!	ax	sw
9!	qq	9z	ss	99	sw	!x	za	sx	9w
!9	qq	z9	ss	99	ws	x!	az	xs	wa
x!	xq	sz	qs	s9	9w	zx	9a	Xs	xw
!x	qx	zs	sq	9 s	w9	xz	a9	Sx	as
a!	9q	az	9 s	x9	ww	9x	a9	wq	sa
!a	q9	za	s9	9x	ww	x9	9a	qw	
!q	aq	!s	ws	w9	aw	wx	sa	as	

2 EMMAS-2S Inspection Strategy

2.1 The Design of EMMAS-2S

The maximum and minimum ant colony optimization wake-up strategy (EMMAS-2S) which based on multi-principle re-processing is based on the maximum and minimum ant colony algorithm and the enumeration algorithm. For the maximum and minimum ant colony algorithm, in order to obtain better solution, Group algorithm to continue the shortcomings of the optimization, increase its search breadth, reduce its randomness. EMMAS-2S uses the enumeration algorithm to improve the MMAS algorithm, and the improved length is 2. Aiming at the shortcomings of MMAS algorithm, we give the concrete improvement method as follows:

(1) The choice of the starting point from the previous random selection into the first non-contract according to the principle of choice, to be selected after all the non-approximate, in the random selection.
(2) The strategy of selecting the next node is that if the starting point adopts the non-contract principle, then the choice of the next node follows the non-contract principle; if the starting point takes the pheromone principle, the next node selection should follow the pheromone principle;
(3) If all the nodes are selected completely, in addition to the starting point and the end point of the node to alternate enumeration;

Theoretically the benefits of improvement are:

(1) Effectively avoid stagnation because the enumeration number of paths is fixed;
(2) To a certain extent, it limits the impact of random number on the convergence rate;
(3) For a single path, in its original degree to increase the breadth of the search;

Multi-rules and reprocessing

Multi-principle means that in EMMAS-2S, the choice of nodes can follow two principles, namely: non-contract principle and stochastic principle. As the random principle for the basic concept of ant colony algorithm for the recognized knowledge, this article is no longer described. Non-contract principle is in accordance with the non-contract to select the node, the non-contractor is not about the number, for example, 9 of the contract (only consider the real number) have 1, 3, 9, 5, 6, 7, 8. According to the principle of non-contract, select the number 2 nodes as the starting node, select all nodes, then select the fourth node as the starting node, and so on. Select the formula for the next node as follows:

$$a_i = (a_{i-1} + a_0) \bmod N, \ (0 < i < N) \tag{10}$$

Where a_i is the node number selected for the i-th, a_{i-1} is the number of the i-1-selected node, i is the number of selected nodes, and N is the total number of nodes. For example, when $a_0 = 2$, N = 9, the node number is $1 \sim 9$, the node selection order: 2, 4, 6, 8, 1, 3, 5, 7, 9; and when $a_0 = 5$, The other conditions are unchanged, then the order of selection of nodes: 5, 1, 6, 2, 7, 3, 8, 4, 9. The final node number in this way is N. When selecting a node, the non-contract principle is first followed, and when the node number of the total node's number is taken as the starting node once, the random principle is followed. The advantage of doing so is to reduce the randomness of the ant colony algorithm from the beginning. And then search is in the original path to modify the starting point other than the nodes. For example, when the first path of $a_0 = 2$, N = 9 is: 2, 4, 6, 8, 1, 3, 5, 7, 9. In the case of expansion, the starting point is still 2, and when the number of references is 2, the remaining ones are: 6, 4, 8, 1, 3, 5, 7, 9. That is, 4 and 6 exchange, to form a new path; 6 and 8 exchange, and to form a new path, and so on. The exchange object is determined by the result of the enumeration algorithm.

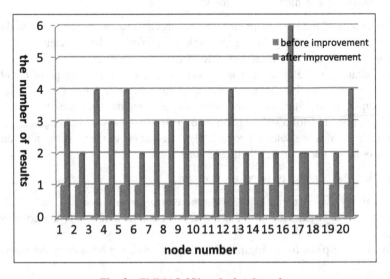

Fig. 3. EMMAS-2S's calculated results

2.2 Implementation of the EMMAS-2S Awakening Strategy and Verification Experiment

The experiment environment is Intel(R) Core(TM)i7-6700KCPU@4.00 GHz, 16 GRAM, 64 bit. The experiment's results as follows:

From Fig. 3: EMMAS-2S calculates 60 result nodes, the success rate is 100%; more 25% than ACO. From Fig. 4: the performance of EMMAS-2S is better than

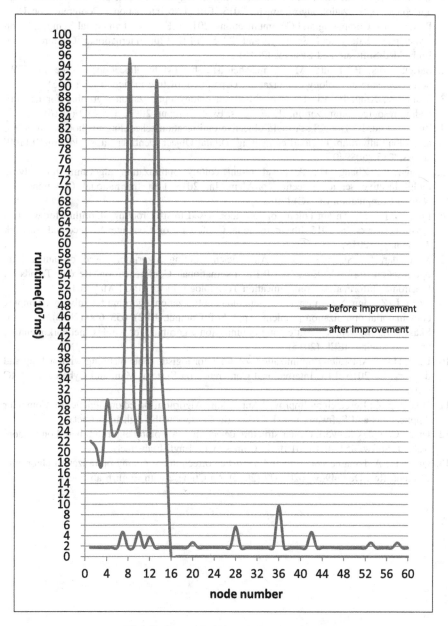

Fig. 4. EMMAS-2S's calculated runtime

ACO, the average value of calculated time is 2.12 time step, decreased 89.79% than ACO. Therefore, the search ability of EMMAS-2S is improved well.

References

1. Chen, Q.: A logistic distribution routes solving strategy based on the physarum network and ant colony optimization algorithm. In: 2015 IEEE 17th International Conference on High Performance Computing and Communications, 2015 IEEE 7th International Symposium on Cyberspace Safety and Security, and 2015 IEEE 12th International Conference on Embedded Software and Systems (2015)
2. Sarigiannidis, P., Louta, M.: A metaheuristic bandwidth allocation scheme for FiWi networks using ant colony optimization, Department of Informatics. IEEE (2015)
3. Wang, Z., Xing, H., Li, T.: A modified ant colony optimization algorithm for network coding resource minimization. IEEE Trans. Evol. Comput. **20**(3), 325–342 (2016)
4. Zuo, L., Shu, L., Dong,S.: A multi-objective optimization scheduling method based on the ant colony algorithm in cloud computing. Digital Object Identifier https://doi.org/10.1109/access.2015.2508940
5. Huang, L., Zhang, B.: A novel bi-ant colony optimization algorithm for solving multi-objective service selection problem. In: 2015 11th International Conference on Natural Computation (ICNC) (2015)
6. Luo, Z., Lu, L.: An ant colony optimization-based trustful routing algorithm for wireless sensor networks. In: 2015 4th International Conference on Computer Science and Network Technology (2015)
7. Majumdar, S., Shivashankarm.: An efficient routing algorithm based on ant colony optimisation for VANETs. In: IEEE International Conference on Recent Trends in Electronics Information Communication Technology, India, 20–21 May 2016
8. Yang, J., Zhuang, Y.: An improved ant colony optimization algorithm for solving a complex combinatorial optimization problem. Appl. Soft Comput. **10**(2), 653–660 (2010)
9. Skakov, E., Malysh, V.: Ant colony optimization algorithms for wireless network planning problem solving. IEEE (2015)
10. Lu, E.H.-C.: Ant colony optimization solutions for logistic route planning with pick-up and delivery. In: 2016 IEEE International Conference on System, Man, and Cybernetics SMC (2016)
11. Huaifeng, Z.: Research on Improved Ant Colony Algorithm Based on Genetics,on Computer Applications and Software, vol. 1 (2011). (in Chinese with English abstract)
12. Di, J.: Complex network cluster structure detection - ant colony algorithm based on random walk. J. Softw. 451–464 (2010). (in Chinese with English abstract)
13. Quan, L.: A dynamic volatility and heuristic correction ant colony optimization algorithm. Comput. Res. Dev. **49**(3), 620–627 (2012). (in Chinese with English abstract)

Improved Asynchronous Energy Saving Mechanism with Mesh-Based Routing for Digital Media Over IEEE 802.15.5-Based Mesh Networks

Li-yong Yuan[1,2(✉)], Gen-mei Pan[1], Xing-Ze Xu[3], Zhen Cheng[1],
and Yi-hua Zhu[1]

[1] School of Computer Science and Technology,
Zhejiang University of Technology, Hangzhou 310023, Zhejiang, China
yuan_zjnu@qq.com, pgm611@126.com,
{zhencheng, yhzhu}@zjut.edu.cn
[2] XingZhi College, Zhejiang Normal University,
Jinhua 321004, Zhejiang, China
[3] Hangzhou Foreign Languages School, Hangzhou 310023, Zhejiang, China
williamxingze991124@outlook.com

Abstract. Energy-efficient data delivery is important for digital media applications based on wireless sensor networks (WSNs). The asynchronous energy saving (ASES) scheme introduced in IEEE 802.15.5 standard, which supports to deliver data using mesh topology, has the shortcoming that the sender and the receivers are required to stay idle listening for too long a period, which wastes energy. In this paper, in addition to remedying this shortcoming, we present the improved asynchronous energy saving mechanism with mesh-based routing (IASES-MR). In the IASES-MR, each node maintains the wakeup schedule information of the nodes within its two-hop neighborhood so that the sender/receivers can wake up just before data delivery starts. This reduces the periods of idle listening and makes the sender/receivers have longer sleeping durations so as to save energy. Moreover, an algorithm for building data delivery route, together with data forwarding rules using mesh topology, are presented to deliver data energy-efficiently. The proposed IASES-MR outperforms the ASES in terms of energy consumed in idle listening periods and end-to-end packet delay.

Keywords: Wireless mesh sensor network · Wireless sensor network
Energy saving · End-to-end delay · Mesh networking · IEEE 802.15.5 standard

1 Introduction

Wireless sensor network (WSN) has been widely used in digital media applications such as healthcare computing, habitat monitoring and the other areas [1]. Contemporary WSNs adopt IEEE 802.15.4 standard [2] in the MAC and PHY layers, which targets low-rate wireless personal area network (WPAN). Usually, tree-based routing protocols, such as the widely-used Collection Tree Protocol (CTP), are applied in

© Springer Nature Singapore Pte Ltd. 2018
J. Li et al. (Eds.): CWSN 2017, CCIS 812, pp. 127–138, 2018.
https://doi.org/10.1007/978-981-10-8123-1_12

gathering data for WSNs. But, they exhibit a critical shortcoming. That is, failure of a branch node prevents its descendant nodes from delivering their data to the sink. This problem is resolved by mesh-based routing [3]. To enable WPAN nodes to maintain stable and scalable wireless mesh topology, IEEE 802.15.5 standard [4] defines the architectural framework that constitutes low-rate mesh network and high-rate mesh network. Considering the former is based on IEEE 802.15.4 standard, which is widely applied in WSNs, we focus on the former and investigate wireless sensor mesh network (WSMN) in this paper.

As sensor nodes typically run on batteries with quite limited energy, energy saving mechanism is crucial for WSMN to have a longer lifetime. To save WSMN node's energy, IEEE 802.15.5 standard introduces the Asynchronous Energy Saving (ASES) that operates with the non-beacon mode supported by IEEE 802.15.4 standard. The ASES provides a node with receiver-initiated mechanism to unicast data and sender-initiated mechanism to broadcast.

The ASES brings in energy efficiency by applying duty cycle. Although the duty cycle significantly reduces nodes' idle listening period [5], energy consumption arising from the idle listening in both the unicast and broadcast mechanisms can further be reduced. This is the motivation of this paper, which has the main contributions as follows:

(1) We propose the improved asynchronous energy saving mechanism with mesh-based routing (IASES-MR), which improves the traditional ASES. With the IASES-MR, a sender is aware of the wakeup schedules of the receivers within 2-hop neighborhood so that the sender has a longer sleeping period to save energy.
(2) The IASES-MR improves the unicast and broadcast mechanisms in the traditional ASES by shortening the period of idle listening based on the wakeup schedules of the receivers, which reduces the energy consumption.
(3) After defining weight of wireless link, we present the algorithm, which uses mesh topology, to build data delivery route towards to low end-to-end delay. Additionally, data packets forwarding rules are designed to deliver data using mesh topology.
(4) We investigate the guard time that overcomes clock drift, guarantees the sender to receive neighbors' wakeup notification messages, and makes the IASES-MR have a lower energy consumption in idle listening (ECIL) than the traditional ASES.
(5) The IASES-MR outperforms the ASES in terms of ECIL and end-to-end packet delay.

The remainder of this paper is organized as follows. In Sect. 2 we survey the related works. The detail of the IASES-MR is described in Sect. 3. Guard time selection to make the proposed IASES-MR outperform the traditional scheme is presented in Sect. 4. Performance evaluation via simulation is given in Sect. 5. We conclude the paper in Sect. 6.

2 Related Works

In IEEE 802.15.5 standard [4], a low rate mesh WPAN standard, the time line of a node is divided into wakeup intervals (WIs). A WI is further subdivided into an active duration (AD) and an inactive duration. In the AD, the node announces that it is active by transmitting a wakeup notification (WN) command. Then, the node waits for possible frame transmission. In the inactive duration, the node enters a low-power or sleeping mode by turning off the receiver circuitry to save energy [4]. With the ASES introduced in IEEE 802.15.5 standard, a node operates with duty cycle, i.e., it alternates active state with inactive state, which is shown in Fig. 1.

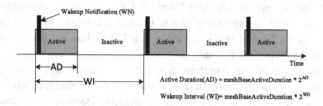

Fig. 1. The structure of WI [4]

In Fig. 1, *meshcBaseActiveDuration* is a constant defined in IEEE 802.15.5 standard; and *WO* and *AO* are the wakeup order and the active order, respectively, which satisfy $0 \leq AO \leq WO \leq 14$. IEEE 802.15.5 standard recommends that all nodes share the same *WO* value. At the beginning of each WI, a wakeup notification (WN) message (a command frame) is transmitted (see Fig. 1).

To cope with the asynchronous ADs of nodes, the ASES uses the receiver-initiated and sender-initiated mechanisms to unicast and broadcast data, respectively. The receiver-initiated mechanism is illustrated in Fig. 2, where node v unicasts to node u after node v receives a WN from node u. The sender-initiated mechanism is shown in Fig. 3, where node w broadcasts to nodes u and v. Node w first wakes them up and keeps them awake by continuously transmitting EREQ frames for a duration longer than one WI, then it broadcasts data.

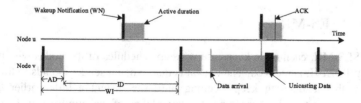

Fig. 2. The receiver-oriented unicast mechanism [4]

From Figs. 2 and 3, we observe energy inefficiency due to the fact that, either the sender has to keep awake to wait for the WN from the receiver (see Fig. 2), or the

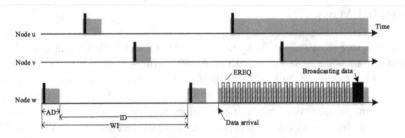

Fig. 3. The sender-initiated broadcast mechanism [4]

earlier waken nodes have to stay idle listening for receiving the broadcast data (see Fig. 3). In a word, there exists energy waste from idle listening (EWIL) in the ASES. Unfortunately, to the best of our knowledge, the EWIL has not been investigated in literatures. This motivates us to study it.

Many efforts are made in literature to reduce the energy waste arising from idle listening. Several protocols were designed for WSNs to mitigate idle listening in receiver-initiated unicast [6]. Using receiver's remaining sleep time to estimate wakeup time, Yang et al. [7] proposed RW-MAC, which was extended by RP-MAC [8] with the feature of frame reordering that uses the next wakeup information of several receivers to reorder the transmission buffer. Basagni et al. [9] used wakeup radio to eliminate idle listening and decreased the delivery delay. Wang et al. [10] analyzed the energy consumption of duty cycled sensor networks with different data rates and designed a light-weight adaptive duty-cycling protocol. However, the above surveyed schemes cannot be applied in the WSMNs based on IEEE 802.15.5 standard, which rides on the MAC layer. Moreover, none of them addresses the aforementioned EWIL problem in ASES.

Aiming at reducing EWIL or ECIL, we propose the IASES-MR. With the IASES-MR, the periods of idle listening in both unicast and broadcast mechanisms are reduced by exploiting the knowledge of wakeup schedules of the neighbors within 2 hops. Furthermore, the guard time that guarantees the sender to receive neighbors' WN messages and enables the IASES-MR to have a lower ECIL is investigated in order to make the IASES-MR function well.

3   The IASES-MR

In the IASES-MR, each node keeps the wakeup schedules of the nodes within 2 hops so that EWIL/ECIL is reduced. The reason is that, when a sender intends to transmit to a receiver, the sender can keep sleeping until the instant a little earlier than the receiver's wakeup time because it has the knowledge of wakeup time of the receiver.

3.1   Initialization of IASES-MR

Each node sets its mesh sublayer parameter *meshASESOn* to *false* in the initial stage, which indicates the nodes in the WSMN initially operate as usual, i.e., they do not operate with the ASES. After obtaining a mesh sublayer address, a node sends several *eHello* messages to inform its neighbors of its wakeup schedule in addition to other necessary information to maintain mesh topology. The *eHello* message, introduced in the IASES-MR, extends the *Hello* message defined in IEEE 802.15.5 standard and used in exchanging connectivity information among neighbors. The format of *eHello* message is illustrated in Fig. 4.

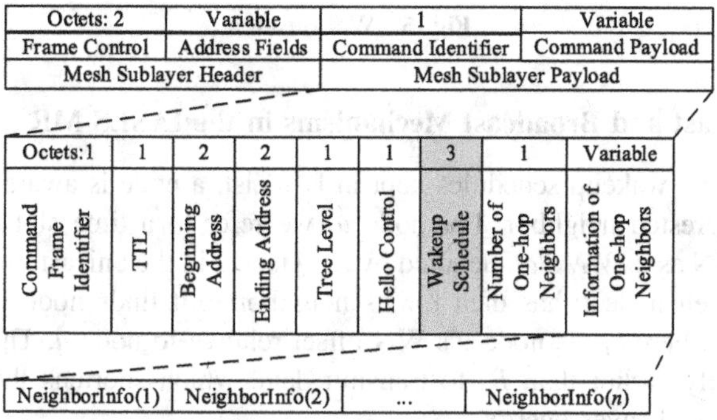

Fig. 4. Format of *eHello* frame

The main difference between the *eHello* and *Hello* frames is that, we add the field "Wakeup Schedule" with shadow (the meaning of the other fields are the same as that in the *Hello* frame defined in IEEE 802.15.5 standard). Moreover, in the case when the field "Number of One-hop Neighbors" is set to n, the field "Information of One-hop Neighbors" contains the fields of NeighborInfo(i) ($i = 1, 2, \ldots, n$) shown in the bottom of Fig. 4. Here, NeighborInfo(i) keeps the information of the i-th neighbor and it contains the fields of "Beginning Address" (2 B), "Ending Address" (2 B), "Tree Level" (1 B), and "Wakeup Schedule" (3 B). Further, each "Wakeup Schedule" field in Fig. 4 is composed of the pair of 4-bit field "AO" and 20-bit field "WN offset" defined as follows.

For nodes u, we use t_u to represent its wakeup time, at which a WN is sent out. Assume node v is a neighbor of node u and wakes up at t_v next to t_u Then, we refer to $t_v - t_u$ as WN offset of node v relative to node u, which is shown in Fig. 5. WN offset is measured by *meshcTimeUnit* (mTU), a constant defined in IEEE 802.15.5 standard [4]. In the sequel, we regard mTU as a time slot, denoted by τ. From [4], a WI consists of L time slots, where $L = 5 \times 2^{WO}$.

A node enters ASES mode by setting *meshASESOn = true* so as to operate with duty cycle after it exchanges *eHello* messages with its neighbors, which makes the node obtain the information of its 2-hop neighborhood. To keep 2-hop neighbors' information, each node maintains a table, called extended neighbor list (EN-List), which appends field of "*wakeup schedule*" to the traditional neighbor list introduced in IEEE 802.15.5 standard [4]. From the EN-List, the node can construct a *connectivity matrix* to indicate whether a pair of nodes is directly connected or not.

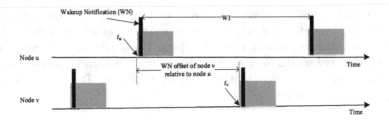

Fig. 5. WN offset

3.2   The Unicast and Broadcast Mechanisms in the IASES-MR

Having the nodes' wakeup schedules kept in EN-List, a node is aware of WN arrival times of an interested neighbor. For node u, we refer to a time slot in which node u sends out a WN as its *WN slot*, denoted by B_u. Hence, in the unicast mechanism in the IASES-MR, when node u has data for its neighbor v, it finds node v's WN slot as $B_v = B_u + \theta_{uv}$, where θ_{uv} is node v's WN offset relative to node u. Thus, node u just wakes up slightly earlier than B_v to transmit data, which shortens the sender's idle listening period and saves energy.

The broadcast mechanism in the IASES-MR is shown in Fig. 6, where node u broadcasts to nodes x, y, z, w, and v. Node u first finds the broadcast time, i.e., the time at which the last neighbor (i.e., node z) wakes up. Then, node u sends *eEREQ* frames to inform its neighbors of the waiting time. During the waiting time, waken receivers are allowed to sleep again until the end of the waiting time, which wakes up the receivers and also triggers node u to broadcast data. Here, *eEREQ* extends *EREQ* by adding a 2-byte field for waiting time. When a neighbor receives an *eEREQ*, it replies with an *EREP* frame to the sender, turns off its radio to sleep, and wakes up at the notified broadcast time. As soon as node u receives the WN message from the last neighbor, it broadcasts the data. It should be stressed that, in Fig. 6, the sender (i.e., node u) stays active only during the period from the instant slightly earlier that s receiver's wake up to the instant of completing *eEREP/EREP* exchange or data broadcasting.

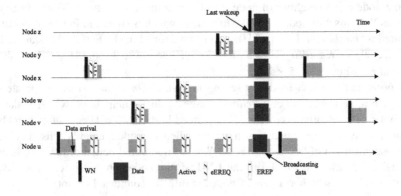

Fig. 6. The broadcast mechanism in IASES-MR

Compared to the original broadcast mechanism in the ASES, the improved broadcast mechanism in the IASES-MR has the following merits. Firstly, the sender only needs to keep awake for a short period for exchanging *eEREQ/EREP* messages with its neighbors, and the sender can sleep in the rest time. Secondly, after finishing *eEREQ/EREP* exchange, a receiver turns off the radio and does not wake up until the instant slightly earlier than the notified broadcasting time, which decreases the receiver's idle listening period. Thirdly, the sender only waits for a period shorter than one WI before broadcasting (at least one WI is required in the traditional ASES), which also saves energy.

3.3   The Routing Mechanism in the IASES-MR

In the IASES-MR, when a node is about to forward a packet, it consults with its EN-List and the *connectivity matrix* to determine the next hop. To find the optimal next hop, we build data delivery route using link weights. Here, we define weight of the link from node u to node v as

$$w(u, v) = L \times \alpha + \theta_{uv}, 0 \leq \alpha \leq 1, \tag{1}$$

where α is a constant for balancing WN offset θ_{uv} and number of time slots L.

Assume v is current node, and nodes u and w are its neighbors. In the EN-List at node v, the WN offsets of the neighbors relative to node v, i.e., θ_{vw} and θ_{vu}, are kept. But, θ_{uw} is not kept. Hence, we use the following expression to calculate it:

$$\theta_{uw} = (\theta_{vw} - \theta_{vu} + L) \bmod L \tag{2}$$

The IASES-MR embeds a mesh-based routing, which proceeds as follows. When a node receives a packet, the receiver checks whether its address matches the packet destination. If yes, the receiver consumes the packet. Otherwise, the receiver forwards the packet according to the following rules.

Rule (i). If the destination matches one of its one-hop neighbors, the receiver delivers the packet directly to the neighbor.

Rule (ii). If the destination's address falls in the address block of a node in the EN-List, the node with the smallest address block that includes the destination is selected as the anchor. Then, the receiver finds the next hop to the anchor using the algorithm *findNextHop* as follows and forwards the packet to the found next-hop node. In the algorithm, we use $N(u)$ to represent the set of the neighbors of node u.

Algorithm: *findNextHop*

Input: *address of the destination, address of the anchor*
Begin:
    $u* = arg\ min\{MinRouteWeight(u) \mid u \in N(anchor)\}$;
    while($u* \notin N(current\ node)$){
        pick **a** node v that satisfies $v \in N(u^*)$ *and*
               $MinRouteWeight\ (v) + w(v, u^*) = MinRouteWeight\ (u^*)$;
        $u* = v$;}
    return u.*
End
Output: *next-hop node*

Here, *MinRouteWeight(u)* represents the smallest weight of the route from the receiver to node *u*, where route weight is defined as the sum of the weights of the links contained in the route.

Rule (iii). If the receiver does not have any information about the destination, it selects the neighbor with the smallest sum of *"tree level"* and *"number of Hops"* in the EN-List as the anchor, and the next hop to the anchor is found by the above *findNextHop* algorithm. Then, the packet is forwarded to the found next-hop node.

4 Guard Time

To avoid missing a receiver's WN message due to clock drift, the sender is required to wake up slightly earlier than the preset wakeup time of the receiver. We refer to the interval from the sender's wakeup instant to the scheduled wakeup instant of the receiver as *guard time* of the sender. In fact, a longer guard time helps in guaranteeing the reception of the WNs from the receivers, whereas it consumes more energy due to a longer idle listening. Inversely, although a shorter guard time saves energy, it may cause the sender to miss the receivers' WNs. Therefore, we should carefully consider guard time to make the IASES-MR function well so as to achieve energy saving.

Next, we address selection of guard time for the unicast and broadcast mechanisms in the IASES-MR.

As well-known, energy consumption in idle listening is the product of listening period and listening power. Assume that the nodes apply the same power under the IASES-MR and the ASES. Thus, energy consumption in idle listening (ECIL) depends on the listening period. As a result, we compare the IASES-MR with the ASES in terms of idle listening period. Without loss of generality, for ease of description, we set power applied in idle listening to 1 unit, so that the energy consumption in the period of idle listening (PIL) is equal to the PIL times 1, i.e., PIL. Hence, in the sequel, we use PIL and ECIL interchangeably.

First, we compare the PIL in the unicast mechanisms in the IASES-MR and the ASES. In the ASES, a sender has to keep listening for entire time slot to avoid missing the receiver's WN. The expected PIL is half of WI. That is, the ECIL is

$$E_{ASES}^{(u)} = 5 \times 2^{(WO-1)}\tau. \tag{3}$$

In the IASES-MR, from view of the sender, arrival time of a receiver's WN is a random variable that obeys a uniform distribution over a time slot with length of $\tau = $ mTU. Hence, the expected PIL of the sender is $t_g + 0.5\tau$, which leads to the ECIL as

$$E_{IASES-MR}^{(u)} = t_g + 0.5\tau. \tag{4}$$

From (3) and (4), we observe that, in the unicast mechanism, we should choose a guard time satisfying

$$\delta \leq t_g < [5 \times 2^{(WO-1)} - 0.5]\tau \tag{5}$$

so as to achieve

$$E_{IASES-MR}^{(u)} < E_{ASES}^{(u)}, \tag{6}$$

i.e., the proposed IASES-MR outperforms the traditional ASES in ECIL for the unicast mechanism. Here, δ is a constant representing the lower bound of clock drift.

Next, we compare the PIL in the broadcast mechanisms in both schemes. Assume the average number of the neighbors of a node is N. In the ASES, to broadcast a data frame, the sender needs to continuously transmit EREQs for a duration longer than one WI to wake up all neighbors. When a receiver receives an *EREQ* message, it keeps listening until receiving the data broadcast by the sender. Averagely, a receiver stays in idle listening for duration of half of WI. Thus, all the receivers contribute $N \times WI/2$ in PIL. Considering the sender stays active for at least one WI, the total ECIL resulting from the ASES is at least as

$$\begin{aligned} E_{ASES}^{(b)} &= 5 \times 2^{WO-1}\tau N + 5 \times 2^{WO}\tau \\ &= 5 \times 2^{WO-1}(N+2)\tau. \end{aligned} \tag{7}$$

In the IASES-MR, the sender unicasts to inform the receivers of the determined broadcast time. Each receiver expends 3 mTU on *eEREQ/EREP* exchange with the sender [4]. So, the expected PIL for all the receivers is totally as $3\tau N$. Considering the sender is involved with all *eEREQ/EREP* exchanges, we have the sender's PIL as $3\tau N$ plus $N \times t_g$ since a guard time is required for each exchange. As a result, we have the ECIL as

$$E_{IASES-MR}^{(b)} = N(6\tau + t_g). \tag{8}$$

From (7) and (8), we observe that, in the broadcast mechanism in the IASES-MR, we should choose a guard time satisfying

$$\delta \leq t_g < 5 \times \frac{2^{WO-1}(N+2)\tau}{N} - 6\tau \tag{9}$$

so as to achieve

$$E_{IASES-MR}^{(b)} < E_{ASES}^{(b)}, \tag{10}$$

i.e., the proposed IASES-MR outperforms the traditional ASES in ECIL for the broadcast mechanism.

5 Performance Evaluation via Simulation

The aim of the IASES-MR is at reducing ECIL or EWIL mentioned in Sect. 1. There are many choices in choosing a guard time t_g to satisfy (5) and (9) so that (6) and (10) hold true. That is, the IASES-MR outperforms the ASES in terms of reduction in ECIL, which agrees with our intuition since we have witnessed a shorter idle listening in the IASES-MR than the ASES.

Next, we compare the IASES-MR with the ASES in end-to-end packet delay via simulation. In simulation, we deploy 400 nodes in a square of 1000×1000 m². For a randomly-generated network topology, a node is randomly selected as the sink. Then, the tree rooted at the sink is formed per IEEE 802.15.5 standard. To compare packet delay, we randomly choose 5000 pairs of nodes and let each pair deliver one packet. We set WO = 8 and AO = 1 for both the IASES-MR and the ASES. The simulation results shown below are from the average over 500 randomly-generated topologies.

Letting α vary from 0 to 1 with step 0.1 and considering different values of radio range R, we have the simulation results shown in Figs. 7 and 8, which reflect the impacts of α and R on the delay ratio and the Average Number of Transmissions (ANT) ratio, respectively. Here, ANT is the total number of transmissions over the number of nodes participating in data forwarding, and the ANT ratio is defined as ratio of the ANT in the IASES-MR to the ANT in the ASES. In addition, the delay ratio is defined as the ratio of the end-to-end packet delay in the IASES-MR to that in the ASES.

From Fig. 7, we have the following observations. Firstly, the end-to-end delay in IASES-MR is smaller than that in the ASES due to the ratio being less than 1. We owe this to the *findNextHop* algorithm in the IASES-MR, which can find a route with a lower delay. Secondly, a smaller α makes the IASES-MR have a smaller delay. The reason is that, from (1), link weight becomes emphasizing on WN offset more than number of slots L when α takes a small value, which helps in reducing delay. Thirdly, for a given α, growth of radio range reduces the delay ratio, i.e., the end-to-end delay in

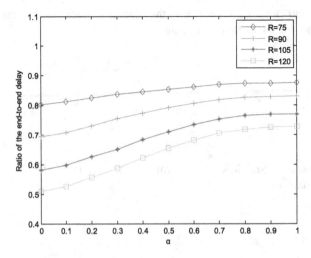

Fig. 7. Delay ratio vs α

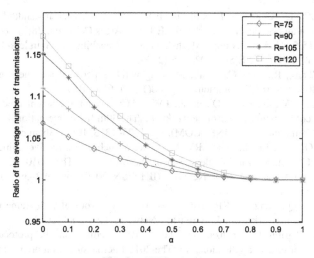

Fig. 8. ANT ratio vs α

the IASES-MR is much better than that in the ASES. This is because a greater radio range makes a node have more neighbors so that the IASES-MR has more choices in building data forwarding route to reduce delay. From Fig. 8, we are aware that the IASES-MR has a higher ANT than the ASES due to the ANT ratio is greater than 1. In other words, the ANT is traded for lower delay in the IASES-MR. Exactly speaking, we trade less than 20% ANT for more than 50% and up to 90% delay. The reason is that, a low delay forwarding path constructed by the IASES-MR generally has more hops so that is occupies a higher ANT than the ASES.

6 Conclusion

In the IASES-MR, nodes exchange wakeup schedule information with their neighbors so that the sender and the receivers have longer sleeping periods before transmitting/receiving data, which reduces energy consumption in idle listening. In addition, the mesh-based routing embedded in the IASES-MR is able to reduce end-to-end packet delay. The IASES-MR is compatible with IEEE 802.15.5 mesh standard and applicable to the applications of delivering digital medium over IEEE 802.15.5 network.

References

1. Estrin, D., Culler, D., Pister, K., et al.: Connecting the physical world with pervasive networks. IEEE Pervasive Comput. **1**(1), 59–69 (2002)
2. IEEE 802.15.4 Working Group: Wireless LAN Medium Access Control (MAC) and Physical Layer (PHY) Specifications for Low-Rate Wireless Personal Area Networks (LR-WPANs). IEEE Std. 802.15.4 (2006)

3. Lee, M.J., Zhang, R., Zheng, J., et al.: IEEE 802.15.5 WPAN mesh standard-low rate part: meshing the wireless sensor networks. IEEE J. Sel. Areas Commun. **28**(7), 973–983 (2010)
4. IEEE 802.15.5 Working Group: Mesh Topology Capability in Wireless Personal Area Networks (WPANs). IEEE Std. 802.15.5 (2009)
5. Lee, M., Zhang, R., Zhu, C., et al.: Meshing wireless personal area networks: Introducing IEEE 802.15.5. IEEE Commun. Mag. **48**(1), 54–61 (2010)
6. Tang, L., Sun, Y., Gurewitz, O., et al.: PW-MAC: an energy-efficient predictive-wakeup MAC protocol for wireless sensor networks. In: The 30th IEEE International Conference on Computer Communications (INFOCOM), pp. 1305–1313. IEEE, Shanghai (2011)
7. Yang, D., Qiu, Y., Li, S., et al.: RW-MAC: an asynchronous receiver-initiated ultra-low power MAC protocol for Wireless Sensor Networks. In: The 2010 IET International Conference on Wireless Sensor Network (IETWSN 2010), pp. 393–398. IEEE, Beijing (2010)
8. Hu, Q., Tian, Q., Tang, Z.: RP-MAC: a passive MAC protocol with frame reordering for wireless sensor networks. Int. J. Wirel. Inf. Netw. **20**(1), 74–80 (2013)
9. Basagni, S., Petrioli, C., Spenza, D.: CTP-WUR: the collection tree protocol in wake-up radio WSNs for critical applications. In: The 2016 International Conference on Computing, Networking and Communications (ICNC 2016), pp. 1–6. IEEE, Hawaii (2016)
10. Wang, J., Cao, Z., Mao, X., et al.: Towards energy efficient duty-cycled networks: analysis, implications and improvement. IEEE Trans. Comput. **65**(1), 270–280 (2016)

Understanding Sensor Data Using Deep Learning Methods on Resource-Constrained Edge Devices

Junzhao Du[1], Sicong Liu[2], Yuheng Wei[2], Hui Liu[1](✉),
Xin Wang[2], and Kaiming Nan[2]

[1] School of Software and Institute of Software Engineering,
Xidian University, Xi'an, China
{dujz,liuhui}@xidian.edu.cn
[2] School of Computer Science and Technology, Xidian University, Xi'an, China
liusc@stu.xidian.edu.cn, yhwei1993@gmail.com, nextowang@gmail.com,
1017954423@qq.com

Abstract. With the development of the Internet of Things, more and more edge devices (such as smart-phones, tablets, wearable devices, embedded devices, gateway equipment and etc.) generate huge amounts of rich sensor data every day. With them, some deep learning based recognition applications provide users with various recognition services on edge devices. However, a fundamental problem these applications meet is how to perform deep learning algorithms effectively and promptly on a resource-constrained platform. Some researchers have proposed completing all computation tasks on the cloud side then returning the results back to edge devices, but such procedure is always time-consuming because of data transmission. In this case, training deep learning models on cloud side and executing the trained model directly on edge devices for inference is a better choice. Meanwhile, the deep learning based mobile applications also need to satisfy the requirements of low latency, low storage and low consumption. To fulfill above objectives, we aim to propose a new deep learning compression algorithm. We conduct comprehensive experiments to compare the proposed light-weight model with other standard state-of-the-art compression algorithms in terms of inference accuracy, process delay, CPU load, energy cost and storage coverage, based on an audio recognition system.

Keywords: Sensor data analysis · Edge computing · Deep learning
Compression method

1 Introduction

The rich sensors on edge devices (such as smart-phones, tablets, wearable devices, embedded devices, and gateway equipment) enable abundant mobile awareness applications [1].

© Springer Nature Singapore Pte Ltd. 2018
J. Li et al. (Eds.): CWSN 2017, CCIS 812, pp. 139–152, 2018.
https://doi.org/10.1007/978-981-10-8123-1_13

Deep learning technologies are popular to analyze sensor data currently, which extract generic representations from raw data to execute classification automatically with the non-linear mapping and outperform traditional data processing methods. In traditional computing mode, edge devices upload the sensor data to powerful servers for data processing, and wait for the responses from server side. However, the speed of data transportation has become the bottleneck for the cloud-based computing paradigm. Therefore, some researchers present to process sensor data directly on edge devices to avoid massive data transmission, reduce the response delay, and make full use of the computing and storage resources of terminals [2].

In this paper, in order to realize deep learning applications on terminals, we explore the novel computing mode which integrates the mobile computing, edge computing [2] and cloud computing mechanisms, training deep learning models accelerated by GPU in the cloud side, loading the trained model to execute offline inference on edge devices so that users could be provided with more intelligent applications. We survey the art-of-the-state compression algorithms for deep learning models to reduce the computational complexity and resource consumption. Furthermore, we implement a sound recognition prototype APP, which adopts different compression algorithms to deep learning models. Based on this APP, we improve the performance of the existing compression algorithms and strategies to the deep learning models. We also quantitatively analyze the performance of deep learning based mobile applications in terms of accuracy, delay, energy consumption, CPU load, and memory usage.

The remaining parts of this paper are organized as follows. We discuss the background and motivations in Sect. 2, introduce the resource constraints of running deep learning models on edge devices and give a survey about deep learning compression algorithms in Sect. 3. We next present the design of a new deep learning models in Sect. 4, and compare the performance of our proposed model with existing deep learning compression algorithms based on our prototype system in Sect. 5. Finally, this paper concludes in Sect. 6.

2   Background and Motivations

2.1   Background of Mobile Recognition Applications

Nowadays, there are rich embedded sensors on edge devices, including motion sensors, environmental sensors and position sensors, etc. Many mobile sensing applications have been developed in academia and industry with these plentiful embedded sensors, such as human activity recognition based on motion sensor data [3]; applications of vehicle recognition based on image and accelerometer [4]; warning hazard identification for pedestrian based on shoe embedded sensor [5]; license plate recognition based on the camera; Cheng et al. [6] exploit the intermittent strong GPS signals for localization; applications of abnormal event monitoring [7] and eye tracking [8] based on the camera data; environmental identification, speech recognition, and sound event recognition based on microphone.

Based on plentiful sensor data, the machine learning methods are used to perform special recognition tasks. The main steps are as follows: sensor data collection, data pre-processing, feature extraction, classification and results feedback etc. The traditional feature extraction is generally designed manually, including time domain features such as mean value, variance, correlation coefficient; frequency domain features such as fast Fourier transform coefficients, frequency domain entropy, and spectral density; etc. However, the features from domain level can not be directly used to characterize the complex and diverse sensor data. The selection and design of the simple classifier also requires the researcher to have a comprehensive understanding and processing skills for the sensor data, for a example, decision tree classifier requires researchers to be familiar with the difference of the sensor data to design the branch basis and threshold [9].

In short, the traditional feature extraction and classification methods often lead to bad features and a poor accuracy, and it is still a challenging problem to extract deep representations from noisy sensor data.

Table 1. Some deep learning based applications in mobile computing area

System	Application	Platform	Model	Functions and advantages of deep learning model
DeepEar [23]	Perception of human activity and context based on microphone	Smart phones	DNN	Improve the classification accuracy based on audio; reduce the impact of environmental noise on the classification.
DeepX [10]	Software accelerator for running deep learning model of mobile devices	Mobile devices	DNN, CNN	Extract high level feature from raw sensor data.
SparseSep [25]	Identifying human activities and context	Mobile, wearable, embedded sensor device	DNN,CNN	Extract the essential features of activity context from data with noise.
Lasagna [11]	Mobile data support applications such as motion recognition	None	convolution RBMs	Extract the multiple resolution and hierarchical human activity features, and extract the deep features of active data to provide semantic search

2.2 Challenges of Deep Learning Based Mobile Applications

Deep learning has a significant improvement in data analysis and recognition. Researchers in computing field have presented some greet deep learning based researches, the detail is shown in Table 1. Running deep learning model always requires powerful computation ability, high energy cost, and high storage usage.

AI researchers prefer to train complex neural networks based on large-scale datasets in order to get a higher accuracy when they use deep learning models to perform special recognition task.

The model of deep learning always contains huge amount of parameters which are learned through a training process. For examples, the 7-layers AlexNet [12] has 192M parameters, and the 22-layers VGG [13] has 1.1G parameters. Obviously, it is necessary to run deep learning based recognition models directly on the edge devices so that it can reduce the delay of data transmission between edge devices and cloud servers, guarantee the mobile applications could work whenever the network is connective or unconnected, and increase the resource utilization of the edge devices. Deep learning based mobile applications should also meet the following requirements: high recognition accuracy, prompt response, low cost of computation and storage, but we find that running deep learning based mobile applications directly on universal edge devices remains a hard problem.

3   Fitting Deep Learning into Edge Devices

To make the large-scale deep learning models fit into some resource constrained devices, the size of model(the number of parameters and network layers, etc.) should be reduced with low accuracy loss. The researches about deep learning model compression algorithms have made some progresses in the past two years in AI communities and mobile computing fields. Deep Neural Networks (DNN) and Convolution Neural Networks (CNNs) are commonly used in recognition applications. These models form a non-linear map from input to output through different neuron connections, weights and biases, which could extract deep features from raw sensor data. In this section, we summarize the existing deep learning compression algorithms for DNN and CNN, and also use some compression techniques to implement model compression on mobile devices.

3.1   Fully-Connected Layer Compression

We firstly study the computing details of two adjacent fully-connected layers, as shown in Fig. 1. It shows the relationship between weight matrix W_{n*m}^{L+1} and

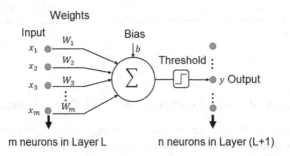

Fig. 1. Computations on fully-connected layers.

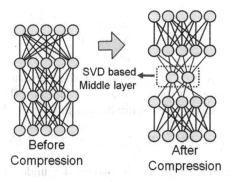

Fig. 2. SVD based compression methods.

bias vector b. There are m neurons in L Layer and n neurons in $(L + 1)$ Layer, so the weight between two fully-connected layers is a two-dimensional matrix of $(n * m)$. The mapping between the input x and the output y is $y = Wx + b$. All the neurons of the Layer L connecting to the same neuron in the layer $(L + 1)$ share the same bias, so the biases between two fully-connected layers form a vector which contains n elements.

SVD Based Compression Method. As shown in Fig. 2, the SVD [14] based fully-connected compression method actually introduces an intermediate layer L'. DeepX [10] uses SVD algorithm to compress the weight parameters of trained models. Specifically, there are m neurons in Layer L and n neurons in Layer $(L + 1)$. Decomposing the weight matrix W_{m*n}^{L+1} between two layers with SVD algorithm, we get $W_{m*n}^{L+1} = U_{m*n} \sum_{m*n} V_{n*n}^T$. As shown in Eq. (1):

$$W_{m*n}^{L+1} = U_{m*c} \sum_{c*c} V_{c*n}^T = U_{m*c} N_{c*n}^T = W_{m*c}^{L'} W_{c*n}^{L+1} \tag{1}$$

We could choose the largest c, but c is still much smaller than n so that the model size is reduced significantly. In implementation, the value of c can be set as a pre-decided value.

Sparse Coding Based Compression Method. According to Fig. 2, Sourav et al. [25] design a sparse code based layer compression method.

Like the SVD algorithm, the sparse coding algorithm decomposes the weight matrix W of the fully-connected layer into two matrix multiplying $W^L \approx B \cdot A$. The sparse matrix factorization problem can be formulated as a sparse dictionary learning problem, where a dictionary $B = \{\beta\}_{i=1}^k$ (with $\beta_i \in R^m$) is learned from the weights W^L of fully-connected layer.

Sparse coding approximates an input $w_i \in R^m$, e.g., a column of W^L, as a sparse linear combination of basis vectors β from the dictionary B, as shown in Eq. (2).

$$w_i = \sum_{j=1}^{k} a_j^i \cdot \beta_j \tag{2}$$

where, a_j^i is a sparse vector, i.e., a sparse matrix consists of multiple sparse vectors. In this paper we use the K-SVD algorithm, and the K-SVD algorithm learns a dictionary by solving the minimization problem in Eq. (3).

$$\min_{B,A} ||W^L - B \cdot A||_2^2 \quad s.t. \forall_i ||a^i||_0 \leq K \tag{3}$$

where A is the sparse code of the weight matrix W^L under the dictionary B and K is the sparsity constraint factor.

3.2   Convolution Layer Compression

In this section, we introduce the compression methods on the convolution layers to reduce the number of parameters of the convolution kernel. While traditional convolution operation is compute-intensive, sparse convolution can significantly reduce the required floating point operations because only the calculations corresponding to the non-zeros of sparse convolution kernel need to be performed.

Holistic SparseCNN. The goal of Holistic SparseCNN [29] is to obtain the trade-offs among the sparsity of model, accuracy and computation speed. The direct sparse convolution algorithm is proposed by the paper, which is introduced as following.

We define the bank of filters as a four-dimensional tensor W with size $M * N * U * V$, the input as a three-dimensional tensor I with size $N * H_{input} * W_{input}$, then we can get a three-dimensional tensor output as O with size $M * H_{output} * W_{output}$ after convolution. The output is computed by Eq. 4.

$$o(m, y, x) = \sum_{n=0}^{N-1} \sum_{u=0}^{U-1} \sum_{v=0}^{V-1} W(m, n, u, v) I(n, y + u, x + v) \tag{4}$$

After some transformation operations, values at (y, x)th position in output tensor cross all channels can be expressed as a Sparse Matrix Vector Multiplication (SpMV), as shown in Eq. (5).

$$o_{(1)}(:, yW_0 + x) = W_{(1)} \cdot (vec(I_{y,x})) \tag{5}$$

where $W_{(1)}$ is a sparse matrix and $I_{y,x}$ is the tensor I with its last two dimensions shifted by (y, x). To get all the values in the output tensor, the convolution operation could be computed as a sparse-matrix-dense-matrix multiplication, where the dense matrix is consisted of the vectors $vec(I)$ with different offsets.

The previous sparse convolution methods often lower tensors to a matrix, which impose extra computation overhead. The direct sparse convolution method directly executes a convolution on tensors without bandwidth-wasting lowering step through operating with a virtual dense matrix $I_{virtual}$.

Sparse Convolution Neural Networks. Equation (6) is a traditional convolution operation whose computation cost is closely relative to the size of input and convolution kernel. If the convolution kernel is sparse, the most of sparse convolution operation algorithms could be utilize to accelerate the calculation.

$$O(y,x,j) = \sum_{i=1}^{m}\sum_{u,v=1}^{s} K(u,v,i,j)I(y+u-1,x+v-1,i) \tag{6}$$

SCNN [15] algorithm uses a initial decomposition over the input channels and the convolution kernels to obtain limited sparsity with very low or no reconstruction error, then adopts a fine-tuning process to get maximum sparsity and minimum recognition loss caused by the former. To achieve SCNN algorithm, the follow steps will explain the whole process in principle with formula. Firstly we convert the tensor I to $J \in \mathbb{R}^{h*w*m}$, and the convolution kernel K is converted to $R \in \mathbb{R}^{s*s*m*n}$, using $P \in \mathbb{R}^{m*m}$ to get $O \approx R * J$, shown in Eq. (7).

$$\begin{aligned} K(u,v,i,j) &\approx \sum_{k=1}^{m} R(u,v,k,j)P(k,i) \\ J(y,x,i) &= \sum_{k=1}^{m} P(i,k)I(y,x,k) \end{aligned} \tag{7}$$

Then for each channel $i = 1, 2, ..., m$, the matrix $R(\cdot,\cdot,i,\cdot)$ is decomposed to generate a matrix $S_i \in \mathbb{R}^{q_i*n}$, and a tensor $Q \in \mathbb{R}^{s*s*q_i}$, where q_i is the number of bases, shown in Eq. (8).

$$\begin{aligned} R(u,v,i,j) &\approx \sum_{k=1}^{q_i} S_i(k,j)Q_i(u,v,k) \\ T_i(y,x,k) &= \sum_{u,v=1}^{S} Q_i(u,v,k)J(y+u-1,x+v-1,i) \end{aligned} \tag{8}$$

After aforementioned conversion operations, the output O could be calculated by Eq. (9),

$$O(y,x,j) \approx \sum_{i=1}^{m}\sum_{k=1}^{q_i} S_i(k,j)T_i(y,x,k) \tag{9}$$

it is noted that q_i is less than s_2, the matrix S_i is a sparse matrix with a large number of 0 elements.

After initial decomposition, a fine-tuning phase is imposed to train the whole network with sparsity constraints to maximize the sparsity of convolution kernel. These sparsity constrains are shown in Eq. (10), where $\|\cdot\|_1$ and $\|\cdot\|_2$ represent the element-wise l_1 and l_2 norms of a matrix.

$$\alpha_1 \sum_{i=1}^{m} \|S_i\|_1 + \alpha_2 \sum_{i=1}^{m}\sum_{j=1}^{q_i} \|S_i(j,\cdot)\|_2 \tag{10}$$

4   Design of a Thinner Deep Learning Model

Inspired by the benchmark of above compression algorithms, we design a new compressed deep learning model named ComNet, which are suitable for the deep learning based mobile recognition applications.

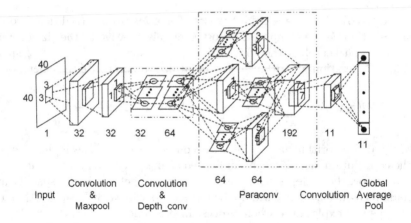

Fig. 3. The architecture of our proposed DL model.

The main components of DNN/CNN are input layer, several hidden layers and output layer, each containing multiple neurons, which can be defined mathematically as a non-linearity mapping function between raw sensor data and the classification categories. Specially, the earliest several hidden layers (fully-connected layers or convolution layers) are known as the extractor to learn the deep representations of diverse raw data, and the last hidden layer (fully-connected layer) is considered the classifier to inference the recognition category. In this paper, we prefer to use convolution layers as the feature extractor because they have the equivalent ability of learning deep represents and lead to less weight parameters. But there are several common choices of convolution kernel size, such as 1×1, 3×3 and 5×5, for us to select. When we chose the kernel size and depth, we do not have some criterion but have the following objectives: the whole model should be accurate, prompt, energy-efficient, and cabinet.

We have some insights towards to the compression of deep learning models, and design a thinner deep learning model with competitive or better accuracy, shown in Fig. 3. To preserve the perception to the details of the raw sensor data, we use the basic operations in $conv1$ and $pool1$, i.e., a 3×3 convolution operation followed by max pooling with a 2×2 pooling window in the first two hidden layers. Instead of the conventional convolution operation, we employ a depth-wise convolution followed by 1×1 convolution in $conv2$ and $conv3$. The channels of a filter in depth-wise convolution are applied separately to each channel of input. That is to say, the multilayer convolution adds more non-linearity to the representation learned by previous layers and also reduces the number of parameters.

We also design the parallel convolution layer, namely ParaConv, which is the combination of a 1×1 convolution layer followed by a 3×3 convolution layer, a max pooling layer followed by a 1×1 convolution layer and a 1×1 convolution layer followed by a 5×5 convolution. The 1×1 kernel leads to less parameters, 3×3 and 5×5 kernels preserve the accuracy. In this way, we can improve the depth of the total model with a small number of parameters. On the other hand, the ParaConv layer can capture multiple resolution of the representations with different kinds of layers and kernels. Overall, in order to greatly reduce the number of parameters involved in a complex neural network, we use a combination of 1×1, 3×3 and 5×5 convolutions. What's more, in the final hidden layer before output layer, we adopt a global average pooling layer instead of traditional fully connected layer in CNN to minimize over-fitting, which is ideal for mapping the low-dimension features to the category.

5 Evaluation

We implement a sound recognition system prototype on Android platform. The system can use above compressed deep learning model to provide a acoustic event notification application, where the acoustic events include knocking door, doorbell ring, fire alarm, smoke alarm, police alert. Firstly, we utilize the prototype to evaluate the performance of above compression algorithms. Then, our proposed compressed deep learning model is also verified by the prototype.

5.1 Prototype System Implementation

The deep learning model in the prototype system is trained on cloud side with GPU acceleration. The edge devices mainly perform sensor data collection, data pre-processing, and loading the trained deep learning model for off-line inference. At present, with the development of deep learning, there are a variety of open source learning frameworks, including TensorFlow [16], Caffe [17], Keras [18], CNTK [19], Torch [20], MXNet [21], Theano [22], Lasagne [11], and Neon. Our prototype system adopts Tensorflow to train the deep learning models. And we also use Tensorflow framework to run the trained deep learning model for inference on Android platform. We collect a large number of audio clips corresponding to aforementioned acoustic events. The majority of these audio clips act as training data, while the remainders act as test data. During the model training process, we adopt the adaptive moment estimation optimization method to learn parameters of model, while initially set the learning rate as $1e-4$. To obtain the sparsity in the convolution kernels, we set parameters which are smaller than threshold 0.0001 as zero in the kernels.

5.2 Load Deep Learning Model from Cache

Since the mobile applications will frequently load the deep learning models for sound recognition task, we explore to load the compressed deep learning model from the cache, which can avoid initializing the model repeatedly and reduce the response delay.

LruCache is a cache tool supported by Android API, which uses the Least Recently Used (LRU) algorithm. It stores the most recently used object in a

Table 2. Memory usage of recent deep models using compression methods for mobile devices

System	Model	Compression method	Layer details	Parameters
DeepEar [23]	DNN	None	5 layers: input, fully-conn*3, output	2,700,299(10.8M)
Deep compression [24]	DNN	pruning	5 layers: input, fully-conn*3, output	300,034(1.2M)
DeepX [10]	DNN	SVD	5 layers: input, fully-conn*3, output	1,955,391(7.8M)
SparseSep [25]	DNN	sparse coding	5 layers: input, fully-conn*3, output	1,033,680(4.1M)
MobiEar [26]	CNN	None	7 layers: input, conv*2, maxpool*2, fully-con, output	430,955(1.6M)
SparseSep [25]	CNN	sparse coding, convolution separation	7 layers: input, conv*2, maxpool*2, fully-con, output	264,972(0.98M)
SCNN [27]	CNN	convolution separation	10 layers: input, conv*5, fully-conn*2, dropout, output	2,543,097(10.2M)
DeepPed [28]	CNN	convolution pruning	10 layers: input, conv*5, fully-conn*2, dropout, output	635,775(2.6M)

"strong reference" in the LinkedHashMap and removes the least recently used object from memory before the cache value reaches the preset value.

In our implementation, the deep learning model is stored in the cache once the APP is loaded. When users start service for classification and content display process repeatedly, the system can directly call the LruCache.get (K, V) method to obtain the cached model. The implementation of the caching strategy is very suitable for reducing the resource consumption of the initialization of the model.

5.3   System Performance

To evaluate the feasibility of running deep learning models directly on edge devices, this section conducts the following experiments. We verify the accuracy, CPU load and inference time of compressed learning models on mobile platform, including our proposed model. Because the resources are limited on mobile platform, we randomly select a small part of test samples to evaluate the performance of a compressed model then get the average performance, instead of using all test data at once.

Table 3 shows the inference accuracy of different compressed deep learning models. Compared with the original model, the accuracy loss of compressed model is very small. And our model, ComNet, achieves satisfactory accuracy 95.6% on acoustic event classification task.

We test the response delay (including the time of loading models and executing inference) of running compressed deep learning models, as shown in Fig. 4. There are two parameters in the figure: model initialization time and model prediction time which represent the rate at which the model reacts instantaneously

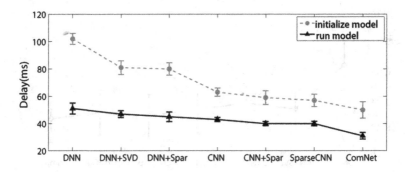

Fig. 4. Response delay.

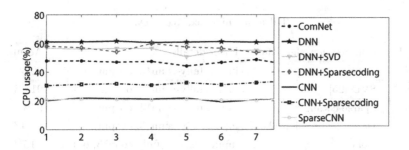

Fig. 5. CPU load on smart-phones.

on the mobile devices. Generally, the response delay is acceptable within 50 ms. Because the compression algorithms reduce the parameter size and simplify computation, the inference time in the model category is significantly reduced, which is reflected in the immediacy.

We also compare the CPU usage on mobile devices among different compressed models through Android Studio CPU monitor. The CPU load is shown in Fig. 5 when running the prototype system on smartphones. Different compression algorithms are different in the CPU load when running deep learning models. Generally, the computational complexity of the fully-connected layer is larger than that of the convolution layer. Therefore, the compression of the fully-connected layer will greatly affect the CPU usage.

The comparison of memory usage of some compression algorithms is shown in Table 2. We can see that each compression algorithm can reduce storage compared with the original model parameters. It's worth mentioning that ComNet only has $1.0M$ parameters, which is much less than others.

There are many platforms for energy consumption testing, such as weTest of Tencent, MTC of Baidu and MQC of Alibaba. We test the mobile phone energy consumption on MTC supported by Baidu. Figure 6 is our comparison of several compression algorithms in the mobile phone energy consumption. We can see that the energy saving when using compression algorithms is obvious.

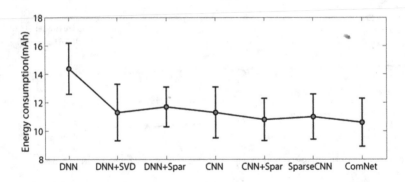

Fig. 6. Energy consumption.

Table 3. Inference Accuracy.

Model	Compression algorithm	Layer details	Accuracy
DNN	None	input, fully-conn*3, output	82.5%
DNN	SVD [25]	input, fully-conn*4, output	91.5%
DNN	Sparse coding [25]	input, fully-conn*4, output	93%
DNN	Deep compression [24]	input, fully-conn*3, output	80.3%
CNN	None	input, conv*5, fully-conn*3, output	84.7%
CNN	Sparse coding, convolution separation [25]	input, fully-conn*3, output	79.6%
CNN	Convolution separation [29]	input, fully-conn*3, output	81.7%
CNN	EIE [30]	input, conv*5, fully-conn*3, output	79.8%
DNN	SVD [10]	input, fully-conn*3, output	81.3%
ComNet	None	Fig. 3	95.6%

The above experiments have proved that it is practical to implement the deep learning technologies on the resource-constrained mobile platform through utilizing the compression methods. And our proposed novel compressed deep learning model improve the performance of previous compression algorithms, which is suitable to run on the mobile platform.

6   Conclusion

In this paper, we present the advantages and challenges when directly using deep learning to realize mobile recognition applications on the local side of resource-constrained edge devices. And then we make a survey about the-state-of-the-art compression algorithms to explore fitting deep learning models into edge devices.

We have implemented a sound recognition prototype system to execute the real-word performance of different compression models in terms of the recognition accuracy, response delay, CPU load and memory usage and energy consumption. On these foundations, we propose a new compressed deep learning model. According to the results of experiments, we could see our model present satisfactory performance in comprehensive acoustic event classification task.

Acknowledgements. This work is partially supported by the National Natural Science Foundation of China (NSFC) under Grant No.61472312 and No.61502374, the Fundamental Research Funds for the Central Universities under Grants JBZ171002, and the CETC shining Star Innovation.

References

1. Hofer, T., Schwinger, W., Pichler, M., Leonhartsberger, G., Altmann, J., Retschitzegger, W.: Context-awareness on mobile devices-the hydrogen approach. In: Proceedings of the 36th Annual Hawaii International Conference on System Sciences, 10-pp. (2003)
2. Shi, W., Cao, J., Zhang, Q., Li, Y., Xu, L.: Edge computing: vision and challenges. IEEE Internet Things J. **3**, 637–646 (2016)
3. Su, X., Tong, H., Ji, P.: Activity recognition with smartphone sensors. Tsinghua Sci. Technol. **19**, 235–249 (2014)
4. Wang, T., Cardone, G., Corradi, A., Torresani, L., Campbell, A.T.: WalkSafe: a pedestrian safety app for mobile phone users who walk and talk while crossing roads. In: Proceedings of the Twelfth Workshop on Mobile Computing Systems & Applications, p. 5 (2012)
5. LiKamWa, R., Zhong, L.: Starfish: efficient concurrency support for computer vision applications. In: Proceedings of 13th Annual International Conference on Mobile Systems, Applications, and Services, pp. 213–226 (2015)
6. Bo, C., Li, X.-Y., Jung, T., Mao, X., Tao, Y., Yao, L.: Smartloc: push the limit of the inertial sensor based metropolitan localization using smartphone. In: Proceedings of 19th Annual International Conference on Mobile Computing and Networking, pp. 195–198 (2013)
7. Gupta, P., Dallas, T.: Feature selection and activity recognition system using a single triaxial accelerometer. IEEE Trans. Biomed. Eng. **61**, 1780–1786 (2014)
8. Duchowski, A.: Eye Tracking Methodology: Theory and Practice. Springer Science & Business Media, London (2007)
9. Swain, P.H., Hauska, H.: The decision tree classifier: design and potential. IEEE Trans. Geosci. Electron. **15**, 142–147 (1977)
10. Lane, N.D., Bhattacharya, S., Georgiev, P., Forlivesi, C., Jiao, L., Qendro, L., Kawsar, F.: Deepx: a software accelerator for low-power deep learning inference on mobile devices. In: 2016 15th ACM/IEEE International Conference on Information Processing in Sensor Networks (IPSN), pp. 1–12 (2016)
11. Liu, C., Zhang, L., Liu, Z., Liu, K., Li, X., Liu, Y.: Lasagna: towards deep hierarchical understanding and searching over mobile sensing data. In: Proceedings of 22nd Annual International Conference on Mobile Computing and Networking, pp. 334–347 (2016)
12. Wikipedia. AlexNet – Wikipedia, The Free Encyclopedia (2017)
13. Wikipedia. VGG Image Annotator – Wikipedia, The Free Encyclopedia (2017)

14. Xue, J., Li, J., Gong, Y.: Restructuring of deep neural network acoustic models with singular value decomposition. In: Interspeech, pp. 2365–2369 (2013)

15. Liu, B., Wang, M., Foroosh, H., Tappen, M., Pensky, M.: Sparse convolutional neural networks. In: Proceedings of IEEE Conference on Computer Vision and Pattern Recognition, pp. 806–814 (2015)

16. Abadi, M., Agarwal, A., Barham, P., Brevdo, E., Chen, Z., Citro, C., Corrado, G.S., Davis, A., Dean, J., Devin, M., et al.: Tensorflow: large-scale machine learning on heterogeneous distributed systems. arXiv Prepr. arXiv:1603.04467 (2016)

17. Jia, Y., Shelhamer, E., Donahue, J., Karayev, S., Long, J., Girshick, R., Guadar-rama, S., Darrell, T.: Caffe: convolutional architecture for fast feature embedding. In: Proceedings of the 22nd ACM international conference on Multimedia, pp. 675–678 (2014)

18. Keras: Deep Learning library for Theano and TensorFlow (2016)

19. Dally, W.J.: CNTK: an embedded language for circuit description, Department of Computer Science, California Institute of Technology, Display File

20. Wikipedia. Torch (machine learning) – Wikipedia, The Free Encyclopedia (2017)

21. Chen, T., Li, M., Li, Y., Lin, M., Wang, N., Wang, M., Xiao, T., Xu, B., Zhang, C., Zhang, Z.: Mxnet: a flexible and efficient machine learning library for heterogeneous distributed systems. arXiv Prepr. arXiv:1512.01274 (2015)

22. Wikipedia. Theano – Wikipedia, The Free Encyclopedia (2016)

23. Lane, N.D., Georgiev, P., Qendro, L.: DeepEar: robust smartphone audio sensing in unconstrained acoustic environments using deep learning. In: Proceedings of the 2015 ACM International Joint Conference on Pervasive and Ubiquitous Comput-ing, pp. 283–294 (2015)

24. Han, S., Mao, H., Dally, W.J.: Deep compression: compressing deep neural net-works with pruning, trained quantization and huffman coding. arXiv Prepr. arXiv:1510.00149 (2015)

25. Lane, N., Bhattacharya, S.: Sparsifying deep learning layers for constrained resource inference on wearables. In: Proceedings of the 14th ACM Conference on Embedded Network Sensor Systems, pp. 176–189 (2016)

26. Liu, S., Du, J.: Poster: MobiEar-building an environment-independent acoustic sensing platform for the deaf using deep learning. In: Proceedings of the 14th Annual International Conference on Mobile Systems, Applications, and Services Companion, p. 50 (2016)

27. Kunz, R., Tetzlaff, R., Wolf, D.: SCNN: a universal simulator for cellular neu-ral networks. In: 1996 Fourth IEEE International Workshop on Cellular Neural Networks and their Applications, CNNA 1996. Proceedings, pp. 255–259 (1996)

28. Tomé, D., Bondi, L., Baroffio, L., Tubaro, S., Plebani, E., Pau, D.: Reduced mem-ory region based deep Convolutional Neural Network detection. In: 2016 IEEE 6th International Conference on Consumer Electronics (ICCE), Berlin, pp. 15–19 (2016)

29. Park, J., Li, S., Wen, W., Li, H., Chen, Y., Dubey, P.: Holistic SparseCNN: forging the trident of accuracy, speed, and size. arXiv Prepr. arXiv:1608.01409 (2016)

30. Han, S., Liu, X., Mao, H., Pu, J., Pedram, A., Horowitz, M.A., Dally, W.J.: EIE: efficient inference engine on compressed deep neural network. In: Proceedings of the 43rd International Symposium on Computer Architecture (2016)

Data Fusion

The Improved Genetic Algorithms for Multiple Maximum Scatter Traveling Salesperson Problems

Wenyong Dong, Xueshi Dong$^{(\boxtimes)}$, and Yufeng Wang

Computer School, Wuhan University, Wuhan, China
dxs_cs@163.com

Abstract. Maximum scatter traveling salesperson problem (MSTSP), as a variant of traveling salesman problem (TSP), has been successfully applied to the practical cases in manufacturing and medical imaging. However, it cannot model the application problems where there are multiple objectives or individuals. This paper proposes a new model named multiple maximum scatter traveling salesperson problems (MMSTSP) for modeling such problems. The paper applies three improved genetic algorithms (GAs) to solve MMSTSP, where three methods are used to improve GA, the first one is greedy initialization for optimization, the second one is climbing-hill algorithm, and the last one is simulated annealing algorithm. Furthermore, many real-world problems can be modeled by MMSTSP, and the scale of constructed model is usually up to large scale, it is necessary to study large scale MMSTSP problem. Therefore, the paper uses the improved GAs to solve the small scale to large scale MMSTSP. By extensive experiments and analysis, it shows that the improved algorithms are effective, and can demonstrate different characteristics in solving the problem.

Keywords: Improved genetic algorithms
Maximum scatter traveling salesperson problem · Greedy algorithm
Hill-climbing · Simulated annealing

1 Introduction

Maximum scatter traveling salesperson problem (MSTSP) is closely related to the bottleneck traveling salesman problem (BTSP) [7–10], which is motivated by the application in manufacturing and medical imaging. However, MSTSP cannot deal with the application where multiple traveling individuals not only have their own exclusive tasks but also share a same starting and ending point. In order to solve this problem, the paper provides a new problem called multiple maximum scatter traveling salesperson problems (MMSTSP), which can cope with the application. Relevant research has proved that genetic algorithm and its variants can demonstrate good performance to solve combination optimization problem, therefore, the paper applies the improved genetic algorithms to solve the problem. The paper utilizes small scale to large scale data to make experiments, the results show that the four genetic algorithms are effective and display distinct characteristics to solve this problem.

© Springer Nature Singapore Pte Ltd. 2018
J. Li et al. (Eds.): CWSN 2017, CCIS 812, pp. 155–164, 2018.
https://doi.org/10.1007/978-981-10-8123-1_14

There are few literatures about MSTSP, and the relevant papers are as follows: Arkin et al. [1] provided the algorithmic study for the problem. It was shown that the maximum scatter TSP is NP-complete problem. MSTSP was proposed in some medical imaging application [1, 2]. Yi-Jen Chiang gave a new approximation results for the MSTSP [3]. The literature [4] also studied many works of MSTSP and its relevant models. However, the mentioned applications of MSTSP can't solve the problem where there are multiple salesmen, individuals or objectives for optimization at the same time. The proposed model MMSTSP can solve this kind of problem.

MSTSP can be also used to model other problems. For one example of MSTSP, there is a falsely accused of a crime who did not commit and facing the death penalty, he escapes from the police and starts a journey across country to avoid capture. He is looking for a tour through his routes network of safe places so that the smallest distance between consecutive locations is as big as possible [4]. The model of this problem is considered to be MSTSP. However, if there are multiple crimes in this example, the problem cannot be modeled by MSTSP. For this case, MMSTSP can model the problem where there are multiple falsely accused of crimes.

The paper gives a novel model called MMSTSP, which can model the problems with multiple individuals and their own exclusive tasks. For extending the application of the problem, this paper applies the improved genetic algorithms to solve the problem, three algorithms are utilized to improve genetic algorithm, the first one is using greedy initialization, the second one is climbing-hill algorithm for optimization, and the last one is based on simulated-annealing. In order to study different scale MMSTSP problem by the algorithms, the paper makes experiment not only using small scale data, but also utilizing large scale. The extensive experiments show that the given algorithms are effective for solving the problem.

The rest of the paper is as follows: the second section gives the definition of MMSTSP and relevant introduction of the model; the third section introduces the three improved genetic algorithms for MMSTSP; the experiments and analysis are in the fourth session; the last one is conclusion and future works.

2   Multiple Maximum Scatter Traveling Salesperson Problems

2.1   The Definition of MMSTSP

The definition of maximum scatter traveling salesperson problem [1–4] is given: there is an edge-weighted complete graph $G = (V, E)$, a cost c_{ij} is the each edge $(i, j) \in E$, Π (G) stands for the collection of Hamiltonian cycle in G. The goal of the problem is to find a Hamiltonian cycle so that the shortest edge is as maximized as possible. By using more detailed words, the objective is to make each point most scattered or far away from the visited points just before or just after in the cycle. The single MSTSP is defined as follows:

Maximize min $\{c_{ij}: (i, j) \in H\}$, subject to $H \in \Pi$ (G)

The MMSTSP problem contains multiple single maximum scatter traveling salesperson problems, which have a same starting and ending point, and it can be used to model the problems where there are multiple salespersons or individuals and their corresponding tasks for optimization at the same time.

When the shared data only includes the depot where the salesmen starts and ends, colored traveling salesman problem can turn into multiple single TSPs with the same depot [5]. For the multiple single TSP problems, we change the goal of the each TSP according to the objective function of MSTSP, thus the multiple single TSP problems can be transformed into multiple single MSTSP problems.

2.2   MMSTSP and Other TSP Variants

Colored traveling salesman problem (CTSP) [5, 6], multiple traveling salesman problems (MTSP), MSTSP are the variants of TSP, there are some differences and similarities of MMSTSP and the TSP variants. For MMSTSP and CTSP, they all have multiple salesmen and multiple tasks, the exclusive cities are visited only by the appointed salesman, but CTSP not only has exclusive cities, but also occupies shared cities, in some condition, CTSP can be transformed into MMSTSP. For MMSTSP and MTSP, they both have multiple salesmen, the cities of MTSP can be accessed by all the salesmen, however, the exclusive cities of MMSTSP are only visited by appoint salesman. For MSTSP and MMSTSP, there is only one salesperson for MSTSP, thus it just models the problem with single objective, but MMSTSP have multiple salesmen and tasks, which can model the problems where there are multiple individuals.

2.3   MMSTSP Theory

Theorem 1: MMSTSP is NP-hard problem

Proof: by its definition, MMSTSP can be modified from CTSP. While the shared cities of CTSP only include a depot which is the starting and ending point, CTSP can be transformed into multiple single TSP problems [5]. We change the objective of the multiple TSP according to the objective of MSTSP, thus CTSP is transformed into MMSTSP. CTSP and TSP has been proved to be NP-hard problem [5]. With the recovery of operations, the time complexity of the problem is not changed, thus MMSTSP is NP-hard problem. On the other hand, MSTSP is proved to be NP-hard problem, MMSTSP is multiple single MSTSP problems which have a same starting and ending point, therefore, MMSTSP is also NP-hard problem.

3   Improved Genetic Algorithms for MMSTSP

3.1   Solution Representation

The paper also utilizes the dual-chromosome coding [5] to represent the solution of MMSTSP. A coding example of MMSTSP with $n = 9$ and $m = 3$ is given in the Fig. 1. Genes 1, 2 and 3 of the city chromosome are the exclusive cities for salesperson 1, genes 4, 5 and 6 are for salesperson 2, and genes 7, 8 and 9 are for salesperson 3. The order cities 2, 3 and 1 are accessed by salesperson 1; cities 6, 5 and 4 are visited by salesman 2; cities 7, 9, and 8 are accessed by salesperson 3.

City chromosome:

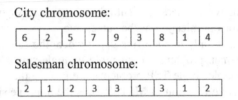

Salesman chromosome:

Fig. 1. Example of dual-chromosome coding for MMSTSP

3.2 Improved Genetic Algorithms

The improved genetic algorithms are genetic algorithm with greedy initialization (GAG), hill climbing genetic algorithm (HCGA) and simulated annealing genetic algorithm (SAGA) [5, 11].

Because greedy algorithm doesn't search all space, it can obtain a good solution in a short time. In the first step of genetic algorithm (GA), greedy algorithm can be used to optimize the individuals of initial population, and the high quality initial population can improve GA to obtain a good solution, the improved algorithm is named as GA with greedy initialization [5].

Because of the characteristic of GAG, the convergence performance of the algorithm is unsatisfactory. To improve the GA search ability, a hill climbing (HC) algorithm is given to optimize GA. Due to its strong ability of local search, and HC can improve the search ability of algorithm.

HC algorithm uses a neighboring search for optimization, and the main idea of the algorithm is as follows: beginning from an initial solution, it generates a new solution by HC. If the new solution is better than the former one, replace it by the latter, otherwise, return back to the beginning and set as the worst, repeat the optimization process until it reaches the highest point [5].

The steps of HC algorithm are as follows:

Step 1: when it performs the swapping, judge whether the i_{th} salesman is equal to the m_{th} salesman, i.e., $i = m$. If it is so, withdraw from this step.

Step 2: two city genes are selected for assigning to i_{th} salesman. Staring from city chromosome a, the individual a_1 is exchanged and obtained.

Step 3: if the fitness value of a_1 is better than the one of a, perform the operation $a = a_1$; otherwise, keep a.

Step 4: carry out the operation $i = i + 1$, and return to step 1.

Simulated annealing (SA) is a probabilistic heuristic algorithm for global optimization problem which can locate a good approximation to global optimum solution. During the process of the search, SA can obtain the good and bad solution based on the Metropolis criterion. It can drop out the local search regions and ensure the good convergence of algorithm, and therefore it is suitable to optimize the GAG. The detailed steps of SA can refer to the literature [5].

Figure 2 is steps of HCGA or SAGA, the first step is to encode and generate initial population, the second step calculates the fitness value, the next step selects the best individual a, the fourth step is optimization operators by hill climbing or simulated annealing. The next step is judgment whether the latter fitness is better than former one,

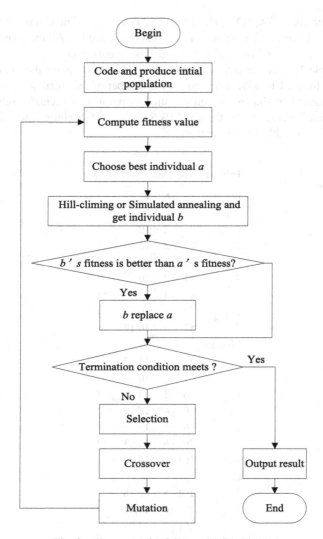

Fig. 2. The steps of HCGA or SAGA [5, 11]

if it meets, *b* replaces *a*, the next step is to judge the stopping condition, if it meets, output results, otherwise perform selection, crossover and mutation operators.

4   Experiments and Analysis

We make some experiments analyze the performance of the algorithms in solving MMSTSP. The experiment computer is based on 3.01 GHz processor and 3.25 GB RAM, and the experiments are developed by Java.

The parameters of GA, GAG, HCGA and SAGA: population 30, crossover rate 0.7, mutation rate 0.1, the detail is shown in the CTSP literature [5]. All the algorithms have same stopping condition. The Table 1 is the experiments data [11].

In the Table 1, there are three different scale data, n stands for the number of city which ranges from 21 to 665, m represents the number of salesmen, it is from 2 to 33, s is the city number of shared set, and e is the city number of exclusive sets [11]. The experiment data is generated by the TSPLIB Symmetric Travelling Salesman Problem Instances which is published in the web.

Table 1. The experiments data

Instance	n	m	e	s
Small				
1	21	2	10	1
2	31	2	15	1
3	31	3	10	1
4	41	2	20	1
5	41	3	13,14	1
6	41	4	10	1
7	51	3	16,17	1
Medium				
8	51	4	12,13	1
9	51	5	10	1
10	76	3	25	1
11	76	4	18,19	1
12	76	5	15	1
13	76	6	12,13	1
14	101	4	25	1
Large				
15	101	5	20,18,21	1
16	101	6	16,17	1
17	101	7	14,15	1
18	206	9	22,23	1
19	431	12	35,36	1
20	547	14	39	1
21	612	23	26,27	1
22	665	33	20,21	1

In the Fig. 3, the top-left figure is GA for MMSTSP, the top-right one is GAG for the problem, the lower-left one is HCGA, and the lower-right one is SAGA. The more information of the four algorithms for the problem with $n = 51$ and $m = 5$ is as follows: GA: the mean solution quality is 19.15, the average solving time is 1.00; GAG: the average solution quality is 18.81, the solving time is 1.00; HCGA: the mean solution quality is 21.10, the mean solving time is 1.91; SAGA: the average solution quality is 17.93, the time is 24.42.

The running interfaces of the four genetic algorithms for MMSTSP with $n = 51$ and $m = 5$ are in the following Fig. 3.

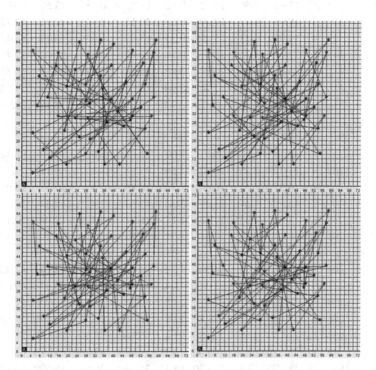

Fig. 3. The interfaces of GA, GAG, HCGA and SAGA for MMSTSP with $n = 51$ and $m = 5$

The following table is experiment results comparison of GA, GAG, HCGA and SAGA for MMSTSP by the three different scale data.

In the Table 2, they are the GA, GAG, HCGA and SAGA for MMSTSP, n is the number of city, m stands for the number of salesperson, the mean represents the average solution quality of the algorithms for running ten times, the time is the average solving time of algorithms for running ten times. The following figures are the mean solution quality of the four algorithms for the problem.

In Figs. 4 and 5, the lateral axis is the number of the instance, for example, the number 1 responds to $n = 21$ and $m = 2$, number 8 responds to $n = 51$ and $m = 4$. Vertical axis represents the average solution quality of the algorithms for the problem.

From Table 2, we can see that GA and GAG have the better solving time, which uses less time than HCGA and SAGA, and SAGA uses the longest solving time in the four algorithms. For solution quality of the four algorithms, HCGA gets the biggest value on mean solution quality, and other three algorithms can obtain the similar solving quality, which can be seen from Figs. 4 and 5.

Table 2. Experiment results comparison of GA, GAG, HCGA and SAGA (Unit km and s)

Instance	n	m	GA		GAG		HCGA		SAGA	
			Mean	Time	Mean	Time	Mean	Time	Mean	Time
Small										
1	21	2	12.91	0.50	12.82	0.52	13.27	0.65	13.60	9.16
2	31	2	18.95	0.67	19.09	0.67	20.15	0.94	19.98	12.47
3	31	3	14.96	0.73	15.59	0.73	15.52	1.00	16.12	13.45
4	41	2	22.01	0.76	22.51	0.76	25.10	1.35	21.04	17.45
5	41	3	20.56	0.90	20.59	0.89	21.30	1.43	20.63	18.53
6	41	4	17.99	0.88	17.26	0.90	18.66	1.47	17.39	19.62
7	51	3	20.72	0.92	20.28	0.93	23.05	1.78	19.96	21.99
Medium										
8	51	4	20.50	0.94	19.77	0.92	21.20	1.86	18.49	23.23
9	51	5	19.15	1.00	18.81	1.00	21.10	1.91	17.93	24.42
10	76	3	17.22	1.25	16.92	1.30	27.03	3.20	16.11	34.56
11	76	4	16.35	1.35	16.05	1.32	25.86	3.32	15.17	35.92
12	76	5	13.60	1.34	13.65	1.35	18.31	3.41	12.37	37.41
13	76	6	14.80	1.34	14.93	1.39	16.71	3.52	12.94	39.11
14	101	4	10.13	1.76	10.04	1.78	14.18	4.87	9.12	45.49
Large										
15	101	5	14.76	1.75	14.38	1.75	24.69	5.03	13.74	47.42
16	101	6	11.66	1.72	11.34	1.74	17.58	5.14	10.93	49.02
17	101	7	8.62	2.01	8.54	1.96	9.82	5.33	7.97	51.52
18	206	9	577.60	4.03	568.80	3.98	1089.50	19.02	686.70	117.07
19	431	12	220.50	9.98	230.60	9.84	665.40	78.90	241.40	270.23
20	547	14	227.30	12.98	240.00	13.21	593.80	134.92	252.70	385.96
21	612	23	181.70	17.47	193.70	18.11	353.90	202.49	188.00	539.47
22	665	33	166.60	21.74	159.00	22.89	388.50	282.90	164.00	698.64

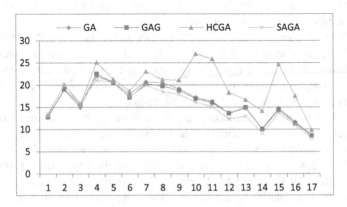

Fig. 4. The average solution quality of the four algorithms for MMSTSP

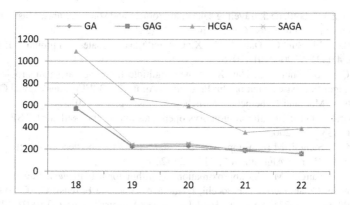

Fig. 5. The average solution quality of the four algorithms for MMSTSP

From the above data and analysis, we can see that the four algorithms are effective in solving the problem. The solving time of SAGA is the longest one. GA and GAG can have similar mean solution quality and solving time, which may be the eclectic selection for solving the problem in the four algorithms. HCGA demonstrates the biggest solution value, and its solving time is longer than GA and GAG.

5 Conclusion and Future Works

In order to solve the problem with multiple salespersons or individuals and their tasks, the paper proposes a novel model MMSTSP, which can model it. For extending the application of the problem, studying advanced algorithms is a significant work, the paper uses the three improved GAs to solve the problem. The extensive experiments shows that the algorithms are effective and can show distinct characteristics.

The future works are as follows: studying more advanced algorithms with better performance to solve the problem would be a future work; although the paper studies the problem by the three different scales, the scale of the problem is still small, and the next work could focus on the larger scale problem.

Acknowledgement. This work is supported by the National Natural Science Foundation of China under Grant No. 61672024, No. 61170305.

References

1. Arkin, E.M., Chiang, Y.J., Mitchell, J.S.B., et al.: On the maximum scatter traveling salesperson problem. SIAM J. Comput. **29**(2), 515–544 (1999)
2. Gutin, G., Punnen, A.P.: The Traveling Salesman Problem and Its Variations, pp. 585–607. Kluwer Academic Publishers, Boston, Dordrecht, London (2002)
3. Chiang, Y.J.: New approximation results for the maximum scatter TSP. Algorithmica **41**, 309–341 (2005)

4. John, L.R.: The bottleneck traveling salesman problem and some variants. Master of Science of Simon Fraser University, Canada, pp. 21–23 (2010)
5. Li, J., Zhou, M., Sun, Q., Dai, X., Yu, X.: Colored traveling salesman problem. IEEE Trans. Cybern. **45**(11), 2390–2401 (2015)
6. Li, J., Qiru, S., Zhou, M., Dai, X.: A new multiple traveling salesman problem and its genetic algorithm-based solution. In: Proceedings of the 2013 IEEE International Conference on Systems Man and Cybernetics, Manchester, U.K, pp. 1–6 (2013)
7. Vairaktarakis, G.L.: On gilmore-gomorys open question for the bottleneck TSP. Oper. Res. Lett. **31**, 483–491 (2003)
8. Kao, M.Y., Sanghi, M.: An approximation algorithm for a bottleneck traveling salesman problem. J. Discrete Algorithms **7**, 315–326 (2009)
9. Kao, M.Y., Sanghi, M.: An approximation algorithm for a bottleneck traveling salesman problem. In: Calamoneri, T., Finocchi, I., Italiano, Giuseppe F. (eds.) CIAC 2006. LNCS, vol. 3998, pp. 223–235. Springer, Heidelberg (2006). https://doi.org/10.1007/11758471_23
10. Ahmed, Z.H.: A hybrid genetic algorithm for the bottleneck traveling salesman problem. ACM Trans. Embed. Comput. Syst. **12**(1), 9:1–9:10 (2013)
11. Dong, X.S., Dong, W.Y., Wang, Y.F.: Hybrid algorithms for multi-objective balanced traveling salesman problem. J. Comput. Res. Dev. **54**(8), 1751–1762 (2017)

Online Multi-label Feature Selection on Imbalanced Data Sets

Jing Liu, Zhongwen Guo[✉], Zhongwei Sun, Shiyong Liu, and Xupeng Wang

Department of Computer Science and Technology,
Ocean University of China, Qingdao, China
guozhw@ouc.edu.cn

Abstract. Feature selection is an important step of data processing. When feature selection is conducted for multi-label classification problem in online learning fashion, it is the problem of online multi-label feature selection. Online feature selection is very appropriate for some actual situations in which the data is not available in advance, the data size is very large or fast running speed is highly demanding. We propose an online multi-label feature selection algorithm in which the data set is divided into many single-label data sets, feature selection is conducted for each single-label data set and the final features are selected from the selected single-label features. As many data sets are imbalanced, we use the basic idea of cost-sensitive learning to combat it. Experiment results corroborate the performance of our algorithm on various data sets and demonstrate that the proposed algorithm can improve online classification performance on imbalanced data sets effectively.

Keywords: Online learning · Feature selection
Multi-label classification

1 Introduction

To obtain useful information from the data, online machine learning algorithms are preferable to traditional ones as they do not require all data to be available in advance and needn't retrain the model from the scratch when new data comes. This kind of algorithms is very scalable and efficient to deal with large-scale streaming data.

Most data in real applications are always high-dimensional and much of them have multiple labels. But not all features are useful and sometimes part of the features are even detrimental for the classification problem. So feature selection is very necessary. Compared with traditional feature selection algorithms, online feature selection algorithms conduct feature selection in the online learning mode which makes this kind of algorithms also have the advantage of online learning algorithms, i.e., high running speed.

In the multi-label feature selection, the common method is to transform the multi-label data set into many single-label data sets and the contribution of

© Springer Nature Singapore Pte Ltd. 2018
J. Li et al. (Eds.): CWSN 2017, CCIS 812, pp. 165–174, 2018.
https://doi.org/10.1007/978-981-10-8123-1_15

each feature is evaluated for each label, then the contribution of each feature is evaluated comprehensively for all labels. Finally, features are selected according to the contribution value. But one problem with this method is that the single-label data sets are always imbalanced. High imbalance level has a detrimental effect on the classification result. So when online feature selection is conducted based on the online learning model, the data imbalance problem inevitably affects the effectiveness of feature selection.

To tackle above challenges, in this paper, we propose an online multi-label feature selection algorithm which can deal with large-scale imbalanced data sets. Extensive experiments are conducted on benchmark data sets and the efficacy of the proposed method is verified.

The rest of this paper is organized as follows. In Sect. 2, the related work is introduced and the proposed algorithm is described in Sect. 3. In Sect. 4, experiments are conducted to demonstrate the effectiveness of the proposed algorithm. In Sect. 5, we conclude our work and point out the future work.

2   Related Work

An online algorithm is very suitable for applications involved with large-scale and high-dimensional data such as computational finance [1], social representations [2] and so on. Online algorithms can be classified into linear online algorithms and nonlinear online algorithms. For example, perceptron algorithm [3] and passive-Aggressive algorithm [4] belongs to the linear algorithm and second-order perceptron algorithm belongs to nonlinear algorithm [5]. Designing algorithms to capture additional information for single features is an effective method to improve the online algorithm's efficiency. This has been implemented in the confidence weighted online learning algorithms [6,7] which are proposed recently. In this paper, we also design the online classifier based on this idea.

There are mainly two kinds of strategies to solve multi-label classification problem, problem transformation strategy and algorithm adaptation strategy [8]. But when the data size is large-scale and high running speed is high-demanding, the former is preferable. Binary relevance is a common-used problem transformation algorithm and used in this paper.

Current various feature selection methods can be divided into three categories. The first category is filter methods [9,10] which select features based solely on the characteristics of the data. The second category is wrapper methods [11] which evaluate features through a predetermined learning algorithm. While the third category, embedded methods [12,13] can be seen as the combination of the first two categories. The feature selection task can be conducted in both batch (or offline) learning fashion and online learning fashion. The latter is preferable when the involved data is large-scale, high-dimensional and most preferable when the data set is not available in advance. In this paper, the feature selection task is conducted in online learning fashion and belongs to the second category.

Data imbalance problem is very pervasive in large-scale data sets. Now many techniques have been crafted to combat it. These techniques can be roughly divided into three categories: resampling, new algorithms and feature selection [14]. But resampling method is appropriate for offline feature selection. In this paper, we use the basic idea of cost-sensitive learning method and feature selection to combat the class imbalance problem in the online feature selection.

3 Methodology

3.1 Problem Setting

In this paper, vector (e.g. w) is denoted by lowercase character, scalar (e.g. y) is denoted by italic lowercase character, the transpose of vector w is denoted by w^T, the Euclidean norm of w is denoted by $\|w\|$. Let $s = (x_i, Y_i)_{i=1}^N$ be a sequence of streaming instance-label pairs (examples) arriving till timestamp N. Each instance x_i is represented by a d-dimensional vector. For binary classification, $Y_i \in \{-1, +1\}$ and if Y_i equals $+1$, then the corresponding pair (x_i, Y_i) is a positive example, otherwise it is a negative one. For multi-label classification, $Y_i = [y_i^1, ..., y_i^k]$. $y_i^j = 1$ if and only if x_i is associated with label j and x_i is a positive example, otherwise it is an negative. k is the number of total labels.

3.2 Online Binary Feature Selection

Online algorithm runs iteratively. On each iteration, when an instance-label pair (x_i, y_i) reaches, the current model is used to predict the label $\tilde{y}_i$ for instance x_i. According to whether $\tilde{y}_i$ is equal to the true label y_i or not, we adopt the update rule of stochastic gradient descent.

A SVM classifier $f(x) = w^T x$ is trained on the data set s. w is a vector and each component of it represents the weight assigned to each feature. The label y_i of each instance x_i is predicted by $sgn(f(x_i))$. w is obtained through solving the following optimization problem in Eq. 1. λ is a regularization parameter to control the model's complexity.

$$\min p(w) = \frac{\lambda}{2}\|w\|^2 + \frac{1}{N}\sum_{t=1}^N l(w; (x_t, y_t)) \tag{1}$$

On each iteration, the parameter w is updated as follows. η is the learning rate.

$$w_{t+1} \leftarrow \begin{cases} (1 - \lambda\eta)w_t + \eta x_t y_t & y_t w_t^T x_t - 1 < 0 \\ (1 - \lambda\eta)w_t & otherwise \end{cases} \tag{2}$$

There is no established theory to set η and λ and they are commonly set from experiment according to experience.

Truncation method is to introduce sparsity during the learning process. We use the truncation algorithm in the literature [15] which project the updated weight vector of each feature to a L2 ball ensuring the largest numerical values are concentrated in its largest element and removing the elements with the smallest numerical values will lead to a small change to the original vector. The projection operation is shown in Eq. 3.

$$w_{t+1} = \min\{1, \frac{\frac{1}{\sqrt{\lambda}}}{\|w_{t+1}\|_2}\}w_{t+1} \tag{3}$$

3.3 Binary Feature Selection on Imbalanced Data Set

The online feature selection in this paper is mainly dependent on the classification model SVM and the basic idea of SVM is to find a hyper-plane in the middle of positive and negative examples. When there are more negative examples than positive ones, the parameter of the classifier is updated more by negative examples. The hyper-plane obtained is closer to the positive examples than the negative ones. Thus the features selected according to the classifier cannot be effective. In addition, some features only have nonzero value on positive examples and they play a key role in the recognition of the positive examples. But the weights of these features are always low because the number of positive examples is small on the whole.

To solve above problem, we resort to the basic idea of cost-sensitive learning and update the classifier's parameter more aggressively when the positive examples are misclassified. Thus larger weights can be assigned to the features which play important role in predicting the positive examples and this also compensates the minority class for the smaller number of examples. Constructing the cost function using the label distribution information has been extensively used in cost-sensitive learning and we also use this method to rectify the model's update rule. Specifically, the update rule in Eq. 2 is rectified as follows.

$$w_{t+1} \leftarrow \begin{cases} (1 - \lambda\eta)w_t + \eta x_t y_t & y_t w_t^T x_t - 1 < 0 \text{ and } y_t = 1 \\ (1 - \lambda\eta)w_t + \eta x_t y_t(1 + \beta_t) & y_t w_t^T x_t - 1 < 0 \text{ and } y_t = -1 \\ (1 - \lambda\eta)w_t & y_t w_t^T x_t - 1 \geq 0 \end{cases} \tag{4}$$

where

$$\beta_t = \frac{p_t}{n_t + p_t} \tag{5}$$

Here, p_t and n_t represent the number of positive and negative examples that have been learned up to timestamp t. So β_t is a parameter that changes with the number of received negative examples and positive examples in real time and the classifier's model is rectified accordingly.

3.4 Online Multi-label Feature Selection

We propose an online multi-label feature selection algorithm (abbr. MOFS). Firstly, the multi-label data set is decomposed into many single-label data sets. Secondly, binary feature selection is conducted with the algorithm in Sect. 3.3 for each label. Thirdly, the weight of each feature for all the labels is averaged up. Finally, truncation algorithm is used to select a predefined number of features. The algorithm is as follows.

```
B = MOFS(S, λ, η, k)
Input  : S    The multi-label training set,
                S = {(x_1, Y_1), (x_2, Y_2), · · · , (x_N, Y_N)};
           λ    Regularization parameter;
           η    Step size;
           k    The number of labels;
Output: B     Selected features;
begin
for t = 1, 2, · · · , N do
    for i = 1, 2, · · · , k do
        if Y_t^i = 1 then
        |   p_i = p_i + 1;
        else
        |   n_i = n_i + 1;
        end
        Predict the label y_t^i for x_t by sign(w_t^i * x_t);
        Update β_t^i according to Eq. 5;
        Update w_t^i according to Eq. 4;
    end
end
w = 0;
for i = 1, 2, · · · , k do
|   w = w + w^i;
end
w = w / N;
Truncate w by Eq. 3;
return the first B features with the largest weight values;
```

Algorithm 1. MOFS

4   Experiment

4.1   Data Sets

Experiments are conducted on eight public benchmark data sets available at the websites of Mulan [15] or UCI machine learning repository [16]. The characteristics of these data sets are listed in Table 1. It can be seen that these data sets are all imbalanced. In the eight data sets, covtype and mnist are data sets used for multi-class classification and we modify these two data sets for binary classification. As for the data set of covtype, we only choose the part of the data which are labeled as 2 and 3 and use the examples labeled as 2 as negative examples and those labeled as 3 as positive examples. As for the data set of mnist, we use the examples labeled as the numbers from 1 to 9 as negative examples and those as 0 as positive examples.

Table 1. Characteristics of the data sets

Data set	Dimension	Example	Negative	Positive
german	24	1000	700	300
svmguide3	21	1243	947	296
magic04	10	19020	12332	6688
a8a	123	32561	24720	7841
mnist	784	70000	63097	6903
ijcnn1	22	141691	128126	13565
codrna	8	271617	181078	90539
covtype	54	319055	283301	35754

4.2   Evaluation Metrics

The number of mistakes is a popular evaluation metric for online algorithms and it is to count up how many mistakes have been made in the learning process of algorithms. The smaller the number of mistakes, the better the algorithms performance is.

Moreover, specificity [17] and geometric mean [18] are also chosen to further evaluate the classifier algorithm's performance on imbalanced data sets. Specificity is used to evaluate the proposed algorithm's performance in the classification of the examples of the minority class. Better classification effect of examples of minority class cannot be obtained at the cost of misclassification of examples of the majority class. So it needs to evaluate the classification performance for the all the examples. In this paper, the geometric mean is used.

In this paper, we also need to evaluate binary classification performance to demonstrate the effectiveness of the proposed feature selection algorithm. The frequently used criterion, F-measure (F1), is chosen in this paper.

4.3   Experimental Results

The data sets in Table 1 are divided into two groups in the experiments. In all experiments, the number of selected features is one tenth of the total features of the data sets.

As the sequence that examples arrive influences the experimental results, we make experiments on each of the data sets 20 times. Each time, we rearrange the sequence of the examples in the data set. And the reported experiment results are the average value over the 20 times of experiment results and same sequences of examples are used for all algorithms for fair comparison.

In the first experiment, we compare the performance of our proposed algorithm (abbreviated as BOFS) with that of the algorithm in literature 15 (abbreviated as OFS). To make a fair comparison, the same values are set to the two parameters, the regularization parameter λ and the learning rate η. Specially, λ

is set to 0.01 and η 0.2 through experiments. The experiment results are shown in Tables 2 and 3.

Table 2. Comparison result of BOFS and OFS on four regular data sets

Data set	Algorithm	Number of mistakes	Specificity	$g - mean$
german	OFS	449.00 82.76	0.56 0.19	0.51 0.07
	BOFS	**418.30 37.60**	**0.61 0.09**	**0.55 0.03**
svmguide3	OFS	400.95 66.80	0.73 0.08	**0.60 0.05**
	BOFS	**391.85 64.01**	**0.75 0.09**	0.60 0.06
magic04	OFS	6023.45 1342.37	**0.61 0.10**	0.66 0.08
	BOFS	**5320.65 660.61**	0.60 0.05	**0.69 0.04**
a8a	OFS	9424.40 2545.85	**0.79 0.17**	0.56 0.11
	BOFS	**9233.15 1518.05**	0.75 0.10	**0.66 0.05**

Table 3. Comparison result of BOFS and OFS on four large-scale data sets

Data set	Algorithm	Number of mistakes	Specificity	g-mean
mnist	OFS	11659.45 6381.63	0.86 0.13	0.66 0.20
	BOFS	**10006.40 4805.18**	**0.87 0.09**	**0.80 0.04**
ijcnn1	OFS	69152.000 11811.76	0.48 0.09	0.63 0.08
	BOFS	**52012.10 2440.61**	**0.61 0.02**	**0.74 0.02**
codrna	OFS	78821.05 287.37	0.67 0.00	0.73 0.00
	BOFS	**78697.60 73.00**	**0.68 0.00**	**0.73 0.00**
covtype	OFS	25270.90 5847.01	**0.98 0.01**	0.61 0.18
	BOFS	**21510.30 5548.05**	0.97 0.02	**0.80 0.10**

From the experiment results, we can find that our proposed algorithm is more efficient than OFS algorithm on the two groups of data sets. On data sets of german, mnist, ijcnn1 and codrna, BOFS algorithm outperforms OFS algorithm on all the three evaluation metrics. On data set svmguide3, BOFS outperforms OFS on number of mistakes and specificity and the OFS algorithm outperforms BOFS algorithm on g-mean. This demonstrates that BOFS improves the classifier's performance on this data set through improving the classifier's classification performance of examples of minority class. On data sets magic04, a8a and covtype, BOFS outperforms OFS on the number of mistakes and g-mean and OFS algorithm outperforms BOFS algorithm on specificity. This demonstrates that BOFS improves the classifier's performance on this data set through improving the classifier's classification performance for examples of the majority class.

All these demonstrate the effectiveness of our proposed algorithm when dealing with imbalanced data sets.

In the second experiments, we compare our proposed algorithm with other two algorithms in literature 15, PE_{trun} and RAND. The experiment results are shown in Tables 4 and 5.

From Tables 4 and 5, it can be seen that our proposed algorithm is more efficient than the other two algorithms on the two groups of data sets. And our

Table 4. Comparison result of three algorithms on four regular data sets

Data set	Algorithm	Number of mistakes	Specificity	g-mean
german	RAND	472.75 16.14	0.54 0.02	0.52 0.02
	PE_{trun}	491.45 27.46	0.51 0.04	0.51 0.03
	BOFS	**418.30 37.60**	**0.61 0.09**	**0.55 0.03**
svmguide3	RAND	563.35 14.65	0.57 0.01	0.52 0.02
	PE_{trun}	512.25 32.67	0.62 0.03	0.54 0.02
	BOFS	**391.85 64.01**	**0.75 0.09**	**0.60 0.06**
magic04	RAND	8686.20 57.29	0.51 0.01	0.54 0.00
	PE_{trun}	8153.15 79.36	0.54 0.01	0.56 0.00
	BOFS	**5320.65 660.61**	**0.59 0.05**	**0.69 0.04**
a8a	RAND	15635.10 94.75	0.50 0.00	0.54 0.00
	PE_{trun}	14086.80 300.49	0.62 0.01	0.50 0.00
	BOFS	**9233.15 1518.05**	**0.75 0.01**	**0.66 0.05**

Table 5. Comparison result of three algorithms on four large-scale data sets

Data set	Algorithm	Number of mistakes	Specificity	g-mean
mnist	RAND	17887.85 111.03	0.7841 0.00	0.55 0.00
	PE_{trun}	16888.45 3945.18	0.77 0.08	0.67 0.10
	BOFS	**10006.40 4805.18**	**0.87 0.09**	**0.80 0.04**
ijcnn1	RAND	52762.80 215.53	**0.65 0.00**	0.49 0.00
	PE_{trun}	104685.30 194.51	0.20 0.00	0.40 0.00
	BOFS	**52012.10 2440.61**	0.61 0.02	**0.74 0.02**
codrna	RAND	128511.55 266.46	0.52 0.00	0.53 0.00
	PE_{trun}	119814.25 248.12	0.54 0.00	0.57 0.00
	BOFS	**78697.60 72.96**	**0.68 0.00**	**0.73 0.00**
covtype	RAND	90650.70 478.49	0.76 0.00	0.54 0.00
	PE_{trun}	52559.85 1250.82	0.92 0.00	0.34 0.02
	BOFS	**21510.30 5548.05**	**0.97 0.01**	**0.80 0.10**

proposed algorithm outperforms the other two algorithms considerably on some data sets. It demonstrates that elaborately designed feature selection method can deal with the imbalanced data sets well. This is the same as that has been proved in literature [19].

In the third experiments, we run two online algorithms, online gradient descent (abbr. OGD) algorithm and classical perceptron algorithm to perform binary classification. The two online algorithm's models are trained only with the features selected by the four algorithms. Two third of each data set is used for feature selection, one third of it is used to obtain the binary classification performance with the selected features. The experiment result is listed in Table 6 and the numbers in the table represent the F1 values of the two classification algorithms.

Table 6. Binary classification performance on four data sets

Classification algorithm	Feature selection algorithm	Data set			
		ijcnn1	mnist	a8a	covtype
OGD	RND	0.17	0.19	0.41	0.26
	PE_{trun}	0.16	0.36	0.17	0.10
	OFS	0.28	0.41	0.38	0.50
	BOFS	**0.31**	**0.54**	**0.50**	**0.69**
Perceptron	RND	0.16	0.19	0.35	0.21
	PE_{trun}	0.16	0.24	0.31	0.10
	OFS	0.20	0.31	0.35	0.37
	BOFS	**0.21**	**0.42**	**0.40**	**0.50**

From Table 6, it can be seen that the two online algorithms perform better with the features selected by our proposed algorithm than by other three algorithms despite the classification algorithms. It demonstrates the effectiveness of our proposed algorithm in dealing with feature selection on large-scale imbalanced data sets.

5   Conclusion

We proposed an algorithm to solve the feature selection problem in online applications. Experiment results demonstrate that our algorithm is effective to deal with online feature selection problem on imbalanced binary and multi-label data sets. As we deal with multi-label data sets without considering the relationship among labels, our next work is to solve this problem.

Acknowledgments. This work is supported by the National Natural Science Foundation of China (NSFC) under the grant number 61379127, 61379128.

References

1. Li, H., Xu, X., Lai, L., Shen, Y.: Online commercial intention detection framework based on web pages. Int. J. Comput. Sci. Eng. **12**(2/3), 176–185 (2016)
2. Perozzi, B., Al-Rfou, R., Skiena, S: Deepwalk: online learning of social representations. In: Proceedings of the 20th ACM SIGKDD International Conference on Knowledge Discovery and Data Mining, pp. 701–710 (2014)
3. Rosenblatt, F.: The perception: a probabilistic model for information storage and organization in the brain. Psychol. Rev. **65**(6), 386–408 (1958)
4. Crammer, K., Dekel, O., Keshet, J., Shalev-Shwartz, S., Singer, Y.: Online passive-aggressive algorithms. J. Mach. Learn. Res. **7**(3), 551–585 (2006)
5. Cesabianchi, N., Conconi, A., Gentile, C.: A second-order perceptron algorithm. SIAM J. Comput. **2375**(3), 121–137 (2002)
6. Wang, J., Zhao, P., Hoi, S.C.H.: Exact soft confidence-weighted learning. In: Computer Science, pp. 107–114 (2012)
7. Crammer, K., Dredze, M., Pereira, F.: Confidence-weighted linear classification for text categorization. J. Mach. Learn. Res. **13**(1), 1891–1926 (2012)
8. Zhang, M.L., Zhou, Z.H.: A review on multi-label learning algorithms. IEEE Trans. Knowl. Data Eng. **26**(8), 1819–1837 (2014)
9. Dash, M., Gopalkrishnan, V.: Distance based feature selection for clustering microarray data. In: Haritsa, J.R., Kotagiri, R., Pudi, V. (eds.) DASFAA 2008. LNCS, vol. 4947, pp. 512–519. Springer, Heidelberg (2008). https://doi.org/10.1007/978-3-540-78568-2_41
10. Karegowda, A.G., Bharathi, P.T.: Enhancing cbir performance using evolutionary algorithm-assisted significant feature selection: a filter approach. Int. J. Appl. Res. Inf. Technol. Comput. **7**(1), 53–59 (2016)
11. Rodrigues, D., Nakamura, R.Y.M., Costa, K.A.P., Yang, X.S.: A wrapper approach for feature selection based on bat algorithm and optimum-path forest. Expert Syst. Appl. **41**(5), 2250–2258 (2014)
12. Chandrashekar, G., Sahin, F.: A survey on feature selection methods. Comput. Electr. Eng. **40**(1), 16–28 (2014)
13. Li-Yeh, C., Ke, C.H., Yang, C.H.: A hybrid both filter and wrapper feature selection method for microarray classification. In: International Multi Conference of Engineers and Computer Scientists, vol. 2168 (2008)
14. Longadge, R., Dongre, S.: Class imbalance problem in data mining review. Int. J. Comput. Sci. Netw. **2**(1), 83 (2013)
15. Wang, J., Zhao, P., Hoi, S.C.H., Jin, R.: Online feature selection and its applications. IEEE Trans. Knowl. Data Eng. **26**(3), 698–710 (2013)
16. Mulan. http://mulan.sourceforge.net/datasetsmlc.html
17. UCI machine learning repository. https://archive.ics.uci.edu/ml/datasets.html
18. Han, C., Tan, Y.K., Zhu, J.H., et al.: Online feature selection of class imbalance via PA algorithm. J. Comput. Sci. Technol. **31**(4), 673–682 (2016)
19. Kubat, M., Matwin, S.: Addressing the curse of imbalanced training sets: one-sided selection. In: International Conference on Machine Learning, pp. 179–186 (1997)
20. Chen, X.W., Wasikowski, M.: FAST:a ROC-based feature selection metric for small samples and imbalanced data classification problems. In: ACM SIGKDD International Conference on Knowledge Discovery and Data Mining, vol. 46, pp. 124–132 (2008)

A Clustering Density Weighted Algorithm of KNN Fingerprint Location Based on Voronoi Diagram

Xiaochao Dang[1,2] , Yili Hei[1] , and Zhanjun Hao[1,2(✉)]

[1] College of Computer Science and Engineering, Northwest Normal University,
Lanzhou 730070, China
zhanjunhao@126.com
[2] Internet of Things Engineering Research Center of Gansu Province,
Lanzhou 730070, China

Abstract. Many existing wireless sensor network localization methods encounter low accuracy and high computational complexity, to address this problem, this paper proposes an improved clustering density weighted algorithm of fingerprint location based on Voronoi diagram. First, the seed points are selected by using a uniform design method within the location region, then the location region is divided based on seed points and Voronoi diagram. At the same time, aiming to estimate the location area accurately, the Dixon's test is employed to filter the gross errors. Finally, considering the problem of low accuracy for traditional K-nearest neighbors (KNN) method, it combines the clustering algorithm and KNN method, proposes a new positioning algorithm with density weighted to obtain the final results. The experiment indicates that the improved algorithm reduces the searching time of fingerprint database effectively on the premise of high positioning accuracy and improves the efficiency without adding any costs of network or energy consumption.

Keywords: Wireless sensor network · Voronoi diagram · Dixon's test
Density weighted

1 Introduction

Wireless Sensor Networks (WSNs) are a kind of network system with low energy consumption, self-organization, diverse structure and an extensive connection [1]. At present, it is widely used in intelligent transportation, military reconnaissance, environmental monitoring, smart home, health monitoring, agricultural control, fire emergency and many other areas; it has very broad application prospects. Determining the location of the event or the location of the data is one of the most basic functions of the sensor networks [2]. Global Positioning System (GPS) is currently the most commonly used and the most accurate positioning system in the world. However, as the shielding of the building to the satellite signal [3], it is difficult to search the satellite signal in the indoor environment. As a result, researchers are forced to seek solutions from the view of the technology of wireless sensor network node localization.

© Springer Nature Singapore Pte Ltd. 2018
J. Li et al. (Eds.): CWSN 2017, CCIS 812, pp. 175–190, 2018.
https://doi.org/10.1007/978-981-10-8123-1_16

In source localization algorithms, according to the measurement of the position parameters of the target, the positioning algorithms can be generally divided into two categories: range-based and range-free. Range-based algorithms are used to calculate the position of the unknown node by measuring the distance or angle information between the nodes. And range-free algorithms are mainly based on the topology information, relationship between nodes and the number of steps between them. Common algorithms for range-free contain Centroid, DV-Hop, Amorphous, MDS-MAP and APIT, and so on [4]. Typical ranging techniques for range-based algorithms include the time of arrival (ToA), time difference of arrival (TDoA), angle of arrival (AoA) and received signal strength indicator (RSSI). The recent work is mainly focused on resorting to finer-grained wireless channel response measurement than RSSI. Different from RSSI, the PHY layer power feature, channel state information (CSI), is able to discriminate multipath characteristics, and thus holds the potential for the convergence of accurate and pervasive indoor location [5]. The fundamental drawback of CSI is that it requires special equipments to achieve positioning, and the research on it stays in the primary phase. Compared with various range-based location methods, localization with RSSI is a very popular technique in wireless sensor networks, because the RSS measurement method does not require time synchronization or the use of an antenna array; it makes a simple and cost-saving method to realize source localization in terms of both software and hardware [6]. The positioning method based on RSSI is generally divided into two categories, the triangle algorithm [7] and fingerprint positioning method [8, 9]. The first method converts the RSSI into a distance between the receiver and the reference point by using wireless signal model [10]. With the distance as constraints, the position of the target is estimated by using the trilateration algorithm. The fingerprint positioning method records the spatial difference or other environment characteristics as the fingerprint of the position; the location of the user is estimated by matching the fingerprint with the location fingerprint database.

In recent years, the localization algorithm based on computational geometry has received extensive attention for its special superiority. Among them, Voronoi diagram based localization scheme is the most representative [11]. The traditional Voronoi diagram based localization algorithm usually uses RSSI as a criterion to measure distance. However, the distance based on RSSI is easy to be influenced by the channel interference and the noise, especially in real indoor environment [12, 13], which as a result, makes it impossible to achieve accurate positioning. There are several methods have been proposed to solve this problem. A hybrid cooperative localization approach is proposed to combine time-of-arrival and received signal strength based fingerprint techniques in the considered scenario in the literature [14]. However, the method greatly increases the computational and energy consumption. Hadzic et al. [15] focused on the method called iterative multilateration, in which once the position is estimated for an unknown node, this node is used as an anchor node whose position is broadcasted to all neighboring nodes. Thus, the method reduces communication cost at the cost of error propagation. Guan et al. [16] first proposes an optimal region selection strategy of Voronoi-based Monte Carlo localization algorithm for WSN, which increases the efficiency and accuracy by adapting the size of Voronoi area during the filtering process. He et al. [17] propose a Voronoi analytical model based on graph theory and apply this model to analyze the fingerprint structure as well as yield proximity information and compute the centroid of the Voronoi vertex in the Voronoi region. Although the method reduces the number of samples and AP access, the positioning accuracy needs to be further improved as the large fluctuations of indoor RSS signal.

In this paper, we propose a clustering density weighted algorithm of KNN fingerprint location based on Voronoi diagram (KNN-CDWV), which mainly discusses using RSSI fingerprinting method for the realization of the position localization, and focuses on reducing the ranging error caused by the environment factors. To the best knowledge, our contributions are as follows:

(a) Voronoi diagram is a proximity graph that is used for first determining the minimum location region, so as to reduce the size of the database and lessen the time cost of the localizing algorithm;
(b) Unlike the traditional fingerprint-based algorithm, this paper combines with the advantages of K-means and KNN to improve the positioning accuracy by using the density weighted algorithm;
(c) We have evaluated the performance of KNN-CDWV using extensive simulation, and the simulation results show that the localization performance of the KNN-CDWV is superior to that traditional KNN algorithm.

The remainder of this paper is organized as follows. Section 2 reviews the related work of localization schemes, including the Voronoi diagram, uniform design and the Dixon's test. Section 3 introduces the proposed approach in detail. Simulation results for the performance evaluation of our proposed approach are presented and discussed in Sect. 4. Then Sect. 5 summarizes and concludes the paper.

2   Preliminaries

2.1   Voronoi Diagram

Voronoi diagram, also known as Thiessen polygon, as a basic geometric structure in computational geometry, is widely used in solving the problem of coverage control and network localization in wireless sensor networks. A Voronoi diagram is a partitioning of a plane regions based on distance to points in a specific subset of the plane. That set of generator points (called seeds) is specified beforehand, and for each seed there is a corresponding region consisting of all points closer to that seed than to any other. These regions are called Voronoi cells.

Assume there are n nodes on the plane, $P = \{p_1, p_2, \ldots, p_n\}$, $2 \leq n < \infty$, which are similar to the points on a graph. Then on this plane, the Euclidean distance of any point $X(x, y)$ and $p_i(x_i, y_i)$ is:

$$d(p_i, X) = ((x_i - x)^2 + (y_i - y)^2)^{1/2} \tag{1}$$

The plane is separated into n Voronoi areas by centering on each p_i, which makes any point X on $V(p_i)$ Voronoi area centering on p_i satisfies the condition of

$$V(p_i, X) = \{x | d(p_i, X) \le d(p_j, X), \forall i \ne j, j = 1, 2, \ldots, n\} \tag{2}$$

For a given set of n generator points, which subdivide points on the plane and generate n subdivision areas according to the proximity principle [18].

2.2 Uniform Design

Uniform design method (UDM) is the experimental design method which combines the number theory and multivariate statistical analysis; this method was jointly proposed by professor FANG Kaitai and professor WANG Yuan in 1978. The core idea of the uniform design is a deterministic method to find uniform distributed point set which replaces random numbers of Monte-Carlo method [19]. It can arrange multifactors and multilevels' analysis experiment with using less experiment times, and the method can avoid the blindness of initial point selection in optimization design.

The specific steps of uniform design are as follows. Firstly, the uniform design table is constructed. Supposing each design table is marked as $U_n(q^s)$ or $U_n^*(q^s)$. U is uniform design; n represents the number of experiment; q is the level of each factor; s is the number of the columns. The uniform design table marked with $*$ indicates that the table has better uniformity and it should be preferred.

For example, $U_6^*(6^4)$ represents that there are six factors and four different levels in six experimentations. In the case of different levels of experimental factors, the method of quasi-level can be used to design the experiment, and the mixed level of uniform design table should be used. Each uniform table is accompanied by another table that indicates how to select the appropriate column from the uniform design table and the uniformity of the experimental scheme. Table 1 is the optional table. However, two columns of the uniform design table in random experimental schemes are usually not equivalent. For instance, we can get the Fig. 1(a) by using column 1 and 3; similarly, get the Fig. 1(b) by using column 1 and 4. We can see the distribution of scattered points in Fig. 1(a) is more evenly than Fig. 1(b). In order to reflect the equilibrium of the experimental arrangement, each uniform design table must have an additional table, such as Table 2. At the same time, by computing the deviation to show the uniformity, the smaller deviation value is, the better the uniformity will be.

Table 1. Uniform design table

No.	Factor1	Factor2	Factor3	Factor4
1	1	2	3	6
2	2	4	6	5
3	3	6	2	4
4	4	1	5	3
5	5	3	1	2
6	6	5	4	1

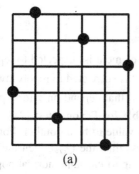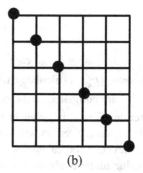

(a)   (b)

Fig. 1. Distribution map

Table 2. Uniform use table

No.	Group	Deviation
2	1 3	0.1875
3	1 2 3	0.2656
4	1 2 3 4	0.2990

2.3 Dixon's Test

In a set of replicate measurements of a physical or chemical quantity, one or more of the obtained values may differ considerably from the majority of the rest. We describe gross error, also known as blunder error or abnormal error. It is the result of several reasons, such as improper instrument operation, results misreading, system failures and environment conditions and so on. If the gross error is not eliminated, it will inevitably lead to the consequences of low measurement repeatability, and if the improper removal of the normal data with large errors, it will result in the measurement of repetitive preferences illusion. In this case there is always a strong motivation to eliminate those deviant values and not to include them in any subsequent calculation (e.g. of the mean value and/or of the standard deviation). This is permitted only when the suspect values can be 'legitimately' characterized as outliers. In statistics, Dixon's Q test, or simply the Q test, is used for identification and rejection of outliers.

The test is applied as follows:

The N values comprising set of observations under examination, which are arranged in ascending order: $x_1 < x_2 < \ldots < x_n$;

The statistic experimental Q-value (Q_{exp}) is calculated [20]. This is a ratio defined as the difference of the suspect value from its nearest one divided by the range of the values (Q: rejection quotient). Thus, for testing x_1 or x_n (as possible outliers), we use the following Q_{exp} value:

$$Q_{exp}^L = \frac{x_2 - x_1}{x_N - x_1} \tag{3}$$

$$Q_{\exp}^{H} = \frac{x_N - x_{N-1}}{x_N - x_1} \qquad (4)$$

where $Q_{\exp}^{H}$ is the outlier factor calculated when the element is suspected to report high values, whereas, $Q_{\exp}^{L}$ is calculated when the element is suspected to report low values. $Q_{\exp}^{H}$ and $Q_{\exp}^{L}$ are compared to the critical value Q_{cric} that depend on α for a particular 'significance level' and is given in the standard table for Dixon's test [21]. The significance level has a direct impact on considering a value to be an outlier. For a given significance level, if the calculated $Q_{\exp}$ value is less than the Q_{cric}, then the extreme rank data value under evaluation is assumed to belong to the same normal population. Otherwise, the data value is considered as an outlier.

3   The Proposed Algorithm

In this section we propose a localization algorithm based on Voronoi diagram, which improves KNN method by using clustering idea. To get the evenly initial points in the positioning area, the uniform design table is structured first. After that, the location region is divided based on seed points and Voronoi diagram. At the same time, aim to estimate the location subarea accurately, the Dixon's test is employed to filter the gross error. Finally, the K-means clustering and weighted density are considered to improve the KNN algorithm.

3.1   Construction of Seed Points

Assume $S_i(x_i, y_i)$ is the reference point in the location area; x is in the interval $[0, a]$, and y is in the interval $[0, b]$, a and b is the size of the location area. We use the optional table of $U_n^*(q^s)$ to construct the initial points. The basic process is as followed.

Step1: Choose the best combination of two columns i and j by query the optional table;

Step2: The first point $S_1(x_1, y_1)$ is constructed, $x_1 = (a/q) \times u_{1,i}, y_1 = (b/q) \times u_{1,j}$;

Step3: The second initial point $S_2(x_2, y_2)$, $x_2 = (a/q) \times u_{2,i}, y_2 = (b/q) \times u_{2,j}$;

Step4: The n-th point $S_m(x_m, y_m)$, $x_3 = (a/q) \times u_{3,i}, y_3 = (b/q) \times u_{3,j}$.

The above points we get are uniformly distributed in range of area S. We define the deviation formula to evaluate the uniformity of the design table. The uniformity is better when the deviation is smaller. If the deviation value exceeds a threshold, we will reconstruct the initial points. In uniform design, the deviation formula is defined as follows:

Assume there are n points $\{s_1, s_2, \ldots, s_n\}$ in C^m, and a vector $Y = (y_1, y_2, \ldots, y_m) \in C^m$; the volume of matrix $[0, Y]$ define as $V(Y) = y_1, y_2, \ldots, y_m$, and the number of points s_i in $[0, Y]$ is defined as n_x; then the deviation of point set $\{s_1, s_2, \ldots, s_n\}$ is:

$$D(s_1, s_2, \ldots, s_n) = \sup_{x \in C^m} \left| \frac{n_x}{n} - V(Y) \right| \tag{5}$$

3.2 Region Division and Decision

Region Division

This section will treat the sample points as independent fingerprint map, and take its RSSI as the character. The region is divided by using the initial points and Voronoi diagram to narrow the search range for the reference points. We select the initial reference points in location area by using uniform design criteria, as shown in Fig. 2(a) and (b) depict Voronoi diagram based on these initial points. We can see that the location area is divided into several convex polygonal sub-regions, the distance between any points and the unique initial point within the polygon area is the shortest.

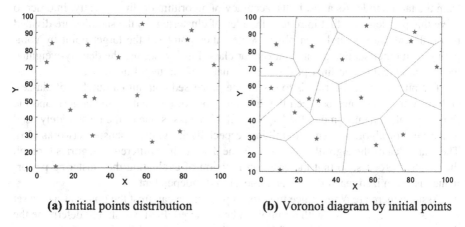

(a) Initial points distribution   **(b)** Voronoi diagram by initial points

Fig. 2. Voronoi diagram

Region Decision

When the target fingerprint is added into the database, the server begins to calculate which Voronoi sub-region it belongs to. However, because the ideal conditions do not exist in real environment, some bad reference points are introduced in the calculation. To solve this problem, we need to filter the gross error by using the Dixon's test before the decision stage to get the correct sub-region.

Assume there are n sample fingerprints in database, arrange this data set in ascending order, let the new data set be $\{RSS_1, RSS_2, \ldots, RSS_n\}$, our interest lies in calculating the outlier factor for every data in data set by using Dixon's test.

Supposing RSS_i is an outlier, it appears unusually far from the rest of the sample. The procedure for testing RSS_i is:

$$
\begin{cases}
r_{10} = \dfrac{RSS_i - RSS_{i-1}}{RSS_i - RSS_n} & r_{11} = \dfrac{RSS_i - RSS_{i-1}}{RSS_i - RSS_{n-1}} \\[3mm]
r_{21} = \dfrac{RSS_i - RSS_{i-2}}{RSS_i - RSS_{n-1}} & r_{22} = \dfrac{RSS_i - RSS_{i-2}}{RSS_i - RSS_{n-2}}
\end{cases}
\tag{6}
$$

The computed value of test statistic RSS_i is then compared with the critical value for a given number of observation n and at a given significance level $\alpha = 0.05$. If computed RSS_i is greater than the respective critical value at a given significance level, RSS_i is said to be false which can then be discarded.

3.3 Improved KNN Algorithm

KNN algorithm has been widely used in search matching because of its low complexity. However, the traditional KNN localization algorithm only selects the former K neighboring samples according to the order and it ignores the distance difference from the target node. As a result, the accuracy of algorithm declines greatly. In order to solve this problem, we first introduce the idea of clustering, so the samples are divided into different classes, and then obtain K neighbor points of the target point by comparing with other sample points in a similar class. Finally, we use the density-weighted method to calculate the final position coordinates of the target node.

The purpose of clustering is to divide the processed data into a number of classes, and make the difference between the different types of elements is the largest, and the same type of elements among the largest [22]. K-means is one of the most widely used in the field of algorithms in data mining, especially in wireless sensor networks [23]. The main idea of the algorithm is to divide the data set into different categories through the iterative process, so that the criterion function of evaluating the clustering performance is optimized, each cluster is compact and independent.

Assume there are N reference fingerprint points; we can treat the points as a data set $U = \{X_i, i = 1, 2, \cdots, N\}$ with a sample to be clustered. First, we should determine the data to divide the class number of K to get the cluster $C = \{C_1, C_2, \ldots, C_k\}$.

In order to get the K, we use a heuristic method to estimate the optimal number of clusters, called Elbow Method. Define the K-means cost function as follows:

$$
J = \sum_{i=1}^{N} \sum_{k=1}^{K} r_{ik} \|x_i - \mu_k\|^2
\tag{7}
$$

where k is supposed to be the clusters' number and x_i is initial reference point, μ_k is the center of class k-th. At the same time, define a class indicator variable $\{r_{nk} | r_{nk} \in \{0, 1\}\}$ representing whether the $x_i (i \in (1, 2, \ldots, N))$ belongs to the class k-th. If it does, the value of r_{nk} is 1, otherwise is 0. The cost function J is the sum of the squares of the distance between each data point and its cluster center. The optimal solution of the K-Means parameter is also aimed at minimizing the cost function.

The pseudo-code of K-means algorithm [24]:

Algorithm: K-Means Algorithm

```
Input: Dataset U = {X_i, i = 1,2,···,N}, cluster number of K
       and limit of iterations MaxIters
Output: The final partition C = {C_1, C_2,...,C_k},
        L = {l(X)|X = 1,2,...,N} represents the set of cluster
        labels of U
Process:
1: foreach C_i ∈ C do
2:    C_i ← X_j ∈ U (e.g. random selection)
3: end
4: foreach X_i ∈ U do
5:    l(X_i) ← argminDistance (X_i, C_j), j ∈ {1,2,...,k}
7: end
8: changed ← false;
9: iter ← 0;
10: repeat
11:    foreach C_i ∈ C do
12:       UpdateCluster(C_i);
13:    end
14:    foreach X_i ∈ U do
15:       minDist ← argminDistance (X_i, C_j), j ∈ {1,2,...,k};
16:       if minDist ≠ l(X_i) then
17:          l(X_i) ← minDist;
18:          changed ← true;
19:       end
20:    end
21:    iter++;
22: until changed=true and iter ≤ MaxIters.
```

After the clustering process is finished, the target point is divided into the nearest sub-cluster by using Euclidean distance. In the traditional KNN algorithm, the selection of the neighboring sample points is only based on its distance from the surrounding sample points. In order to improve the accuracy of the positioning results, density weighed localization algorithm is proposed. The density weighted positioning algorithm assigns a higher weight to a reference point with a larger density value, while a smaller reference point gives a smaller weight.

Assume there are M sample points in cluster $C_m = \{x_i, i = 1, 2, \ldots, M\}$, and define the density function as the points x_i:

$$dens(x_i) = \sum_{m=1}^{M} \exp\left(-\frac{\|x_i - x_m\|^2}{\partial^2}\right) \tag{8}$$

where ∂ represents the effective radius of the neighborhood, and define the mean square distance:

$$\partial = \sqrt{\frac{1}{M(M-1)} \sum_{i=1}^{M} \sum_{j=1}^{M} \|x_i - x_j\|^2} \tag{9}$$

The weight w_i of an object x_i is:

$$w_i = \frac{dens(x_i)}{\sum_{x_j \in C_m} dens(x_j)} \tag{10}$$

The final coordinates of target point is defined as:

$$(x, y) = \frac{\sum_{i=1}^{M} \left(\frac{1}{w_i} \times (x_i, y_i)\right)}{\sum_{i=1}^{M} \frac{1}{w_i}}. \tag{11}$$

4 Experiment and Analysis

In order to evaluate the performance of the proposed algorithm in real indoor environment, experiments are conducted in the lab of 12 m × 8 m. The layout is shown in Fig. 3, where there are 4 APs denoted by triangles and located in different locations, besides, according to conclusion in [25], the 3D measurements at 1 m height show the best results, so all the experiments are conducted at the height of 1 m. Black dots are on the behalf of the points of reference. Black squares represent the points to be located. The RSSI will be measured by taking a common 802.15.4 Transmitter-Receiver with a pair of TI CC2530 and a laptop. The sampling frequency is 30 samples/min, and collect the RSSI signal for 3 min at each reference points, then construct the fingerprint database by taking the average value of RSSI feature.

4.1 Cluster Number Determination

In this phase, the optimal number of cluster is determined by using elbow method. Through the classification of the reference points, we can see from Fig. 4, the cost

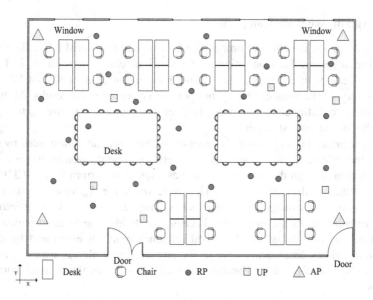

Fig. 3. Layout of the experimental environment

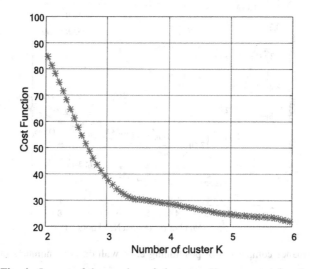

Fig. 4. Impact of the number of cluster on K-means cost function

function decreased sharply when the number of cluster K changed from 2 to 3. After beyond 3, the change is significantly reduced. So the elbow is 3, that is, $K = 3$ is the best number of cluster.

4.2   Location Accuracy Comparison

Now let us examine the effect of proposed algorithm and traditional KNN algorithm on positioning accuracy. For convenience, the value of cluster number is 3. The first simulation deals with comparing the relative localization error of KNN-CDWV with the KNN varying the number of neighbor points in calculating the results. At the same time, in order to distinguish the K value in K-means algorithm, we use K_n to represent the number of the nearest neighbor.

It can be noticed in Fig. 5 that the positioning error is greatly influenced by the K_n. With the increase of K_n, the process of localization can be realized by the best nearest nodes selection through the node positioned; as a result, the error of KNN-CDWV and KNN algorithm is declining greatly. However, when the K_n value exceeds 3, the positioning error of two algorithms increases sharply due to the bad points introduced into the calculation. At the same time, because we divided the location region before the localization, and the effect of the bad reference points is eliminated by density-weighted algorithm, localization error of the proposed algorithm is always lower than that of a classical algorithm. Therefore, we take $K_n = 3$ as the optimal number of neighbor.

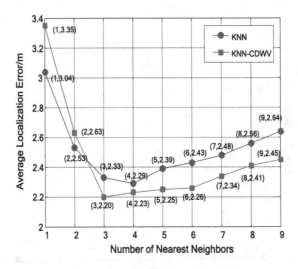

Fig. 5. Performance comparison of positioning error with different numbers of neighbors

The accuracy measure is the cumulative distribution function (CDF) of the position error with the number of reference points changing. In order to reduce the interference of the random error in the experiment, we take the average of 30 tests as the final result. From the results displayed in Fig. 6, we can see that the proposed improved algorithm achieves significantly better positioning accuracy than the traditional algorithm, and the error is always within $3m$. This is because the KNN-CDWV calculates the coordinates by using the improved density weighted method compared to the classical average method. As a result, the cumulative probability curves of these methods also show that the proposed density weighted localization method outperforms the traditional localization methods.

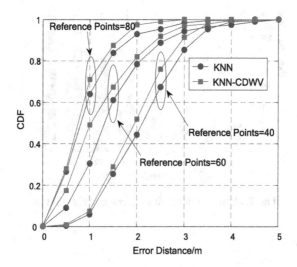

Fig. 6. Experiment result in CDF

4.3   Location Time Comparison

In addition to positioning accuracy, algorithm execution time is an important positioning indicator. In this phase, the average time consumption is used to evaluate the algorithm performance. The number of reference points is set to 80, and the ratio of the total time consumed by all the target points to the total number of points is measured in the MATLAB platform. Assume that t_i is the time of the point i consumed in the process of the localization; the average location time of S points can be defined as equation:

$$\bar{t} = \frac{1}{S}\sum_{i=1}^{S} t_i \tag{12}$$

The Fig. 7 shows the effect number of the target points. It is clear that the positioning time increases with the change of target number. It is mainly caused by the searching and matching process. Because we divided the location region, which greatly reduced the amount of the calculation and the searching space, the KNN-CDWV localization algorithm is faster when vary the target number.

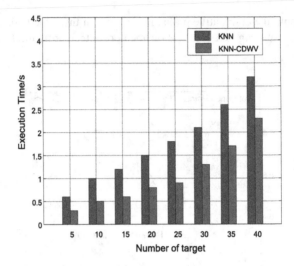

Fig. 7. Experiment result in average execution time

5 Conclusion

In order to address the problem that the existing fingerprint localization algorithm has low positioning accuracy, this paper proposes a clustering density weighted algorithm of KNN fingerprint location based on Voronoi diagram (KNN-CDWV). The algorithm selects the initial points by using uniform design method, and divides the location region based on these seed points and Voronoi diagram. The Dixon's test is introduced to filter the gross error before sub-region decision. On one hand, the search region is narrowed greatly, and improves the positioning efficiently. Finally, in order to improve the positioning accuracy of traditional KNN algorithm, we combine the K-means cluster method and density weighted method to calculate the final position of the target points. Extensive experiments are conducted in practical environment to evaluate the performance of our proposed algorithm, and the results have demonstrated that KNN-CDWV is effective in accurately estimating target positions. In our future work, we will focus on improving the applicability of the algorithm for outdoor positioning, and further reducing the positioning error and the complexity.

Acknowledgements. This work was supported by the National Natural Science Foundation of China under Grant No. 61363059, No. 61762079, and No. 61662070, Key Science and Technology Support Program of Gansu Province under Grant No. 1604FKCA097 and No. 17YF1GA015, Science and Technology Innovation Project of Gansu Province under Grant No. 17CX2JA037 and No. 17CX2JA039.

References

1. Qian, Z.H., Wang, Y.J.: Internet of Things-oriented wireless sensor networks review. J. Electron. Inf. Technol. **35**(1), 215–227 (2013)
2. Labraoui, N., Gueroui, M., Aliouat, M.: Secure DV-HOP localization scheme against wormhole attacks in wireless sensor networks. Trans. Emerg. Telecommun. Technol. **23**(4), 303–316 (2012)
3. Vaghefi, R.M., Buehrer, R.M.: Cooperative source node tracking in non-line-of-sight environments. IEEE Trans. Mob. Comput. **16**(5), 1287–1299 (2017)
4. Yassin, A., Nasser, Y., Awad, M., Raulefs, R.: Recent advances in indoor localization: a survey on theoretical approaches and applications. IEEE Commun. Surv. Tutor. **19**(2), 1327–1346 (2017)
5. Yang, Z., Zhou, Z., Liu, Y.: From RSSI to CSI: indoor localization via channel response. ACM Comput. Surv. **46**(2), 1–32 (2014)
6. Kaemarungsi, K., Krishnamurthy, P.: Analysis of WLAN's received signal strength indication for indoor location fingerprinting. Pervasive Mob. Comput. **8**(2), 292–316 (2012)
7. Cho, H.H., Lee, R.H., Park, J.G.: Adaptive parameter estimation method for wireless localization using RSSI measurements. J. Electr. Eng. Technol. **6**(6), 883–887 (2011)
8. Liu, C.Y., Wang, J.: A constrained KNN indoor positioning model based on a geometric clustering fingerprinting technique. Wuhan Univ. J. Nat. Sci. **39**(11), 1287–1292 (2014)
9. Li, Q., Li, W., Sun, W., Li, J., Liu, Z.: Fingerprint and assistant nodes based Wi-Fi localization in complex indoor environment. IEEE Access **4**, 2993–3004 (2017)
10. Yao, Y., Han, Q., Xu, X., Jiang, N.: A RSSI-based distributed weighted search localization algorithm for WSNs. Int. J. Distrib. Sens. Netw. **11**(4), 1–8 (2015)
11. Swangmuang, N., Krishnamurthy, P.: An effective location fingerprint model for wireless indoor localization. Pervasive Mob. Comput. **4**(6), 836–850 (2008)
12. Xue, W., Qiu, W., Hua, X., Yu, K.: Improved Wi-Fi RSSI measurement for indoor localization. IEEE Sens. J. **17**(7), 2224–2230 (2017)
13. Mao, K.J., Wu, J.B., Jin, H.B.: Indoor localization algorithm for NLOS environment. Acta Electronica Sinica **44**(5), 1174–1179 (2016)
14. He, Z., Ma, Y., Tafazolli, R.: A hybrid data fusion based cooperative localization approach for cellular networks. In: 7th International Wireless Communications and Mobile Computing Conference (IWCMC), Turkey, pp. 162–166. IEEE Press (2011)
15. Hadzic, S., Rodriguez, J.: Utility based node selection scheme for cooperative localization. In: Proceedings of 2011 International Conference on Indoor Positioning and Indoor Navigation (IPIN), Portugal. IEEE Press (2011)
16. Guan, Z., Zhang, Y., Zhang, B., Dong, L.: Voronoi-based localisation algorithm for mobile sensor networks. Int. J. Syst. Sci. **47**(15), 1–8 (2015)
17. He, C., Guo, S., Yang, Y.: Voronoi diagram based indoor localization in wireless sensor networks. In: Proceedings of 2015 IEEE International Conference on Communications (ICC), UK, pp. 3269–3274. IEEE Press (2015)
18. Guan, Z., Zhang, B., Dong, L., Chai, S.: An optimal region selection strategy for WSNs localization based on Voronoi diagram. In: Proceedings of 34th Chinese Control Conference (CCC), China, pp. 7759–7764. IEEE Press (2015)
19. Fang, K.T.: Uniform Design and Uniform Design Table. Scientific Press, China (1994)
20. Shrivastava, S., Rajesh, A., Bora, P.K.: Sliding window Dixon's tests for malicious users' suppression in a cooperative spectrum sensing system. IET Commun. **8**(7), 1065–1071 (2014)

21. Verma, S.P., Quiroz-Ruiz, A.: Critical values for six Dixon tests for outliers in normal samples up to sizes 100, and applications in science and engineering. Revista Mexicana de Ciencias Geolgicas **23**(2), 133–161 (2006)
22. Zhong, Y.Z., Wu, F., Zhang, J., Dong, B.: WiFi indoor localization based on K-means. In: Proceedings of 2016 International Conference on Audio, Language and Image Processing (ICALIP), China, pp. 11–12. IEEE Press (2016)
23. Manisekaran, S.V., Venkatesan, R.: Cluster-based architecture for range-free localization in wireless sensor networks. Int. J. Distrib. Sens. Netw. **10**(4), 1–8 (2014)
24. Zhou, Z.H.: Machine Learning. Tsinghua University Press, China (2016)
25. Habaebi, M.H., Khamis, R.O., Zyoud, A., Islam, M.R.: RSS based localization techniques for ZigBee wireless sensor network. In: Proceedings of 2014 International Conference on Computer and Communication Engineering (ICCCE), Malaysia, pp. 72–75. IEEE Press (2014)

Detecting Bogus Messages in Vehicular Ad-Hoc Networks: An Information Fusion Approach

Jizhao Liu$^{(\boxtimes)}$, Heng Pan, Junbao Zhang, Qian Zhang,
and Qiusheng Zheng

School of Computer Science, Zhongyuan University of Technology, No. 41,
West Zhongyuan Road, Zhengzhou, Henan, People's Republic of China
liujizhao2009@163.com

Abstract. In Vehicular ad hoc networks (VANETs), vehicles are allowed to broadcast messages for informing nearby vehicles about road condition and emergent events, such as traffic congestion or accident. It leaves a backdoor in which inside attackers can launch false information attacks by injecting bogus emergency messages to mislead other vehicles, and potential threats on road safety can be caused. This paper presents a multi-source information fusion approach to detect bogus emergency messages, in which each vehicle uses its on-board sensor data and received beacon messages to perceive the traffic condition and calculates its belief on credibility for received emergency messages. Moreover, the proposed approach provides enhanced robustness against collusion attacks by integrating an outlier detection mechanism in which a clustering algorithm is performed to filter out the colluder whose behavior deviates largely from others. The simulation results show validity of our approach, higher significantly detection rate can be achieved comparing to the existing threshold based scheme.

Keywords: Vehicular ad-hoc networks · Security · False information attacks
Information fusion

1 Introduction

Vehicular ad-hoc networks (VANETs) [1], consisting of on-board units (OBUs), roadside units (RSUs) and a central trusted authority (TA), are drawing more and more attentions from academia and industry, since various kinds of applications can be provided to improve road safety and efficiency of transportation system [2]. In VANETs, vehicles are able to perceive the occurrence of some emergent events by using their on-board sensors (i.e. airbag explosion, hard braking, or accident) and send an emergency message to the vehicles in the vicinity for the drivers to take reaction in time. A potential threat is that the rich functionality provided by VANETs may be abused by inside attackers [3]. Motivated by the purpose of selfishness or malicious attacks, an inside attacker can launch a false information attack by sending bogus emergency messages to claim inexistent events. Since inside attackers commonly have certificate and other security parameters distributed by TA and legal signatures can be

© Springer Nature Singapore Pte Ltd. 2018
J. Li et al. (Eds.): CWSN 2017, CCIS 812, pp. 191–200, 2018.
https://doi.org/10.1007/978-981-10-8123-1_17

generated, the existing VANETs security framework proposed in IEEE 1609.2 standard [4], which is built on entity authentication and message integrity protection technology, is unable to resist this kind of attack. In real-world traffic scenario, the occurrence of abnormal traffic events commonly lead to a change in traffic condition [5, 6]. For example, in a car collision accident scenario, crashed cars may result in lane blocking, which make the vehicles behind the accident site to take an emergent evasion maneuver for avoiding secondary collisions, such as hard brake or lane changing. The vehicles that have passed the accident site will take an acceleration action. It provides us with novel methods to detect bogus emergency messages. In this paper, we propose a false information detection scheme which is based on information fusion technology, in which vehicles collect information from multiple available sources for perceiving traffic condition. We conduct a simulation to evaluate the performance of the proposed scheme, the results prove that fusion of multi-sources information can improve effectively detection accuracy.

The remainder of this paper is organized as follows. We discuss the related work in Sect. 2. Section 3 gives a system model and some basic conceptions. The detailed description of the proposed approach is shown in Sect. 4. Section 5 presents the simulation setup and the results analysis. Finally, we draw concluding remarks in Sect. 6.

2 Related Work

In recent years, various technologies have been proposed, including network modeling, threshold scheme and data centric method. Network modeling based methods [7–10] try to build and maintain a network model that is used to verify reliability of received information. Golle et al. [7] proposed a general approach to detect and correct malicious data in VANETs. In the proposed approach, each vehicle constructs a VANETs model using the data collected from its own sensors. When receiving a message from other nodes, the vehicle tests validity using its own model. Enormous store and communication resource consumption make this approach expensive and impractical. Ghosh et al. [8] conducted a root-cause analysis for misbehavior of node in VANET. A cause-tree is firstly constructed, and then a successive logical reduction is used to take a decision which indicates the root-cause of a misbehavior node.

Threshold schemes include works in [11, 12]. Raya et al. [11] proposed a distributed algorithm, named local eviction of attackers by voting evaluators to evaluate the credibility of vehicle nodes. In this approach, each node collects information from its neighbors, and compare the neighbors' behavior with the average behavior. In [12], a vehicle accepts a message only if the number of received messages reporting the same information exceeds a given threshold. This scheme is sample and easy to implement. But it is hard to set optimized value for the threshold in highly-dynamic VANETs scenario.

In data centric schemes [13, 14], vehicles try to evaluate the reliability of the received message, instead to calculate the reputation value of its sender. Ruj et al. [13] proposed a data-centric misbehavior detection scheme in VANETs. Authors argue that it is unnecessary to classify a vehicle as honest or malicious. Besides, reputation based schemes [15–17] have proposed to evaluate reliability of messages and their senders. In reputation management system, vehicles location privacy may be disclosed because of the a unique communication ID they used. For solving this problem, Dietzel et al. [18] applied the information entropy and the majority rule to the reputation accumulation algorithms, and proposed hidden-zone strategy and k-anonymity strategy to defend the reputation link attack during pseudonym changes. Wang et al. [19] proposed a bandwidth-efficient protection mechanism for in-network aggregation based on data-consistency checking by combining data mining techniques to detect false information with a filtering technique for forwarding paths that limits the influence of attackers on aggregated data. Falasi et al. [20] use similarity as a metric to establish and maintain trust relationships among the vehicles and propose a trust management system aiming to detect false safety event messages from abnormal vehicles in VANETs.

3   Preliminaries

3.1   VANETs Model

As shown in Fig. 1, a traffic scenario with 3 lanes freeway is established in which vehicles are equipped with wireless node and various kinds of on-board sensors (GPS, accelerometer, etc.) that enable them to obtain the information about motion status, such as position, speed and instantaneous acceleration. We also assume that vehicles exchange periodically information with their neighbors using beacon broadcasting for them to achieve the state of the neighbors. For example, a vehicle can calculate easily the traffic density around it by counting the number of the senders in its communication range based on received beacon messages. Also, it can calculate the vehicular average speed. In the case of an emergent event, such as a traffic accident, the vehicle creates an emergency message that indicates event type, time, position etc.

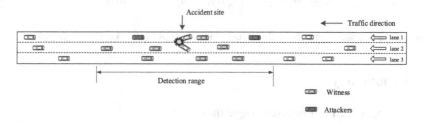

Fig. 1. System model

3.2   Adversary Model

We assume there are a percentage of inside adversaries in VANETs which can launch a false information attack by sending a bogus emergency message in which reported event may be inexistent, or with a wrong type, position and time. Also, we assume there may be collusion attacks in which multi attackers can launch false information attack in a cooperative style. After one of attackers sends a bogus emergency message, its colluders try to submit bogus evidence to compromise the intrusion detection system for them to obtain inaccurate results.

3.3   Dempster-Shafer Theory

Let $\Theta = \{\omega_1, \omega_2, \ldots \omega_n\}$ be a frame of discernment, in which all elements are assumed to mutually be exclusive and exhaustive. The basic belief assignment (BBA) is a mapping $2^\Theta \mapsto [0, 1]$ defined by:

$$\sum_{A \subseteq \Theta} m(A) = 1 \tag{1}$$

where, $m(A)$ is numerical value which represents the belief assigned to A for any given $A \subseteq \Theta$. The belief function is defined as:

$$\text{bel}(A) = \sum_{\phi \neq B \subseteq A} m(B) \ \forall A \subseteq \Theta \tag{2}$$

where, $bel(A)$ represents the sum of belief in all subsets of A. Given two BBAs m_1 and m_2, a combination operation [21] can be performed on them using the conjunctive combination rule.

$$(m_1 \otimes m_2)(A) = \sum_{B,C \subseteq \Theta, B \cap C = A} m_1(B) m_2(C) \tag{3}$$

A metric distance is used to quantify the degree that two given BBAs are dissimilar. Jousselme et al. [22] proposed a principled metric distance, and a geometrical interpretation of BBA is given. The distance between two BBAs m_1 and m_2, termed by $d_{BBA}(m_1, m_2)$, is defined as follows.

$$d_{BBA}(m_1, m_2) = \sqrt{\frac{1}{2}(\vec{m}_1 - \vec{m}_2)D(\vec{m}_1 - \vec{m}_2)^T} \tag{4}$$

where, D is a matrix and its each element are $D = |A \cap B|/|A \cup B| \ \forall A, B \subseteq \Theta$.

4   Methodology

4.1   Overview of the Proposed Algorithm

Aiming to providing high detection accuracy and enhanced robustness against collusion attacks, we propose a multi-source information fusion based detection scheme which use a two-layer information fusion framework (Fig. 2). The first layer is inner-node fusion in which each single witness vehicle fuses the collected information from its own multiple kinds of on-board sensors and received beacon messages. A witness calculates a BBA representing the degree that this kind of data supports or rejects the received emergency message. Then, all of generated BBAs are combined into a single BBA to represent the vehicle's attitude. Since we assume there may be colluded attackers who can inject false BBAs to support bogus emergency message, a verifying mechanism is necessary to find the BBAs deviated significantly from others.

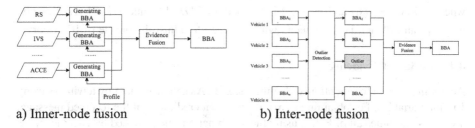

a) Inner-node fusion   b) Inter-node fusion

Fig. 2. Information fusion framework

This work is done in the second layer fusion, in which all BBAs generated by witnesses are combined to make final decision.

4.2 Input Description

We assume there are k available information sources for each vehicle, denoted by $S = \{s_1, s_2 \ldots s_k\}$. In practice, the following variables can be exploited to characterize traffic condition: **Related Speed (RS)** is the speed different between the current vehicle and the vehicle on its front, **Inter-Vehicle Spacing (IVS)** is the distance between a vehicle to its neighbors ahead, and **Acceleration: (ACCE)** is the speed change of a vehicle on a time window.

4.3 Creation of Belief

Let $\Theta = \{H, F\}$ be a discernment frame, in which H and F represent the received message is honest and false respectively. The basic belief assignment can be defined as $m : P(\{T, F\}) \to [0, 1]$, $m(\varnothing) = 0$. Where, $m(\{H\})$ and $m(\{F\})$ represent the masses that the observation data of witness supports a positive or negative result respectively, and $m(\{H, F\})$ represents the credibility of the received message which cannot be determined only depending on the available observation data. We use a *mean deviation function* to quantify the degree that a traffic variable deviates its value under normal pattern. Let X is a random variable, if its expectation $E(x)$ and standard variance σ_X exists, the mean deviation function $\xi(X)$ can be defined as

$$\xi(x) = \frac{|x - E(x)|}{\sigma_X} \tag{5}$$

By using of Eq. (6), a witness vehicle can create a BBA m for traffic variable s_i to represent its attitude on the credibility of the received message.

$$\begin{cases} m_H(s_i) = \exp(-\gamma^1 \xi(s_i)^{\beta^2}) \\ m_F(s_i) = \exp(-\gamma^2 \xi(s_i)^{\beta^2}) \\ m_{F,H}(s_i) = 1 - m(F) - m(H) \end{cases} \tag{6}$$

where, $m_H(s_i)$, $m_F(s_i)$ and $m_{F,H}(s_i)$ is the belief of $\{H\}$, $\{F\}$ and $\{H, F\}$ respectively. $\gamma^1, \beta^1, \gamma^2$ and β^2 are the parameters which is used to adjust the profile of BBA curve.

4.4   Fusion of Evidence

According to the aforementioned definitions, k BBAs can be created by a witness using k traffic variables. For obtaining a final decision on credibility of the received message, a witness combines all of BBAs using the combination rule provided by D-S theory, as shown in Eq. (3):

$$m = \sum_{j=1}^{k} \otimes m_j \tag{7}$$

Here, m can be considered as the attitude of a witness vehicle on credibility of the recipient emergency message. Each witness broadcasts its BBA to its neighbors, and it also receives BBAs sent by each of their neighbors. Then, it fuses all of received and its own BBAs by a combination operation given in Eq. (7), and its output is denoted by m^*. Finally, we use maximum belief rule to as the decision-making approach. The detailed algorithm is given in Table 1.

Table 1. The proposed detection algorithm

Algorithm 1: Detection Algorithm
1   **for** each **msg** received **do**
2   update v_i, p_i
3   update v_{i-1}, p_{i-1}
4   calculate s_1, s_2, ... s_k
5   **for** i=1 **to** k **do**
6   calculate BBA m_i
7   combinate k BBAs get m^*
8   **if** max[m*]=$m\{H\}$
9   accept data
10   **else if** max[m*]=$m\{F\}$
11   reject data
12   **else**
14   report node

Since we assume there may be colluded adversaries among the witnesses to inject bogus BBAs to support the false emergency message, BBAs received by a witness should be evaluated before being combined. Firstly, a distance metric $d_{BBA}(m_i, m_j)$ can be used to quantify the dissimilarity between any two given BBAs provided by witness i and j according to Eq. (4) in which a high value represents two BBAs are largely deviated to each other. Then, we use density based outlier detection algorithm DBSCAN [23] to filter out the BBAs deviated largely from of others, the remains BBAs are use in the second layer fusion.

5 Simulation and Results Analysis

In this section, we turn the proposed approach into a simulation to evaluate its performance from three aspects: accuracy, delay, and robustness against collusion attacks. Besides, we compare it with existing threshold based scheme proposed in [12]. We employ the traffic simulation software SUMO to build realistic traffic scenario and generate vehicular traces. The proposed algorithm is implemented on a NS-2 simulator. The *detection rate* (DR) is defined as the probability that a bogus message is successively detected. The *false positive rate* (FPR) is the probability that an honest message is detected as a false one. The *detection delay* (DD) is the time span from the time the message is sent to it is detected successively. We investigate the impact of the vehicular density, the number of lanes, and number of the blocked lanes on the performance of the proposed algorithm. The vehicular density ranges from 10 to 100 vehicles/km/lane.

Firstly, we evaluate DR of the proposed approach under various level of traffic stress with various numbers of lanes (NL) and blocked lanes (NBL). Figure 3 shows the DR of with various vehicular densities. Firstly, we observed that NL and NBL have significant impact on the performance of the proposed approach. In general, more blocked lanes, higher DR is achieved. DR is significantly lower when only one lane is block. It is mainly because that NBL has a significant impact on the degree of traffic disturbance phenomenon. The similar trend can be seen in Fig. 4. FPR is high under one blocked lane scenarios. Moreover, DR under middle vehicular density is higher than other density settings.

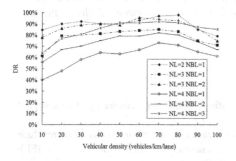 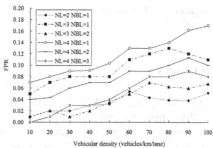

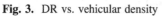

Fig. 3. DR vs. vehicular density   **Fig. 4.** FPR vs. vehicular density

In Fig. 5, we evaluate the performance of the proposed algorithm under various percentage of attackers and compare it with the threshold-based scheme. We observe that the DR of the proposed algorithm only slightly decreases with increasing percentage of attackers. In comparison, DR of the threshold based scheme decrease significantly under high attacker percentage, since it is incapable for detecting effectively colluded attackers. Figure 6 shows the DD of the proposed algorithm under various vehicular densities. We notice that detection delay increase at approximately linear speed. Under maximum density of 100 vehicles/km/lane, the delay reaches 1900 ms.

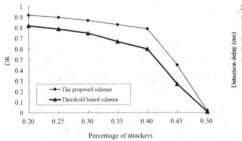

Fig. 5. DR vs. percentage of attackers

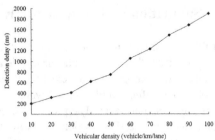

Fig. 6. Detection delay

6 Conclusion

Aiming to providing high detection accuracy and enhanced robustness against collusion attacks, we propose a multi-source information fusion based detection algorithm that uses a two-layer information fusion framework. The first layer is responsible to fuse information from multiple kinds of on-board sensors and received beacon messages, and create a belief on credibility of the emergency message. The second layer integrates an outlier detection mechanism which is used to detect colluded attacker and improve detection accuracy. We evaluate the performance of the proposed algorithm by simulation experiment. The results prove higher significant average detection rate can be achieved by our algorithm comparing to the existing threshold based scheme.

Acknowledgement. This work was partially supported by Chinese National Natural Science Foundation (U1504614) and Key Research Project of Higher Education of Henan Province (18A520052).

References

1. Hartenstein, H.: VANET: Vehicular Applications and Inter-Networking Technologies. Wiley, Chichester (2010)
2. De Fabritiis, C., Ragona, R., Valenti, G.: Traffic estimation and prediction based on real time floating car data. In: Proceedings of the 11th International IEEE Conference on IEEE Intelligent Transportation Systems, pp. 197–203 (2008)

3. Raya, M., Hubaux, J.P.: Securing vehicular ad hoc networks. J. Comput. Secur. Spec. Issue Secur. Ad Hoc Sensor Netw. **15**(1), 39–68 (2007)

4. IEEE Std. 1609.2-2013: IEEE Standard for Wireless Access in Vehicular Environments Security Services for Applications and Management Messages, April 2013. http://standards. ieee.org/ndstds/standard/1609.2-2013.html

5. Thajchayapong, S., Garcia-Trevino, E.S., Barria, J.A.: Distributed classification of traffic anomalies using microscopic traffic variables. IEEE Trans. Intell. Transp. Syst. **14**(1), 448–458 (2013)

6. Pan, T.L., Sumalee, A., Zhong, R.X.: Short-term traffic state prediction based on temporal-spatial correlation. IEEE Trans. Intell. Transp. Syst. **14**(3), 1242–1254 (2013)

7. Golle, P., Greene, D., Staddon, J.: Detecting and correcting malicious data in VANETs. In: Proceedings of the 1st ACM International Workshop on Vehicular Ad Hoc Networks, pp. 29–37. ACM (2004)

8. Ghosh, M., Varghese, A., Gupta, A., Kherani, A.A., Muthaiah, S.N.: Detecting misbehaviors in VANET with integrated root-cause analysis. Ad Hoc Netw. **8**(7), 778–790 (2010)

9. Abumansoor, O., Boukerche, A.: Towards a secure trust model for vehicular ad hoc networks services. In: Proceedings of the Global Telecommunications Conference (GLOBECOM 2011), pp. 1–5. IEEE (2011)

10. Wu, Q., Domingo-Ferrer, J., Gonzalez-Nicolas, U.: Balanced trustworthiness, safety, and privacy in vehicle-to-vehicle communications. IEEE Trans. Veh. Technol. **59**(2), 559–573 (2010)

11. Raya, M., Papadimitratos, P., Aad, I., Jungels, D.: Eviction of misbehaving and faulty nodes in vehicular networks. IEEE J. Sel. Areas Commun. **25**(8), 1557–1568 (2007)

12. Chen, L., Ng, S.L., Wang, G.: Threshold anonymous announcement in VANETs. IEEE J. Sel. Areas Commun. **29**(3), 605–615 (2011)

13. Ruj, S., Cavenaghi, M.A., Huang, Z., Nayak, A., Stojmenovic, I.: On data-centric misbehavior detection in VANETs. In: Proceedings of the 2011 IEEE Vehicular Technology Conference, pp. 1–5. IEEE (2011)

14. Wu, A., Ma, J., Zhang, S.: RATE: a RSU-aided scheme for data-centric trust establishment in VANETs. In: Proceedings of the 2011 7th International Conference on Wireless Communications, Networking and Mobile Computing (WiCOM), pp. 1–6. IEEE (2011)

15. Li, Q., Malip, A., Martin, K.M., Siaw, N.G., Zhang, J.: A reputation-based announcement scheme for VANETs. IEEE Trans. Veh. Technol. **61**(9), 4095–4108 (2012)

16. Dhurandher, S.K., Obaidat, M.S., Jaiswal, A., Tiwari, A., Tyagi, A.: Vehicular security through reputation and plausibility checks. IEEE Syst. J. **8**(2), 384–394 (2014)

17. Sedjelmaci, H., Senouci, S.M.: A new intrusion detection framework for vehicular networks. In: Proceedings of the 2014 IEEE International Conference on Communications (ICC), pp. 538–543. IEEE (2014)

18. Dietzel, S., Gürtler, J., Heijden, R.V.D., et al.: Redundancy-based statistical analysis for insider attack detection in VANET aggregation schemes. In: Vehicular Networking Conference, pp. 135–142. IEEE (2014)

19. Wang, J., Zhang, Y., Wang, Y., et al.: RPRep: a robust and privacy-preserving reputation management scheme for pseudonym-enabled VANETs. Int. J. Distrib. Sens. Netw. **12**(3), 1–15 (2016)

20. Al Falasi, H., Mohamed, N., El-Syed, H.: Similarity-based trust management system: data validation scheme. In: Abraham, A., Han, S.Y., Al-Sharhan, S.A., Liu, H. (eds.) Hybrid Intelligent Systems. AISC, vol. 420, pp. 141–153. Springer, Cham (2016). https://doi.org/10. 1007/978-3-319-27221-4_12

21. Mahler, R.P.S.: Statistical Multi Source-Multi Target Information Fusion. Artech House Inc., Norwood (2007)
22. Jousselme, A.L., Grenier, D., Bossé, É.: A new distance between two bodies of evidence. Inf. Fusion **2**(2), 91–101 (2001)
23. Birant, D., Kut, A.: ST-DBSCAN: an algorithm for clustering spatial–temporal data. Data Knowl. Eng. **60**(1), 208–221 (2007)

A Synchronization Detection and Time Delay Estimation Algorithm Based on Fractional Fourier Transform

Yu Deng[1], Fei Yuan[1(✉)], En Cheng[1], Jinwang Yi[2], and Ye Li[3]

[1] Key Laboratory of Underwater Acoustic Communication and Marine
Information Technology, Ministry of Education, Xiamen University, Xiamen,
Fujian, China
yuanfei@xmu.edu.cn
[2] Xiamen University of Technology, Xiamen, Fujian, China
[3] Shandong Computer Science Center
(National Supercomputer Center in Jinan), Jinan, Shandong, China

Abstract. Synchronization signal detection and time delay estimation are worth studying in underwater acoustic positioning. This paper proposes a signal capture algorithm first, which uses matching filter method with an adaptive dynamic threshold calculated by real time orthogonal sliding correlation. Fractional Fourier Transform (FRFT) is used to re-examine signals over the adaptive threshold and eliminate the false alarm signal for its characteristics which can separate signal and noise at a proper fractional order. Moreover, FRFT is also used to correct the time delay with its characteristics of time shift and frequency shift. The experiment result shows that the algorithm proposed decreases the false alarm probability and time delay error effectively.

Keywords: Fractional Fourier Transform · Adaptive dynamic threshold
Time delay estimation · Underwater acoustic positioning

1 Introduction

The time delay estimation is a critical parameter in underwater acoustic positioning. Traditional underwater acoustic positioning system typically sets a static threshold to capture synchronization signal at the underwater acoustic receiver based on the matching filter method, and estimates distance based on the time delay between the anchor node and the positioned node [1, 2]. However, static thresholds may prove insufficient in underwater environment as the underwater acoustic channel can be highly variable. Besides, conventional method usually sets a static threshold which is insufficient to capture synchronization signal, in another word, which may increase the missed detection possibility or increase the false alarm probability [3, 4], and then affect the time delay evaluating eventually. Therefore, this paper proposes an algorithm to detect synchronization signal and estimate the time delay based on Fractional Fourier Transform. The simulation results show that the algorithm proposed reduces the false alarm probability and time delay error effectively which is more adapt to the complicated and variable underwater environment.

© Springer Nature Singapore Pte Ltd. 2018
J. Li et al. (Eds.): CWSN 2017, CCIS 812, pp. 201–210, 2018.
https://doi.org/10.1007/978-981-10-8123-1_18

The rest of this paper is organized as follows: In Sect. 2, we will describe the system model of this paper. Then, in Sect. 3, we will introduce the background knowledge of the detection scheme in detail, explain how to detect synchronization signal with FRFT re-examination and correct time delay. Following that, we will present simulation result in Sect. 4. Finally, we will draw conclusions according to it.

2   System Model

Figure 1 shows a block diagram of the synchronization detection and time delay estimation algorithm based on FRFT. The algorithm mainly consists of two parts: the upper part of the diagram uses matching filter principle, setting the adaptive dynamic threshold to capture the synchronization signal; the second part of the diagram can re-examine the synchronization results and then correct the time delay error based on FRFT characteristics, which can achieve good separation between signal and noise at an appropriate order.

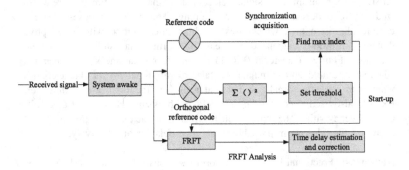

Fig. 1. The block diagram of the algorithm

According to the block diagram of the algorithm shown in Fig. 1, the overall process of the algorithm includes the following operations:

1. When the system is awakened, the received signal is firstly matched by convolution on the upper branch, and the orthogonal correlation result is used as an adaptive dynamic threshold to capture the synchronization signal.
2. When the correlation result exceeds to the adaptive dynamic threshold, the FRFT re-examination is initiated immediately.
3. Re-examine the captured synchronization signal, if the signal captured is judged as a false alarm signal, this signal would be eliminated in this step, and return to step 1 to continue convolution calculation; if the synchronization signal passes the re-examination, then fixes the time delay error according to the FRFT characteristics of the peak offset.

Traditional matching filter method typically sets a static estimated threshold in the time domain. However, static thresholds may prove insufficient in underwater environment as the underwater acoustic channel can be highly variable, the possibility of missing synchronization signal would increase if the static threshold is too high, and the possibility of capturing false alarm signal would increase if the static threshold is too low. In order to solve the problem of static threshold, we propose to use a signal capture algorithm which can capture synchronization signal using matching filter method with an adaptive dynamic threshold calculated by real time orthogonal sliding correlation. FRFT re-examination would be started up immediately to judge whether it is false alarm signal or not, when corresponding result exceeds to the dynamic threshold. Since FRFT can separate signal and noise in an appropriate fractional order, we can analyze the captured synchronization result and eliminate the false alarm signal effectively, and correct the time delay error according to the peak offset. The missed detection and false alarm possibility can be improved effectively with the coordination of matching filter method and FRFT analysis. Since the calculation cost of matching filter method is lower than FRFT, the algorithm proposed can save system energy as well.

3 Synchronization Signal Detection and Correction Based on FRFT

Capturing synchronization accurately is the key issue of underwater acoustic communication, its essence is to judge when the synchronization arrives, by comparing the decision statistic with the preset threshold. Currently, the synchronization signal is typically added before the valid data in underwater acoustic communication [5, 6], and Linearly Frequency Modulated (LFM) is widely used in the synchronization of underwater acoustic communication because of its anti-Doppler effect and good autocorrelation characteristics [5, 7].

Traditional synchronization method is to set a static threshold according to the noise level of the channel, which cannot meet the requirements of communication quality for modern people [8]. Therefore, choosing the appropriate decision statistic and decision threshold will be a key factor that affects the system performance. To solve this problem, this paper proposes a synchronization detection and time delay estimation algorithm based on FRFT. The algorithm is divided into two parts, the first part is based on matching filter method, and the next part of the FRFT analysis and calculation will be started up when the matching result exceeds to the adaptive dynamic threshold. The FRFT re-examination will be used to eliminate the false alarm signal after that. The algorithm uses Two-Part structure in conjunction, and solves the contradiction between the possibility of missing detection and false alarm signal effectively, obtains a better synchronization detection result.

3.1 Synchronization Signal Capture

The received signal consists of two parts: signal and noise. The signal is expressed as a LEM sequence. The noise is expressed as the Gaussian white noise with mean 0 and the variance n_0:

$$R(t) = x(t - \tau) + n(\tau) \tag{1}$$

For traditional matching filter method, the cross-correlation result between the received signal and the local replicated signal includes both signal correlation result and the noise correlation result, as shown in Eq. (2). So we find the maximum value of the cross-correlation peak, then compare the peak with a static threshold, which is set according to the noise level of underwater environment. If the peak is higher than the static threshold, we think the synchronization work is successful; otherwise, the synchronization signal hasn't been captured. Since the underwater acoustic channel can be highly variable, static threshold cannot meet the requirement of communication quality. This paper uses orthogonal correlation result as an adaptive dynamic threshold, which is shown in Eq. (3). We can see that, the cross-corresponding result of valid signal and orthogonal reference sequence is 0, the cross-correlation result between the orthogonal reference sequence and the received signal contains solely noise correlation result. We set the adaptive dynamic threshold according to the real-time orthogonal correlation results. It can dynamically estimate underwater noise and adapt to the underwater acoustic channel environment better.

$$C(t) = R(t) * r(t) = \sum_{j=0}^{N-1} R'(t)r(t+j) = \sum_{j=0}^{N-1} x'(t - \tau)r(t+j) + \sum_{j=0}^{N-1} n'(t)r(t+j) \tag{2}$$

$$C_0(t) = R(t) * r_0(t) = \sum_{j=0}^{N-1} R'(t)r_0(t+j) = \sum_{j=0}^{N-1} n'(t)r_0(t+j) \tag{3}$$

Where $C(t)$ is the cross-correlation value of received signal $R(t)$ and local replicated signal $r(t)$, $C_0(t)$ is the cross-correlation value of received signal $R(t)$ and local orthogonal reference sequence $r_0(t)$ [9].

By comparing the Eq. (2) with Eq. (3), we can evaluate the real-time noise level of underwater acoustic channel according to the adaptive dynamic threshold based on Eq. (3). If the result of the cross-correlation exceeds to the dynamic threshold, it probably indicates the synchronization signal arrives, then we need start up FRFT re-examination to judge whether the valid synchronization signal arrives, and eliminate the interference of false alarm signals.

3.2   FRFT Analysis and Correction

Re-examination of Synchronization Signal Based on FRFT

Recently, FRFT is applied extensively to separate the overlapping LFM signals in signal processing application. For a given LFM signal (frequency slope is constant), there is a fractional order to achieve a good signal and noise separation, so that the energy of LFM gathers at a maximum value. Therefore, depending on the fractional aggregation characteristics of LFM signal, we can detect signal effectively. At the same time, FRFT also has frequency shift characteristics, which is suitable for detecting with LFM signal with Doppler frequency offset.

The p-order FRFT can be defined as the following linear integral form:

$$X_p(u) = \int\limits_{-\infty}^{+\infty} \tilde{K}_p(u,t)x(t)dt \tag{4}$$

Where $K_p(u,t) = A_\alpha e^{\left[j\pi(u^2 \cot\alpha - 2utcsc\alpha + t^2\cot\alpha)\right]}$, $A_\alpha = \sqrt{1 - jcot\alpha}$, $\alpha = \frac{p\pi}{2}$, $p \neq 2n$, n is an integer.

The variable substitution can be simplified as:

$$X_p(u) = \sqrt{\frac{1 - j\cot\alpha}{2\pi}} e^{\frac{\cot\alpha u^2}{2}} \int\limits_{-\infty}^{+\infty} e^{-j\csc\alpha ut} e^{\frac{\cot\alpha t^2}{2}} x(t)dt \tag{5}$$

When the chirp signal frequency $k = -\cot\alpha = \cot\left(\frac{p\pi}{2}\right)$,

$$X_p(u) = A_\alpha e^{j\pi u^2 \cot\alpha} \delta(u - f_0 \sin\alpha) \tag{6}$$

When the frequency of chirp matches with the order of FRFT, chirp signal exhibits obvious impulse peak characteristic in p-order FRFT domain. Based on FRFT fractional aggregation characteristics, the other branch of the algorithm is designed to eliminate the false alarm signal, as shown in Fig. 2.

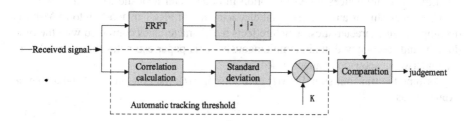

Fig. 2. The schematic diagram of FRFT re-examination

U is the square of the module value of the received sequence after FRFT operations at the corresponding order. Where $F(p)$ is the FRFT result of the LFM signal, $F(n)$ is the FRFT result of the noise. Let the noise-related $2|F(p)F(n)| + F^2(n) = N_1$, then equation can be simplified as:

$$U = |F(p) + F(n)|^2 = F^2(p) + 2|F(p)F(n)| + F^2(n) = F^2(p) + N_1 \tag{7}$$

$$R = std(R_{st}) \tag{8}$$

Where R_{st} is the signal cross-correlation result, R is the standard deviation of R_{st}. The synchronization detection can be simplified as a comparison of U and KR, if $U > KR$ means synchronization signal arrives, otherwise we think that synchronization signal has not yet arrived, and continue to search until successful detection of synchronization sequence. Where K is a scale factor and can be determined according to the actual situation.

When the LFM signal arrives at the receiver, its FRFT will exhibit energy aggregation and have a waveform similar to the correlation peak. Therefore, the cross-correlation result is used as the decision threshold, its standard deviation can reflect its peak characteristic and we convert it to the same window-length as FRFT, so the peak of FRFT will exceed to the threshold, when the most part of the effective signal locates in the window. According to the above analysis, we can re-examine the synchronization signal.

Time Delay Correction Based on FRFT

In the above, we set an adaptive dynamic threshold based on matching filter method and make re-examination according to FRFT characteristic, which improves the accuracy of synchronization signal detection and reduces the probability of false alarm signal detection and missing detection greatly. After that, we further utilize the characteristics of FRFT to estimate the time delay in the underwater acoustic channel.

In actual work, the length of received signal is generally longer than that of local replica signal. We utilize the length of replica signal as a sliding window length, to process the longer received signal, so it is hard to make the synchronization signal completely align with the sliding window start point, and the effective signal is generally spanning several adjacent windows. Therefore, there is a certain time delay error between the start point of capturing sliding window and the actual signal arrival point, this time delay influences time calculation in underwater acoustic location as well.

Frequency shift is another essential characteristic of FRFT in addition to LFM-basis decomposition characteristics, which reflects the characteristics combined with the time domain and frequency domain simultaneously. This paper estimates the time delay in the underwater acoustic channel based on it.

Assume the transmit signal is $x(t)$ and noise is $n(t)$, then the received signal can be expressed as

$$R(t) = A_0 x(t - \tau_0) e^{j2\pi\varepsilon_0(t-\tau_0)} + \sum_{i=1}^{N-1} A_i x(t - \tau_i) e^{j2\pi\varepsilon_i(t-\tau_i)} + n(t) \qquad (9)$$

Where A_0 is direct path attenuation coefficient, A_i is the attenuation coefficient of i th path, N is intrinsic line number, τ_0 is the time delay of direct path, τ_i is the time delay of i th path, ε_0 is Doppler frequency offset of direct path, ε_i is Doppler frequency offset of i th path. The FRFT of Eq. (9) is:

$$R_p(u) = A_0 X_p(u - \varepsilon_0 \sin\alpha - \tau_0 \cos\alpha) \exp\left(j\pi\tau_0^2 \sin\alpha\cos\alpha - j2\pi(u - \varepsilon_0 \sin\alpha)\tau_0 \sin\alpha\right)$$
$$\exp\left(-j\pi\varepsilon_0^2 \sin\alpha\cos\alpha - j2\pi u\varepsilon_0\cos\alpha\right) + \sum_{i=1}^{N-1} A_i X_P(u - \varepsilon_i \sin\alpha - \tau_i \cos\alpha) \qquad (10)$$
$$\exp\left(-j\pi\varepsilon_i^2 \sin\alpha\cos\alpha - j2\pi u\varepsilon_i\cos\alpha\right) \exp\left(j\pi\tau_i^2 \sin\alpha\cos\alpha - j2\pi(u - \varepsilon_i \sin\alpha)\tau_i \sin\alpha\right)$$

It can be seen from the Eq. (10), the FRFT module value of received signal is $|R_p(u)|^2$, when the best fractional order is p, which forms a series of peaks in the corresponding u domain. The direct path acoustic coordinates shifts $\varepsilon_0 \sin \alpha + \tau_0 \cos \alpha$ relative to standard direct acoustic coordinates, the peak of the multipath signal shifts $\varepsilon_i \sin \alpha + \tau_i \cos \alpha$ (i = 1, ..., N – 1) [10], relative to the direct path. When there is no Doppler shift, the direct path acoustic coordinates shifts $\tau_0 \cos \alpha$ relative to the standard direct acoustic coordinates [11]. Therefore, the time delay can be expressed as:

$$\Delta t = \frac{\Delta u}{\cos \alpha} \ or \ \Delta t = \frac{\Delta u - \varepsilon_0 sin\alpha}{cos\alpha} \tag{11}$$

Where $\alpha = \frac{p\pi}{2}$, the value of p is a discrete normalized value when making Matlab discrete calculation.

4 Simulation Experiment

In order to evaluate the performance of the algorithm, the algorithm is simulated in the Bellhop multipath channel model. In the simulations, the parameters of detection signal and the Bellhop channel are shown in Table 1. The channel model with Gaussian white noise is shown in Fig. 3.

Table 1. Simulation parameters

LFM signal parameters		Bellhop model related parameters	
Frequency band (kHz)	20–30	Launch distance (m)	1000
Duration (s)	0.2	Send transducer depth (m)	10
Sampling rate (Hz)	102400	Receive transducer depth (m)	10
		Send signal center frequency (Hz)	25000

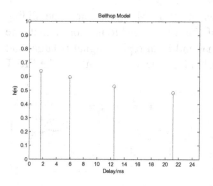

Fig. 3. Bellhop channel model

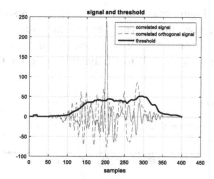

Fig. 4. The simulation of adaptive dynamic threshold

Figure 4 shows the simulation diagram of adaptive dynamic threshold, the dotted line in the figure represents the orthogonal correlation result, and the solid line represents the matching correlation result. The result shows that the dynamic adaptive threshold performs well in evaluating the level of noise, it changes with the noise in underwater acoustic channel, the correlation results are basically below the threshold, which meet the requirements of adaptive dynamic threshold. When the suspected synchronization signal appears, the correlation result is much higher than the threshold, we think that suspected synchronization signal has been captured and start up FRFT detection immediately to re-examine whether or not it is false alarm signal.

We compare the different performances on Matlab both when false alarm signal comes and effective signal comes. As the sliding window shown in Fig. 5, most of the noise signal is filtered by the adaptive dynamic threshold. However, due to the disturbance of the noise, the peak of noise sometimes exceeds to the dynamic threshold, so system starts up re-examination to filter out the false alarm signal. As Fig. 5(b) shows, the peak obtained by FRFT is far lower than the threshold, and the false alarm signal is successfully eliminated at this step.

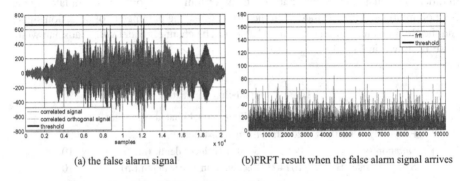

(a) the false alarm signal   (b)FRFT result when the false alarm signal arrives

Fig. 5. Eliminating the false alarm signal

Figure 6(a) shows the simulation results when the LFM signal enters the sliding window. In this case, due to the presence of the valid synchronization signal, the cross-correlation result of synchronization signal and local replica signal is large, and the peak exceeds to the dynamic adaptive threshold, so the system starts up the FRFT

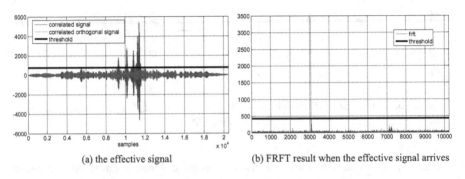

(a) the effective signal   (b) FRFT result when the effective signal arrives

Fig. 6. Capturing the effective signal

re-examination. As Fig. 6(b) shows, the FRFT calculation filters out most of the noise and it has the impulse peak characteristic, so we can determine that the synchronization signal arrives.

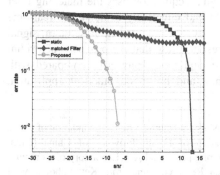

Fig. 7. Comparison of false alarm probabilities of different synchronization signal detection algorithms

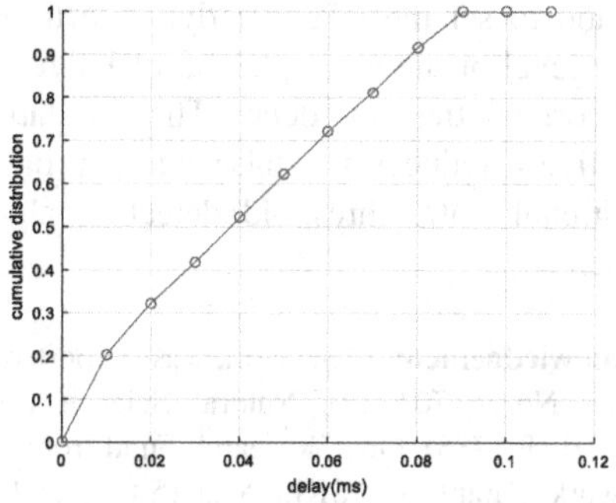

Fig. 8. Error distribution probability

Figure 7 shows comparison of false alarm probabilities of three types of synchronization detection algorithms under different signal-to-noise ratio, including static threshold detection method, matched filter method with adaptive dynamic threshold detection and the algorithm proposed in this paper. It can be seen that the traditional one performs badly when signal-to-noise ratio is poor, because it is difficult to distinguish whether the signal arrives or not. When the signal-to-noise ratio is higher than a certain value, the false alarm probability of the algorithm decreases rapidly because the peak of noise is mostly lower than the threshold value. Therefore, the algorithm is not adaptable. The adaptive dynamic threshold algorithm adjusts the real time threshold according to the size of the noise power, and it has better performance than the static threshold algorithm when the SNR is poor. However, since the threshold setting is related to the noise power, when SNR is high, false alarm phenomenon can't be eliminated completely, influenced by noise disturbance phenomenon, and the possibility of false alarm signal approaches at a certain value.

The algorithm proposed in this paper combines the adaptive dynamic threshold algorithm and FRFT algorithm. It has better performance both in the case of poor SNR and great SNR, when the SNR is greater than −10 dB, the probability of false alarm of proposed algorithm is less than 0.1.

The difference between the synchronized position and the ideal position is the synchronization error. It can be visually seen by the error distribution probability in Fig. 8: after the time delay correction, the time delay can be controlled in 0.1 ms range, which can effectively improve the accuracy of underwater acoustic position.

5 Conclusions

In this paper, a synchronization detection and time delay estimation algorithm is proposed. The algorithm is divided into two parts: synchronous signal acquisition and FRFT re-examination. The synchronization signal acquisition uses the matching filter method to set the adaptive dynamic threshold and effectively evaluate the real-time noise level of the channel. The FRFT re-examination eliminates the false alarm signal and corrects the time delay. The simulation results show that the proposed algorithm effectively reduces the false alarm probability and time delay error compared with traditional static threshold detection algorithm, and has good practical application value.

Acknowledgement. This work was supported by National Natural Science Foundation of China (Grant No. 61701422), Natural Science Foundation of Fujian Province of China (Grant No. 2017J01785), Open Research Fund from Shandong provincial Key Laboratory of Computer Network (Grant No. SKLCN-2015-01), and Open Research Fund from Key Laboratory of Underwater Acoustic Communication and Marine Information Technology Ministry of Education (Xiamen University) (Grant No. 201602).

References

1. Quan, Y., et al.: An adaptive threshold detection algorithm for linearly-frequency modulated signals based on signal power in underwater acoustic communication. Appl. Acoust. **32**(2), 116–121 (2013)
2. Hu, K.-X., Hu, A.-M.: Characteristic analysis of linearly-frequency modulated signal. Space Electron. Technol. **4**(1), 56–59 (2007)
3. Huang, W.-Q.: Study on signal detection and adaptive threshold in digital receiver. Diss., Chongqing University (2010)
4. Wu, Y.-C., Chen, T.T.: Adaptive threshold detection scheme in gliding window. J. Syst. Simul. **20**(10), 2770–2773 (2008)
5. Sun, W.-Q: Studies on underwater acoustic localization technique in shallow water and its application. Diss., Ocean University of China (2007)
6. Dai, R.-T., Wang, Q.-C: The development and application of modern underwater acoustic communications. Sci. Mosaic, 241–242 (2008)
7. Chen, K.-Y.: A survey on for underwater wireless sensor network technology. Diss., Xiamen University (2013)
8. Huang, Y.-W.: Research on long-range source localization by matched field processing in shallow water. Diss., Harbin Engineering University (2005)
9. Li, Y., et al.: A new hardware design scheme of symbol synchronization for an underwater acoustic receiver. IEEE (2011)
10. Yang, G.: Research on multi-parameter estimation algorithm of underwater acoustic channel based on FRFT. Diss., Ocean University of China (2010)
11. Yin, J.-W., Hui, J.-Y., Cai, P., Wang, Y.-L.: Underwater acoustic channel parameter estimation based on fractional Fourier transforms. Syst. Eng. Electron. **27**(71), 486–489 (2007)

Segment Clustering Based Privacy Preserving Algorithm for Trajectory Data Publishing

Li Fengyun[1(✉)], Xue Junchao[1], Sun Dawei[2], and Gao Yanfang[1]

[1] School of Computer Science and Technology, Northeastern University,
Shenyang 110819, China
lifengyun@mail.neu.edu.cn
[2] School of Information Engineering,
China University of Geosciences, Beijing 100083, China

Abstract. In recent years, privacy preserving data publishing has become a hot research point in the area of privacy preserving. The (k, δ)-anonymity model exploited the inherent uncertainty of the trajectory acquisition system, but could not consider the case that the uncertain threshold of trajectory was variable in practical applications. Therefore, the (k, δ)-anonymity model was improved, and a (k, Δ)-anonymity model with variable threshold was proposed. Furthermore, in the traditional cluster-constraint based trajectory anonymous algorithm, the whole trajectory was taken as the basic unit for clustering. Although the probability that attacker can identify the trajectory of a specific user can be reduced to $1/k$, the anonymous group was vulnerable to the re-clustering attack as the anonymous group lacks diversity. Aiming at this problem, a segment clustering based trajectory privacy preserving algorithm was proposed. The trajectories were partitioned into segments based on the principle of Minimum Description Length. And then, these segments were made anonymous based on the cluster-constraint strategy. Simulation results show that the proposed method can improve the security, and have better performance in terms of data quality and data availability.

Keywords: Privacy preserving · Trajectory data publishing
Segment clustering · Uncertainty · Trajectory anonymous

1 Introduction

In recent years, with the increasing popularity of mobile communication technologies, location technologies and location-based services, service providers and research institutes have accumulated a large amount of user trajectory data for research, analysis and distribution [1]. In addition, trajectory data are distributed to the academic institutions and commercial research institutions, for the purpose of exploring the academic value and commercial value of trajectory data, and applying in urban planning, behavioral pattern analysis and business decision-making [2]. The issue of privacy preserving has a great significance in the development of release trajectory data, and has become a hot research point [3]. However, due to the characteristics of large-scale

© Springer Nature Singapore Pte Ltd. 2018
J. Li et al. (Eds.): CWSN 2017, CCIS 812, pp. 211–221, 2018.
https://doi.org/10.1007/978-981-10-8123-1_19

and high-dimensional trajectory data, as well as rich background knowledge, the study of trajectory privacy preserving is facing serious challenge [4, 5].

Over the years, people have done a lot of researches on issues of privacy preserving based on trajectory data [6–9], most of researches are based on the traditional k-anonymity model to disturb trajectory data, release in a manner of generalize or feature. The most commonly used method in trajectory privacy preserving schemes is k-anonymity model. K-anonymity model [10] is a privacy preserving technology that is proposed by Sweeney for relational data. The k-anonymous model divides recorded attributes into quasi-identifier (QI) and sensitive attributes. By anonymizing the quasi-identifier of each record in the database, there is any record in the database which has the same quasi-identifier with k–1 records at least [11]. For k-anonymization of relational data sets, generalization and suppression techniques are commonly used, which eventually reduces the probability that attackers use quasi-identifiers to identify specific users from anonymized databases to 1/k. However, due to the characteristics of high dimension, spatiotemporal correlation and abundant background information of trajectory data, the trajectory data cannot be divided into fixed quasi-identifiers and sensitive attributes. These k-anonymization methods for relational data cannot be effectively applied to the trajectory dataset.

Abul et al. [12] first put forward the problem of converting the anonymity of the trajectory into the clustering constraint of the trajectory, so as to realize the privacy preserving base on k-anonymity, and also put forward the (k, δ)-anonymous model that utilizes uncertainty of the localization system. Abul clusters the trajectories according to the Euclidean distance in the same time period, and obtains a cluster group formed by a plurality of trajectories with similar distances. Then, the trajectories are distorted in the clustering group. Finally, for any one trajectory, there are more than k-1 other trajectories that are the same with it under the uncertainty threshold δ in the processed trajectory dataset. Then, Abul proposed the improved W4M algorithm, which replaced the Euclidean distance used as the similarity function of trajectory clustering by using EDR. They improved the deficiency of Euclidean distance requiring that each trajectory should be defined in the same time interval, so that the trajectories of different time range can be clustered together, combining with a cluster group.

Saygin [13] also takes the strategy of first cluster and then constraints. Firstly, clustering trajectories, and then generalized releasing each trajectory cluster group. In each clustering group, the generalized publishing means that every position point is covered by a rectangular area in each sampling time, and only publishing the generalized track which are composed of the rectangular areas. In addition, this scheme also aims at the generalized intersections attack which may exist in the generalization of trajectory cluster group, and proposes the publish strategy of disturbance while publishing rein trajectory cluster groups. Although this algorithm has a high degree of privacy preserving, it can only support simple aggregation analysis and it is not suitable for other applications, such as behavior pattern discovery and association rules mining.

The above clustering constraint based privacy preserving schemes all take the whole trajectory as a basic unit for clustering [14]. Although the probability that an attacker can identify the trajectory of a particular user according to the specific location information can be reduced to 1/k, they ignored the problem of large trajectory distortion in the constraint process caused by clustering the trajectory as a whole, as well as the problem that the constrained cluster group has insufficient trajectory diversity in the clustering groups after constraints, so they cannot effectively prevent re-clustering attacks.

Aiming at the above problems, a segment clustering based privacy preserving algorithm (UPG for short) is proposed based on the (k, Δ)-anonymous model. In the algorithm, the trajectories are partitioned into segments based on the principle of Minimum Description (MDL for short), and then the segments are anonymized based on clustering constraint strategy.

2 Model Definition

2.1 (k, Δ)-Anonymity Model

Definition 1 ((k, Δ)-anonymity model): Given a trajectory database D in which the uncertainty threshold is variable, the anonymity threshold k, and the uncertainty threshold function Δ: τ → R, (k, Δ)-anonymity model requires that for the trajectory database D which satisfies $\forall \tau \in D$, there exists an anonymity set $S \subseteq D$ containing at least k trajectory and it makes τ∈S. Besides, all the trajectories in S are similar under the conditions of uncertainty threshold. Where the uncertainty threshold of anonymity set S is:

$$\delta_S = \min\{\Delta(\tau)|\tau \in S\} \tag{1}$$

For different uncertain trajectory databases, the uncertainty threshold function Δ: τ → R in the model definition has a variety of different realization forms. In some trajectory database, the uncertain trajectory threshold is determined according to the position the prediction model used during the sampling process. During sampling process, trajectory database determines a consistent uncertainty threshold with the moving objects firstly, and saves it in the trajectory properties, and then stores each trajectory sampling location. The uncertainty threshold function $\Delta(\tau)$ simply queries the property value corresponding to records τ as the uncertainty threshold. In some trajectory database systems, they don't use the prediction model for trajectory sampling. The uncertainty of trajectory is mainly produced by the communication system. In that case, the uncertainty size of each trajectory is mainly related to the communication quality. In such systems, the uncertainty threshold function $\Delta(\tau)$ can obtain the appropriate uncertainty threshold by calculating the distance between the trajectory τ and the base stations in communication system.

2.2 Attack Model

Definition 2 (re-clustering attacks): The re-clustering attacks aim at the published trajectory database that has been clustered and anonymized, by using the same clustering algorithm as the former anonymization process or the same clustering parameters for re-clustering clustering, it may find the cluster group characteristics of original database before publishing, so as to get useful information about the users.

The specific process of the second clustering attack is as follows: Firstly, the attacker uses the same clustering algorithm as the anonymization process to clustering the published anonymous trajectory database. Then, using the background knowledge of the attacking object, identifying the clustering group where the attacking object is located, and establishing the corresponding relationship between the attacking goal and the clustering group. Finally, according to the characteristics of the clustering group, the user's private information is further obtained.

3   Segment Clustering Based Trajectory Data Privacy Preserving Algorithm

3.1   UPG Algorithm Design

UPG algorithm tracks the trajectory in the trajectory database according to the principle of Minimum Description Length, and divides each trajectory into multiple trajectory segments. And then, the algorithm clusters these trajectory segments. In the process of clustering, the UPG algorithm takes these trajectory segments as independent trajectories, and assigns them to multiple cluster groups according to the similarities, so that the trajectories in the same cluster group are similar in distance, and the number of trajectory segments in a group is limited to between k and 2k–1. After the clustering phase, different segments of the same trajectory can be located in different clusters. Finally, the UPG algorithm performs spatial perturbation-based constraint processing on the trajectory segments in the diffident clustering group, so that the trajectory segments are indistinguishable from each other.

UPG algorithm (see Algorithm 1) mainly includes the following three stages:

(1) Trajectory segmenting stage: Based on the trajectory segmenting algorithm, the trajectories in the original trajectory database are segmented based on the MDL principle and according to the trajectory behavior characteristics. And then, the generated trajectories are segmented into multiple equivalent D_T, Each of these equivalence classes consists of the track segments defined at the same time interval.

(2) Trajectory clustering stage: In this stage, the greedy strategy is used to cluster the trajectory segments. The algorithm takes the equivalent D_T as the input, and clusters the trajectories segments in D_T into several clusters. In the meantime, the suppression technique that can enhance the overall effect of clustering is introduced. The trajectories in clustering group are located in a small radius cylinder by deleting some abnormal trajectories after clustering.

(3) Spatial perturbation stage: This stage uses the point-based spatial perturbation technique by moving the positions of a few trajectory nodes in the cluster, so as to transform each cluster group into a corresponding (k, Δ) -anonymous set. In the stage of spatial perturbation, the UPG algorithm maintains the availability of trajectory data as much as possible while satisfying (k, Δ) - anonymity requirements.

Algorithm 1. UPG algorithm.

Input: D, k, δ,π
Output: D'
1. Initialize(*Max_Trash*)
2. $D' \leftarrow \varnothing$
3. $D^{ec} \leftarrow$ UPG_part(D, π)
4. for all $D_T \in D^{ec}$ do
5. if ((|$D_T \geq k$|) do

6. $Trash\_quota(T) \leftarrow \left| \dfrac{D_T}{D} * Max\_Trash \right|$

7. $\gamma \leftarrow$ UPG_clust(D_T, k, Trash_quota(T))
8. $D' \leftarrow D' \cup UPG\_str(\gamma, \Delta)$

The inputs to the UPG algorithm are the original trajectory database D, the anonymous threshold k, the uncertainty threshold function Δ, and the time granularity π. The parameter Max_Trash is used to limit the suppression of abnormal trajectory segments during trajectory segmented clustering, and is defined as the maximum number of deleted track segments. Its value is automatically initialized in the first line of the algorithm (Most of the time, the size is 10% of the size of the trajectory database) (line 1). The database to be released D' is initialized to empty (line 2). First, the UPG algorithm divides the trajectory in the original trajectory database D into several equivalent classes according to the time granularity π (line 3). Then, for each equivalence class whose trajectory segmentation number is greater than k, the UPG algorithm performs clustering. And ensuring that there are at least k trajectories in each cluster group (lines 4–7). Finally, the UPG algorithm performs spatial perturbation on each cluster and re-combines the trajectories for publishing (line 8).

3.2 Trajectory Segmenting Algorithm

The first step of UPG algorithm is to segment the original trajectory database into several equivalence classes. Each equivalence class is composed of the track segments defined at the same time interval. That means each trajectory segment in an equivalence class has the same start time and finish time. In order to solve the weighing problem of accuracy and simplicity, the MDL principle which is widely used in information theory is introduced [15]. The trajectory segment problem is converted into a minimum description length problem to be solved, and can use the least number of segments to describe the characteristics of the trajectory.

If the traditional trajectory segmentation algorithm is used directly in the original trajectory database, the result is usually a large number of trajectory equivalence classes with a very small scale [16]. If doing the clustering constraint operation on these equivalent trajectories which is composed of few trajectory segments, it can only get the poor quality of the anonymous trajectory set. In order to solve the above problems, UPG algorithm improved the traditional trajectory segmentation algorithm, with a small loss of data in exchange for the upgrade of the equivalent class size. In the improved trajectory segmentation algorithm, the integer parameter π is introduced, and only the node whose timestamp is an integral multiple of π can be selected as the sensitive node of the trajectory, while the traditional segmentation algorithm does not consider the dimension of time. For example, if the sampling frequency of the original trajectory data is once per minute, under the condition of $\pi = 60$, only the sampling node at the time of the whole point is selected as the sensitive node. Therefore, in the trajectory segmentation result, the start and end moments of a trajectory segment are all at the time of the integral point.

The algorithm starts from the nodes whose first sampling time is the integer multiple of π. For the sampling nodes located at time interval π, our algorithm calculates the MDL cost of choosing it as feature node and not as a feature node separately. Then, the trajectory segment between the two feature nodes is putted into corresponding equivalence classes. The algorithm abandons those parts of the trajectory located besides the first feature node and the last feature node for simple. At last, all the trajectory segments are putted into corresponding equivalence classes.

3.3   Trajectory Segment Clustering Algorithm

The clustering stage of UPG algorithm adopts the greedy strategy to cluster the trajectories. The trajectory clustering algorithm clusters the trajectories D_T which are defined in the same time interval π into a cluster group, and with a size between k and 2k–1. It uses the Euclidean distance as the similarity (distance) function of the clustering stage. The input of the algorithm is the segmented trajectory set D_T, anonymous threshold k and the maximum number of suppression trajectory $Trash_{max}$, the detailed clustering process is as follows:

Step 1   In the initial stage, initialize the constant max_radius and assign the alternative cluster center set Active to D_T, and randomly select a trajectory from Active as the center trajectory of cluster groups τ_c.

Step 2   Then, select k to 2k–1 trajectories from D_T which is the nearest with τ_c to form a cluster group p_i.

Step 3   If the distances from all trajectories in p_i to the cluster center τ_c are less than the constant max_radius, then the trajectories of p_i will be removed from D_T and Active set, and p_i will be add to the cluster group set γ. Otherwise, remove τ_c from the Active set.

Step 4   If $|D_T| \geq k$ or Active is not null, then turn to Step 2. Otherwise, try to add the remaining trajectories of D_T to nearest cluster group in γ. If the distance from the trajectory to any cluster group is greater than a given constant max_radius, the trajectory will be deleted. Finally, if the number of be deleted trajectories is greater than a given constant max_trash, then go to Step 1 to re-clustering. Otherwise, return to the cluster group set γ.

The greedy algorithm used in the clustering phase cannot guarantee to generate the optimal clustering results. Moreover, since the center locus in Step 1 is randomly selected, the result of the algorithm is random. In practice, the clustering stage is usually limited according to the actual situation of the trajectory database. For example, the distance between the trajectories in the generated clustering group cannot exceed one constant. This constant is expressed as max_radius. The distance between any cluster trajectory and the cluster center trajectory should be less than max_radius. This is to ensure the similarity of clusters and ensure better results in the constraint phase. If the result of clustering does not meet the specified conditions, the algorithm simply discards the result and performs the clustering again until the result of the clustering is met.

4 Experiment

4.1 Experimental Setup

The experiments were performed using the trajectory data generated by a network-based mobile object simulation generator which is provided by Brinkhoff in [17] as experimental data. The generated trajectory dataset used in the experiment consisted of 100000 trajectories and represented Germany Oldenburg City's urban road conditions in one day, so in the experiment the trajectory data set is represented by OLDEN.

Table 1 is the statistical information of the trajectory dataset OLDEN, where MBB_radius (D) represents the length of the diagonal of the smallest covered rectangle in dataset D, |D| represents the number of trajectories, |Dec| represents the equivalence class D_T in dataset D, Max_pop represents the maximum number of trajectories in the equivalence class, Max_time represents the maximum time interval in the dataset, and Size represents the actual size of the data. The constant max_radius used in the clustering phase in the UPG algorithm is the 0.5% of MBB_radius (D).

Table 1. Statistics of OLDEN

Parameter name	Parameter value
MBB_radius(D)	35779.3
|D|	100000
|Dec|	435
Max_pop	3499
Max_time/min	141
Size/Mb	220

All the experiments were performed on a quad-core PC compatible machine with Intel(R) Core(TM) 2 Quad 2.83 GHz processor, 4 GB of RAM, and Windows 7 platform. The algorithm is implemented in C language. In the experiment, the traditional NWA algorithm and the UPG algorithm were respectively used to protect the trajectory database from privacy, and the anonymous results of the algorithm were analyzed and compared from two aspects of data quality and data availability.

4.2 Data Discernibility

Data Discernibility (DM for short) is an important indicator of the quality of data in anonymous databases. It represents the indistinguishable degree between each of the data elements in the results of the original database after anonymous treatment. In order to compare the DM of the anonymous result between UPG algorithm and NWA algorithm, the experimental dataset D is anonymized separately. The parameters of UPG algorithm are as follows: the minimum threshold number of trajectories in a single anonymous group is k, the time interval $\pi = 5$, the uncertainty threshold function $\Delta(t) \in [100,500]$, and the uncertainty threshold δ of NWA is fixed at 200. Figure 1 shows the test results of DM obtained by UPG algorithm and NWA algorithm.

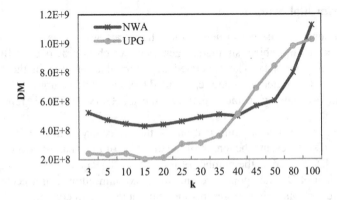

Fig. 1. DM of anonymity result

As can be seen from Fig. 1, the DM values of NWA and UPG both increase with the increase of k. This is because the size of anonymous group increases with the increase of k, the anonymous group size $|p_i|$ increases continually and in the anonymous result more elements become indistinguishable. Under the condition that k is less than 40, the DM of anonymous result is kept at a very low level, which is obviously better than NWA algorithm. This is because clustering constraints after segmentation can effectively solve the problem of unitary feature in the anonymous group. Even if the clustering constraint operation makes the trajectory segmentation in the anonymous group become indistinguishable, the trajectories made up of the various segments can still be distinguished from each other. However, when the value of k is greater than 40, more trajectory segments will be deleted as the value of k increases in the clustering stage. In the UPG algorithm, the deletion of a segment will lead to the deletion of an entire trajectory, so the $|p_n|$ value in UPG algorithm grows faster, and DM value increased rapidly in the range of k = 40 to 50. But due to the limit of Max_Trash parameter, when k = 50, the upper limit $|p_n|$ will not continue to increase. After that, the change of DM value is mainly affected by the size of anonymous group $|p_n|$, and the increase is relatively gentle.

Generally speaking, the DM value of anonymous result of UPG algorithm is less than that of NWA algorithm. The algorithm guarantees the data discernibility of released trajectory data set to be kept at a low level by trajectory segmentation, under the condition of variable threshold. This experiment explains the validity of the data generated by UPG algorithm to some extent.

4.3 The Degree of Information Distortion

Figure 2 shows the test results of the degree of information distortion between NWA and UPG at different values of k. As can be seen from Fig. 2, the information distortion of UPG algorithm under all k values is less than that of NWA algorithm. The average degree of information distortion of UPG algorithm is 14346211044, which is only 80% of the NWA algorithm. This is because the UPG algorithm is based on the (k, Δ)-anonymous model with variable trajectory uncertainty threshold. In UPG algorithm, during the stage of spatial perturbation, each cluster group can be converted to the anonymous group which meets the requirements by moving the positions of few trajectory nodes in the cluster, and this can reduce the degree of information distortion. In Fig. 2, the degree of information distortion of the two algorithms increases continuously with the increase of the uncertainty threshold k. This is because the number of trajectories in the anonymous group increases with the increase of k, which leads to the fact that in order to ensure the indistinguishability between the trajectories in a group, it requires more point-based spatial perturbations.

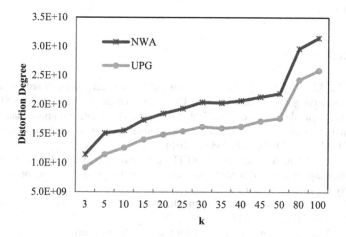

Fig. 2. The degree of information distortion

As a whole, the UPG algorithm is obviously superior to the NWA algorithm in the degree of information distortion. Under the uncertain threshold, the UPG algorithm obviously reduces the information distortion level.

5 Conclusions

The problem of privacy preserving is crucial in the development of trajectory data publishing and has become a research hotspot. But due to its large scale, high dimension and abundant background knowledge, the research of trajectory privacy preserving is facing a serious challenge.

Based on the existing research, the feature unitary problem of the anonymous group that exists in the traditional clustering constrained based strategy trajectory privacy preserving scheme is analyzed, and gives the definition of the re-clustering attacks against the features of anonymously published database. In order to solve the feature unitary problem of anonymous group, a segment clustering based algorithm (UPG algorithm) is proposed. In the UPG algorithm, the trajectory is segmented firstly, and then the trajectory segment is used as the basic unit for clustering constraints. The segments of a same trajectory are located in different segmented anonymous groups, and this can effectively solve the problem of unitary feature. For the proposed trajectory privacy preserving algorithm, the performance of the algorithm is the best. The experiment results showed that the algorithm can effectively protect the user's privacy under the premise of ensuring data quality and data availability.

Acknowledgement. This work is supported by the National Natural Science Foundation of China (No. 61602106), the Doctor Research Start-up Fund of Liaoning Province (No. 201601014).

References

1. Zhang, L., Liu, Y., Wang, R.C.: Location publishing technology based on differential privacy-preserving for big data services. Chin. J. Commun. **37**(9), 46–54 (2016)
2. Zhang, L., Cormode, G., Procopiuc, C.M., Srivastava, D.: PrivBayes: private data release via Bayesian networks. In: ACM SIGMOD International Conference on Management of Data, pp. 1423–1434. ACM Press, Snowbird (2014)
3. Elahe, G.K., Mahdi, A., Fatemeh, D.: PPTD: preserving personalized privacy in trajectory data publishing by sensitive attribute generalization and trajectory local suppression. Knowl. Based Syst. **94**, 43–59 (2016)
4. Huo, Z., Meng, X.F.: A trajectory data publication method under differential privacy. Chin. J. Comput. **40**(115), 1–9 (2017)
5. Chen, R., Xiao, Q., Zhang, Y.: Differentially private high-dimensional data publication via sampling-based inference. In: 21th ACM SIGKDD Conference on Knowledge Discovery and Data Mining (SIGKDD), pp. 129–138. ACM Press, Sydney (2015)
6. Gidofalvi, G., Huang, X., Pedersen, T.B: Privacy-preserving data mining on moving object trajectories. In: International Conference on Mobile Data Management, pp. 60–68. IEEE Press, Mannheim (2007)
7. Yarovoy, R., Bonchi, F., Lakshmanan, L.V.S.: Anonymizing moving objects: how to hide a MOB in a crowd. In: 12th International Conference on Extending Database Technology, pp. 72–83. ACM Press, Saint Petersburg (2009)
8. Hoh, B., Gruteser, M., Xiong, H.: Achieving guaranteed anonymity in GPS traces via uncertainty-aware path cloaking. IEEE Trans. Mob. Comput. **9**(8), 1089–1107 (2010)

9. Abul, O., Bonchi, F., Nanni, M.: Anonymization of moving objects databases by clustering and perturbation. Inf. Syst. **35**(8), 884–910 (2010)
10. Sweeney, L.: k-anonymity: a model for protecting privacy. Int. J. Uncertain. Fuzziness Knowl. Based Syst. **10**(5), 557–570 (2002)
11. Arunkumar, S., Srivatsa, M., Rajarajan, M.: A review paper on preserving privacy in mobile environments. J. Netw. Comput. Appl. **53**, 74–90 (2015)
12. Abul, O., Bonchim, F., Nanni, M.: Never walk alone: uncertainty for anonymity in moving objects databases. In: 24th IEEE International Conference on Data Engineering (ICDE 2008), pp. 376–385. IEEE Press, Cancun (2008)
13. Khalil, A.H., Benjamin, C.M.F., William, K.C.: Privacy-preserving trajectory stream publishing. Data Knowl. Eng. **94**, 89–109 (2014)
14. Nergiz, M.E., Atzori, M., Saygin, Y.: Towards trajectory anonymization: a generalization-based approach. In: SIGSPATIAL ACM GIS 2008 International Workshop on Security and Privacy in GIS and LBS, pp. 52–61. ACM Press, Irvine (2008)
15. Grunwald, P.D., Myung, I.J., Pitt, M.A.: Advances in Minimum Description Length: Theory and Applications, pp. 20–28. MIT Press, Cambridge (2005)
16. Li, F., Gao, F., Yao, L., Pan, Y.: Privacy preserving in the publication of large-scale trajectory databases. In: Wang, Y., Yu, G., Zhang, Y., Han, Z., Wang, G. (eds.) BigCom 2016. LNCS, vol. 9784, pp. 367–376. Springer, Cham (2016). https://doi.org/10.1007/978-3-319-42553-5_31
17. Brinkhoff, T.: Generating traffic data. IEEE Data Eng. Bull. **26**(2), 19–25 (2003)

Direction-of-Arrival Estimation of Near-Field Sources Based on Two Symmetric Nested Arrays with Enhanced Degrees of Freedom

Shuang Li[1](✉) ⓘ, Shunren Hu[1] ⓘ, Wei Liu[1] ⓘ, Xiaoxiao Jiang[2] ⓘ,
and Wei He[3] ⓘ

[1] Chongqing University of Technology, Chongqing 400054, China
lis@cqut.edu.cn
[2] Shanghai University of Engineering Science, Shanghai 201620, China
[3] Shanghai Institute of Microsystem of Information Technology,
Shanghai 200050, China

Abstract. This paper addresses the underdetermined direction-of-arrival estimation problem in the near-field. Placing two identical nested arrays symmetrically is one easy way to perform underdetermined direction-of-arrival estimation. However, by using such an array with $N = 2(N_1 + N_2)$ sensors, where N_1 and N_2 denotes the number of sensors in each level of the two nested arrays, only $N_2(N_1 + 1) - 1$ source can be detected. In this paper, a novel direction-of-arrival estimation is proposed. More specifically, we have proved that by employing the same array, at most $(N_2 + 1)(N_1 + 1)$ sources can be resolved. Simulation results are given to demonstrate the effectiveness and efficiency of the proposed method.

Keywords: Direction-of-arrival estimation · Symmetric nested array
Near-field · Degrees of freedom

1 Introduction

Direction-of-arrival (DOA) estimation using sensor arrays is one of the most important topics in array signal processing, which has significant application in wireless sensor network. For example, it can be used to track a maneuvering target in wireless microphone array sensor networks.

In recent years, the DOA estimation problem has drawn many researchers' attentions. However, there are still some issues to be solved. For instance, a far-field assumption is made in most literatures so that the waves radiated by the sources can be regarded as plane wave. The assumption is true when the sources are located relatively far from the array. But in some cases, where the sources or the array are moving, the sources and the array are probably close to each other. Therefore, the far-field assumption does not hold.

In order to solve this problem, many source localization methods are proposed in the near-field, such as maximum likelihood methods [1], higher-order-based methods [2–4] and sparse-based methods [5–7] and so forth. However, some of these methods

© Springer Nature Singapore Pte Ltd. 2018
J. Li et al. (Eds.): CWSN 2017, CCIS 812, pp. 222–233, 2018.
https://doi.org/10.1007/978-981-10-8123-1_20

suffer poor resolution from heavy aperture loss [8]. Some require large computational cost because of computation of cumulants [2–4] or sparse signal recovery [5–7]. Besides, these methods cannot identify more sources than sensors.

In the far-field, there are many literatures to deal with the underdetermined DOA estimation problem, such as nested arrays [9], co-prime arrays [10] and super nested arrays [11]. However, there are only a few methods being capable to resolve more sources than sensors in the near-field since most of existing methods require the physical array to be symmetric. One can easily think of combining two identical nested arrays or co-prime arrays to improve the degrees of freedom (DOF). By exploiting two symmetric co-prime arrays, Liang and Han [12] proposed a near-field source localization method, which improved the array aperture and can be applicable to underdetermined case for DOA estimation. Based on nested array, the authors proposed one array geometry called compressed symmetric nested array (CSNA) [13], which is obtained by getting rid of some elements from two identical nested arrays. Compared with the simple way of combining two identical nested arrays symmetrically, the DOA estimation method based on CSNA can achieve higher resolution and identify more sources with the same number of sensors.

For convenience, if an array is constructed by placing two identical nested arrays symmetrically, we call it symmetric nested array (SNA). The contributions of this paper are as follows:

(1) A theorem is given to verify that an SNA can achieve more DOF than that of the nested array contained in the SNA, i.e. Given a SNA with $2N = 2(N_1 + N_2)$ sensors, where N_1 and N_2 denote the number of sensors in the inner and outer ULAs, respectively, the difference co-array of the SNA contains a ULA with $2(N_2 + 1)(N_1 + 1) + 1$ elements, while the difference co-array of the nested array contained in SNA is a filled ULA with $2N_2(N_1 + 1) - 1$ elements.

(2) A novel underdetermined DOA estimation method is proposed by using this theorem in the near-field.

2 Data Model for Physical and Virtual Array

2.1 Data Model for Physical Array

Consider this case in which K near-field sources impinge on a symmetric linear array with $N = 2g$ sensors (Here, we assume N is even.), as depicted in Fig. 1. The sensors are assumed to be located at a linear grid with a smallest spacing d. Let $l = \{l_{-g}, \cdots, l_{-2}, l_{-1}, l_1, l_2, \cdots, l_g\}d$ denote the position vector of the array elements, where all l_i for $i = -g, \cdots, -1, 1, \cdots, g$ should be integers. Then the signal observed by the ith sensor can be expressed as

$$x_i(t) = \sum_{k=1}^{K} s_k(t) \exp(j\frac{2\pi}{\lambda}(r_{i,k} - r_k)) + n_i(t), \, t = 1, 2, \cdots, T; i = -g, \cdots, -1, 1, \cdots, g \quad (1)$$

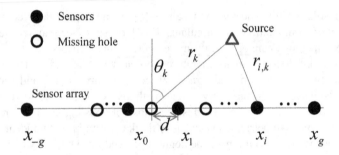

Fig. 1. Array geometry for near-field source

where

$$r_{i,k} = \sqrt{r_k^2 + l_i^2 d^2 - 2l_i dr_k \sin \theta_k} \tag{2}$$

stands for the range between the ith sensor and the kth source, r_k denotes the distance from the kth source to the reference point of the array, $s_k(t)$ is the kth source signal, $n_i(t)$ refers to the additive noise received by the ith sensor, λ represents the wavelength of the sources and θ_k denotes the direction-of-arrival of the kth source.

Define

$$\tau_{i,k} \triangleq \frac{2\pi}{\lambda}(r_{i,k} - r_k) \tag{3}$$

According to the Fresnel approximation, it can be represented as

$$\tau_{i,k} = l_i \omega_k + l_i^2 \varphi_k \tag{4}$$

where

$$\omega_k = -\frac{2\pi d}{\lambda} \sin \theta_k \tag{5}$$

and

$$\varphi_k = \frac{\pi d^2}{\lambda r_k} \cos^2 \theta_k \tag{6}$$

Substituting (4) into (1), we get

$$x_i(t) = \sum_{k=1}^{K} s_k(t) \exp(jl_i \omega_k + jl_i^2 \varphi_k) + n_i(t), \tag{7}$$

$$t = 1, 2, \cdots, T; i = -g, \cdots, -1, 1, \cdots, g$$

Let $x(t) = [x_{-g}(t), x_{-g+1}(t), \cdots, x_g(t)]^T$, $s(t) = [s_1(t), \cdots, s_2(t), s_K(t)]^T$ and
$n(t) = [n_{-g}(t), n_{-g+1}(t), \cdots, n_g(t)]^T$ denote the received signal vector, the source signal vector and the received noise vector, respectively, (7) can be rewritten in a compact form as

$$x(t) = As(t) + n(t), t = 1, 2, \cdots, T \tag{8}$$

where $A = [a(r_1, \theta_1), a(r_2, \theta_2), \cdots, a(r_K, \theta_K)]$ denotes   the   array   manifold   and
$a(r_k, \theta_k) = [e^{j\tau_{-u,k}}, e^{j\tau_{-(u-1),k}}, \cdots, e^{j\tau_{u,k}}]^T$ is steering vector.

To make the following derivation simple, some assumptions are made as follows:

(A1) The sources are non-Gaussian, and mutually uncorrelated.

(A2) The noise is additive Gaussian one, either white or colored, and independent of the sources.

(A3) The array is a non-uniform linear array with underlying grid $d \leq \frac{\lambda}{4}$ to avoid manifold ambiguity.

In this paper, we only focus on solving the following DOA estimation problem: Given the observed signals $\{x(t), t = 1, 2, \cdots, T\}$, find the azimuth $\theta = [\theta_1, \theta_2, \cdots, \theta_K]^T$.

2.2   Data Model for Virtual Array

The forth order cumulants of the observed signals can be defined as

$$\begin{aligned}
cum(x_m(t), x_n^*(t), x_p(t), x_q^*(t)) &= E\{x_m(t)x_n^*(t)x_p(t)x_q^*(t)\} \\
&- E\{x_m(t)x_n^*(t)\}E\{x_p(t)x_q^*(t)\} - E\{x_m(t)x_p(t)\}E\{x_n^*(t)x_q^*(t)\} \\
&- E\{x_m(t)x_q^*(t)\}E\{x_n^*(t)x_p(t)\}, \ m, n, p, q \in (-g, -1) \cup (1, g)
\end{aligned} \tag{9}$$

Under the above assumptions (A1) and (A2), and by utilizing the properties of cumulants, we have

$$cum(x_m(t), x_n^*(t), x_p(t), x_q^*(t)) = \sum_{k=1}^{K} e^{j[(l_m - l_n + l_p - l_q)\omega_k + (l_m^2 - l_n^2 + l_p^2 - l_q^2)\varphi_k]} c_{4,sk} \tag{10}$$

where $c_{4,sk} = cum(s_k(t), s_k^*(t), s_k(t), s_k^*(t))$ represents the kurtosis of the kth source signal.

Let $n = -m$ and $p = -q$, then

$$\begin{cases} l_n = l_{-m} = -l_m \\ l_p = l_{-q} = -l_q \end{cases} \tag{11}$$

Substituting (11) into (10), we obtain

$$cum(x_m(t), x^*_{-m}(t), x_{-q}(t), x^*_q(t))$$

$$= \sum_{k=1}^{K} e^{j(l_m - l_q)2\omega_k} c_{4,sk}, m, q = -g, \cdots, -1, 1, \cdots, g \tag{12}$$

The right side of (12) can be regarded as the correlation between the mth and qth sensor output of a virtual far-field array, which is just the difference co-array of the original array.

3   Array Structures and One Existing Method

3.1   Nested Array

Nested array [9] is a concatenation of two ULAs: inner one and outer one, where the inner ULA has N_1 elements with intersensor spacing d_1 and the outer ULA has N_2 elements with spacing $d_2 = (N_1 + 1)d_1$. More specifically, it is a linear array whose sensor location is presented by the union of the two sets $S_{inner} = \{md_1, m = 1, 2, \cdots, N_1\}$ and $S_{outer} = \{n(N_1 + 1)d_1, n = 1, 2, \cdots, N_2\}$. It has been shown that the difference co-array of such a nested array is a filled ULA with $2N_2(N_1 + 1) - 1$ elements, which indicates that the DOF of a nested array is increased to $2N_2(N_1 + 1) - 1$. Through the use of KR product and classic subspace-based DOA estimation methods, up to $O(N^2)$ far-field sources can be detected with a N-elements nested array. However, it cannot be directly used in the near-field since in the derivation of (12) the original array is assumed to be symmetric.

3.2   Symmetric Nested Array

In order to make use of the advantages of nested array in the near-field, a simple idea is to place two identical nested arrays symmetrically, named symmetric nested array (SNA) [13]. The sensor position of a symmetric nested array can be given by the union of the two sets $S_{inner} = \{md_1, m = -N_1, -N_1 + 1, \cdots -1, 1, \cdots N_1\}$ and $S_{outer} = \{n(N_1 + 1)d_1, n = -N_2, -N_2 + 1, \cdots, -1, 1, \cdots, N_2\}$. Apparently, according to the properties of nested array, we know that the difference co-array of a SNA contains a ULA with $2N_2(N_1 + 1) - 1$ elements, which implies the DOF of a SNA with $2(N_1 + N_2)$ sensors can be increased to $2N_2(N_1 + 1) - 1$ in the near-field.

To clearly show the SNA, an example is given in Fig. 2, where the number of sensors in each level of each nested array is 2. i.e. $N_1 = N_2 = 2$.

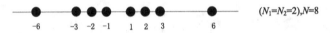

Fig. 2. A symmetric nested array with 8 elements

3.3   One Existing Method: The Original SNA Method [13]

It has been shown in (12) that the correlation of the difference co-array of the physical array is obtained in the near-field. If a physical array sensors are spatially located in such a way that the elements in the set of $\{l_m - l_q, -g \leq m, q \leq g\}$ represent every integer from 0 to $\tilde{N}$, where $\tilde{N} \leq N(N-1)/2$, then we attain $\tilde{N}+1$ autocorrelation lags given by

$$c(u) = c(l_m - l_q) = \sum_{k=1}^{K} e^{j(l_m - l_q)2\omega_k} c_{4,sk}, u = 0, 1, \cdots, \tilde{N} \tag{13}$$

Interestingly, these correlation lags are similar with those corresponding to a ULA of $\tilde{N}+1$ sensors for the same source scene in the far-field.

Hence, we can construct a toeplitz matrix:

$$C = \begin{bmatrix} c(0) & c(1) & \cdots & c(\tilde{N}) \\ c^*(1) & c(0) & \cdots & c(\tilde{N}-1) \\ \vdots & \vdots & \ddots & \vdots \\ c^*(\tilde{N}) & c^*(\tilde{N}-1) & \cdots & c(0) \end{bmatrix} \tag{14}$$

where the matrix C behaves like the conventional covariance matrix of the sensor output of a ULA with $\tilde{N}+1$ elements whose steering vector can be expressed as $\tilde{a}(\theta_k) = [1, e^{j2\omega_k}, \cdots, e^{j2\tilde{N}\omega_k}]$.

Obviously, for an SNA with $N = 2(N_1 + N_2)$ sensors, where N_1, N_2 refer to the numbers of each level of the nested array in the SNA, its difference co-array should contains a ULA with $2N_2(N_1+1) - 1$ elements. It indicates that we can obtain such a matrix C in (14), where $\tilde{N} = N_2(N_1+1) - 1$. Hence, by exploiting the conventional MUSIC method [14], $N_2(N_1+1) - 1$ near-field sources can be processed. Take the SNA in Fig. 2 as an example, the difference co-array of this SNA contains 11 elements. By exploiting the existing method, only 5 sources can be detected. In the following section, we will verify that the difference co-array of a SNA contains a ULA with more sensors, and thus can resolve more sources. For example, the difference co-array of the SNA in Fig. 2 contains a ULA with 19 elements. Therefore, 9 sources can be identified.

4   The Proposed Method

Theorem 1: Given an SNA with $N = 2(N_1 + N_2)$ sensors, where N_1 and N_2 denote the number of sensors in the inner and outer ULAs, respectively, the difference co-array of the SNA contains a ULA with $2(N_2+1)(N_1+1)+1$ elements.

Proof: We assume the sensor positions of the SNA is given by the union of the sets $S_{inner} = \{md, m = -N_1, -N_1+1, \cdots -1, 1, \cdots N_1\}$ and $S_{outer} = \{n(N_1+1)d, n = -N_2, -N_2+1, \cdots, -1, 1, \cdots, N_2\}$. According to the properties of nested array, the difference co-array of each of the two contained nested arrays is a filled ULA with $2N_2(N_1 + 1) - 1$ elements, whose location is given by

$$S_{NA} = \{nd, n = -N_2(N_1 + 1) + 1, -N_2(N_1 + 1) + 2, \cdots, N_2(N_1 + 1) - 1\} \quad (15)$$

Note that the difference co-array of any array is symmetric. Therefore, what we only need to prove is there are virtual sensors in the positions given by the sets

$$\{nd, n = N_2(N_1 + 1), \cdots, (N_2 + 1)(N_1 + 1)\}$$

To express conveniently, we use $\{\vec{x}_i, i = -N_2(N_1 + 1), \cdots, -(N_1 + 1), -N_1, \cdots, -1, 1, \cdots, N_1, N_1 + 1, , N_2(N_1 + 1)\}$ to be the position vector of the original array, then the difference co-array is given by keeping the distinct values of the set $\{\vec{x}_i - \vec{x}_j\}$. Then, we have

i. $\vec{x}_i - \vec{x}_j = N_2(N_1 + 1)$, when $i = (N_2 - 1)(N_1 + 1)$ and $j = -(N_1 + 1)$;
ii. $\vec{x}_i - \vec{x}_j = N_2(N_1 + 1) + 1, N_2(N_1 + 1) + 2, \cdots, (N_2 + 1)(N_1 + 1)$,   when $i = N_2(N_1 + 1)$ and $j = -1, -2, \cdots, -(N_1 + 1)$.

Thus, $\vec{x}_i - \vec{x}_j$ occurs at most once from $N_2(N_1 + 1)$ to $(N_2 + 1)(N_1 + 1)$. The theorem has been proved. ∎

According to Theorem 1, since by using an SNA with $N = 2(N_1 + N_2)$ sensors, we can obtain a virtual ULA with $2(N_2 + 1)(N_1 + 1) + 1$ elements, we can form a matrix $\bar{C}$ similar with C as

$$\bar{C} = \begin{bmatrix} c(0) & c(1) & \cdots & c(\bar{N}) \\ c^*(1) & c(0) & \cdots & c(\bar{N} - 1) \\ \vdots & \vdots & \ddots & \vdots \\ c^*(\bar{N}) & c^*(\bar{N} - 1) & \cdots & c(0) \end{bmatrix} \quad (16)$$

where $\bar{N} = (N_2 + 1)(N_1 + 1)$ and the matrix $\bar{C}$ also can be considered as the conventional covariance matrix of the sensor output of a ULA with $\bar{N} + 1$ elements whose steering vector is $\bar{a}(\theta_k) = [1, e^{j2\omega_k}, \cdots, e^{j2\bar{N}\omega_k}]$.

Just like the original SNA method, we can utilize the conventional MUSIC method to find the DOAs of the sources. Let V denote the noise space spanned by the eigenvalues of the matrix $\bar{C}$ corresponding to small eigenvalues. The spatial spectrum can be defined as

$$P(\theta) = \frac{1}{\bar{a}^H(\theta)VV_n^H\bar{a}^H(\theta)} \quad (17)$$

At last, the DOAs can be found by searching the first K peaks of the spatial spectrum $P(\theta)$.

From the above derivation, we know the number of source the proposed method can identify is $\bar{N} = (N_2 + 1)(N_1 + 1)$ for a given number of sensors $N = 2(N_1 + N_2)$. Thus, it can be easily deduced that when $N_1 = N_2$, we can gain the largest value of

$\bar{N} = N^2/16 + N/2 + 1$. Besides, compared with the original SNA method, $N_1 + 2$ more sources can be detected by employing Theorem 1.

Remarks: Regarding the number of sources that can be detected for a fixed number of sensors $N = 2g$, we make a comparison with several methods in Table 1. As we can see, the proposed method can process more sources than the method in [13], both of which are based on SNA.

Table 1. The number or sources that different methods can detect for $2g$ sensors

Different array geometries and methods	The maximum number of sources to be able to detect
ULA (Two-stage MUSIC) [2]	$2g - 1$
SNA without further improve DOF [13]	$g^2/4 + g/2 - 1$, when g is even
	$(g^2 - 3)/4 + g/2$, when g is odd
CSNA [13]	$g^2/2 + g - 1$, when g is even
	$g^2/8 + g/2 - 1/2$, When g is odd
The proposed method: SNA with further improve DOF	$g^2/4 + g + 1$

5   Simulation Results

In this section, several numerical experiments are given to illustrate the effectiveness and efficiency of the proposed method in terms of estimation error and resolution. Several approaches are compared with the proposed method, including two-stage MUSIC method which is based on ULA, the original SNA method and the method based on CSNA [13]. In the following figures, we use ULA (Two-stage MUSIC method), SNA (The original SNA method), CSNA (the method based on CSNA) and SNA-FI (the proposed method, FI denotes further increasing of DOF) to represent these methods, respectively.

In all the experiments, we consider this scenario that two near-field sources impinge on 3 different linear arrays with 8 elements: a ULA, an SNA in Fig. 2 and a CSNA. The underlying grid of SNA and CSNA should be equal to the intersensor spacing of the ULA. From Table 1, the numbers of sources that the ULA, SNA, CSNA and SNA-FI methods can be resolved are 7, 5, 11, 9, respectively. Therefore, it can be deduced that if we sort the four methods in terms of resolution, the descended order should be CSNA, SNA-FI, ULA and SNA. This result will be verified in the latter.

5.1   RMSE

In the first example, we investigate the root mean square error (RMSE) of the four methods as a function of SNR. The RMSE is defined as

$$RMSE = \sqrt{\frac{1}{KN_{mc}} \sum_{q=1}^{K} \sum_{i=1}^{N_{mc}} (\hat{\theta}_{q,i} - \theta_{q,i})}$$

where N_{mc} denotes the number of Monte Carlo trials and $\hat{\theta}_{q,i}$ and $\theta_{q,i}$ denote the estimate DOA and the real DOA of the qth signal in the ith trial. We assume the two sources are located at $\{21\lambda, -25.4°\}$ and $\{16\lambda, -14.7°\}$. When SNR varies from 5 dB to 15 dB with a step 1 dB, the RMSE of the four methods is depicted in Fig. 3 by averaging 500 Monte Carlo trials and computing 5000 snapshots. It has been shown that after further increasing the DOF for SNA, the proposed method has a lower RMSE than the original SNA method. Besides the proposed method achieves a close error compared to the methods based on ULA and CSNA.

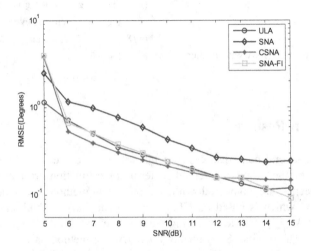

Fig. 3. RMSE versus SNR

Subsequently, we make a comparison for the RMSE of the four methods at different number of snapshots. We keep all the parameters the same as before except SNR = 20 dB. Figure 4 illustrates the RMSE of the four methods versus the number of snapshots. According to Fig. 4, the method based on CSNA has a smallest error among these methods. Moreover, the proposed method shows similar RMSE compared with two-stage MUSIC method, both of which achieve a lower variance than the original SNA method.

5.2 Resolution

In this subsection, we evaluate the resolution with regard to different SNR and different number of snapshots. The two source are closely spaced at $\{21\lambda, -3°\}$ and $\{17\lambda, 3°\}$ so as to make a better comparison. The two sources are considered to be resolved in a

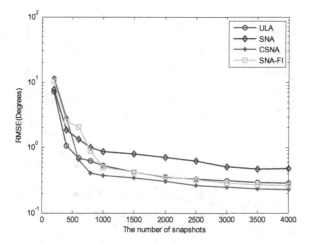

Fig. 4. RMSE versus the number of snapshots

trial if both $\left|\hat{\theta}_2 - \theta_2\right|$ and $\left|\hat{\theta}_1 - \theta_1\right|$ are smaller than $|\theta_2 - \theta_1|/2$, where θ_1 and θ_2 denote the true DOAs and $\hat{\theta}_1$ and $\hat{\theta}_2$ denote the estimating DOAs. The detection probability of the four methods versus SNR is depicted in Fig. 5, where the number of snapshots is $T = 4000$ and 500 Monte Carlo trials are carried out. It can be easily discovered the method based on the CSNA achieve highest resolution. Besides, the proposed method shows better resolution than the other two methods. The resolution ability of the four methods as a function of the number of snapshots is plotted in Fig. 6, where the parameters are kept as before except the SNR = 10 dB. The same results can be acquired from Figs. 5 and 6.

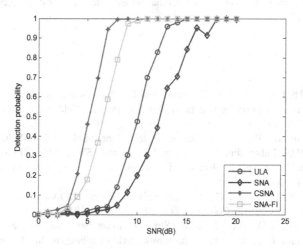

Fig. 5. Resolution ability with regard to SNR

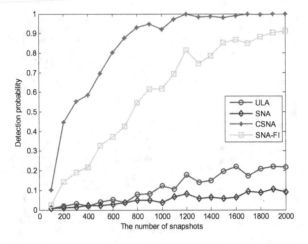

Fig. 6. Resolution ability versus the number of snapshots

6   Conclusions

In this paper, a novel direction-of-arrival estimation is proposed, where we have proved that given a symmetric nested array, which is to place two identical nested arrays symmetrically, we can further improve the degrees of freedom, i.e. with such an array with $2N = 2(N_1 + N_2)$ sensors, where N_1 and N_2 denotes the number of sensors in each level of the two nested array, $(N_2 + 1)(N_1 + 1)$ source can be detected. Both the DOF and the resolution have been clearly increased in the proposed method. Future research will involve the design of the new array structure for the near-field.

Acknowledgments. This work was supported in part by Chongqing Research Program of Basic Research and Frontier Technology of China under grant No. cstc2015jcyjA40055 and cstc2016jcyjA0515.

References

1. Chen, J.C., Hudson, R.E., Yao, K.: Maximum-likelihood source localization and unknown sensor location estimation for wideband signals in the near-field. IEEE Trans. Sig. Process. **50**(8), 1843–1854 (2002)
2. Liang, J., Liu, D.: Passive localization of mixed near-field and far-field sources using two-stage MUSIC algorithm. IEEE Trans. Sig. Process. **58**(1), 108–120 (2010)
3. Liang, J., Liu, D.: Passive localization of near-field sources using cumulant. IEEE Sens. J. **9** (8), 953–960 (2009)
4. Li, J., Wang, Y., Le Bastard, C., et al.: Simplified high-order DOA and range estimation with linear antenna array. IEEE Commun. Lett. **21**(1), 76–79 (2017)
5. Qin, S., Zhang, Y.D., Wu, Q., et al.: Structure-aware bayesian compressive sensing for near-field source localization based on sensor-angle distributions. Int. J. Antennas Propag. **2015**, 15 (2015)

6. Tian, Y., Sun, X.: Passive localization of mixed sources jointly using MUSIC and sparse signal reconstruction. AEU Int. J. Electron. Commun. **68**(6), 534–539 (2014)
7. Hu, K., Chepuri, S.P., Leus, G.: Near-field source localization using sparse recovery techniques. In: 2014 International Conference on Signal Processing and Communications (SPCOM), pp. 1–5. IEEE (2014)
8. Xie, J., Tao, H., Rao, X., et al.: Comments on near-field source localization via symmetric subarrays. IEEE Sig. Process. Lett. **5**(22), 643–644 (2015)
9. Pal, P., Vaidyanathan, P.: Nested arrays: a novel approach to array processing with enhanced degrees of freedom. IEEE Trans. Sig. Process. **58**(8), 4167–4181 (2010)
10. Vaidyanathan, P.P., Pal, P.: Sparse sensing with co-prime samplers and arrays. IEEE Trans. Sig. Process. **59**(2), 573–586 (2011)
11. Liu, C.-L., Vaidyanathan, P.: Super nested arrays: linear sparse arrays with reduced mutual coupling-part I: fundamentals. IEEE Trans. Sig. Process. **64**(15), 3997–4012 (2016)
12. Liang, G., Han, B.: Near-field sources localization based on co-prime symmetric array. J. Electron. Inf. Technol. **01**(1), 135–139 (2014). (In chinese)
13. Li, S., Xie, D.: Compressed symmetric nested arrays and their application for direction-of-arrival estimation of near-field sources. Sensors **16**(11), 1939 (2016)
14. Schmidt, R.: Multiple emitter location and signal parameter estimation. IEEE Trans. Antennas Propag. **34**(3), 276–280 (1986)

Finding the Minimal Sufficient Set in Causal Graph Under Interventions: A Dimension Reduction Method for Data Analysis

Mengjiao Pan and Qingsong Cai[✉]

Computer and Information Engineering,
Beijing Technology and Business University, Beijing 100048, China
10011316280@st.btbu.edu.cn, caiqs@btbu.edu.cn

Abstract. One of the ultimate goals of data analysis is to uncover the inherent causality in data. Pearl's causal graph model provides the fundamental framework for measuring changes caused by external interventions that are commonly used to reveal the causality. Although the criteria and algorithms of atomic intervention for evaluating causal effects have been proposed in previous studies, the research of causal effects under conditional intervention remains inadequate. In this paper, we propose a criterion to combine the back-door criterion of atomic intervention with conditional intervention when the treatment variable is unique. Under the criterion, the derived minimal sufficient sets under atomic intervention (a-MSSs) can be converted into the one under conditional intervention (c-MSSs). The calculation of c-MSSs can remarkably decrease the complexity of target data analysis regarding data dimension reduction. Based on those steps, we also develop an algorithm to implement the conversion. Case studies demonstrate that our algorithm can enumerate both a-MSSs and c-MSSs effectively when a causal graph is given, which validates the effectiveness of our proposed scheme.

Keywords: Causal graph · Atomic/conditional intervention
Minimal sufficient set · Data dimension reduction

1 Introduction

Uncovering relations from massive data is becoming a significant and hot research field. Most of the current research focused on data correlativity issues. [1–3]. However, inferring causality is one of the ultimate goals of data analysis, which is known as causal inference [4,5]. Causality analysis serves uniquely in telling us how a distribution of the causal effect would vary when external conditions are changed by interventions [6]. The simplest type of external intervention, atomic intervention, is one in which a single variable is forced to take on some fixed value. Although atomic intervention is simple to analyze, it is unreasonable

© Springer Nature Singapore Pte Ltd. 2018
J. Li et al. (Eds.): CWSN 2017, CCIS 812, pp. 234–244, 2018.
https://doi.org/10.1007/978-981-10-8123-1_21

to force all variables to achieve the same value. Conditional intervention [7] is that the value of a variable is determined by a function on a set of variables. Pearl demonstrated the causal effect of conditional intervention can be obtained by calculating the conditional probability of atomic. Based on this concept, there are some ready-made algorithms [8]. However, the conditional independent (CI) relationship [9] among variables is absent in them, which leads to the complexity of the expression. For deriving a relatively simple expression, Na Shan [10] proposed the back-door criterion of conditional intervention, which considered the CI relationship in the case of single treatment variable.

The criterion provides a graphical method of evaluating causal effects by selecting a subset of these variables in our study for adjustment. Such a set of variables is called a "sufficient set" [9]. The analysis dimension of observation data can be effectively reduced by finding the sufficient sets. Discovering the minimal sufficient sets from these sets will further facilitates the reduction of data dimension. Textor [11–14] and Kyono [15] respectively proposed algorithms to enumerate the minimal sufficient sets in causal graph. However, these algorithms can only be used for atomic intervention, but not for conditional.

In this paper, we combine the atomic intervention with conditional intervention, and establish the mapping relationship according to the similarities and differences of the back-door criteria in the two external intervention cases. Based on this mapping, we propose a criterion that converts the resulting minimal sufficient sets under atomic intervention (a-MSSs) to minimal sufficient sets under conditional intervention (c-MSSs) when the treatment variable is unique. We also propose an algorithm to list all a-MSSs and c-MSSs respectively, and explain its usage and application in data analysis via specific causal graphs. The rest of this paper is organized as follows. Section 2 defines the preliminaries. Section 3 analyzes the minimal sufficient set under conditional intervention. Section 4 presents the pseudocode for algorithm. Case studies on specific causal graphs are given in Sect. 5, and Sect. 6 ends with conclusion and discussion.

2   Preliminaries

A graph is a tuple $G = (V, E)$ of a set of vertices V denoting the variables and a set of edges E denoting the relations among these variables. We use the following notions in the causal graph literatures to support the thesis and the reader is referred to the tutorials by Pearl [4,7] for more detail.

The causal graph is a directed acyclic graph (DAG) with causal hypothesis. Pearl established the back-door criterion [7] based on the causal graph framework to identify the causal effect under atomic intervention. Where the atomic intervention is denoted by $do(X = x)$, or $do(x)$ for short, which signifies that a single variable X is forced to take on some fixed value x.

Definition 2.1 (Back-door Criterion). *Given a causal graph $G = (V, E)$ and three pairwise disjoint vertex sets $X, Y, Z \subseteq V$. Z satisfies the back-door criterion relative to (X, Y) if*

(1) no node in Z is a descendant of X, and
(2) Z blocks every path between X and Y which contains an arrow into X.

The path described in the property (2) is called back-door path [6]. The implication of finding a sufficient set Z by the back-door criterion is that the effect of X on Y can be identified by the adjustment formula [9]:

$$P(y|do(X = x)) = \sum_z P(y|x, z)P(z). \tag{1}$$

The moral graph G^m is used to find the equivalent undirected form of a DAG. The following is the definition of its corresponding criterion [11, 16].

Definition 2.2 (Moral Graph Criterion). *Given a causal graph $G = (V, E)$ and three pairwise disjoint vertex sets $X, Y, Z \subseteq V$. Z satisfies the moral graph criterion relative to (X, Y) if two conditions hold:*

(1) $Z \subseteq An(X \cup Y) \setminus De(X)$.
(2) Z separates X and Y in the ancestor moral graph $(G_{\underline{X}}[An(X \cup Y)])^m$.

Where the $G_{\underline{X}}$ is obtained by deleting from G all arrows emerging from X. The ancestor set $An(v)$ contains all ancestors of v (this includes v). And, the descendant set $De(v)$ is the set of all descendants of v.

Within this paper, the neighborhood of X is the set of vertices that are adjacent to some vertices in X and include vertices in X, denoted by $N(X)$. The notation $G[X]$ denotes the subgraph of G induced by X. Conversely, the notation $G[V \setminus X]$ denotes the subgraph of G formed by deleting from G all vertices in X and all edges incident to its vertices. To separate the nonadjacent vertices between $x \in X$ and $y \in Y$ in the undirected graph, we define $x - y$ separator as follows: A vertex set S is a $x - y$ separator if x and y belong to different connected components of $G[V \setminus S]$. For a $x - y$ separator S, we write $C_x(S)$ (respectively, $C_y(S)$) for the connected component of $G[V \setminus S]$ containing x (respectively, y). A $x - y$ separator is a minimal $x - y$ separator if there is no proper subset of it that is also a $x - y$ separator.

3   Minimal Sufficient Set Under Conditional Intervention

Conditional intervention is one in which the value of a single variable X is determined by a function on the set of variables Z, denoted by $do(X = g(Z))$. Each node in the conditional set Z is observable and no node in Z is a descendant of X, and g is a function of Z to X.

Definition 3.1 (Back-door Criterion of Conditional Intervention).
Given a causal graph $G = (V, E)$ and four disjoint vertex sets $X, Y, Z, W \subseteq V$. W satisfies the back-door criterion of conditional intervention relative to (X, Y) if

(1) no node in W is a descendant of X, and
(2) $W \cup Z$ blocks all back-door paths between X and Y.

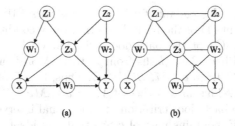

(a)   (b)

Fig. 1. (a) Graphical model illustrating the back-door criterion of conditional intervention. (b) The ancestor moral graph corresponding to (a).

Finding a set W, which satisfies the back-door criterion of conditional intervention, means the effect of X on Y identifiable, via the adjustment formula:

$$P(y|do(X = g(Z))) = \sum_{z} \sum_{w} P(y|w, z, x = g(Z))P(w, z). \qquad (2)$$

The set W satisfying the Definition 3.1 is a sufficient set under conditional intervention which denoted by $c - SS(W)$, or c-SS for short. W is a c-MSS, also written as $c - MSS(W)$, if there is no proper subset of W that is also a c-SS. In addition, a-MSS is also denoted as $a - MSS(Z)$.

Definition 3.2 (Atomic to Conditional Criterion (A2CC)). *Given a causal graph $G = (V, E)$ and four disjoint vertex sets $X, Y, Z, W \subseteq V$. W satisfies the atomic to conditional criterion relative to (X, Y) if convert as follows:*

(1) List all $a - MSS(Z')$ without considering the conditional set Z.
(2) Compute $W = a - MSS(Z') \setminus Z$.
(3) Remove all W_j which satisfies $W_i \subseteq W_j$ from the family set F_c.

Where Z' represents Z in Definition 2.1, not the conditional set Z. $0 \leq i \neq j \leq count(F_c)$. F_c is the set that contains the results obtained from the property (2) of the A2CC.

Theorem 3.1. *Let G represent a causal graph. Then W is a c-MSS relative to (X, Y) in G if and only if W satisfies the A2CC relative to (X, Y) in G.*

Lemma 3.1. *Given a causal graph $G = (V, E)$ and three pairwise disjoint vertex sets $X, Y, Z \subseteq V$, listing a minimal sufficient set $a - MSS(Z')$ without considering the conditional set Z, $W = a - MSS(Z') \setminus Z$ is a set satisfying the back-door criterion of conditional intervention relative to (X, Y).*

Proof. The set $a - MSS(Z')$ satisfies the back-door criterion because it is a minimal sufficient set without considering the conditional set Z. By the property (1) of the back-door criterion we have that no element in $a - MSS(Z')$ is a descendant of X. Moreover, $a - MSS(Z') \setminus Z \subseteq a - MSS(Z')$. Thus, no element in $a - MSS(Z')\setminus Z$ is a descendant of X. This means the set $W = a - MSS(Z')\setminus Z$ satisfies the statement (1) of the back-door criterion of conditional intervention.

By the property (2) of the back-door criterion we have that the set $a - MSS(Z')$ blocks all back-door paths from X to Y. Moreover, $a - MSS(Z') \subseteq a - MSS(Z') \cup Z$, $W \cup Z = a - MSS(Z') \cup Z$. Thus, $W \cup Z$ blocks all back-door paths from X to Y. This means the set $W = a - MSS(Z') \setminus Z$ satisfies the statement (2) of the back-door criterion of conditional intervention.

The family set F_c contains part of c-SSs that can identify the causal effect of X on Y. And some sets in F_c, but not all, are c-MSSs. Assuming the conditional set $Z = \{Z_1, Z_2\}$ we see, for example that, in Fig. 1(a), the sets $\{Z_3, W_2\}$, $\{Z_2, Z_3\}$, $\{Z_1, Z_3\}$ and $\{W_1, Z_3\}$ are given by $c - MSS(Z')$. (The details will be described in part V.) The c-SSs $\{Z_3, W_2\}$, $\{Z_3\}$, $\{Z_3\}$ and $\{W_1, Z_3\}$ are computed by $a - MSS(Z') \setminus Z$. Only the set $\{Z_3\}$, apparently, is a c-MSS.

Proof (Theorem 3.1). Suppose that the set W satisfies the A2CC relative to (X, Y) in G. We have proved that the set $W = a - MSS(Z') \setminus Z$ is a c-SS from Lemma 3.1. After removing all W_j satisfying $W_i \subseteq W_j$ from F_c, assuming a set W_p in F_c is not a minimal set satisfying the back-door criterion of conditional intervention, a proper subset W_p' of W_p satisfies the back-door criterion of conditional intervention. $W_p = a - MSS(Z') \setminus Z$, $W_p' = Sub(W_p)$. $W_p' \cup Z$ blocks all back-door paths in G. Then there is at least one minimal sufficient set $a - MSS'(Z') = Sub(W_p' \cup Z)$. Moreover, there is $W_p'' = a - MSS'(Z') \setminus Z$ in F_c. And $W_p'' \subset W_p$, a contradiction. It directly follows that W is a minimal set satisfying the back-door criterion of conditional intervention. This implies that W is a c-MSS relative to (X, Y) in G.

Lemma 3.2. $c - MSS(W) \equiv \emptyset$ *if the conditional set Z is a sufficient set that satisfies the back-door criterion.*

Proof. First, Suppose that the set $W = \emptyset$, it directly follows that no node in W is a descendant of X. Then, $W \cup Z = Z$, and Z is a sufficient set satisfying the back-door criterion. Thus, $W \cup Z$ blocks all back-door paths from X to Y. Moreover, even if there are some nonempty sets S_i in F_c, S_i will be removed from F_c due to $\emptyset \subseteq S_i$.

4   The Algorithm

In this section, we present the algorithm for listing all a-MSSs or c-MSSs that can identify the causal effect of treatment X on outcome Y. In the following, the set of latent variables is denoted by L. According to the proof of Textor [11], it is known that obtaining a-MSSs by the moral graph criterion is equivalent to obtaining by the back-door criterion. Given a causal graph $G = (V, E)$ and four vertex sets $X, Y, Z, L \subseteq V$, in order to enumerate all minimal sufficient sets, we first construct the ancestor moral graph $G^m := (G_{\underline{X}}[An(X \cup Y)])^m$ according to the Definition 2.2. Then starting the algorithm to list all minimal sufficient sets

---

Algorithm 1. ListMinSuf_AtoConI

Input: Four vertex sets, X, Z, L and N from a causal graph G and the corresponding ancestor moral graph G^m.

Output: All minimal sufficient sets under atomic or conditional intervention.

1: **if** $Z = \emptyset$ **then**
2:     $ListMinSuf\_AtoI(X, Z, L, N)$;
3: **else**
4:     **if** $V(C_x(Z)) \cap N = \emptyset$ **then**
5:        output $\emptyset$;
6:     **else**
7:        $F_a := ListMinSuf\_AtoI(X, Z, L, N)$;
8:        **for** $i = 0$ to $count(F_a)$ **do**
9:           $W_i := F_a[i] \setminus Z$
10:       **end for**
11:       $F_c = \{W_1, W_2 \cdots W_n\}$;
12:       **if** exist $W_i \subseteq W_j$ in F_c **then**
13:          delete W_j;
14:       **end if**
15:       output F_c;
16:     **end if**
17: **end if**

Algorithm 2. MinSep_UndirGra

Input: Vertex set X from a graph with vertices x and y such that $G[X]$ is connected and $X \cap N[y] = \emptyset$.

Output: Minimal vertex separators.

1: compute $N(X)$;
2: delete the vertex set $N(X)$ from G;
3: $V := V(C_y(N(X)))$;
4: output $N(V)$;

---

by calling: ListMinSuf_AtoConI($\{x\}, Z, L, N[y]$), which requires as subroutines MinSep_UndirGra and ListMinSuf_AtoI.

The subroutine MinSep_UndirGra uses the $x - y$ separator property in the undirected graph G^m to enumerate the minimal vertex separators. Another subroutine ListMinSuf_AtoI computes the result by constructing a tree that is pruned when conditions are not satisfied. Here, the outcomes of the two subroutines are denoted as MVS and F_a, respectively.

5   Case Studies

We demonstrate our method with the following two causal graphs, the first of which we have already used in the previous sections.

Algorithm 3. ListMinSuf_AtoI

Input: Four vertex sets, X, Z, L and N from a causal graph G and the corresponding
  ancestor moral graph G^m.
Output: All minimal sufficient sets under atomic intervention.
1: $MVS := MinSep\_UndirGra(X)$;
2: $X^* := V(C_x(MVS))$;
3: **if** $X^* \cap N = \emptyset$ **then**
4:     $X := X^*$;
5:     **if** $N(X) \setminus N \neq \emptyset$ **then**
6:         Let v be a vertex in $N(X) \setminus N$;
7:         $ListMinSuf\_AtoI(X \cup \{v\}, Z, L, N)$;
8:         $ListMinSuf\_AtoI(X, Z, L, N \cup \{v\})$;
9:     **else**
10:        **if** $MVS \cap L = \emptyset$ **then**
11:            output MVS;
12:            $\{F_a = \{MVS\}.\}$
13:        **end if**
14:    **end if**
15: **end if**

5.1   Classical Causal Graph Model

The classical causal graph model in Fig. 1 was retrieved from Pearl [9]. Figure 2
shows a tree to list the family set of the model when the conditional set $Z = \{Z_1, Z_2\}$ and the latent set $L = \emptyset$. At the start of the algorithm (depicted as
the root of the tree), the vertex set X is $\{X\}$, and the neighborhood N of Y
is $N(Y) = \{Y, W_2, W_3, Z_3\}$. In the figure below, the vertices in X (respectively,
N) are enclosed by an red (respectively, blue) oval to show how X (respectively,
N) changes depending on where we are in the tree.

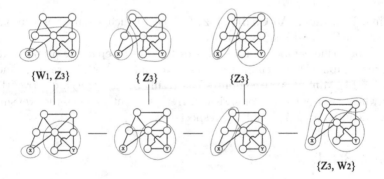

Fig. 2. Tree to list the family set of the classical causal graph model. (Color figure
online)

Since Z and $V(C_x(Z)) \cap N$ are nonempty sets, we calculate the sets W_1, $\cdots$, W_n in the family set F_c as follows: the minimal vertex separator MVS in undirected graph obtained by the Algorithm 2 is $\{W_1, Z_3\}$. Then we compute that the vertex set of the component that contains $\{X\}$ in subgraph $G[V \setminus MVS]$ is $\{X\}$. Because of the intersection of the assigned set X^* and the neighborhood set N is null, the algorithm will properly select an available vertex adjacent to X (either W_1 or Z_3 in this instance) to be added to the set X or N according to the sixth to eighth line of Algorithm 3. We choose vertex W_1 here. The algorithm then creates two children of the root. For the left child, vertex W_1 is added to X. In the figure, we draw it on the right side of the root. Similarly, we draw the right child on top of the root, which is growing set N by adding W_1.

Given the vertex sets X, Z, L and N for the left and right children of the root, the algorithm again computes MVS and X^*, finds an adjacent vertex v not in N, and creates left and right children. Here, the adjacent vertex v of the right child of the root is absent. So in this instance, judge whether MVS contains latent variables. Since the answer is no, the algorithm outputs the MVS to F_a. According to the ninth line of Algorithm 1, we calculate the set W_i in F_c. The leaf level of the tree has 4 leaves, in this case, the "grandchildren" of the root. The leaves output the sufficient sets under conditional intervention $\{Z_3, W_2\}$, $\{Z_3\}$, $\{Z_3\}$, and $\{W_1, Z_3\}$, which are written below the leaves as shown in Fig. 2. These are all sets in the family F_c. They satisfy $\{Z_3\} \subseteq \{Z_3, W_2\}$, $\{Z_3\} \subseteq \{Z_3\}$ and $\{Z_3\} \subseteq \{W_1, Z_3\}$. Thus, only the set $\{Z_3\}$ is a minimal sufficient set under conditional intervention after removing $\{Z_3, W_2\}$, $\{Z_3\}$, and $\{W_1, Z_3\}$ from F_c.

Table 1 shows all the cases that the conditional set Z may appear, and the corresponding outputs from the algorithm. Only when the set Z is empty, the results in the family set F_a are a-MSSs, the other cases are c-MSSs. In order to evaluate the causal effect of X on Y, only two variables need to be adjusted under atomic intervention, and only 0 or 1 variable is required under conditional intervention.

Table 1. Minimal sufficient sets of the classical causal graph model.

Z	F_c	Z	F_c	Z	F_c
$\{Z_1\}$	$\{Z_3\}$	$\{Z_2, W_2\}$	$\{Z_3\}$	$\{Z_2, Z_3, W_1\}$	$\emptyset$
$\{Z_2\}$	$\{Z_3\}$	$\{Z_3, W_1\}$	$\emptyset$	$\{Z_2, Z_3, W_2\}$	$\emptyset$
$\{W_1\}$	$\{Z_3\}$	$\{Z_3, W_2\}$	$\emptyset$	$\{Z_2, W_1, W_2\}$	$\{Z_3\}$
$\{W_2\}$	$\{Z_3\}$	$\{W_1, W_2\}$	$\{Z_3\}$	$\{Z_3, W_1, W_2\}$	$\emptyset$
$\{Z_1, Z_2\}$	$\{Z_3\}$	$\{Z_1, Z_2, Z_3\}$	$\emptyset$	$\{Z_1, Z_2, Z_3, W_1\}$	$\emptyset$
$\{Z_1, Z_3\}$	$\emptyset$	$\{Z_1, Z_2, W_1\}$	$\{Z_3\}$	$\{Z_1, Z_2, Z_3, W_2\}$	$\emptyset$
$\{Z_1, W_1\}$	$\{Z_3\}$	$\{Z_1, Z_2, W_2\}$	$\{Z_3\}$	$\{Z_1, Z_2, W_1, W_2\}$	$\{Z_3\}$
$\{Z_1, W_2\}$	$\{Z_3\}$	$\{Z_1, Z_3, W_1\}$	$\emptyset$	$\{Z_1, Z_3, W_1, W_2\}$	$\emptyset$
$\{Z_2, Z_3\}$	$\emptyset$	$\{Z_1, Z_3, W_2\}$	$\emptyset$	$\{Z_2, Z_3, W_1, W_2\}$	$\emptyset$
$\{Z_2, W_1\}$	$\{Z_3\}$	$\{Z_1, W_1, W_2\}$	$\{Z_3\}$	$\{Z_1, Z_2, Z_3, W_1, W_2\}$	$\emptyset$
Z	F_a			Z	F_c
$\emptyset$	$\{W_1, Z_3\}; \{Z_1, Z_3\}; \{Z_2, Z_3\}; \{Z_3, W_2\}$		$\{Z_3\}$	$\{W_1\}; \{Z_1\}; \{Z_2\}; \{W_2\}$	

This significantly reduces the analytical dimension of the observation data compared with the six covariates that need to be considered.

5.2   Effect of Warm-up Exercises on Injury

In Fig. 3, a causal map of variables that are associated with Warm-up exercise and Injury is shown. This is a realistic graph retrieved from Shrier and Platt [17]. In this example, we are interested in how the algorithm can be used to list a-MSSs and c-MSSs when the causal graph includes latent variables.

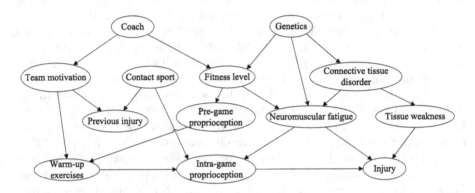

Fig. 3. Causal graph: the effect of warm-up exercises on injury.

When estimating the causality between Warm-up exercise and Injury, there are too many covariates associated with Warm-up exercise and Injury that need to be analyzed. In this case, the complexity of the analysis is high due to the number of dimensions of observation data. More unfortunately, there is a potential variable (Genetics) in these covariates. Completely correct genetic data is likely to be absent in multi-dimensional observation data because it is difficult to obtain due to cost and other reasons. For this example, we decide to include the "Connective tissue disorder" in the conditional set Z when we state the case of conditional intervention. And the "Genetics" is a latent variable in the set L. We obtain Table 2 by the algorithm, which enumerates all minimal sufficient sets under atomic and conditional interventions.

Take the first and second items in the table as an example. According to the Eqs. (1) and (2), the causal effect under atomic intervention that denoted as $P(Injury| do(Warm\text{-}up\ exercises))$ can be estimated by adjusting on Fitness level and Team motivation or by adjusting on Neuromuscular fatigue and Tissue weakness. Another, the causal effect under conditional intervention that denoted as $P(Injury| do(Warm\text{-}up\ exercises = g(Connective\ tissue\ disorder)))$ can be estimated by adjusting on Fitness level and Team motivation or by adjusting individually on Neuromuscular fatigue. In reality, the sufficient set is usually chosen with less variables and easy to measure which can reduce the workload and increase the efficiency of statistical analysis.

Table 2. Minimal sufficient sets of the causal graph in Fig. 3.

a-MSS ($Z = \emptyset$)	c-MSS ($Z = \{$Connective tissue disorder$\}$)
1 Fitness level, Team motivation	1 Fitness level, Team motivation
2 Neuromuscular fatigue, Tissue weakness	2 Neuromuscular fatigue
3 Neuromuscular fatigue, Connective tissue disorder	3 Pre-game proprioception, Team motivation
4 Pre-game proprioception, Team motivation	4 Coach, Fitness level
5 Coach, Fitness level	5 Coach, Pre-game proprioception
6 Coach, Pre-game proprioception	

6 Conclusion and Discussion

This paper reviews criteria of sufficient set as well as separation operations presented in causal graph related literatures and presents a criterion based on previous work to extract the minimal variable sets for adjustment when the external intervention is conditional. We develop an algorithm to uncover the minimal sufficient sets under both atomic and conditional interventions in the causal graph. Although there are several research approaches aiming at inferring the causality in observation data, the approach proposed in our work is fairly effective in terms of intuition and verifiability. By the properties of criteria on a DAG, we can conveniently recover the causality between the treatment and the outcome when external interventions are imposed. It is worth mentioning that this is particularly useful when we analyze the multi-dimensional observation data.

Next, we will investigate other criteria (such as front-door criterion, instrument variable, etc.) or external random interventions to better integrate causal theory with data analysis methodology.

References

1. Han, J., Pei, J., Kamber, M.: Data Mining: Concepts and Techniques. Elsevier, Amsterdam (2011)
2. Bechini, A., Marcelloni, F., Segatori, A.: A MapReduce solution for associative classification of big data. Inf. Sci. **332**(C), 33–55 (2016)
3. Li, L., Lu, R., Choo, K.K.R., Datta, A., Shao, J.: Privacy-preserving-outsourced association rule mining on vertically partitioned databases. IEEE Trans. Inf. Forensics Secur. **11**(8), 1847–1861 (2016)
4. Pearl, J.: An introduction to causal inference. Int. J. Biostat. **6**(2), 1–62 (2010)
5. Imbens, G.W., Rubin, D.B.: Causal Inference in Statistics, Social, and Biomedical Sciences. Cambridge University Press, Cambridge (2015)
6. Wang, J., Mueller, K.: The visual causality analyst: an interactive interface for causal reasoning. IEEE Trans. Visual. Comput. Graph. **22**(1), 230–239 (2016)

7. Pearl, J.: Causal diagrams for empirical research. Biometrika **82**(4), 669–688 (1995)
8. Shpitser, I., Pearl, J.: Identification of conditional interventional distributions. In: Proceedings of the Twenty-Second Conference on Uncertainty in Artificial Intelligence, pp. 437–444 (2006)
9. Bareinboim, E., Pearl, J.: Causal inference and the data-fusion problem. Proc. Natl. Acad. Sci. **113**(27), 7345–7352 (2016)
10. Shan, N.: Causal inference based on causal network. Northeast Normal University (2010)
11. Textor, J., Liskiewicz, M.: Adjustment criteria in causal diagrams: an algorithmic perspective. In: Proceedings of the Twenty-Seventh Conference on Uncertainty in Artificial Intelligence, pp. 681–688 (2012)
12. Perković, E., Textor, J., Kalisch, M., Maathuis, M.H.: A complete generalized adjustment criterion. In: Proceedings of the 31st Conference on Uncertainty in Artificial Intelligence, pp. 682–691 (2015)
13. Textor, J.: Drawing and analyzing causal dags with dagitty. Nucleic Acids Res. **32**(10), 3220–3227 (2015)
14. Textor, J., Hardt, J., Knüppel, S.: DAGitty: a graphical tool for analyzing causal diagrams. Epidemiology **22**(5), 745–751 (2011)
15. Kyono, T.M.: Commentator: a front-end user-interface module for graphical and structural equation modeling. Ph.D. thesis, University of California, Los Angeles (2010)
16. Lauritzen, S.L., Dawid, A.P., Larsen, B.N., Leimer, H.G.: Independence properties of directed Markov fields. Networks **20**(5), 491–505 (2010)
17. Shrier, I., Platt, R.W.: Reducing bias through directed acyclic graphs. BMC Med. Res. Methodol. **8**(1), 70 (2008)

Mobile Computing and Social Services

LDA-TIM: An Approach for Individual Sentiment Prediction in Social Networks

Wenxin Kuang and Ming Zhao$^{(\boxtimes)}$

Department of Software, Central South University, Changsha 410083, China
{wenxinkuang,meanzhao}@csu.edu.cn

Abstract. Social networks like Facebook and SINA have been rapidly growing and accumulating a sheer volume of data such as social links between the users, user claims, and their comments. The work is motivated by the proliferation of social networks and large amounts of information that is voluntarily broadcast on them, which generates an interest in finding ways to predict individual sentiment that applies in public sentiment warning, advertisement, and recommendation. However, the traditional user sentiment prediction model has shortcoming of high complexity, which renders inefficiencies of individual sentiment prediction in social networks. To tackle this challenge, in this study, we develop an individual sentiment prediction method LDA-TIM based on the individual interest preferences and social influence. Then, based on the objective function we trained a logistic regression classifier to predict individual sentiment polarity. Finally, extensive experiments are conducted to evaluate the performance of our approach by using two large-scale real-world data collected from SINA. The experimental results on the two large-scale-real-word data set both reveal that each of the components are critical to obtaining satisfactory performance on our data. Experiments show the F1-Measure value of the individual sentiment approach can reach 70.99%.

Keywords: Keywords social network
Individual sentiment prediction · Logistic regression · Recommendation

1 Introduction

The wide use of computers and the mobile devices sparks the boom of the social networks. The use of social networking platforms, such as Facebook twitter and SINA, bridges the gap between the physical world and the digital online world. According to eMarketer's (www.emarketer.com) latest statistics, 2016 Britain will have half of the population on a regular basis using Facebook. It means that, there will be an average of 33.2 million people in the UK to use at least the monthly social network, from 49.5% in 2015 to 50.1% in 2016. SINA, the most popular social networking platform, active users reached 236 million per month, and daily active users had 106 million, an increase of 32% at the end of the fourth quarter in 2016. Sustained increase in the number of social network users

© Springer Nature Singapore Pte Ltd. 2018
J. Li et al. (Eds.): CWSN 2017, CCIS 812, pp. 247–261, 2018.
https://doi.org/10.1007/978-981-10-8123-1_22

has created critical conditions for the public sentiment warning, advertisement, and recommendation.

It is greatly significant to uncover the underlying social network operating mechanism and the law of information diffusion to obtain valuable information for the users. As we know that the behavior of users will affect the dissemination of information in social networks and crucial for the performance of recommendation system. Kempe et al. present a panorama of three classic information dissemination models and uncover the law of information Diffusion in the social network [1].

Unlike traditional networks, nodes in social networks are humans. Emotion is one of the important characteristics of mankind. The sentiments of a user plays an important role in understanding the individual activities. Individual sentiments are beneficial for exploring the social networks and its applications, such as recommendation and information diffusion. Bollen et al. point out that individual emotions can profoundly affect the user's behavior and decision-making [2]. They studied the feelings of Twitter users and revealed to us how emotions affect the stock market ups and downs. Lei et al. mine individual sentiment information from reviews to help us understand how it influences a user's preferences and makes an accurate recommendation [3]. The status of individual sentiment will not only affect their behavior and decision-making but also will even impact fluctuations in the market economy.

However, the sheer volume of information in the online social networks often undermines the users' ability to choose the things or activities that best fit their interests. To address the aforementioned questions, in this paper, we aim to propose a new method to predict individual sentiment in the social network. We present an emotional predictive function, which mainly uses the user's personal information, such as interest tags, friends number etc. We provide a formal definition for the notion of individual interest preferences and social influence first. Then we develop two instantiation functions based on individual interest preferences and social influence. At last, we will use the final training of the classification model based on our proposed functions to achieve the purpose of individual sentiment prediction. The main contribution of the paper can be listed as follows.

We propose a user sentimental prediction approach, which is based on two formal definitions for the notion of individual interest preferences function and social influence function. The individual interest preferences and social influence are mined from the individual claims and comments, respectively. We will discuss this in detail in a later chapter.

A final training of the classification model based on the proposed functions is designed to predict individual sentiment. Extensive experiments are conducted to evaluate the performance of our approach using large-scale real-world data sets collected from SINA. The experiments results on the two large-scale-real-word data set both reveal that each of the components are critical to obtaining satisfactory performance on our data substantially outperforming models that consider each of the factors alone.

We point out promising research topics for future work. This article presents a panorama of the individual sentiment prediction with a balanced depth, facilitating research into this important research theme.

The road map of the paper is as follows. After discussing related work in more details (Sect. 2), we give a formalization of the problem and approach overview (Sect. 3). We then describe how to use the final training of the classification model based on our proposed functions to predict individual sentiment (Sect. 4). In Sect. 5, we subject our system to thorough experimental analysis using two real datasets. We point out promising research topics for future work in Sect. 6.

2   Related Work

With the arrival of Web2.0 era and the soaring information, social network platform has become popular. Social network as one of the typical applications of Web2.0 is highly valued by a growing number of educational researchers. Vastardis et al. have made a detailed introduction to the concept, structure, social attribute, and application of social network [4]. To find the law of information dissemination from a large amount of information, Kempe et al. shown the model of information dissemination. He summed up the three classic information dissemination model [1]. Since Kempe et al.'s seminal work, extensive researches have been done on influence maximization [5–7]. Guille et al. also made a detailed introduction to the proliferation of information in social networks [8]. Many factors can affect the proliferation of information in social networks, such as the underlying structure of the social network [6] and the content of the information itself, etc. Srivastava et al. first time put forward a unified information dissemination model and summarized the law of information dissemination [9].

As the work to explore information dissemination progress, people began to realize that the social network is different from the original virtual network. The node in the social network is human beings, therefore, the social network of users' various complex behavior is likely to affect the dissemination of information. Such the characteristics of social attributes-emotion, which was critical for us to better understand for the social network. Bollen et al. have raised a research upsurge of emotion. They revealed to us how emotions affect the stock market ups and downs and showed to us how user's emotions affect their behavior and decision-making [2]. Through carefully analyzed and studied the individual sentiment, researchers found that the user's emotional state will affect their behavior and decision-making [2, 10, 11]. Gong et al. is also a relatively early start to study how to use the user's history claims information and the user's emotional status information to predict the user's behavior, but their understanding of this relationship is still fragmentary [10].

A body of research began to study emotional prediction [2, 3, 10–13]. Lei et al. focus how to build the emotional lexicon, but its performance in the prediction is not very well, since they had reckoned without the social influence which discussed in our work [3]. Zhang et al. only consider how to predict the user's emotion from the text, and emotional polarity is only positive and negative [11].

Comparatively speaking, the neutral emotion be put into our study with best comprehensive benefits. In recent years, some researchers have studied the image emotion [14,15]. Wang et al. mainly studied how to obtain the user's emotional state from the image and developed a model to predict the emotions hidden in the picture but the model complexity is more higher than our work [12]. If we grasp the emotional state of users in the social network accurately, which will facilitate the understanding of the running mechanism of social networks, we can get a better application performance, for illustrate, the public sentiment warning, advertisement social recommendation [15–21].

This paper uses the insights from the above work and develops a new emotion prediction approach to accurately grasp the emotion state of users in social networks. To the best of our knowledge, this is the first attempt to conjointly individual interest preferences, frequency, and social influence to accurately grasp the individual emotional state.

3   Problem Definition and Approach Overview

3.1   Preliminaries

The time-varying social network can be denoted as a graph $G^t = (U^t, E^t, M^t)$, where U^t is a set of $|U| = N$ users at time t and $v \in U$ represents an individual in the social network $|U| = N$, N is the number of users. $E^t \subset U^t \times U^t$ is a bunch of relationships between users at time t which will be changing over time. $e_{i,j}$ represents the relationship between the user v_i and v_j, here, we define that if the user v_i followed to the v_j, there is a relationship between them and $e_{i,j} \in E^t$. M^t are claims posted by all the users in the social network, and $m_i^t \in M^t$ represents that the user v_i post a microblog/claim m at the time t. To make it more general, we give the definition of individual interest preferences and social influence.

Definition 1. *Individual interest preference* $T_i^t(m)$ *is the user's interest tendency about a microblog/claim when he saw it which only generated from the user's personal interests. For example, if a user likes a particular singer he may be attached to the songs which were sung by that singer. Here, we use* $T_i^t(m)$ *represents the interest preference of user* v_i *when he saw a microblog* m *at the time* t.

Definition 2. *Social influence* $I_i^t(m)$ *is another kind of user emotion tendency which is only influenced by his friends in the social network. For instance, a user may want to eat a kind food that many of his friends recommend to him. Notation that we only consider the sentiment polarity made by his friends.* $I_i^t(m)$ *represents the social influence that for a microblog* m, *user* v_i *received from his friends at time* t.

Definition 3. *Individual sentiment is* $v_i^{'}$ *target emotion which is a combination of individual interest preference and social influence.*

Learning task $y_i^t(m)$: Given a time-varying social network G^t, we aim to find a function for predicting emotions of all unlabeled microblogs.

$$f(V, E^t, M^t, Y^t | G^t) = f(T_{i,m}^t, I_{i,m}^t) \rightarrow Y_i^{t+1} \tag{1}$$

3.2   Approach Overview

We will overview the main idea of the prediction method in this part. First, we extract all the data in the social network. Next, we provide a formal definition for the notion of individual sentiment and develop two instantiation functions: based on individual interest preferences and social influence. We aggregate the terms associated with the user, including user's self-interest tags and themes, history claims, and user comments for claims etc. into the corresponding document. Based on all the textual data aforementioned we try to give a formal definition for individual interest preferences which presents in Sect. 4.1. Then, we try to establish the social influence function in Sect. 4.2. Finally, based on the objective function we trained a logistic regression classifier to predict individual sentiment. Figure 1 is a snapshot of the framework for individual sentiment prediction process.

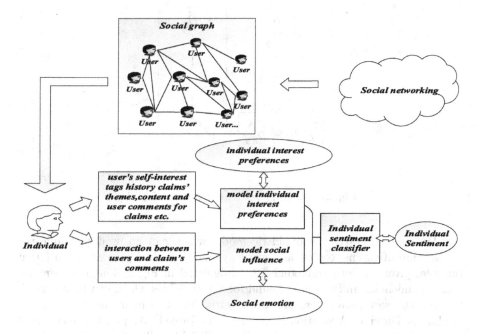

Fig. 1. Framework of individual sentiment prediction

4   Individual Sentiment Prediction Model

4.1   Individual Interest Preferences Function

Extract Individual Interests Preference. According to the user's self-interest tags, history claims' themes, content, and user comments for claims etc. We will use all the textual data aforementioned to establish the personal vocabulary corpus, then we can give a formal definition for individual interest preferences. Yang et al. considered only with obvious emotional vocabulary words when modeling individual interest preferences [13]. However, some words do not have a clear emotional polarity, and it contains the meaning of emotional polarity. To illustrate, as we all know, when we meet word "happy", we know it delivers a positive sentiment to us obviously, and the word "sad" are opposite. But for a word "sunshine" maybe represents a positive sentiment can be overlooked. Due to the different language habits of users, some words may be regarded as a different polarity. To solve the above problems, we extract individual interest preference from users' self document by using LDA (Latent Dirichlet Allocation).

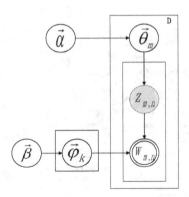

Fig. 2. The graphical representation of LDA

LDA is a generative probabilistic model which can be used to mimic the relationship of claims, topics, and words, generating observed data from latent variables given model parameters [22] as depicted in Fig. 2. The arrows represent dependencies and the $w_{m,n}$ stand for the variables which can be observed. Instead, the rest parameters are latent variables. The main notation used in the Latent Dirichlet Allocation is as showed in Table 1. We profile the claims of users as documents and then perform latent Dirichlet allocation (LDA) to learn individual preference over topics. However, the problem is these documents are usually too short to reflect individual interest performance. We aggregate the terms associated with the user, including user self-interest tags and themes, history claims, and user comments for claims etc. into the corresponding document.

Table 1. Key notation in latent Dirichlet allocation

Symbol	Definition
Voc	The set of words in claims posted by individual in the dictionary
$w_{m,n}$	The nth word in m^{th} claims of user v_i and $w_{m,n} \in Voc$
d_m	The document/claims of the user v_i', each individual
τ	The number of topics which is a constant set up by experience
θ_m	Topic distribution of the individual v_i
φ_k	Word distribution of the kth topic v_i
α	Dirichlet prior to distribution θ_m
β	Dirichlet prior to distribution φ_k

We treat words in individual history claims as words in LAD model and individual expression patterns are equivalent to topic. We design the set of individual document and the individual expression habits which calls the distribution of individual topic preference as our input and output respectively. In this paper, we empirically assign $\tau = 50$. We learn the LDA model by conduct a Gibbs sampling algorithm to obtain the individual topic preference. Later in Sect. 5.3, we will analyze the effect of the number of topics on predicting individual sentiment.

Instantiation the Function of Individual Interest Preferences. We will model individual interest preferences by using the result in the above section which reflect individual topic preferences words. We found that when we analyze individual interest preferences, as in real life, users' emotion can be divided into many categories but to simplify the problem and facilitate theoretical analysis, the emotion polarity can be broadly separated into positive and negative. Therefore, we assume that the user has three main kinds of emotion polarity, namely, positive (such as like), negative (such as hate), neutral (such as indifferent). First, we will calculate each word's probability of sentiment polarity in the claims/microblog for the individual. Then, we use the defined function to estimate individual interest preferences. The probability that vocabulary w describes the user's positive emotion can be calculated as follows:

$$p_i^+(w) = \frac{|\{m|m \in M_i, y_i(m) > 0, w \in m\}|}{|\{m|m \in M_i, w \in m\}|} \tag{2}$$

where $p_i^+(w)$ is the probability that vocabulary w has a positive effect for individual. M_i refers to a document for all the words extracted from user v_i' document, including his microblogs and comment which he posted before and $w \in m \in M_i$. $y_i(m) > 0$ means user v_i have a positive attitude to a claim m. $p_i^-(w)$ represents the probability that word w have a negative impact on individual v_i which can be calculated as follows:

$$p_i^-(w) = \frac{|\{m|m \in M_i, y_i(m) < 0, w \in m\}|}{|\{m|m \in M_i, w \in m\}|} \tag{3}$$

$p_i^*(w)$ represents the probability that word w have a neutral impact on individual v_i. The formal definition is as follows

$$p_i^*(w) = \frac{|\{m|m \in M_i, y_i(m) = 0, w \in m\}|}{|\{m|m \in M_i, w \in m\}|} \tag{4}$$

Namely, we can provide the Individual interest preferences function with the form

$$T_i^t(m) = \sum_{k=1, w_k \in m}^{n} [p_i^+(w_k) - p_i^-(w_k) - p_i^*(w_k)] \tag{5}$$

According to the superposition of positive neutral, and negative emotional states of all words, we can obtain individual interest preferences function $T_i^t(m)$, n is the number of words in an unlabeled microblogs.

4.2   Social Influence Function

The definition for social influence is inspired from the observation that behavioral changes in individuals are frequently affected by their intimate friends. If user v_i follows with v_j, v_j' activities, such as he post a claim or retweet an microblog, are visible to v_i. Then v_i can decide whether to retweet it or not. Here, we define that v_i is the follower of v_j and v_j is the followee of v_i and v_j is v_i' friend. In addition to being affected by their own preferences, a user's emotion will also be influenced by other friends in its ego social network. The impact of different friends on the user is different, which depends on the degree of intimacy between a pair of users and their similarity to the same event.

In this paper, we use $freq(v_i, v_j)$ as the frequency of interaction between users. We define that once v_i and v_j satisfy any of the following condition, an interaction will be created between them: (1) if user v_j pushed a claim, the user v_i retweet it or give it a comment. (2) if user v_j pushed a claim, the user v_i give a 'like' behavior. The interaction between v_i and v_i can be calculated as follows:

$$freq(v_i, v_j) = \frac{|\{l_{(v_i,v_j)}|v_j \in F(v_i)\}|}{\sum_{k=0}^{k} |\{l_{(v_i,v_k)}|v_k \in F(v_i)\}|} \tag{6}$$

Note that $freq(v_i, v_j)$ not equal to $freq(v_j, v_i,)$. $F(v_i)$ means a set of v_i' followees. k is the number of v_i' followees. l_{v_i,v_k} represents the number of interaction between user and, and refer to the number of interaction between user v_i and v_k.

We use $simi(v_i, v_j)$ as the similarity between users (probability of having similar emotions between a pair of users). Based on the sentiment state of their history, the emotional similarity is calculated as follows:

$$simi(v_i, v_j) = \sum_{k=1, v_j \in F(v_i)}^{s, s<N} \hbar$$

$$\hbar = \frac{|\{m_k|y_i(m) \cap y_j(m) > 0, m_k \in M(i), m_k \in M(j)\}|}{|\{m_k|m_k \in M(i), m_k \in M(j)\}|} \qquad (7)$$

where s refers to the number of claims which v_i, v_j have the same emotion. $M(i)$ is the a set of microblog comments is the microblog set commented by user v_i in historical dataset and $y_i(m)$ is the user v_i' emotion value for the commented microblog m. We assume that if v_i see a new claim m, he can also meet all his friend's comments for this claim.

To sum up, when user v_i see a new claim he will generate an emotion which comes from social influence $I_i^t(m)$:

$$I_i^t(m) = \sum_{\substack{0<t'<t, \\ 0<j<n, \\ v_j \in F(v_i)}}^{N} sign(y_j^{t'}(m)) \times (freq(v_i, v_j) + simi(v_i, v_j)) \qquad (8)$$

4.3 Sensitivity Weight Assignment

Individual interest preferences and the social influence are instantiated as aforementioned. However, everyone has his own personalities that some people are more sensitive. If a user's individual interest preferences are consistent with the final sentiment for most of the time, we regard that the user is more assertive. By contrast, if a user's final sentiment are more consistent with his friends, we can conclude that the user is more sensitive. Weighted calculation formula for individual interest preferences:

$$\gamma = \frac{1}{n} \sum_{\substack{k=1, \\ m_k \in M}}^{n} \frac{|\{T_i(m_k) \times y_i(m_k) + |T_i(m_k) \times y_i(m_k)|\}|}{2|T_i(m_k) \times y_i(m_k)|} \qquad (9)$$

Weighted calculation formula for individual interest preferences:

$$\beta = \frac{1}{n} \sum_{\substack{k=1, \\ m_k \in M}}^{n} \frac{|\{I_i(m_k) \times y_i(m_k) + |I_i(m_k) \times y_i(m_k)|\}|}{2|I_i(m_k) \times y_i(m_k)|} \qquad (10)$$

n is the number of microblogs created by individual v_i. To summarize, the final definition of the user's emotional objective function is as follows:

$$f(T_{i,m}^t, I_{i,m}^t) = \gamma \times T_i^t(m) + \beta \times I_i^t(m) \qquad (11)$$

4.4 Individual Sentiment Prediction and Social Recommendation

To predict individual emotion accurately, we can handle it as a classification problem: given a claim m, user v_i will see that claim and the comments which given by all his friends at time t. The main question is to classify individual sentiment state at the time $t'(t' > t)$ namely the value of $y_i^t(m)$. Using the emotional objective function $f(T_{i,m}^t, I_{i,m}^t)$ defined above as evidence to predict $y_i^t(m)$. $y_i^t(m) = 1$ means the user v_i have a positive emotion toward claims m, then we can utilize the result to do retweet behavior prediction or built a user satisfied recommendation system. Here, we choose logistic regression classifier to predict individual sentiment.

$$P(y_i^t(m) = 1 | \overrightarrow{x}_{v,m,t}) = \frac{1}{1 + e^{-(\mu \times \overrightarrow{x}_{v,m,t} + \omega)}} \tag{12}$$

where $\overrightarrow{x}_{v,m,t}$ is the feature vector of user v_i. μ and ω are weights of the features which can be learned by maximizing the likelihood objective function:

$$L(y|\mu, \varepsilon) = \prod_{\substack{v \in U, \\ m \in M}} P(y = 1 | \overrightarrow{x}_{v,m,t}) \prod_{\substack{v \in U, \\ m \in M}} P(y = 0 | \overrightarrow{x}_{v,m,t}) \tag{13}$$

5   Experiments

5.1   Experimental Setup

Throughout experiments using two large real datasets crawled from SINA microblog (http://weibo.com) demonstrate the effectiveness of our proposed approach in contrast to state-of-the-art event competitors from the literature. User in SINA is able to share their own interests and mood or other things with their friends by pushing claims. Sometimes they may be far away from their friend in the physical world, but they are capable of catching friends up on the latest microblogs which posted by their friends. The latest published data show that the number of registered users of SINA microblog have more than 560 million. Since it is difficult to capture such a large amount of data in a short time, here, we sampled the data and randomly selected 100 sets of users, including their followees and followees' followees. The final data set was extracted from 1269743 user data, and they were able to constitute a small core social network. In order to improve the efficiency of the experiment, we excluded some less active users. We finally choose the users who have more followees and at least post or retweet more than 40 claims within the period of the past ten days from December 11th to 20th, 2014. At last, we selected 94759 users and they produced a total of 760498551 claims. Picture sentiment is more confusing, which is beyond our considerations. The data set also removed claims that contained only pictures, videos or less than five characters. We Selected 529387443 claims and its following comments which we called DataSet_1. Considering the novelty and diversity of experiment data, we collect the data from SINA in the same way. We sampled the data and randomly selected 100 sets of users, including their followees and followees' followees. The difference is that we crawl the data, namely DataSet_2, within the period of the past ten days from January 11th to 20th, 2016. Finally we selected 98347 users and their 834549146. Then we mark sentiment polarity for all claims and comments manually. To get an accuracy sentiment polarity result, we invite three microblogging emotional marker to label the emotional polarity for the two datasets collected from SINA. Finally, we check the consistency of the result by conducting a Kappa test. For claims, which is inconsistent with the emotional tagging, we determine its polarity of belonging according to the voting principle of High-voting.

5.2 Analysis Performance of Sentiment Prediction

As our emotional predict method is based on LDA and an objective function $f(T_{i,m}^t, I_{i,m}^t)$ which described in Eq. (11), the individual emotion prediction method can be named LDA-TIM. We compare the proposed model with alternative baseline methods for emotion prediction. The data configuration for the baseline algorithms is the same as our model. The prediction performance of the model is evaluated by using Precision, Recall, and F1-Measure. The three baseline methods are as follows:

Table 2. Comparison of different baseline methods (%)

Method	DataSet_1			DataSet_2		
	Precision	Recall	F1	Precision	Recall	F1
LDA-TIM	70.96	71.02	70.99	73.52	70.23	70.87
SVM_Simple	50.68	47.36	48.96	45.68	47.46	46.55
SVM	64.51	53.43	58.45	60.50	74.55	66.79
Naïve Bayes	48.18	53.63	50.76	72.35	58.06	64.42

Simple Support Vector Machine (SVM_Simple): This method train the classification model which only use the information of individual interest preferences to classify the individual sentiment.

Support Vector Machine (SVM): This method directly uses the same visual features as our model to train a classifier.

Naïve Bayes (Naïve Bayes): This method uses the same information as SVM, but uses a naive Bayesian classifier.

From Table 2, we can see the performance comparison between the three baseline methods and the methods proposed in this paper. From the results, we can see that the F1-Measure score of LDA-TIM method proposed by us is higher than the other three baseline methods, which shows that our proposed method can get better user emotion prediction performance. The F1-Measure score of SVM method is higher than the SVM_Simple method, which shows that it is not enough to consider the individual interest only and social influence is essential to predict individual sentiment accurately. Even if the social influence factors are added, the predictive results of the SVM model are barely satisfactory. The LDA-TIM method proposed in this paper takes into account the individual interest preferences and the social influence, which shows a significant higher score on prediction accuracy and F1-Measure than other three method.

5.3 Analysis of Extracting Individual Interests

In this part, we set up an experiment to test the impact of extracting individual interest topic election on experimental results. If few number of topics were selected, we can hardly extract individual real interest preference, and F1-Measure score of the model will be greatly reduced, which can be illustrated in Fig. 3. On the other hand, a little size of topics will weak the predictive performance of the LDA-TIM model, which completely neglects the individual characteristic, and depress the F1-Measure score of emotion classification. On the other hand, increasing the number of topics improperly leads to the emergence of noise topics, which will cause a bad influence on emotion prediction, since it maybe result in the emergence of the topic fragmentation. As depicted in Fig. 3, the performance of SVM_Simple, which not take the advantage of extract users' interest preference, has been flat to predict individual emotion. Unlike SVM_Simple, the SVM make use of the two factors as LDA-TIM, and the prediction performance has been greatly improved.

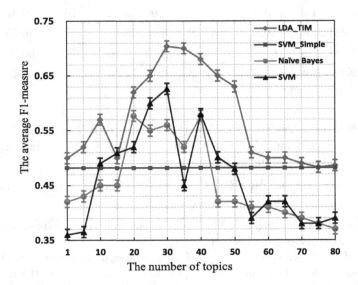

Fig. 3. The contribution of extracting individual interests performance

We can conclude that if we select fewer topics, we can hardly extract individual real interest performance, and the model F1 will be significantly reduced.

Only when the number of topics reaches 20+, the average F1 has been significantly improved. From the results, we can see that the F1-Measure score of LDA-TIM method proposed by us is higher than the other three baseline methods, and it can also get better prediction performance. Obviously, in order to obtain the accurate personal interest, it is necessary to use the LDA to extract individual interest performance. For our LDA-TIM method, when we choose about 30 topics, the average F1 will reach the peak.

5.4   Analysis of Contribution Factors

Figure 4 shows the change of Precision, Recall, and F1-Measure in the process of extracting various factors for two datasets. The extraction order is as follows: the extraction of individual interest preferences (TIM_Intr), pulling away the social influence (TIM_Infl). In order to prove that the frequency of interaction between users is essential to the definition of social influence function, we also exclude user interaction frequency (TIM_Freq). When we define the social influence (only considering the similarity between users). It shows in Fig. 4 that individual sentiment prediction should be determined by both individual interest preferences and social influence, and neither is dispensable. When the factor of social influence is extracted, the F1 will drop sharply by 0.24 and 0.26 on DateSet_1 and DataSet_2 respectively. Which verifies that the nodes in the social network are different from traditional networks since the nodes in social networks are humans. The nodes in the social network have the characteristics of social attributes like human beings. In order to improve the social influence modeling, we add the factors of interaction frequency between users. As shown in the Fig. 4, we found that if the user interaction frequency to be considered the LDA-TIM prediction method can get a higher F1-Measure score than not considering the interaction frequency. In conclusion, the frequency of interaction between users is particularly important for modeling Social influence.

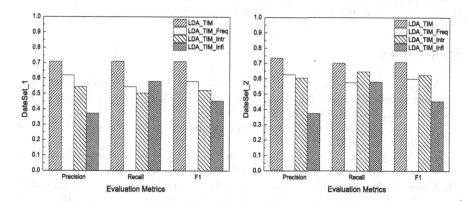

Fig. 4. Contribution of different factor functions. LDA_TIM_Freq excludes frequency factor, LDA_TIM_Intr excludes individual interest preference factors and the LDT_TIM_Infl excludes social influence factors

For the same claims, most individual sentiments are consistent with their friend, which implies that the proportion of social influence in predicting the user's emotion is slightly greater than the individual interest preference, but after adding the fact of personal interest preference the LDA-TIM will achieve a considerable performance. It can be observed that when we ignored any one factor, the value of the three evaluation indicators have an obvious decline in both datasets. As the results, if we neglect any factors, the value of indicators start to decline.

In general, the predictive power of the model is the strongest when only considering the individual interest and the whole social influence. Ignoring any factor could weaken the prediction ability of the model.

6   Conclusion

The work is motivated by the proliferation of social networks and the wealth of information that is voluntarily broadcast on them, which generates interest in finding ways to predict individual sentiment that applies to public sentiment warning, advertisement, and recommendation.

In this paper, we have proposed an individual sentiment prediction method to jointly consider the individual interest preferences and social influence. In particular, we use the LDA to capture the individual interests preference more accurately. Then we predict individual sentiment by training a logistic regression classifier. Finally, the results of the experiments on two large-scale-real-word data sets reveal that each of the components (individual interest preferences, frequency, and social influence) are critical to obtaining satisfactory performance on our data. Substantially outperforming models that consider each of the factors in isolation.

Acknowledgments. The research is supported by "National Natural Science Foundation of China" under Grant No.61572526 and "The Fund of Graduate Student Independent Innovation Project" under Grant No.2017zzts617.

References

1. Kempe, D., Kleinberg, J., Tardos, É.: Maximizing the spread of influence through a social network. In: ACM SIGKDD International Conference on Knowledge Discovery and Data Mining, pp. 137–146 (2003)
2. Bollen, J., Mao, H., Zeng, X.: Twitter mood predicts the stock market. J. Comput. Sci. **2**(1), 1–8 (2010)
3. Lei, X., Qian, X., Zhao, G.: Rating prediction based on social sentiment from textual reviews. IEEE Trans. Multimedia **18**, 1910–1921 (2016). IEEE Press
4. Vastardis, N., Yang, K.: Mobile social networks: architectures, social properties, and key research challenges. IEEE Commun. Surv. Tutor. **15**(3), 1355–1371 (2013)
5. Xiong, X., Jiang, D., Wu, Y., He, L., Song, H., Lv, Z.: Empirical analysis and modeling of the activity dilemmas in big social networks. IEEE Access **5**(99), 967–974 (2016)

6. Foroutan, N., Hamzeh, A.: Discovering the hidden structure of a social network: a semi supervised approach. IEEE Trans. Comput. Soc. Syst. **4**(1), 14–25 (2017)
7. Wu, L., Ge, Y., Liu, Q., Chen, E., Hong, R., Wang, M., Du, J.: Modeling the evolution of users' preferences and social links in social networking services. IEEE Trans. Knowl. Data Eng. **29**(6), 1240–1253 (2017)
8. Guille, A.: Information diffusion in online social networks. In: SIGMOD/PODS Ph.D. Symposium, pp. 31–36 (2013)
9. Srivastava, A., Chelmis, C., Prasanna, V.K.: Influence in social networks: a unified model? In: IEEE/ACM International Conference on Advances in Social Networks Analysis and Mining, pp. 451–454 (2014)
10. Gong, J., Tang, J., Fong, A.C.M.: ACTPred: activity prediction in mobile social networks. Tsinghua Sci. Technol. **19**(3), 265–274 (2014)
11. Zhang, Y., Tang, J., Sun, J., Chen, Y., Rao, J.: MoodCast: emotion prediction via dynamic continuous factor graph model. In: IEEE International Conference on Data Mining, pp. 1193–1198 (2010)
12. Wang, X., Jia, J., Tang, J., Wu, B., Cai, L., Xie, L.: Modeling emotion influence in image social networks. IEEE Trans. Affect. Comput. **6**(3), 286–297 (2015)
13. Yang, Y., Cui, P., Zhu, W., Yang, S.: User interest and social influence based emotion prediction for individuals, pp. 785–788 (2013)
14. Caldelli, R., Becarelli, R., Amerini, I.: Image origin classification based on social network provenance. IEEE Trans. Inf. Forensics Secur. **PP**(99), 1 (2017)
15. Wang, Z., Liao, J., Cao, Q., Qi, H.: Friendbook: a semantic-based friend recommendation system for social networks. IEEE Trans. Mob. Comput. **14**(3), 538–551 (2015)
16. Stepan, T., Morawski, J.M., Dick, S., Miller, J.: Incorporating spatial, temporal, and social context in recommendations for location-based social networks. IEEE Trans. Comput. Soc. Syst. **PP**(99), 1–12 (2016)
17. Lou, P., Zhao, G., Qian, X., Wang, H., Hou, X.: Schedule a rich sentimental travel via sentimental POI mining and recommendation. In: IEEE Second International Conference on Multimedia Big Data, pp. 33–40 (2016)
18. He, R., Mcauley, J.: Ups and downs: modeling the visual evolution of fashion trends with one-class collaborative filtering. In: International Conference on World Wide Web, pp. 507–517 (2016)
19. Dey, S., Mitra, P., Gupta, K.: Recommending repeat purchases using product segment statistics. In: ACM Conference on Recommender Systems, pp. 357–360 (2016)
20. Ge, M., Elahi, M., Ricci, F., Massimo, D.: Using tags and latent factors in a food recommender system. In: International Conference on Digital Health, pp. 105–112 (2015)
21. Rubinstein, R.Y.: The score function approach for sensitivity analysis of computer simulation models. Math. Comput. Simul. **28**(5), 351–379 (1986)
22. Blei, D.M., Ng, A.Y., Jordan, M.I.: Latent Dirichlet allocation. J. Mach. Learn. Res. **3**, 993–1022 (2003)

Real-Time Road Traffic State Prediction Based on SVM and Kalman Filter

Peng Qin[1(✉)], Zhenqiang Xu[1,2], Weidong Yang[1], and Gang Liu[1]

[1] School of Information Science and Engineering,
Henan University of Technology, Zhengzhou, China
289291366@qq.com
[2] The PLA Information Engineering University, Zhengzhou, China

Abstract. Road traffic prediction offers traffic guidance for travelers and relieves traffic jams with effective information. In this paper, a real-time road traffic state prediction based on support vector machine (SVM) and the Kalman filter is proposed. In the proposed model, the well-trained SVM model predicts the baseline travel times from the historical trips data; the Kalman filtering-based dynamic algorithm can adjust travel times by using the latest travel information and the estimated values based on SVM. Experimental results show that the real-time road traffic state prediction based on SVM and the Kalman filter is feasible and can achieve high accuracy.

Keywords: TTP · SVM · Kalman filter

1 Introduction

Road travel time provides travelers with effective information from urban traffic control departments, which conducts a reasonable traffic induction, and is the main basis of improving the utilization rate of the traffic. TTP (Travel Time Prediction) has become the research focus, and many experts and scholars both of the foreign and domestic are studying this problem.

In recent years, with the rapid development of intelligent transportation system, the related research also got great progress. At present, a lot of researches of travel time prediction at home and abroad especially is based on travel time. Deb Nath et al. [1], Chowdhury et al. [2], and Chang et al. [3], respectively adopted K means clustering method, the improved moving average method and improved Bias classifier and rule based classifier to predict travel time, but those require very large amount of data samples. Based on the historical and real-time data, Chien and Kuchipudi [4] used Kalman filter algorithm to predict the travel time, in which the accuracy is very high, but the accuracy of this method in the none peak period is low. Tu et al. [5] also considered factors of space and time respectively by using historical data of linear regression analysis and grey theory model of expressway vehicle travel time prediction, which gets the final prediction speed of the two kinds of prediction speed weighted, and gets the predicted travel time with the road length divided by the speed prediction. Zhu et al. [6] got the distribution rules of traveling time in the particular time span through adopting statistical analysis methods of historical data, from which he got the final

© Springer Nature Singapore Pte Ltd. 2018
J. Li et al. (Eds.): CWSN 2017, CCIS 812, pp. 262–272, 2018.
https://doi.org/10.1007/978-981-10-8123-1_23

traveling time, but poor adaptability, statistical analysis of historical data fitting based on distribution function are not known distribution function in all cases, so the prediction accuracy in this case is difficult to guarantee. Yang et al. [7] proposed a Fuzzy Expressway travel time prediction model, the application of this model to achieve high prediction accuracy of the need to consider many factors. This paper considers the impact of traffic flow and sharing, but has not formed a system of weight allocation method. Yang et al. [8] adopted the sharing data through the pattern to match the travel time to predict the traveling time of city expressway. This model is based on historical data, but when matching needs compared one by one, time consuming, and update the database in real time, it is not dynamic. Therefore, the model of anti-jamming ability is not enough.

The above methods for the prediction of travel time also have the following problems and challenges:

(1) Large sample data;
(2) In direct prediction, adopting other parameters in the traffic flow forecast after the travel speed and then calculating travel time;
(3) The influence factors and the parameters (weight distribution) of the selected subjectivity;
(4) Generality of model is poor.

To solve the above problems, this paper establishes two comprehensive prediction models based on support vector machine theory and Kalman filter algorithm to predict the travel time, which not only can overcome the dependence of the amount of training data, but also has strong anti-jamming ability. Compared the predicted results with ARIMA prediction method and Kalman filter prediction method to verify the accuracy of the model, this paper analyzes the applicability of the SVM and Kalman filter integrated forecasting model proposed in different periods.

2 Travel Time Prediction Model Based on SVM and Kalman Filtering

2.1 Initial Travel Time Prediction Model Based on Support Vector Regression Theory

The support vector machine theory includes linear support vector machine classification algorithm, nonlinear support vector machine classification algorithm and linear support vector regression algorithm, nonlinear support vector regression algorithm. Currently, these algorithms have been applied in many fields to realize the classification and regression forecast object characteristic value, and simultaneously achieves good results. The travel time of vehicles changes with time and is not a simple linear relationships, will not be increased without limit, nor without limit decreases. A given road travel time is fluctuated in a range. Therefore, using the least squares regression simple and similar methods of travel time prediction is not reasonable. And the nonlinear regression of SVM theory can solve this problem. So this paper uses the nonlinear support vector machine regression theory.

If the learning sample set (training set) $S = \{(x_i + y_i), x_i \in R^n, y_i \in R^n\}_{i=1}^l$ is nonlinear, change the input sample space of nonlinear transformation to another high dimensional feature space, construct the linear regression function in the feature space, and the nonlinear transform is realized by defining appropriate kernel function $K(x_i, y_i)$. Where $K(x_i, y_i) = \phi(x_i)^T \phi(x_j)$, $\phi(x)y$ is a nonlinear function. Therefore, the problem of nonlinear regression function is reduced to the following optimization problem:

$$\min \frac{1}{2} \|w\|^2 \tag{1}$$

The constraint condition is

$$\|w^T \phi(x_i) + b - y_i\| \le \varepsilon, i = 1, 2, \cdots, l \tag{2}$$

The lagrange dual problem for this problem is

$$\min \frac{1}{2} \sum_{i=1}^l \sum_{j=1}^l \left(\alpha_i^* - \alpha_i\right) \left(\alpha_j^* - \alpha_j\right) K(x_i, x_j) + \varepsilon \sum_{i=1}^l \left(\alpha_i^* - \alpha_i\right) - \sum_{i=1}^l y_i \left(\alpha_i^* - \alpha_i\right) \tag{3}$$

The constraint condition is

$$\sum_{i=1}^l \left(\alpha_i^* - \alpha_i\right) = 0 \tag{4}$$

$$\alpha_i, \alpha_i^* \ge 0, i = 1, 2 \cdots, l \tag{5}$$

The nonlinear function is obtained by solving the dual problem. When the constraint condition can't be achieved, two slack variables are introduced:

$$\xi_i, \xi_i^* \ge 0, i = 1, 2 \cdots, l \tag{6}$$

The problem to be optimized should be:

$$\min \frac{1}{2} \|w\|^2 + C \sum_{i=1}^l \left(\xi_i + \xi_i^*\right) \tag{7}$$

The constraint condition is

$$w^T \phi(x_i) + b - y_i \le \xi_i + \varepsilon, i = 1, 2, \cdots, l \tag{8}$$

$$y_i - w^T \phi(x_i) - b \le \xi_i^* + \varepsilon, i = 1, 2, \cdots, l \tag{9}$$

In this formula $C > 0$ is the penalty factor, where the greater the C is, the more the errors come from the big data point. Lagrange can be used to solve the constrained optimization problem of multiplier method for Lagrange's function is constructed as follows:

$$L(w, b, \alpha, \alpha^*) = \frac{1}{2}\|w\|^2 + C\sum_{i=1}^{l}(\xi_i + \xi_i^*) - \sum_{i=1}^{l}\alpha_i[\varepsilon + \xi_i - y_i + w^T\phi(x_i) + b]$$
$$- \sum_{i=1}^{l}\alpha_i^*[\varepsilon + \xi_i^* + y_i - w^T\phi(x_i) - b]y - \sum_{i=1}^{l}(\beta_i\xi_i + \beta_i^*\xi_i^*) \tag{10}$$

According to the optimization theory, the L respectively for w, b, ξ_i, ξ_i^* partial differential and make them 0, get

$$\begin{cases} w = \sum_{i=1}^{l}(\alpha_i - \alpha_i^*)\phi(x_i) \\ \sum_{i=1}^{l}(\alpha_i - \alpha_i^*) = 0 \\ C - \alpha_i - \beta_i = 0 \\ C - \alpha_i^* - \beta_i^* = 0 \\ i = 1, 2, \cdots, l \end{cases} \tag{11}$$

Substitute formula (11) into formula (10), the dual optimization problem solves the nonlinear regression function.

2.2 Dynamic Prediction Model Based on Kalman Filter

Kalman filtering can be described as: using the observation data vector $y(1), y(2), \cdots y(n)$, the $n \geq 1$ of each component of the least squares estimation. Kalman prediction model is used to predict the travel time. First, establish the prediction model as follows:

Through the average travel time from any of $(k, k-1, \cdots k-n+1)$ to predict the time of the vehicle during the $k+1$ moment, this paper takes into account the specific situation of the traffic, and takes 4 times $(k, k-1, k-2, k-3)$ as the influencing factors on the prediction of the model as shown in (12):

$$T(k+1) = H_0(k)T(k) + H_1(k)T(k-1)$$
$$+ H_2(k)T(k-2) + H_3(k)T(k-3) + w(k)2 \tag{12}$$

In the formula, $T(k+1)$ is the prediction of the travel time of the road section; $H_i(k)(i = 0, 1, 2, 3)$ is the system parameter matrix; $w(k)$ is the zero mean white noise, which indicates the system observation noise, and the covariance matrix is $R(k)$. Define the state vector (13):

$$A(k) = [T(k), T(k-1), T(k-2), T(k-3)]$$
$$x(k) = [H_0(k), H_1(k), H_2(k), H_3(k),]^T \tag{13}$$
$$y(k) = T(k+1)$$

The formula (12) can be transformed into the state equation and observation equation of the Kalman system, such as formula (14):

$$x(k) = \varphi(k, k-1)x(k-1) + u(k-1)$$
$$y(k) = A(k)x(k) + w(k) \tag{14}$$

In the formula, $x(k)$ is the state vector; $y(k)$ is the observation vector; $\varphi(k, k-1)$ is a state transition matrix; $u(k-1)$ is the process noise, and the covariance matrix is $Q(k-1)$;$w(k)$ is the observation noise, and the covariance matrix is $R(k)$;$u(k-1)$ and $w(k)$ are uncorrelated zero mean white noise.

By calculating, we can get the prediction value of the travel time of the next section of the road, as shown in Eq. (15).

$$T(k+1) = A(k)\hat{x}(k) \tag{15}$$

2.3   Dynamic Prediction Model Based on SVM-Kalman Filtering

The influence factors of road travel time are very complex, including the weather, the vehicle running time, intersection delay, road conditions, and other emergency situations, which may lead to the nonlinear variation of travel time.

The SVM model has a strong nonlinear prediction ability and can be applied to the prediction of the model, while the real-time performance of the Kalman filter can make up the defect very well that SVM can't effectively reflect the real time prediction (Fig. 1).

The dynamic model is a combination of static and dynamic adjustment. The support vector machine (SVM) is used as the basis of forecasting, which is off-line

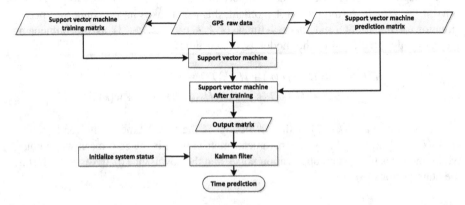

Fig. 1. Dynamic prediction model based on SVM-Kalman filter.

prediction. The trained support vector machine maps out the road travel time to be predicted from a large number of historical data. However, the SVM model can't effectively adjust the emergency, so this paper introduces the Kalman filter dynamic algorithm as the model. The link travel time predicted by support vector machine is used as the initial travel time, and then the initial travel time matrix is input to the Kalman filter to dynamically adjust the results.

The Kalman filter dynamic algorithm uses the update equation to add the latest observations into the prediction vector, which will effectively improve the prediction accuracy of the dynamic model.

The specific steps by using this model are shown as follows:

(1) According to the principle of support vector machine and the influence factors of travel time, each division of the line will travel the whole line which is divided into n sub sections, with each of the two adjacent partition points away for a sub section;

(2) Select the support vector machine type, kernel function and loss function. This model regards the SVM-support vector regression as the basic algorithm, with Gauss RBF kernel function, the epsilon insensitive loss function as the loss function;

(3) The data are divided into two parts: the first part is for the training matrix, comprehensive training model to support vector regression; the other is for prediction matrix to the prediction and test results, the same training matrix and prediction matrix format;

(4) Through cross validation to determine the parameters of support vector regression optimization, use the training matrix according to optimized parameters of support vector machine for training, and the trained support vector machine regression to predict the initial travel time;

(5) The initial travel time matrix is input into the Kalman filter, and the results are adjusted dynamically.

3   Experimental Results and Analysis

3.1   Evaluating Indicator

In order to determine the SVM-Kalman filtering dynamic model, single SVM model, using two kinds of evaluation index below the forecast results for evaluation: mean absolute error, MAE, mean absolute percentage error, MAPE root mean square error, RMSE. The formula is shown in formula (16).

$$MAE = \frac{\sum |\text{Observed value–predicted value}|}{N}$$
$$MAPE = \frac{1}{N} \sum \frac{|\text{Observed value–predicted value}|}{\text{Observed value}} \cdot \qquad (16)$$
$$RMES = \sqrt{\frac{\sum (\text{Observed value–predicted value})^2}{N}}$$

3.2   Data Acquisition

Two sets of road speed and volume data were adopted in this study (Table 1). To achieve a better performance, the road traffic state data under the same running mode were extracted for training and prediction. The road traffic speed and volume data captured on June 15 and 16, 2011 were extracted as historical road traffic state data to train optimal parameters. The road traffic speed and volume data captured on June 22, and 23, 2011 were extracted to make a road traffic state prediction. June 15 and 22 were Wednesday, June 16 and 23 were Thursday. Therefore, we used the training parameters based on the data of June 15 and 16 to predict in real time the road traffic speed and volume values of June 22 and 23.

Table 1. Road segment information

ID	Road segment
LB1170a	Xiaojie Bridge East to Dongzhimen Bridge
LB3750d	White Bridge to Guangqumen Road

The traffic speed and volume data collection interval was 2 min.

3.3   Analysis of Experimental Results

From Figs. 2, 3, 4 and 5 and Tables 2, 3, 4 and 5, we see that:

(1) The road traffic state (speed and volume) predictions based on the SVM–Kalman model are superior to those according to other two algorithms. From Figs. 2, 3, 4 and 5, the accuracy and stability of speed and volume predicted based on the SVM–Kalman model are superior to those based on the other two algorithms for all the segments. We find that for all experiment road segments, the accuracy and stability of speed and volume predicted based on the SVM–Kalman model are superior to those based on the pure ARIMA model and Kalman filter. The stability of speed and volume predicted based on the SVM–Kalman model is inferior to that from expectation maximization. Tables 2, 3, 4 and 5 shows that the SVM–Kalman model is strikingly superior to the pure ARIMA model.

(2) The accuracy of speed prediction is higher than that of volume prediction. The regularity of the change in volume is determined mainly by the regularity of people's travel origin-destination (OD). However, for different dates, people's travel OD changes randomly. So, the regularity of change in volume has a certain random property. The regularity of change in speed is affected not only by the regularity of people's OD travel but also by the running status of road infrastructure. Thus, the change in speed shows high regularity. The accuracy of speed is consequently higher than that of volume when they are estimated on the basis the other guaranty of road traffic.

(3) There are still some errors in predicting road traffic states using this algorithm. There are two main reasons for these errors:

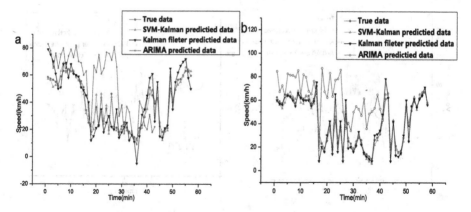

Fig. 2. Speed prediction results of LB1170a on June 22(a), 23(b)

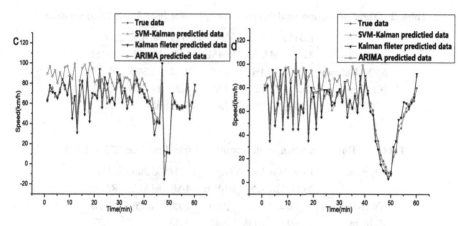

Fig. 3. Speed prediction results of LB3750d on June 22(c), 23(d)

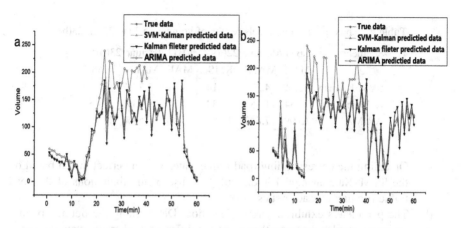

Fig. 4. Volume prediction results of LB1170a on June 22(a), 23(b)

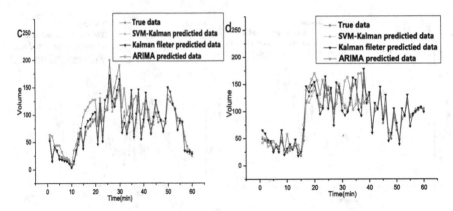

Fig. 5. Volume prediction results of LB3750d on June 22(a), 23(b)

Table 2. Three prediction models results of speed on June 22(a), 23(b) segment

	LB1170a June 22(a)			LB1170a June 23(b)		
	MAE	MAPE	RMSE	MAE	MAPE	RMSE
SVM-Kalman	1.79	5.1%	2.58	2.34	3.39%	2.5
Kalman	5.82	10.32%	7.99	6.25	14.42%	5.02
ARIMA	19.94	29.9%	24.48	24.77	38.89%	23.6

Table 3. Three prediction models results of speed on June 22(c), 23(d)

Segment	LB3750d June 22(c)			LB3750d June 23(d)		
	MAE	MAPE	RMSE	MAE	MAPE	RMSE
SVM-Kalman	1.96	1.71%	2.09	2.06	1.75%	2.16
Kalman	5.69	4.67%	5.45	6.43	7.29%	6.37
ARIMA	13.24	12.02%	17.78	14.15	17.09%	17.55

Table 4. Three prediction models results of volume on June 22(a), 23(b)

Segment	LB1170a June 22(a)			LB1170a June 23(b)		
	MAE	MAPE	RMSE	MAE	MAPE	RMSE
SVM-Kalman	1.81	4.37%	3.14	1.89	3.73%	3.05
Kalman	3.54	11.85%	8.33	6.38	9.63%	7.46
ARIMA	15.99	17.82%	17.59	35.43	16.53%	29.53

(a) Obtaining the corresponding road traffic states with a perfect match based on the SVM–Kalman model is difficult, because of the limitations of the road traffic running characteristics.

(b) The parameters exhibit a certain deviation. Determining the optimal parameters is irregular, because they vary for different road traffic state data sets.

Table 5. Three prediction models results of volume on June 22(c), 23(d)

Segment	LB3750d June 22(c)			LB3750d June 23(d)		
	MAE	MAPE	RMSE	MAE	MAPE	RMSE
SVM-Kalman	5.27	9.33%	7.01	5	8.04%	5.4
Kalman	10.87	14.49%	12.81	11.15	12.37%	13.7
ARIMA	22.27	27.19%	19.36	19.7	18.9%	15.4

The selected optimal parameters are determined based on historical road traffic state data. Therefore, the current optimal parameters maybe different from the historical optimal parameters.

4 Conclusions

Three conclusions can be drawn by comparing the real-time prediction analysis results of the SVM–Kalman model with those from the pure ARIMA model, the Kalman filter.

(1) The mean absolute relative prediction error of speed data based on the proposed algorithm is lower than those of the pure ARIMA model and the Kalman filter, indicating that the proposed algorithm has a higher accuracy.

(2) According to the maximum absolute relative error of the prediction, traffic state prediction based on the SVM–Kalman model performs admirably in tracking trends in the variation of the traffic state. The mean relative error sum of squares signifies that the proposed algorithm is more stable than the pure and Kalman filter.

(3) The proposed algorithm is easy to implement on a computer, and is suitable for online prediction of the road traffic state, because it has fewer variable types and dynamic cumulative values compared with SVM–Kalman methods. Considering the remarkable performance of the proposed algorithm, we will explore traffic state prediction based on spatial–temporal correlations in our next research.

References

1. Deb Nath, R.P., Lee, H.-J., Chowdhury, N.K., Chang, J.-W.: Modified K-means clustering for travel time prediction based on historical traffic data. In: Setchi, R., Jordanov, I., Howlett, Robert J., Jain, Lakhmi C. (eds.) KES 2010. LNCS (LNAI), vol. 6276, pp. 511–521. Springer, Heidelberg (2010). https://doi.org/10.1007/978-3-642-15387-7_55

2. Chowdhury, N.K., Nath, R.P.D., Lee, H., Chang, J.: Development of an effective travel time prediction method using modified moving average approach. In: Velásquez, Juan D., Ríos, Sebastián A., Howlett, Robert J., Jain, Lakhmi C. (eds.) KES 2009. LNCS (LNAI), vol. 5711, pp. 130–138. Springer, Heidelberg (2009). https://doi.org/10.1007/978-3-642-04595-0_16

3. Chang, J., Chowdhury, N.K., Lee, H.: New travel time prediction algorithms for intelligent transportation systems. J. Intell. Fuzzy Syst. **21**(1, 2), 5–7 (2010)

4. Chien, S.I.J., Kuchipudi, C.M.: Dynamic travel time prediction with real-time and historic data. J. Transp. Eng. **129**(6), 608–616 (2003)
5. Tu, J., Li, Y., Liu, C.: A vehicle traveling time prediction method based on grey theory and linear regression analysis. J. Shanghai Jiaotong Univ. (Science) **14**(4), 486–489 (2009)
6. Zhu, Y., Cao, Y.R., Du, S.: Travel time statistical analysis and prediction for the urban freeway. J. Transp. Syst. Eng. Inf. Technol. **7**(1), 93–98 (2009)
7. Yang, Z.S., Bao, L.X., Zhu, G.H.: An urban express travel time prediction model based on fuzzy regression. J. Highway Transp. Res. Dev. **21**(3), 78–81 (2004)
8. Yang, Z.S., Dong, S., Li, S.M., et al.: Traffic travel time forecast based on pattern match of occupancy date. In: Proceedings of the 2006 Annual Meeting of ITS, pp. 231–233 (2006)
9. Wen, X.S.: Pattern Recognition and Condition Monitoring. Science Press, Beijing (2007)
10. Yang, H., Zhu, Y.S.: Parameters selection method for support vector machine regression. Comput. Eng. **35**(13), 218–220 (2009)

An Efficient Routing Algorithm Based on Interest Similarity and Trust Relationship Between Users in Opportunistic Networks

Xueyang Qin[1,2], Xiaoming Wang[1,2(✉)], Yaguang Lin[1,2],
Liang Wang[1,2], and Lichen Zhang[1,2]

[1] Key Laboratory of Modern Teaching Technology,
Ministry of Education, Xi'an 710062, China
wangxm@snnu.edu.cn
[2] School of Computer Science, Shaanxi Normal University,
Xi'an 710119, China

Abstract. In opportunistic networks, due to the randomness of node moving and the uncertainty of network topology, it's a challenging issue to establish a complete communication link between the source and the destination node. Fortunately, the "store-carry-forward" strategy can be used to solve this problem. However, such forwarding strategy heavily relies on the cooperation among nodes. Thus, the selection of a proper relay node has a great impact on the performance of the whole network. In this paper, considering the differences between users' interest and the variability of interest with the change of time, firstly, we propose a dynamic update and calculation method of the value of interests, and then establish a calculation model of interest. Secondly, according to the Ebbinghaus forgetting curve and the ability of users to forward messages, we propose a dynamic calculation method of the trust value of users and establish a model for computing trust relationships. Finally, we propose an efficient routing algorithm based on interest similarity and trust relationship (BIST) between users. The simulation results show that our proposed algorithm has better routing performance, and it validates the correctness and validity of our proposed models and algorithm.

Keywords: Interest similarity · Opportunistic network · Routing algorithm
Trust relationship

1 Introduction

Opportunistic network (OppNet) is a kind of self-organizing network which does not need a complete communication path between the source and the destination node. [1] Unlike the traditional wireless ad hoc networks, OppNet doesn't need to establish a complete end-to-end communication path, and it adopts the "store-carry-forward" strategy to communicate between nodes [2–4]. In addition, OppNet can also deal with some difficult problems which have not been solved in the wireless network [5]. For instance, it would be quite advantageous to interconnect mobile search and rescue nodes in some disaster areas (where basic communication facilities have been

© Springer Nature Singapore Pte Ltd. 2018
J. Li et al. (Eds.): CWSN 2017, CCIS 812, pp. 273–284, 2018.
https://doi.org/10.1007/978-981-10-8123-1_24

destroyed by flooding, earthquakes, hurricanes, or wildfires), allow message exchange in underdeveloped areas (remote towns and villages interconnected by wireless networks), and permit scientific monitoring of wilderness areas (remote monitoring of various forms of wildlife) [6]. Therefore, the study of OppNet is still an open and meaningful problem. Currently, the hot topic of OppNet mainly includes routing protocols, mobility models and cache management. Among of these, routing protocol is the most important part. An ideal routing protocol can not only improve the delivery rate of messages, but also reduce the delay of messages. Thus, how to design an efficient routing is essential to maintain the performance of the entire network.

To solve this problem, some scholars have proposed some routing algorithms [7–12]. Such routing algorithms can be divided into two categories according to the consideration of the context information, namely context-ignorant routing algorithm and context-aware routing algorithm. In general, when the whole network connectivity is extremely poor, the robustness of context-aware routing algorithm is better than context-ignorant routing algorithm. The main reason is that context-ignorant routing algorithm does not consider context information of users when it selects relay nodes. On the contrary, the context-aware routing algorithm uses the context information to select a proper relay node. Yet, all of above context-aware routing algorithms only consider a single aspect and neglect the diversity of user's attributes. A single attribute can't fully represent the user's current state. To better represent the current state of a user, it is necessary to consider two or more attributes of the user.

In this paper, we consider two attributes of a user, including interest information and trust information. For each user in the network, its interests are different at different moment, which means that the user receives different messages. Based on this view, we propose a dynamic update and calculation method of users' interest, and then establish a calculation model of interest. In order to improve the availability of the network, according to the Ebbinghaus forgetting curve and the ability of users to forward messages, we establish a calculation model of the users' trust value. Finally, we propose an efficient routing algorithm based on interest similarity and trust relationship (BIST) between users.

The rest of this paper is organized as follows. In Sect. 2, we discuss the related works. In Sect. 3, we provide our system model. In Sect. 4, we present our BIST routing algorithm. The simulation results and discussions are presented in Sect. 5. In Sect. 6, we conclude the paper.

2   Related Works

In opportunistic networks, routing is a challenge problem and completely different from the traditional network. An ideal routing algorithm can provide reliable message transmission, even when the network connection is intermittent or an end-to-end path does not exist. Moreover, the connection between users may appear uncertain without the pre-information in the opportunistic network, therefore, how to design a perfect routing algorithm is particularly critical. As we have mentioned in Sect. 1, the existing routing algorithms can be divided into two categories, namely context-ignorant routing algorithm and context-aware routing algorithm.

Currently, epidemic is the most typical context-ignorant routing algorithm based on flooding [13]. It sends the same copies of a message over multiple paths to reduce the impact of a single path failure. Thus, when the network resource is unlimited, it can increase the possibility of successful message delivery. However, the large transmission overhead and required buffer size render it inappropriate in most opportunistic networks.

In order to reduce the overhead of flood routing, Controlled Flooding routing algorithm is proposed based on the controlling of message copies, such as time-to-live, kill time, and passive cure [14]. Compared with Epidemic routing algorithm, Controlled Flooding routing algorithm can achieve a better routing performance.

Similarly, Spyropoulos et al. have proposed the Spray and Wait routing algorithm to control the impact of flooding routing [15]. The Spray and Wait consists of two phases: In the "Spray" phase, the source node sprays L copies of the messages over the network; in the "Wait" phase, nodes with message copies forward the messages directly to the destination nodes. This routing algorithm can drastically reduce the network traffic due to it limits the number of copies of the same message. However, the value of L is difficult to determine. The larger the value is, the higher the network overhead is; the smaller the value is, the lower the delivery rate of the message is.

In context-aware routing algorithm, Prophet routing algorithm is a probability prediction based routing algorithm, which estimates the transmission probability of each link to the destination node [16]. It can well reduce the overhead of flood routing, but the initial probability of message transmission between nodes is difficult to determine accurately.

Leguay et al. have proposed MobySpace routing algorithm [17], which is defined as a multi-dimensional Euclidean space where each axis indicates that a pair of nodes are interconnected and the distance between nodes is the contact probability. However, in order to build a better MobySpace, it is clear that all the axis information and node information are required in the virtual space.

ONSIDE routing algorithm is proposed based on the interest and socially-aware [18]. In this algorithm, when two nodes meet, they exchange message lists and interest lists. Based on this information, each node decides which message should be transmitted. ONSIDE reduces the overhead ratio to a certain degree, but it does not consider the change of the interests.

In this paper, we further consider the context information such as the interest and trust of nodes. Correspondingly, we propose the BIST routing algorithm. In BIST routing algorithm, if the interest similarity between a node and the destination node is high and the trust value is also high, then we choose the node as the relay node.

3 System Model

In this section, we mainly introduce our system model, which includes two sub-models, interest model and trust model. In the interest model, according to the receiving history messages, nodes update and calculate their own interest information. In the process of message transmission, nodes update the other nodes' interest information by exchanging interest record. In the trust model, we evaluate the trust value of nodes in two direct and indirect ways, as illustrated in Fig. 1.

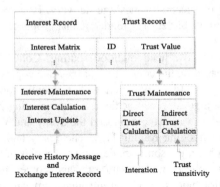

Fig. 1. System model.

Besides, we assume that all mobile nodes are carried by human and the links between nodes are described as an undirected graphs where denotes a set of nodes and denotes a set of edges [19]. For the sake of convenience, in the following article, we use the user instead of the node. For any user N_i in the network, we use $Q_1^i, Q_2^i \ldots Q_r^i \ldots Q_n^i$ to represent the n different kinds of interests, where Q_r^i is the r - th interest of N_i. We use the matrix $R_i^t = \left[q_1^i, q_2^i, \ldots q_s^i \ldots, q_n^i \right]$ to represent the weight of each interest of N_i at t moment, where q_s^i is the importance of s - th interest to N_i, and the greater the value is, the more the user likes the interest. We define $\sum\limits_{s=1}^{n} q_s^i = 1$.

3.1   The Update and Calculation Model of User's Interest

For any message m in the network, we use $k_1, k_2, \ldots k_r \ldots, k_n$ to represent the n different kinds of context classification, where k_r denotes the r - th context classification of the message m. We use the matrix $p_m = \left[w_1^m, w_2^m, \ldots w_r^m \ldots, w_n^m \right]$ to represent the weight of the message m in each context classification, where w_r^m is the degree of correlation between r - th context classification and the message m. The greater the value is, the higher the correlation degree is. We define that $\sum\limits_{r=1}^{n} w_r^m = 1$.

In opportunistic networks, the interest of each user is different and its interest changes over time. This is mainly because the users may be interested in different contents at different time. Research shows that users are more likely to receive messages that they are concerned. Therefore, the interest of a user can be reflected from the historical messages received by the user. In view of this, we consider that the change of a user's interest is related to the change of the message, and the latest information reflects the user's current interest. We use an attenuation function $f_{(t_\varsigma, t_\xi)}$ to represent the impact factor of the messages on users during the time period $(t_\varsigma, t_\xi) \cdot f_{(t_\varsigma, t_\xi)}$ is defined as follows:

$$f_{(t_\varsigma, t_\xi)} = \int_{t_\varsigma}^{t_\xi} e^{-\frac{1}{2}t} dt \tag{1}$$

Where t_ς is the current moment and t_ξ is the last moment.

For each user N_i in the network, we assume that N_i receives q messages $m_1, m_2, m_r, \ldots, m_q$ during the time (t_ς, t_ξ), we use $k_r^{(t_\varsigma, t_\xi)} = \frac{1}{q}\sum_{j=1}^{q} w_r^j$ to represent the average weight of q messages in r - th context classification. Therefore, the matrix $d^i = \left[k_1^{(t_\varsigma, t_\xi)}, k_2^{(t_\varsigma, t_\xi)}, \ldots, k_n^{(t_\varsigma, t_\xi)} \right]$ can be used to represent the average weight of the q messages in each content classification, where $\sum_{r=1}^{n} k_r^{(t_\varsigma, t_\xi)} = 1$.

For ease of calculation, we select the last three equal time slots to update user's interests. As shown in Fig. 2, t_0 is the current time, t_1 is the last time, and so on.

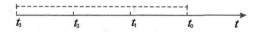

Fig. 2. Time windows

The received message of the user can be represented by a $3 \times n$ matrix D in three time periods $(t_0, t_1), (t_1, t_2), (t_2, t_3)$ as follows:

$$D = \begin{bmatrix} k_1^{(t_0,t_1)} & k_2^{(t_0,t_1)} & \cdots & k_n^{(t_0,t_1)} \\ k_1^{(t_1,t_2)} & k_2^{(t_1,t_2)} & \cdots & k_n^{(t_1,t_2)} \\ k_1^{(t_2,t_3)} & k_2^{(t_2,t_3)} & \cdots & k_n^{(t_2,t_3)} \end{bmatrix} \tag{2}$$

Based on this, we use the attenuation function $f_{(t_\varsigma, t_\xi)}$ and matrix D to define the variation degree R_i of the user's interest matrix (where R_i is a matrix with n elements. Each element represents an interest of the user and the value of each element indicates the degree of change in the corresponding interest) as follows:

$$\begin{aligned} R_i &= [f(t_0, t_1), f(t_1, t_2), f(t_2, t_3)] \times D \\ &= [f(t_0, t_1), f(t_1, t_2), f(t_2, t_3)] \times \begin{bmatrix} k_1^{(t_0,t_1)} & k_2^{(t_0,t_1)} & \cdots & k_n^{(t_0,t_1)} \\ k_1^{(t_1,t_2)} & k_2^{(t_1,t_2)} & \cdots & k_n^{(t_1,t_2)} \\ k_1^{(t_2,t_3)} & k_2^{(t_2,t_3)} & \cdots & k_n^{(t_2,t_3)} \end{bmatrix} \\ &= [f(t_0, t_1) \cdot k_1^{(t_0,t_1)} + f(t_1, t_2) \cdot k_1^{(t_1,t_2)} + f(t_2, t_3) \cdot k_1^{(t_2,t_3)}, \\ &\quad \ldots, f(t_0, t_1) \cdot k_n^{(t_0,t_1)} + f(t_1, t_2) \cdot k_n^{(t_1,t_2)} + f(t_2, t_3) \cdot k_n^{(t_2,t_3)}] \end{aligned} \tag{3}$$

In order to evaluate the interest of N_i, we use the user's interest at t_3 moment and formula (3) to calculate the user's interest $R_i^{t_0}$ at the current t_0 moment.

$$R_i^{t_0} = (1 - \theta) \cdot R_i^{t_3} + \theta \cdot R_i \qquad (4)$$

Where $\theta \in [0, 1)$ is a weight for the variation degree R_i of interest matrix and $R_i^{t_3}$ is an interest matrix with n elements at t_3 moment. Each element represents an interest of the user and the value of each element indicates the degree of the user liking the interest.

On the basis of user's interest update, the similarity $S_{(i,j)}$ between N_i and N_j at t moment can be defined as follow:

$$
S_{(i,j)} = \frac{R_i^t \times (R_j^t)^T}{R_i^t \times (R_i^t)^T + R_j^t \times (R_i^t)^T - R_i^t \times (R_j^t)^T}
$$
$$
= \frac{\sum\limits_{s=1}^{n} q_s^i \cdot q_s^j}{\sum\limits_{s=1}^{n} q_s^i \cdot q_s^i + \sum\limits_{s=1}^{n} q_s^j \cdot q_s^j - \sum\limits_{s=1}^{n} q_s^i \cdot q_s^j} \qquad (5)
$$

Where R_i^t is an interest matrix with n elements at current t moment. $(R_i^t)^T$ is the transpose of N_i interest matrix R_i^t, $(R_j^t)^T$ is the transpose of N_j interest matrix R_j^t. From formula (5) we can see that $S_{(i,j)}$ gets the minimum value 0 when N_i and N_j have no common interest. $S_{(i,j)}$ reaches the maximum value 1 when N_i and N_j have the same interest.

3.2   The User's Trust Calculation Model

In this section, we mainly introduce user's trust model, including the calculation of message importance and the trust value of a user. In opportunistic networks, the more messages a user transmits, the higher the trust value is [20, 21]. In order to accurately evaluate a user's trust value, if a user N_j successfully forwards the message receiving from the user N_i to the relay node (or destination node), N_i increases the trust value for N_j, otherwise, N_i reduces the trust value for N_j. In addition, if two users have not met for a long time, then the trust value of each other will reduce. In order to further describe this situation. Assuming that the trust value of N_i for N_j is related to the memory of N_i for N_j, which is a k coefficient linear relationship with the Ebbinghaus memory forgetting curve $y = 1 - 0.56t^{0.06}$, the trust value of N_i for N_j will gradually decrease until it becomes stable.

As we know, the importance of a message is different for different users, and will change at different moment. Considering the timeliness of messages, we define the importance $I_{(m,d)}$ of the message m to the destination N_d as follows:

$$I_{(m,d)} = \alpha e^{-(t-t_s)} \cos\left(R_d^t, p_m\right)$$

$$= \alpha e^{-(t-t_s)} \frac{\sum\limits_{r=1}^{n} q_r^d \cdot w_r^m}{\sqrt{\sum\limits_{r=1}^{n} (q_r^d)^2} + \sqrt{\sum\limits_{r=1}^{n} (w_r^m)^2}} \tag{6}$$

Where $\alpha \in (0, 1)$ is a constant, R_d^t is the interest matrix of N_d at t moment, and p_m is a matrix representing the weight of the message m in each context classification. Respectively, t_s is the creation time of message m and t is the current moment.

Assuming that N_i forwards message m with importance $I_{(m,d)}$ to N_j at time t_α, and N_i encounters N_j at current moment t_0, we define the trust value $T_{i,j}^{t_0}$ of N_i for N_j at time t_0 as follows:

$$T_{i,j}^{t_0} = \max\{k \cdot [1 - 0.56(t_0 - t_\alpha)^{0.06} \cdot T_{i,j}^{t_\alpha} \pm \varphi I(m,d), T_c\} \tag{7}$$

Where $k \in (0, 1]$ is a constant, $T_{i,j}^{t_\alpha}$ represents the trust value of N_i for N_j at time t_α, $\varphi \in (0, 1)$ is a reward coefficient. Moreover, T_c is a constant, which represents the minimum trust value of N_i for N_j when they haven't seen each other for a long time.

We use a continuous function $f_{(x)}$ to fully describe the trust value of N_i for N_j, which is limited in the range $(0, 1)$, and $f_{(x)}$ can be calculated by:

$$f_{(x)} = \begin{cases} 1 - e^{-\lambda x} & , x \geq T \\ 0 & , otherwise \end{cases} \tag{8}$$

Where $\lambda \in (0, 1)$ is a constant, the value of x represents the trust value $T_{i,j}^t$. When they encounter each other for the first time, we define $f_{(x)} = 0.5$. Since the trust value of a user dynamically varies from 0 to 1, we use the median between 0 and 1 to define $f_{(x)}$, therefore, $f_{(x)} = 0.5$. T_ϕ represents the minimum trust value that the user forwards message, we assume that the user doesn't have the forwarding ability when the trust value is smaller than T_ϕ.

To describe user's trust clearly, we also consider the transitivity of user trust. Assuming that the trust value of N_i for N_r is $T_{i,r}^t$, and the trust value of N_r for N_j is $T_{r,j}^t$ at time t. The trust value of N_i for N_j can be updated at time t as follows:

$$T_{i,j}^t = T_{i,j}^t + (1 - T_{i,j}^t) \cdot (T_{i,r}^t - T_{i,j}^t) \cdot (T_{r,j}^t - T_{i,j}^t) \cdot \gamma$$
$$s.t. \; T_{i,r}^t \geq T_{i,j}^t, T_{r,j}^t \geq T_{i,j}^t \tag{9}$$

Where $\gamma \in (0, 1)$ is a constant, the formula (9) represents that if N_i trust N_r very much and N_r trust N_j very much, then the trust value of N_i for N_j will increase.

4 The BIST Routing Algorithm

Based on the discussion mentioned above, we propose an efficient routing algorithm based on interest similarity and trust relationships between users according to the interest and trust model. In order to improve the delivery ratio of the messages, for any message m in the network, if the importance $I_{(m,d)}$ of the message is great and the remaining time to live (TTL) is small, the number of copies will increase correspondingly. In the process of forwarding a message, the maximum number of copies R_m of the message is defined as follows:

$$R_m = \left\lceil I_{(m,d)} \cdot e^{\frac{k}{TTL}} \right\rceil \tag{10}$$

Where k is a constant coefficient.

In BIST, if a user with high interest similarity and trust value, it will be selected as a relay node. Algorithm 1 illustrates our scheme in details.

Algorithm 1. The BIST routing algorithm

Begin:
1: for each message m_i of N_i do
2: compute $I_{(m,d)}$
3: for m_i sort by $I_{(m,d)}$ in descending order
4: select the message m of max $I_{(m,d)}$
5: for each neighbor N_j of N_i do
6:   if (the destination $N_d = N_j$)
7:     N_i transmits m to N_j
8:   else
9:     if (N_j does not have m)
10:       N_j computes $S_{(j,d)}$ with N_d
11:       if ($S_{(m,d)} \geq S_\phi$)
12:         N_i computes $T'_{i,j}$ with N_j
13:         if ($T'_{i,j} \geq T_\phi$)
14:           place N_j into a queue Q
15: for queue Q sort by $S_{(m,d)} * T'_{i,j}$ in descending order
16: computing R_m of message m
17: select the first $\min\{R_m, C(Q)\}$ nodes transmits m
End

In BIST routing algorithm, we choose the most important message m of all messages (lines 1–3). For each neighbor N_j of N_i, we calculate the interest similarity and trust value(where S_ϕ represents the minimum similarity between nodes that can put forward messages.), and then place the eligible users in queue Q (lines 10–14). Finally, N_i calculates the copies of the message and forwards the message (lines 16–17).

5 Performance Evaluations

5.1 Metrics and Simulation Setup

In this paper, we use the Opportunistic Network Environment (ONE) simulation [22] to evaluate the performance of our proposed BIST routing algorithm. In the experiment, we compare our proposed routing algorithm BIST with Epidemic, Spray and Wait and ONSIDE. We compare these routing algorithms using the following three different metrics:

Delivery Ratio: The ratio of messages that have been delivered to the destination nodes to the messages generated by the source nodes.

Average Latency: The average time duration from messages are generated until they are received.

Overhead Ratio: The ratio of the total number messages created by source nodes to the total number messages forwarded by all nodes.

The simulation parameters are shown in Table 1.

Table 1. Simulation setup

Parameter	Default value
Simulation time	43200 s
Warmup time	10000 s
Transmission speed	10 Mbps
TTL	200 min
Message size	0.5 MB–1 MB
Transmission range	50 m
Walking speed	1.0 m/s–1.5 m/s
Message interval	25 s–35 s

5.2 Performance Results

(a) **Delivery Ratio:** The simulation results are shown in Fig. 3. In general, with the increase of the number of nodes or buffer size, the delivery ratio of all the routing algorithms increases gradually. In Fig. 3(a), whether it is in the sparse network or dense network, the delivery ratio of BIST routing is very high. When the number of nodes is large (>350), the delivery ratio of BIST routing algorithm is better than others. The main reason is that when the number of nodes increases, the source nodes are easier to select the relay node with high interest similarity and trust value. In Fig. 3(b), when the cache size of nodes is large (>40), the delivery ratio of BIST routing is better than other routing algorithms, because the larger the buffer space, the more messages it can store so that relay nodes can be accurately evaluated when it is selected.

(b) **Average Latency:** Figure 4 shows that with the increasing number of nodes or buffer size, average latency of the all routings decreases gradually. This is mainly because when the number of nodes in the network increases, there will be more

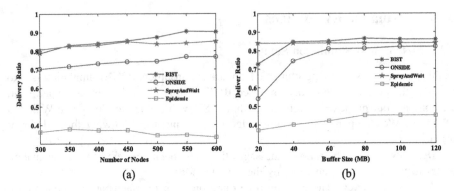

Fig. 3. Impact of the Number of Nodes and Buffer Size on delivery ratio.

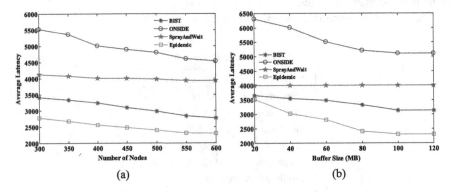

Fig. 4. Impact of the Number of Nodes and Buffer Size on average latency.

nodes involved in the message transmission, which is conductive to reduce the delay in message transmission. Besides, when a single node's buffer size increases, the node can store more messages, which means that a copy of the same message retained in the network increases. Therefore, when the node's buffer size increases, the average latency will be reduced. Compared with other algorithms, Epidemic algorithm has the lowest average latency, because it is a flooding based routing algorithm. BIST algorithm is much better than Spray and Wait and ONSIDE. This is mainly because our proposed trust model guarantees the selection of reliable relay nodes.

(c) **Overhead Ratio:** The simulation results show that in terms of overhead ratio, BIST algorithm is obviously better than other three algorithms in Fig. 5. The main reason is that BIST algorithm can reduce the copies of messages and choose proper relay nodes with higher interest similarity and trust value by our proposed models.

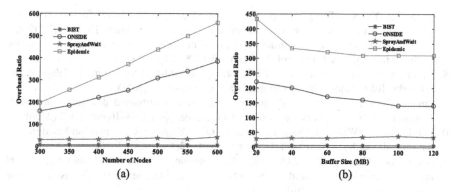

Fig. 5. Impact of the Number of Nodes and Buffer Size on overhead ratio.

6 Conclusions

In this paper, we propose an efficient opportunistic routing algorithm based on interest similarity and trust value between users. In the process of calculating interest similarity of the users, we establish a calculation model of updating the users' interest based on the characteristic of dynamic changing interest. We also establish a trust model to evaluate trust value of users. The simulation results show that BIST has a better routing performance in comparison with Epidemic, Spray and Wait, and ONSIDE algorithms, which verifies the correctness and validity of our proposed model and algorithm. In the future work, we will further investigate routing optimization problems and security issues like malice and selfishness of users.

Acknowledgments. This work is supported by the National Natural Science Foundation of China (Grant Nos. 61373083, 61402273); the Program of Shaanxi Science and Technology Innovation Team of China (Grant No. 2014KTC-18); the 111 Programme of Introducing Talents of Discipline to Universities (Grant No. B16031).

References

1. Xiao, M., Wu, J., Huang, L.: Community-aware opportunistic routing in mobile social networks. IEEE Trans. Comput. **63**(7), 1682–1695 (2014)
2. Kolios, P., Friderikos, V., Papadaki, K.: Energy-efficient relaying via store-carry and forward within the cell. IEEE Trans. Mobile Comput. **13**(1), 202–215 (2014)
3. Bhorkar, A., Naghshvar, M., Javidi, T.: Opportunistic routing with congestion diversity in wireless ad hoc networks. IEEE/ACM Trans. Netw. **24**(2), 1167–1180 (2016)
4. Trifunovic, S., Kouyoumdjieva, S.T., Distl, B., et al.: A decade of research in opportunistic networks: challenges, relevance, and future directions. IEEE Commun. Mag. **55**(1), 168–173 (2017)
5. Wang, X., Lin, Y., Zhang, S., Cai, Z.: A social activity and physical contact-based routing algorithm in mobile opportunistic networks for emergency response to sudden disasters. Enterp. Inf. Syst. **11**(5), 597–626 (2017)

6. Chen, L., Yu, C., Tseng, C., et al.: A content-centric framework for effective data dissemination in opportunistic networks. IEEE J. Sel. Areas Commun. **10**, 761–772 (2008)
7. Mendes, P.M., Moreira, W.: Structural analysis of social-aware opportunistic networks. Ichthyol. Res. Official J. Ichthyol. Soc. Jpn. **60**(1), 85–88 (2013)
8. Hui, P., Crowcroft, J., Yoneki, E.: BUBBLE rap: social-based forwarding in delay-tolerant networks. IEEE Trans. Mobile Comput. **10**(11), 1576–1589 (2011)
9. Liu, Y., Yan, L., Liu, K., et al.: Incentives for delay-constrained data query in mobile opportunistic social networks. In: Control Conference, pp. 10363–10368. IEEE (2016)
10. Liu, J., Wan, J., Wang, Q., Deng, P., Zhou, K., Qiao, Y.: A survey on position-based routing for vehicular ad hoc networks. Telecommun. Syst. **62**(1), 15–30 (2016)
11. Allen, S.M., Chorley, M.J., Colombo, G.B.: Exploiting user interest similarity and social links for micro-blog forwarding in mobile opportunistic networks. Pervasive Mobile Comput. **11**(2), 106–131 (2014)
12. Jang, K., Lee, J., Kim, S.K., Yoon, J.H., Yang, S.B.: An adaptive routing algorithm considering position and social similarities in an opportunistic network. Wirel. Netw. **22**(5), 1537–1551 (2016)
13. Vahdat, A., Becker, D.: Epidemic routing for partially-connected ad hoc networks. Master thesis (2000)
14. Harras, K.A., Almeroth, K.C., Belding-Royer, E.M.: Delay Tolerant Mobile Networks (DTMNs): controlled flooding in sparse mobile networks. In: Boutaba, R., Almeroth, K., Puigjaner, R., Shen, S., Black, James, P. (eds.) NETWORKING 2005. LNCS, vol. 3462, pp. 1180–1192. Springer, Heidelberg (2005). https://doi.org/10.1007/11422778_95
15. Spyropoulos, T., Psounis, K., Raghavendra, C.S.: Spray and wait: an efficient routing scheme for intermittently connected mobile networks. In: ACM SIGCOMM Workshop on Delay-Tolerant Networking, pp. 252–259. ACM (2005)
16. Lindgren, A., Doria, A., Schelén, O.: Probabilistic routing in intermittently connected networks. ACM Sigmobile Mobile Comput. Commun. Rev. **7**(3), 239–254 (2004)
17. Leguay, J., Friedman. T., Conan, V.: DTN routing in a mobility pattern space. In: Proceedings of the 2005 ACM SIGCOMM Workshop on Delay-Tolerant Networking, pp. 276–283 (2005)
18. Ciobanu, R.I., Marin, R.C., Dobre, C., Cristea, V.: Interest-awareness in data dissemination for opportunistic networks. Ad hoc Netw. **25**, 330–345 (2014)
19. Shu, J., Zeng, L., Liu, L.: Random graph model for opportunistic sensor networks based on divided area. Commun. Comput. Inf. Sci. **418**, 179–190 (2014)
20. Yao, L., Man, Y., Huang, Z., Deng, J., Wang, X.: Secure routing based on social similarity in opportunistic networks. IEEE Trans. Wirel. Commun. **15**(1), 594–605 (2016)
21. Bo, W., Chuanhe, H., Layuan, L.: Trust-based minimum cost opportunistic routing for Ad hoc networks. J. Syst. Softw. **84**(12), 2107–2122 (2011)
22. Conti, M., Giordano, S.: Mobile ad hoc networking: milestones, challenges, and new research direction. IEEE Commun. Mag. **52**(1), 85–96 (2014)

A Routing Algorithm Based on the Prediction of Node Meeting Location in Opportunistic Networks

Xinyan Wang[1,2], Xiaoming Wang[1,2(✉)], Lichen Zhang[1,2],
Yaguang Lin[1,2], and Ruonan Zhao[1,2]

[1] Key Laboratory of Modern Teaching Technology,
Ministry of Education, Xi'an 710062, China
wangxm@snnu.edu.cn
[2] School of Computer Science,
Shaanxi Normal University, Xi'an 710119, China

Abstract. The opportunistic network is a kind of self-organizing network which makes use of the meeting opportunities created by moving nodes to realize short-distance wireless communication, in which the dynamic characteristics of the network topology often result in low communication efficiency. To improve the efficiency of messages transmission, firstly we combine the Markov model to establish a node location prediction model and a distance prediction and calculation model between nodes respectively in order to accurately predict the location of the nodes at the next moment and calculate the distance between nodes; secondly based on the significance and timelessness of messages, a priority based buffer management strategy is proposed to realize the efficient use of buffer. Finally in this paper we propose an efficient opportunistic network routing algorithm, named LIBR, based on the prediction of node meeting location to forward the messages. Compared with the well-known routing algorithms, the simulation results show that our proposed algorithm can significantly improve the delivery ratio, reduce the overhead ratio and average delay of messages.

Keywords: Buffer management · Opportunistic network · Routing
Markov model

1 Introduction

The opportunistic network is a kind of self-organizing network that does not need a complete link between the source and the destination node, and uses the meeting opportunities created by moving nodes to realize short-distance wireless communication [1]. Due to the influence of high latency, sparse node density, node mobility and other factors, the topology of opportunistic network is dynamically volatile. In order to realize communication between the source and the destination node, the "store-carry-forward" strategy is used to transfer messages to the destination node [2].

The traditional wireless network establishes routing table according to the state information of the current network, and maintains it according to the change of the

© Springer Nature Singapore Pte Ltd. 2018
J. Li et al. (Eds.): CWSN 2017, CCIS 812, pp. 285–295, 2018.
https://doi.org/10.1007/978-981-10-8123-1_25

network state, meanwhile data transmission depends on a stable end-to-end connection, but the opportunistic network can maintain efficient data transmission when the network topology is dissociated. So the Opportunity network can solve the problem of frequent fracture of communication links between the source and the destination node caused by network split, delay, sparse distribution of nodes and limited communication capacity [3]. And it can meet the communication need in emergency environment, such as disaster rescue and bad communication environment. So the opportunistic network has an important position and research significance in the military and civil communication fields [4], and also has been used in environment monitoring, vehicular ad hoc networks [5], military ad hoc transmission, remote areas transmission and disaster rescue [6].

Most of the existing routing algorithms consider the encounter probability, contact time and other historical information, and ignore the situation where the nodes moving lead to the change of actual location [7], so that these algorithms can't get the actual location information of the nodes and predict the location of the nodes in the future. In this paper, we consider the most important performance metrics: delivery ratio of messages, overhead ratio of messages, and average delay of messages. Obviously, it implies that we can achieve a better routing performance when the delivery ratio is higher, overhead ratio and average delay of messages is lower.

Our main contributions are summarized as follows:

- We firstly combine the Markov model to establish a node location prediction model to predict the location of the nodes at the next moment. The core of this model is to establish two order Markov transition probability matrix.
- We establish a distance prediction and calculation model between nodes to predict and calculate the distance at the next moment, on the basis of which the message carrying node decides the specific forwarding process.
- Based on the significance and timelessness of messages, we propose a priority based buffer management strategy, which decides the forwarding priority of messages and realizes the efficient use of buffer size.
- We propose a routing algorithm LIBR (Location Information Based Routing) to improve delivery ratio of messages, decrease overhead ratio of messages and average delay of the messages, and realize better routing performance.

The remainder of the paper is organized as follows: in Sect. 2 we discuss the related works. In Sect. 3, we introduce the routing algorithm LIBR in detail. In Sect. 4, we verify the correctness and validity of our proposed models and algorithm through a large number of simulation experiments. Finally we conclude the paper and raise future research directions in Sect. 5.

2 Related Works

The location information of the nodes is a useful information that can help network routing. Currently, the existing routing algorithms based on node location information mainly are GLS (Grid Location Service), LAR (Location Aided Routing), LOTAR (Location Trace Aided Routing) and GPSR (Greedy Perimeter Stateless Routing) etc. [8].

The GLS algorithm is a hierarchical routing algorithm. It divides the whole network into different grids according to level. The nodes in the first-level grid use the two-hop geographical-location information packets to keep touch with other nodes, and the nodes out the first-level grid select the nodes as location servers to update and query the geographical location information [9]. In LAR algorithm, the source node determines the expected area of the destination node by using the geographical location information of the destination node, and the request area according to its current location information, and then initiate a routing request. When the other nodes receive the request packets, they determine whether to forward the request according to the request area carried by packets, thus to control the routing query region and improve the efficiency of routing query [10]. LOTAR is a kind of location trace aided routing algorithm, which is similar to the LAR algorithm. This algorithm does not initiate a routing discovery process by the source node, but find a node with the latest geographic location information of the destination node, which initiates the routing discovery process [11]. GPSR algorithm does not need to maintain routing table. It uses geographic location information to transfer messages to the neighbor node which is nearest to the destination node [12].

All these algorithms improve routing performance by seeking the location information of the destination node and the neighbor nodes. However, due to the actual location of the node changes at the time, the performance of such algorithms will decline.

To improve the routing performance, in this paper we use two order Markov model to predict the location of destination node at the next moment. Subsequently the node location prediction model and the prediction and calculation model [13] of distance between nodes are established. Meanwhile we propose a priority based buffer management strategy to realize the use efficiency of buffer. Finally we propose a routing algorithm LIBR based on node meeting location prediction.

3 The Routing Algorithm Based on the Prediction of the Node Meeting Location

In opportunistic network, the mobility of the nodes results in that the location information of nodes changes at any time. In order to predict the location of the nodes at the next moment, we combine the Markov model to establish a node location prediction model, and propose a distance prediction and calculation model between the nodes to calculate the angle formed by the moving speed and the distance between nodes at the next moment, and then based on the significance and timelessness of messages, we propose a priority based buffer management strategy. Finally we propose the LIBR routing algorithm.

3.1 The Node Location Prediction Model

The nodes are constantly moving, so the position at the next moment is not only related to its current position, but also to its previous position. So in this paper we use two order Markov model [14] to predict the location.

Supposing that the location variable X of the node is a random variable, and the sequence of random variable X_i constitutes a homogeneous Markov process [15]. Two order Markov prediction model requires that X_i meets the following conditions:

$$P\{X_{i+1} = l | X(1, n) = L\} = P\{X_{i+1} | X_i X_{i-1} = l_i l_{i-1}\} \tag{1}$$

where $L = l_1 l_2 \cdots l_n$ represents the historical position sequence of the sampling nodes and l_i represents the location of the node at i moment.

We can calculate the appropriate sampling interval ΔT according to the average speed of node itself and the size of network scenarios in the process of location recording, and ΔT can be calculated by:

$$\Delta T = \frac{\omega}{\bar{v}} \times \rho \tag{2}$$

where ω represents the minimum distance between nodes in the network scenarios, $\bar{v}$ represents the average speed of nodes, and ρ represents the scaling factor that controls the sampling accuracy.

Two order Markov location prediction model predicts the location of the node at the next moment according to the current location L_{cur} and previous moment location L_{pre}. The core of this model is to establish two order Markov transition probability matrix P and the row vector of matrix P represents the context location of the nodes, that is, the location at the previous moment and current moment, the column vector of matrix P represents the location L_{next} that may occur at the next moment, P is denoted by:

$$P = \begin{bmatrix} P_{11} & \cdots & P_{1j} & \cdots & P_{1n} \\ \vdots & \ddots & \vdots & \ddots & \vdots \\ P_{i1} & \cdots & P_{ij} & \cdots & P_{in} \\ \vdots & \ddots & \vdots & \ddots & \vdots \\ P_{m1} & \cdots & P_{mj} & \cdots & P_{mn} \end{bmatrix} \tag{3}$$

where $m = n^2$, the element P_{ij} represents the probability of the nodes moving to the location at the next moment represented by column vector in the current state represented by row vector. The transition probability is calculated by:

$$P(X_{i+1} = l | L) = \frac{T_{AB}}{T_A} \tag{4}$$

where T_A represents the times of A in the whole sampling process L, T_{AB} represents the times of AB in the whole sampling process, and A represents the last moment and the current moment location of the nodes, B represents the next moment location, AB represents these three locations.

According to the corresponding row vector of the destination node in the transition probability matrix P, we find the location represented by the corresponding probability P_{ij} in the row, so we can get the location prediction result of the current destination node, which denotes the location of the destination node at the next moment.

3.2   The Prediction and Calculation Model of Distance Between Nodes

After we obtain the aforementioned prediction result, in this section, we first consider the moving speed of the nodes at the moment, and then predict and calculate the distance between the nodes at the next moment.

Supposing that the moving speed of the node carrying messages C, the neighbor nodes N and the destination node D is respectively denoted by $\vec{v_c}, \vec{v_n}, \vec{v_d}$. The angles formed by moving speed of the node C and the node N with the node D are denoted by θ_c and θ_n, they are calculated as follows:

$$\cos\theta_c = \cos\langle \vec{v_c}, \vec{v_d} \rangle = \frac{\vec{v_c} \times \vec{v_d}}{|\vec{v_c}||\vec{v_d}|} \tag{5}$$

$$\cos\theta_n = \cos\langle \vec{v_n}, \vec{v_d} \rangle = \frac{\vec{v_n} \times \vec{v_d}}{|\vec{v_n}||\vec{v_d}|} \tag{6}$$

that is $\theta_c = \cos^{-1}\left(\frac{\vec{v_c} \times \vec{v_d}}{|\vec{v_c}||\vec{v_d}|}\right)$, $\theta_n = \cos^{-1}\left(\frac{\vec{v_n} \times \vec{v_d}}{|\vec{v_n}||\vec{v_d}|}\right)$, the calculating of angles are shown in Fig. 1, where θ_c represents the angle formed by moving speed of the node carrying messages and the destination node and $\theta_{n1}, \theta_{n2}, \theta_{n3}$ represent the angle formed by moving speed of the neighbor nodes and the destination node.

After considering the angles of the node moving speed, we calculate and compare θ_c and θ_n, and then determine whether they are in the range of $(0, \frac{\pi}{2}]$ according to the calculation result when we select the relay node.

The locations of the node C at the previous moment and the current moment are denoted by $c1(c1_x, c1_y)$ and $c(c_x, c_y)$, the locations of the node N at the previous moment and the current moment are denoted by $n1(n1_x, n1_y)$ and $n(n_x, n_y)$, the location of the node D at the current moment is denoted by $d(d_x, d_y)$. So the average moving speed of the node C and its neighbor node N are calculated by (here we use average speed within the sampling interval instead the instantaneous speed):

$$\overline{v1} = \frac{\sqrt{\left(c_x^2 - c1_x^2\right) + \left(c_y^2 - c1_y^2\right)}}{\Delta T} \tag{7}$$

$$\overline{v2} = \frac{\sqrt{\left(n_x^2 - n1_x^2\right) + \left(n_y^2 - n1_y^2\right)}}{\Delta T} \tag{8}$$

We denote the location of the node C, the node N and the node D at the next moment by $c2(c2_x, c2_y)$, $n2(n2_x, n2_y)$ and $d2(d2_x, d2_y)$, that is $c2(c_x + \Delta T \times \overline{v1}_x, c_y + \Delta T \times \overline{v1}_y)$ and $n2(n_x + \Delta T \times \overline{v2}_x, n_y + \Delta T \times \overline{v2}_y)$, the distance between the node

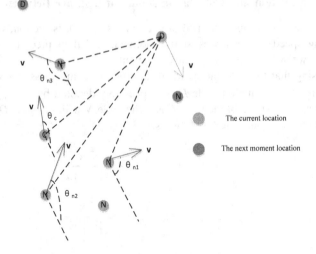

Fig. 1. The calculation of angles of the moving speed.

C and the node N with the node D at the next moment are denoted by S_c and S_n, and they can be calculated by:

$$S_c = \sqrt{\left(d2_x - \left(c_x + \Delta T \times \overline{v1_x}\right)\right)^2 + \left(d2_y - \left(c_y + \Delta T \times \overline{v1_y}\right)\right)^2} \tag{9}$$

$$S_n = \sqrt{\left(d2_x - \left(n_x + \Delta T \times \overline{v2_x}\right)\right)^2 + \left(d2_y - \left(n_y + \Delta T \times \overline{v2_y}\right)\right)^2} \tag{10}$$

3.3   A Priority Based Buffer Management Strategy

The buffer size of each node is limited, so when the message arrives the buffer, the effective management of buffer can achieve a priority of message forwarding and select messages to be dropped reasonably to avoid the overflow of buffer.

We synthetically consider the importance level $L(m_i)$ and the timelessness $T(m_i)$ of the message to calculate the message priority:

Supposing that the message contents created in the network is various, we set an importance level $L(m_i)$ for each messages. A higher $T(m_i)$ means a greater importance of the message. Then $T(m_i)$ is calculated by:

$$T_c = t_c - t_s \tag{11}$$

$$T(m_i) = \begin{cases} \frac{T_c}{TTL}, & T_c < 0.95TTL \\ 0, & otherwise \end{cases} \tag{12}$$

where T_c represents the existing time of the message, t_c represents the current time, t_s represents the created time of the message, TTL represents the time-to-live.

So the final priority P_m is calculated by:

$$P_m = L(m_i) \times \alpha + (1 - (T(m_i) \times \beta))\tag{13}$$

where α and β represent the weights of $L(m_i)$ and $T(m_i)$, and $\alpha + \beta = 1$.

3.4   The LIBR Routing Algorithm

In our proposed LIBR routing algorithm, the node carrying messages selects proper relay nodes and determines the forwarding priority of messages, then enters the message forwarding phase, so the node carrying messages determines the specific forwarding process according to the number of copies κ carried by itself. The LIBR routing algorithm is described in Table 1.

Table 1. The LIBR routing algorithm.

1. Begin
2. if N is the destination node
3. C transmits message to N
4. else compute P_{ij} of D by using eq.(1) - eq.(4);
5. then compute θ_c and θ_n ;
6. if ($\theta_c \in \left[0, \frac{\pi}{2}\right]$)∥($\theta_n \in \left[0, \frac{\pi}{2}\right]$)
7. compute S_c and S_n ;
8. then compute P_m ;
9. if ($\kappa = 1$)
10. C will not forward messages;
11.else if ($\kappa > 1$) then
12.if ($S_c = S_n$)
13. C forwards $\left\lfloor \frac{\kappa}{2} \right\rfloor$ copies while keeping $\left\lceil \frac{\kappa}{2} \right\rceil$;
14.else if ($S_c > S_n$)
15. C forwards messages with higher P_m ;
16.else if ($S_c < S_n$)
17. C carries messages itself;
18.End

In Table 1, from first line to third line, the node carrying messages determines whether a neighbor node is the destination node and then forward messages; the fourth line first predicts the location of the destination node; from fifth line to seventh line, we calculate the angle formed by moving speed and the distance between nodes at the next moment; the single copy forwarding process is from eighth line to ninth line; the multiple copy forwarding process is from tenth line to eighteenth line.

4 Simulation Experiment and Result Analysis

In this paper, we use the Opportunistic Network Environment (ONE) simulator [16] to evaluate the correctness and validity of our proposed models and algorithm. Then we compare the LIBR algorithm with the routing algorithms such as FirstContact, DirectDelivery, Epidemic in terms of delivery ratio of messages, overhead ratio of messages, average delay of the messages based on Shortest Path Map Based Movement model. In this paper, the overhead ratio of messages refers to the ratio of the total times that all messages are forwarded minus the number of messages arriving at their destination nodes over the number of messages arriving at their destination nodes. And we choose the buffer size of the nodes, the number of nodes and the interval of message generation as the factors that impact the routing performance, the specific simulation parameters are listed in Table 2.

Table 2. The specific parameters in our simulations.

Parameter	Default value	Range
Simulation size	4500 m × 3500 m	——
Transmit speed	250 Kbps	——
Transmit range	10 m	——
Simulation time	12 h	——
Moving speed	0.5 m/s–1.5 m/s	——
Time-to-Live (TTL)	100 s	——
Messages size	50 KB	——
Sampling interval	5 s	——
Node buffer size	60 M	20 M–120 M
Number of nodes	300	100–600
Message interval	20 s	10 s–35 s

4.1 Impact of Buffer Size on Routing Performance

Figure 2 is the variation rules of delivery ratio, overhead ratio and the average delay of messages of the four routing algorithms with the change of buffer size.

From Fig. 2, we note that LIBR achieves the highest delivery ratio, the smallest average delay and the overhead ratio is relatively low, which is higher than that of DirectDelivery. The main reason, we believe, is that our prediction of location information results in more possibilities of meeting with the destination node, and reduces the blindness of forwarding. Meanwhile based on our proposed models, we can select proper relay node to forward the messages. So the overhead ratio and the average transmission delay declines. Compared with other three routing algorithms, the delivery ratio of FirstContact routing algorithm is the lowest, and the average delay of

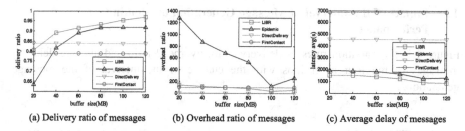

(a) Delivery ratio of messages   (b) Overhead ratio of messages   (c) Average delay of messages

Fig. 2. Impact of buffer size on routing performance.

messages is the highest, so FirstContact has a better routing performance in the small load network.

4.2 Impact of the Number of Nodes on Routing Performance

Figure 3 is the variation rules of delivery ratio, overhead ratio and the average delay of messages of the four routing algorithms with the change of the number of the nodes.

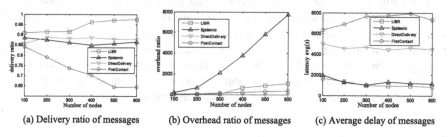

(a) Delivery ratio of messages   (b) Overhead ratio of messages   (c) Average delay of messages

Fig. 3. Impact of the number of nodes on routing performance

From Fig. 3, we note that the delivery ratio of LIBR routing algorithm is the highest. Compared to Epidemic routing, its overhead ratio is much low and the average delay is relatively low with the increase of the number of nodes. Due to the fact that with the increase of the number of nodes, the meeting probability will increase between nodes, so in this case the average delay of messages and consumption of network resources will shorten. The delivery ratio of LIBR routing algorithm has a significant increase before the number of nodes reaches 400, when the number of nodes is greater than 400, the network load increases accordingly due to the network node density is too large and the network resources are limited.

The delivery ratio of FirstContact routing declines rapidly, and its average delay is the highest, because the meeting opportunities with the destination node will decrease with the change of the number of nodes, so FirstContact is suitable for sparse network.

4.3   Impact of the Interval of Message Generation on Routing Performance

Figure 4 is the variation rules of delivery ratio, overhead ratio and average delay of messages of the four algorithms with the change of the interval of the message generation.

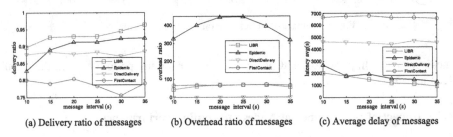

(a) Delivery ratio of messages   (b) Overhead ratio of messages   (c) Average delay of messages

Fig. 4. Impact of the interval of message generation on routing performance

From Fig. 4, we note that the delivery ratio increases with the increase of the interval of message generation. The main reason, we believe, is that when the interval reduces, it adopts redundant control measures. Instead when the interval of message generation is smaller than 15 s, Epidemic routing algorithm don't take any redundancy strategy, so the dropped packet of messages increases gradually. Thus we come to a conclusion that the LIBR routing algorithm can preferably adapt to the change of the interval of message generation, and the overall performance is good.

5   Conclusions

In this paper we propose a routing algorithm LIBR based on the prediction of the node meeting location, in which this algorithm firstly selects the proper relay node based on the node location prediction model and the calculation model of distance between nodes, and determines the forwarding priority according to the buffer management strategy, then finishes the full forwarding process. Furthermore we verify the correctness and validity of our proposed models and algorithm, and the simulation results show that the proposed algorithm LIBR has better routing performance in opportunistic networks with higher node density and limited buffer space. Follow-up we will further consider the historical information of time, and put forward the efficient routing algorithm of time and space historical meeting information combined in opportunistic networks.

Acknowledgments. This work is supported by the National Natural Science Foundation of China (Grant Nos. 61373083, 61402273); the Program of Shaanxi Science and Technology Innovation Team of China (Grant No. 2014KTC-18); the 111 Programme of Introducing Talents of Discipline to Universities (Grant No. B16031).

References

1. Xiao, M., Wu, J., Huang, L.: Community-aware opportunistic routing in mobile social networks. IEEE Trans. Comput. **63**(7), 1682–1695 (2014)
2. Kimura, T., Matsuda, T., Takine, T.: Location-aware store-carry-forward routing based on node density estimation. IEICE Trans. Commun. **98**(1), 99–106 (2015)
3. Azam, K.N., Chowdhury, M.Z.: Opportunistic system approach for capacity enhancement and congestion mitigation in advanced wireless networks. In: International Conference on Electrical Information and Communication Technology, pp. 341–346. IEEE (2016)
4. Koulali, S., Sabir, E., Taleb, T., et al.: A green strategic activity scheduling for UAV networks: a sub-modular game perspective. IEEE Commun. Mag. **54**(5), 58–64 (2016)
5. Conti, M., Giordano, S.: Mobile ad hoc networking: milestones, challenges, and new research directions. IEEE Commun. Mag. **52**(1), 85–96 (2014)
6. MartíN-Campillo, A., Crowcroft, J., Yoneki, E., et al.: Evaluating opportunistic networks in disaster scenarios. J. Netw. Comput. Appl. **36**(2), 870–880 (2013)
7. Pirozmand, P., Wu, G., Jedari, B., et al.: Human mobility in opportunistic networks: characteristics, models and prediction methods. J. Netw. Comput. Appl. **42**, 45–58 (2014)
8. Wang, N., Yoneki, E.: Impact of social structure on forwarding algorithms in opportunistic networks. In: Mobile and Wireless Networking, pp. 82–88. IEEE (2011)
9. Luo, J., Hu, J., Wu, D., et al.: Opportunistic routing algorithm for relay node selection in wireless sensor networks. IEEE Trans. Ind. Informat. **11**(1), 112–121 (2015)
10. Ciobanu, R.I., Dobre, C., Cristea, V.: Reducing congestion for routing algorithms in opportunistic networks with socially-aware node behavior prediction. In: International Conference on Advanced Information Networking and Applications, pp. 554–561. IEEE Computer Society (2013)
11. Shen, H., Zhao, L.: ALERT: an anonymous location-based efficient routing protocol in MANETs. IEEE Trans. Mob. Comput. **12**(6), 1079–1093 (2013)
12. Kumar, N., Chilamkurti, N., Rodrigues, J.J.P.C.: Learning automata-based opportunistic data aggregation and forwarding scheme for alert generation in vehicular ad hoc networks. Comput. Comun. **39**, 22–32 (2014)
13. Wang, X., Chen, M., Kwon, T., et al.: Mobile traffic offloading by exploiting social network services and leveraging opportunistic device-to-device sharing. IEEE Wirel. Commun. **21**(3), 28–36 (2014)
14. Becchetti, L., Clementi, A., Pasquale, F., et al.: Flooding time in opportunistic networks under power law and exponential intercontact times. IEEE Trans. Parall. Distr. **25**(9), 2297–2306 (2014)
15. Li, F., Shi, P., Wu, L., et al.: Quantized control design for cognitive radio networks modeled as nonlinear semi-Markovian jump systems. IEEE Trans. Ind. Electron. **62**(4), 2330–2340 (2015)
16. Dhurandher, S.K., Borah, S., Woungang, I., et al.: EDR: an encounter and distance based routing protocol for opportunistic networks. In: International Conference on Advanced Information Networking and Applications, pp. 297–302. IEEE (2016)

A Cooperative Optimization Method for Mobile User Data Offloading

Guangsheng Feng[1](✉), Dongdong Su[1], Junyu Lin[2], Fumin Xia[1], Hongwu Lv[1], and Huiqiang Wang[1]

[1] College of Computer Science and Technology,
Harbin Engineering University, Harbin, China
fengguangsheng@hrbeu.edu.cn
[2] Institute of Information Engineering, Chinese Academy of Sciences, Beijing, China

Abstract. We study the problem of mobile data offloading in a cooperative cellular network where the cellular network can offload a fraction of data traffic to its cooperative WiFi networks. To measure the metric of *user satisfaction* towards offloading scheme, an S-shaped function is introduced to capture the user utility, namely, the user satisfaction function. Therefore, the first objective is to maximize the user satisfaction. Considering the cooperation and competition among cellular and WiFi networks, the operator has to given up partial benefit to the cooperative partners. Therefore, optimal pricing is the other consideration of this work. The mobile data offloading problem is formulated as a joint optimization of "min-max" problem, which is converted into a bi-level optimization problem, where the upper level is to minimize the *operator benefit* loss and the lower one is to maximize the user satisfaction. Simulation results show that the proposed method achieves the near-optimal solutions with limited iterations.

Keywords: Mobile data offloading · Utility function · User satisfaction

1 Introduction

Mobile data offloading is one of cooperative transmission technologies, in which the network operators can offload partial traffic through the free or charging cooperative partners, e.g., WiFi hotspots, without interference to the data consumers. Different from the traditional way of transmission only through one BS or WiFi hotspots, user data can be delivered concurrently through multi-operator networks, and the traffics belong to the same session and same destination from different paths are aggregated on the terminal device.

One representative of mobile data offloading is BT Fon community [1], co-founded by BT and Fon in 2007, wherein BT invited 3 million home users to join the community and share their free/charging idle bandwidth resources. Existing

© Springer Nature Singapore Pte Ltd. 2018
J. Li et al. (Eds.): CWSN 2017, CCIS 812, pp. 296–306, 2018.
https://doi.org/10.1007/978-981-10-8123-1_26

studies on mobile data offloading can generally be classified into two major categories, namely, infrastructure-assisted and infrastructure-free schemes [2]. The
first type of scheme utilizes some existing facilities with communication, calculation and storage capabilities for data transmission, e.g., WiFi hotspot [3] and
Internet of Vehicles [4]. The second one refers to infrastructure-free offloading,
wherein the cooperative transmission is implemented via other local networks
composed by various mobile terminals, e.g., delay tolerance networks (DTN) [5]
and device to device (D2D) networks [6].

In perspective of incentive cooperation, designing effective strategies to moti-
vate the partner participating in data offloading becomes a research hotspot currently. Generally, such approaches leverage economic principle, e.g., benefit sharing [7] or unilateral benefit maximization [8], on the incentive strategies where
sharing the idle bandwidth resources for data offloading. In this work, we also
study the data offloading in consideration of the incentive cooperation among
cellular and WiFi networks. Different from the existing work where only one
type of participation partner is considered, we study this problem incorporating
different types of partners. To facilitate the description of the user satisfaction,
we incorporate the S-shaped utility function into the system design. Our system's objective is to maximize all users' satisfaction and minimize all operators'
benefit loss for giving up a fraction of user traffic to other cooperative partners,
and thus the offloading problem is then formulated as a "Min-Max" optimization
problem.

2 System Model

2.1 Network Model

Considering an LTE-A network scenario, there are I ($I \in \mathbb{Z}^+$) mobile users and
K ($K \in \mathbb{Z}^+$) WiFi access points in one cell. We assume that each UE is equipped
with LTE and WiFi interfaces, such that both can provide transmission services
to users through their own links. Moreover, we assume that the cellular and WiFi
operators can work cooperatively towards our offloading mode, i.e., the cellular
BS can offload a fraction of traffics to the WiFi access points such that the users
can obtain sufficient transmission bandwidth.

Considering that different mobile users possibly have different traffics
demand, we divide the user traffic demand into J types ($J \in \mathbb{Z}^+$). We use
f_{ij} to denote the user i's traffic demand of type j. The total amount of data
traffic required by all I users is $\sum_{i=1}^{I} \sum_{j=1}^{J} f_{ij}$. In our model, we assume that
$\sum_{i=1}^{I} \sum_{j=1}^{J} f_{ij}$ reaches to or exceeds the limit of cellular network capacity, but
it is less than the capacity summation of cellular and WiFi networks. The total
amount of data traffic provided by the cellular network is $\sum_{i=1}^{I} \sum_{j=1}^{J} f_{ij0}$, and
that provided by WiFi networks is $\sum_{i=1}^{I} \sum_{j=1}^{J} \sum_{k=1}^{K} f_{ijk}$.

2.2   A Two-Stage Offloading Strategy

In our work, we assume that the unit price of traffics is set by each network operator independently. Each user knows the location, unit price and other related information, so that it can make decision independently according to their observations. And meanwhile, the cellular and WiFi networks can adjust the unit price to ensure their own benefits. Basically, this offloading strategy can be depicted by a two-stage decision process.

Stage I: the cellular and WiFi networks adjust the unit prices and broadcast them to all users in the coverage area.

Stage II: according to the unit price announced in Stage I, each user will reallocate their data traffic for maximization of their satisfaction.

Notice that the cellular and WiFi networks will continuously adjust their own unit prices to guarantee the benefits in consideration of the users' choice in Stage II. When the unit prices are announced in Stage I, all the users will determine the amount of data traffic from different networks. Therefore, the above two stages interact with each other, and it forms a process of iterative change. In this process, user i's type j traffic is formed by both the cellular and the WiFi networks, which is given by

$$f_{ij} = f_{ij0} + \sum_{k=1}^{K} f_{ijk}. \tag{1}$$

Notice that f_{ij} is also the type j data traffic amount required by user i.

3   Problem Description

3.1   Maximization Problem of User Satisfaction

Considering that the traditional utility function cannot show completeness of users' preferences [9], an S-shaped utility function is adopted to evaluate the user satisfaction in the mobile offloading scheme [10]. Such a utility function means that the user utility curve changes like *S shape* with the user getting more required resources, and it is more suitable to depict the user satisfaction thanks to the good marginal effect, as shown in Fig. 1, where it shows the user satisfaction versus resource amount. Before the resource amount reaches to the user's expectation, the utility function is concave with the resource amount increasing. Thereafter, it becomes convex.

According to [9], the S-shaped utility function of cellular network (denoted by subscript "0"), namely $U(f_{ij0})$, is defined by

$$U(f_{ij0}) = \frac{1}{1 + e^{-a_{i0}(f_{ij0} - d_{ij0})}}, \tag{2}$$

and the utility function of WiFi network k, namely $U(f_{ijk})$, is defined as

$$U(f_{ijk}) = \frac{1}{1 + e^{-a_{ik}(f_{ijk} - d_{ijk})}}, \tag{3}$$

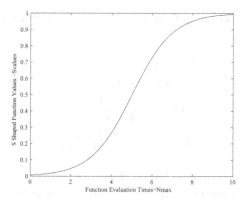

Fig. 1. An S-shaped utility function to depict the user satisfaction.

where a_{i*} represents user i's preference factor to BS/WiFi *. Notice that * denotes BS if $* = 0$, and otherwise it denotes WiFi k given $* = k$. Parameter a_{i*} can be used to adjust the convergence speed of the S-shaped utility function. A larger value of a_{i*} means that user i prefers to network * rather than other networks. d_{ij*} denotes the access threshold, meaning that user i expects a certain amount of type j traffics from network *, such that it can get a basic access service from the specific network.

The access thresholds are set by the corresponding networks, and also corresponding to the expected utility function values. When the traffics from one network below the access threshold, it has to achieve the access guarantee urgently, so the utility function is concave. Otherwise, the user has achieved the basic access guarantee and the utility function is convex. Since $U(f_{ij0})$ and $U(f_{ijk})$ are the S-shaped utility functions, both follow the cumulative effect of the general utility function and have the first derivative that is greater than zero. Therefore, the utility functions $U(f_{ij0})$ and $U(f_{ijk})$ are quasi-convex.

According to the principle of economic supply [11], the commodity price will rise as the goods supply increases. The slope of the corresponding supply curve is positive and can be approximated in a straight line. Similarly, to ensure a higher cumulative effect of the cellular and WiFi networks, the access threshold (d_{ij0} or d_{ijk}) will be improved as the increasing amount of data traffic provision (f_{ij0} or f_{ijk}). As the principle shows, the larger f_{ij0} or f_{ijk} are, the larger d_{ij0} or d_{ijk} are. d_{ij0} and d_{ijk} can be defined as $d_{ij0} = q_{i0} \times f_{ij0}$ and $d_{ijk} = q_{ik} \times f_{ijk}$, where q_{i*} is the access slope, representing the percentage of the access threshold to the amount of data traffic that is required by user i. To simplify our formulation, we substitute the d_{ij0} and d_{ijk}'s formula into (2) and (3), respectively, and we can obtain that

$$U(f_{ij0}) = \frac{1}{1 + e^{-a_{i0}(f_{ij0} - q_{i0}f_{ij0})}}, \tag{4}$$

$$U(f_{ijk}) = \frac{1}{1 + e^{-a_{ik}(f_{ijk} - q_{ik}f_{ijk})}}. \tag{5}$$

Then, we use the following (6) and (7) to further simplify $U(f_{ij0})$ and $U(f_{ijk})$, we can obtain that

$$h_{i0} = a_{i0}(1 - q_{i0}), \tag{6}$$

$$h_{ik} = a_{ik}(1 - q_{ik}), \tag{7}$$

$$U(f_{ij0}) = \frac{1}{1 + e^{-h_{i0}f_{ij0}}}, \tag{8}$$

$$U(f_{ijk}) = \frac{1}{1 + e^{-h_{ik}f_{ijk}}}, \tag{9}$$

where h_{i*} denotes user i's sensitivity of the data traffic service provided by the network *. A larger value of h_{i*} means a faster convergence speed of the utility function. According to the first derivative of the utility functions $U(f_{ij0})$ and $U(f_{ijk})$, both of them are monotonically increasing. When $f_{ij0} \geq 0$ and $f_{ijk} \geq 0$, the two order derivatives of $U(f_{ij0})$ and $U(f_{ijk})$ are negative, which means that $U(f_{ij0})$ and $U(f_{ijk})$ are convex in the defined domain.

In the offloading problems, the user's expenses are crucial [12]. Each user need to pay the fees to the networks according to their usage in Stage II and the announced unit price in Stage I. To represent the price sensitivity to the data traffic provided by the cellular and WiFi networks, the price sensitive functions $P(f_{ij0})$ and $P(f_{ijk})$ are represented by $P(f_{ij0}) = b_{i0}c_{i0}f_{ij0}$ and $P(f_{ijk}) = b_{ik}c_{ik}f_{ijk}$.

Parameters b_{i*} represents user i's sensitivity to the unit price of network *, which is a constant. In this work, $U(f_{ij0})$ and $U(f_{ijk})$ describe the user's satisfaction of the service provided by the cellular WiFi networks, and the price sensitive functions, i.e., $P(f_{ij0})$ and $P(f_{ijk})$, are used to describe the satisfaction with expenses. Combined the user's satisfaction with expense and service, the user's satisfaction function can be represented by $SF = \sum_{i=1}^{I} \sum_{j=1}^{J} [U(f_{ij0}) + \sum_{k=1}^{K} U(f_{ijk}) - P(f_{ij0}) - \sum_{k=1}^{K} P(f_{ijk})]$.

The strategy to reallocate traffics in Stage II is to maximize user's payoff, which can be formulated as the maximization of the user's satisfaction. Mathematically, the optimal solution of allocation is to the maximization **Problem 1**.

Problem 1: User's Satisfaction Maximization Problem.

$$\max \quad SF$$

$$s.t. \quad (1), f_{ij0} \geq 0, f_{ijk} \geq 0$$

$$var : \quad \{\sum_{i=1}^{I} \sum_{j=1}^{J} f_{ij0}, \sum_{i=1}^{I} \sum_{j=1}^{J} \sum_{k=1}^{K} f_{ijk}\} \in F$$

3.2   Minimization Problem of the Network Benefit Loss

The traffic allocation in Stage I has an impact on the revenue of cellular and WiFi networks. Thus, the corresponding networks will adjust the unit price to attract more users to use their transmission services. Price discounts are one of the most commonly used methods. Notice that the price discount will also result in a loss of the benefit of networks.

The cellular benefit loss: to attract more users to use the cellular transmission service, the cellular operator will conduct a discount price on the standard unit price, which can lead to the benefit loss of the cellular operator. For cellular network, we denote c_0 and c_{i0} the standard unit price and the discount unit price to user i. The discount unit price c_{i0} is no larger than the c_0. Therefore, the cellular benefit loss can be represented by $H_1 = \sum_{i=1}^{I} \sum_{j=1}^{J} (c_0 - c_{i0}) f_{ij0}$.

The WiFi benefit loss: when the cellular network is overloaded, it will seek the offloading partners from the cooperative WiFi networks. Similar to the benefit loss of cellular network, the WiFi benefit loss can also be caused because of the price competition. Correspondingly, the WiFi benefit loss can be represented by $H_2 = \sum_{i=1}^{I} \sum_{j=1}^{J} \sum_{k=1}^{K} (c_k - c_{ik}) f_{ijk}$, where c_k and c_{ik} are the WiFi's standard unit price and discount unit price. Consequently, the total benefit loss can be represented by $H(c) = H_1 + H_2$, and the minimization of benefit loss problem can be formulated as the **Problem 2**.

Problem 2: Minimization Problem of the Profit Loss

$$\min H(c)$$
$$s.t.\, 0 < c_{i0} < c_0, 0 < c_{ik} < c_k$$
$$var: \left(\sum_{i=1}^{I} c_{i0}, \sum_{i=1}^{I} \sum_{j=1}^{J} c_{ik} \right) \in C \tag{10}$$

4   The Solution of Bi-Level Optimization Problem

After the networks announce the unit prices, the corresponding unit price becomes constant. Therefore Problem P1 is a convex optimization problem, which can be solved by KKT conditions, which are given by (11)–(14).

$$\sum_{j=1}^{J} \sum_{i=1}^{I} \left\{ b_{i0} c_{i0} - \frac{h_{i0} e^{-h_{i0} f_{ij0}}}{(1 + e^{-h_{i0} f_{ij0}})^2} + \lambda \right\} \geq 0, \tag{11}$$

$$\sum_{k=1}^{K} \sum_{j=1}^{J} \sum_{i=1}^{I} \left\{ b_{ik} c_{ik} - \frac{h_{ik} e^{-h_{ik} f_{ijk}}}{(1 + e^{-h_{ik} f_{ijk}})^2} + \lambda \right\} \geq 0, \tag{12}$$

$$\sum_{j=1}^{J} \sum_{i=1}^{I} \left\{ b_{i0} c_{i0} - \frac{h_{i0} e^{-h_{i0} f_{ij0}}}{(1 + e^{-h_{i0} f_{ij0}})^2} + \lambda \right\} = 0, \tag{13}$$

$$\sum_{k=1}^{K} \sum_{j=1}^{J} \sum_{i=1}^{I} \left\{ b_{ik} c_{ik} - \frac{h_{ik} e^{-h_{ik} f_{ijk}}}{(1 + e^{-h_{ik} f_{ijk}})^2} + \lambda \right\} = 0. \tag{14}$$

Since Stage I and Stage II can form an iterative process in conjunction with **Problem 1** and **Problem 2**, it is necessary to ensure that the benefit loss of the cellular and the WiFi networks is minimized after the completion of allocation. Therefore, **Problem 2** can be seen as a bi-level optimization problem based on **Problem 1**. Mathematically, it can be described as **Problem 3**.

Problem 3: The Bi-Level Optimization Problem

$$\min \ \sum_{i=1}^{I}\sum_{j=1}^{J}\left((c_0 - c_{i0})f_{ij0} + \sum_{k=1}^{K}(c_k - c_{ik})f_{ijk}\right)$$

$$s.t. \ (10)-(14)$$

$$var: \ \left\{\sum_{i=1}^{I}\sum_{j=1}^{J}f_{ij0}, \sum_{i=1}^{I}\sum_{j=1}^{J}\sum_{k=1}^{K}f_{ijk}\right\} \in F \tag{15}$$

$$\left\{\sum_{i=1}^{I}c_{i0}, \sum_{i=1}^{I}\sum_{j=1}^{J}c_{ik}\right\} \in C$$

All the KKT conditions (11)–(14) are the function of f_{ij0}, f_{ijk} and λ, which depend on c_{i0} and c_{ik}. Therefore, **Problem 3** can be converted into **Problem 4**.

Problem 4: Minimization Problem of the Profit Loss when the traffic usage is known

$$\min \ H(c)$$

$$s.t. \ (10)$$

$$var: \ \left\{\sum_{i=1}^{I}c_{i0}, \sum_{i=1}^{I}\sum_{j=1}^{J}c_{ik}\right\} \in C$$

The solution of **Problem 4** is based on the condition that the data traffics are known. As we can see from Stage II, the multi-users data traffics usage is based on the initial unit price announced by the multi-operators in Stage I. Thus, solving **Problem 4** is equivalent to solve **Problem 5**.

Problem 5: Minimization Problem of the Profit Loss when the unit price at Stage I is known

$$\min \ H(c)$$

$$s.t. \ (1), (11)-(14)$$

$$var: \ \left\{\sum_{i=1}^{I}\sum_{j=1}^{J}f_{ij0}, \sum_{i=1}^{I}\sum_{j=1}^{J}\sum_{k=1}^{K}f_{ijk}\right\} \in F, \lambda$$

Problem 5 can be seen as the simplified problem of **Problem 3** when the unit price at Stage I is known. Since the condition (1) is a linear condition, and conditions (11)–(14) are the KKT conditions of a convex-optimization **Problem 1**, **Problem 5** is also a convex optimization problem. Because the utility functions $U(f_{ij0})$ and $U(f_{ijk})$ are quasi-convex and the price sensitive functions $P(f_{ij0})$ and $P(f_{ijk})$ are linear, the second order derivative of the satisfaction function SF is negative. Therefore, the maximum value of SF exists. Similarly, the solution of **Problem 5** is also presented.

Problem 5 can be solved after the values of f_{ij0}, f_{ijk} and λ are obtained. And we can get them by solving the KKT conditions (11)–(14). First, according to conditions (13) and (14), we can represent the parameters f_{ij0} and f_{ijk} as the combination of c_{i0}, c_{ik} and λ, which are given by $f_{ij0} = \max\{f_{ij0}(c_{i0}, \lambda), 0\}$ and $f_{ijk} = \max\{f_{ijk}(c_{ik}, \lambda), 0\}$.

Moreover, according to (11) and (12), we can obtain the upper and lower bounds of λ, which is given by $\frac{h_{i0}e^{h_{i0}f_{ij0}}}{(1+e_{i0}^h f_{ij0})^2} - b_{i0}c_{i0} \leq \lambda \leq 1$. According to the dichotomy, the values of f_{ij0} and f_{ijk} can be determined by substituting λ into (1). According to the (13) and (14), the upper and lower bounds of λ can be given by $0 \leq \frac{\lambda + b_{i0}c_{i0}}{h_{i0}} \leq 1$.

DYCORS is an algorithm that can solve the optimization problem with high dimensional bounds [13]. The basic idea of the DYCORS is to establish an agent model of the objective function in each iteration, and generate an experimental solution by dynamic coordinate perturbation method. The optimal solution is obtained by perturbing a small fraction of the local optimal solution at present. When the coordinate probability of the local optimal solution is reduced to the given threshold, it can be considered as the optimal solution.

Ma et al. [12] used the DYCORS algorithm to solve offloading problem. The difference with literature [12] lies in our work has combined with the economic supply principle to describe S-shaped utility function, and further convert it into a quasi-convex function for processing. Another difference is that our work allows more than one networks. However, [12] only uses the cellular network to solve offloading problem, which means that they has lost the cooperation of other networks.

5   Simulation Results

There are four WiFi hotspots and a single cellular BS in our experiment, i.e., $K = 4$. Under the ideal conditions, the transfer rate of 4G cellular downlink can reach to 100 Mbps, and that of WiFi can reach to 54M [14]. To simplify the calculation, we set that there are three type of user traffics, which are 5M, 10M and 15M, respectively. Meanwhile, there are three different types of traffic sensitivity parameters and unit price sensitivity parameters for h_{i0}, h_{ik}, b_{i0} and b_{ik}, which

Table 1. Three types of traffic sensitivity parameters

	h_{i0}	h_{i1}	h_{i2}	h_{i3}	h_{i4}	b_{i0}	b_{i1}	b_{i2}	b_{i3}	b_{i4}
LOW	0.3	0.5	0.1	0.4	0.7	0.6	0.8	0.5	0.7	0.9
MID	0.6	1	0.2	0.8	1.4	0.6	0.8	0.5	0.7	0.9
HIGH	0.9	1.5	0.3	1.2	2.1	0.6	0.8	0.5	0.7	0.9

are LOW, MID and HIGH, as shown in Table 1. The maximum evaluation times of $N_{\max}$ is 300.

To generate initial discount unit price for c_{i0} and c_{ik}, the values of their unit price's lower and upper bounds are set in advance. The upper values are 1.5, 1.3, 1.2, 2 and 1.6. The lower values are 0.5, 0.3, 0.6, 0.4 and 0.2. We also set the values of standard unit prices for c_0, c_1, c_2, c_3 and c_4 as 2, 1.5, 1.6, 2.4 and 1.8.

We analyze the results of the bi-level problem when the users are the same type and their data traffic demand f_{ij} is setting consistent with the three specific types. Furthermore, we choose the LOW type of the traffic sensitivity parameters for h_{i0} and h_{ik}, and the unit price sensitivity parameters for b_{i0} and b_{ik}.

The results of **Problem 2** are shown in Fig. 2. With the evaluation iterations increasing, the results towards to converge. Moreover, when the data traffic demand of f_{ij} increases, the value of $H(c)$ nearly increases identically.

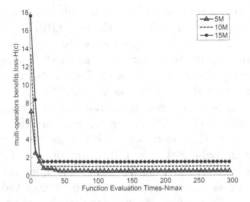

Fig. 2. The results of problem 2 when users are same but traffics demand is different.

The results of **Problem 1** are shown in Fig. 3. With the function evaluation times increasing, the results converge rapidly. Moreover, when the data traffic demand f_{ij} increases, the corresponding convergence result of SF is nearly decreased as equal.

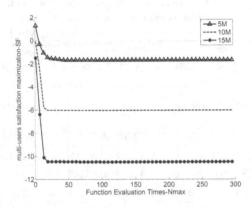

Fig. 3. The results of problem1 when users are same but traffics demand is different.

6 Conclusion and Remarks

We proposed the bi-level optimization problem for mobile data offloading based on the cooperation of multi-operators and single cellular operator. The user satisfaction maximization problem is firstly simplified to a quasi-convex problem. Combined with the user satisfaction maximization problem, we then introduced the DYCORS algorithm to solve the multi-operators benefits loss minimization problem. Moreover, we also verified the performance of the proposed method under different situations, the proposed method can converge quickly.

Acknowledgement. This work is supported by the National Natural Science Foundation of China (No. 61502118 and 61402127), the Fundamental Research Fund for the Central Universities (No. HEUCF170602) and the Natural Science Foundation of Heilongjiang Province (No. F2016028, F2016009, F2015029).

References

1. FON Wireless. http://www.fon.com
2. Wang, N., Wu, J.: Opportunistic WiFi offloading in a vehicular environment: waiting or downloading now? In: IEEE INFOCOM 2016, pp. 1–9. IEEE (2016)
3. Pyattaev, A., Johnsson, K., Andreev, S., et al.: 3GPP LTE traffic offloading onto WiFi direct. In: 2013 IEEE Wireless Communications and Networking Conference Workshops (WCNCW), pp. 135–140. IEEE (2013)
4. Alsharif, N., Cspedes, S., Shen, X.: iCAR: intersection-based connectivity aware routing in vehicular ad hoc networks. In: 2013 IEEE International Conference on Communications (ICC), pp. 1736–1741. IEEE (2013)
5. Li, Y.Q., Zhang, J.B., Gan, X.Y., et al.: A contract-based incentive mechanism for delayed traffic offloading in cellular networks. IEEE Trans. Wirel. Commun. **15**(8), 5314–5327 (2016)
6. Andreev, S., Pyattaev, A., Johnsson, K., et al.: Cellular traffic offloading onto network-assisted device-to-device connections. IEEE Commun. Mag. **52**(4), 20–31 (2014)
7. Iosifidis, G., Gao, L., Huang, J., et al.: A double-auction mechanism for mobile data-offloading markets. IEEE/ACM Trans. Network. **23**(5), 1634–1647 (2015)
8. Apostolaras, A., Iosifidis, G., Chounos, K., et al.: A mechanism for mobile data offloading to wireless mesh networks. IEEE Trans. Wirel. Commun. **15**(9), 5984–5997 (2016)
9. Li, N., Chen, L., Dahleh, M.A.: Demand response using linear supply function bidding. IEEE Trans. Smart Grid **6**(4), 1827–1838 (2015)
10. Guo, Z., Baruah, S.K.: A neurodynamic approach for real-time scheduling via maximizing piecewise linear utility. IEEE Trans. Neural Netw. Learn. Syst. **27**(2), 238–248 (2016)
11. Gao, L., Iosifidis, G., Huang, J., et al.: Economics of mobile data offloading. In: 2013 Proceedings IEEE INFOCOM, pp. 3303–3308. IEEE (2013)
12. Ma, Q., Liu, Y.F., Huang, J.: Time and location aware mobile data pricing. IEEE Trans. Mob. Comput. **15**(10), 2599–2613 (2016)

13. Regis, R.G., Shoemaker, C.A.: Combining radial basis function surrogates and dynamic coordinate search in high-dimensional expensive black-box optimization. Eng. Optim. **45**(5), 529–555 (2013)
14. Zhang, X., Jia, M., Chen, L., et al.: Filtered-OFDM-enabler for flexible waveform in the 5th generation cellular networks. In: 2015 IEEE Global Communications Conference (GLOBECOM), pp. 1–6. IEEE (2015)

Inferring the Most Popular Route Based on Ant Colony Optimization with Trajectory Data

Hong Zhang[1,2], Wei Huangfu[1,2(✉)], and Xiaoyan Hu[3]

[1] School of Computer and Communication Engineering, University of Science and Technology Beijing, Beijing 100083, China
huangfuwei@ustb.edu.cn
[2] Beijing Engineering and Technology Research Center for Convergence Networks and Ubiquitous Services, Beijing 100083, China
[3] China Mobile Group Design Institute Co., Ltd., Beijing 100080, China

Abstract. The development of big data technologies makes it possible to derive valuable information from the history trajectory data. An algorithm is proposed to discover the most popular route from the given source to the given destination in this paper. The region is latticed into regular grids and then the history trajectories are discretized according to the aforementioned grids. Afterwards, the most popular route is determinated by the ant colony optimization method, where the actions of the ants are inspired by the statistics of the history trajectories which lead to the destination or at least near the destination. The grid size and the ant colony parameters are adjustable to fulfil the requirements of the solution precision and the computation complexity. The experiments are performed on the real vehicle trajectory dataset and the results meet our common sense of the popular routes.

Keywords: Trajectory data · Route Inference
·The most popular route

1 Introduction

With the rapid development of the location-tracking technologies and the location based services in the last decade, spatio-temporal data have attracted more and more attentions from academe and industry [1–3]. The trajectory data, i.e. the records of the paths of moving objects, such as persons, vehicles, animals and nature phenomena [4], which are generated by GPS (Global Positioning System) modules or other similar devices, are one of the most important kinds of spatio-temporal data. In this paper, we use p to represent a point and use a sequence of points to represent a trajectory; then a trajectory is denoted as $p_1 \rightarrow p_2 \rightarrow p_3 \rightarrow \ldots p_n$ [5]. These trajectories give hints on how objects usually travel between locations [6].

© Springer Nature Singapore Pte Ltd. 2018
J. Li et al. (Eds.): CWSN 2017, CCIS 812, pp. 307–318, 2018.
https://doi.org/10.1007/978-981-10-8123-1_27

Our work is to discover a route on the basis of the history trajectories which are produced by similar moving objects, named the most popular route (MPR) [6]. The most popular route is usually not the shortest or the fastest route but the route which the objects pass with high probability. In many cases, the shortest or the fastest route can not reflect the whole scenarios related to objects' preferences or habits. Whereas, the most popular route will make great benefit to travel planning, track tracing, animal migration behavior studying, weather forecasting and so on.

In this paper, a new algorithm is proposed to discover the MPR between two given locations. We first lattice the region and discretize the history vehicle trajectories, and then use the ACO (Ant Colony Optimization) method [7] to discover the MPR, where the transfer probabilities between adjacent steps of the ants are derived from the statistics of the history trajectories.

The remainder of this paper is organized as follows. We discuss the related work in Sect. 2. Then we introduce the new algorithm of route discovering process in Sect. 3. We demonstrate the rationality and practicality of our algorithm by conducting experiments on real data in Sect. 4. Conclusion and the future work are in Sect. 5.

2   Related Work

The route discovering problem is relevant to data processing [8], trajectory clustering [9–11], trajectory prediction [12–14], trajectory pattern mining [15,16] etc. The definition of route in our work is similar to that in hot route discovery algorithms [17,18]. An on-line algorithm is developed in [17] to discover hot motion routes. Li et al. implement an algorithm which is based on density to search hot routes [18]. However, these works aim at finding routes that are popular in the whole region, not the one between two given locations.

The purpose of route inferring [1,4,6,19] is to discover the route between two given locations. Banerjee et al. construct a Network-Mobility-Model based on road network and history trajectories of vehicles, and then use the model to infer routes [1]. Zheng et al. propose HRIS (History based Route Inference System) to derive the most popular k paths from one location to another [4]. Yet, [1] and [4] need the information of road network to infer routes, and thus cannot apply in non-network situation. RICK (Route Inference framework based on Collective Knowledge) [19] infers route without network and gives the top-k routes which sequentially pass through the given location sequence in the given time span.

The problem of discovering popular route between two locations is investigated in [6]. The authors retrieve a directional transfer network from history trajectories and import popularity indicators to decide the next node of the route in the search phase to discover the most popular route between two given locations. Here the nodes are the clusters generated from the locations in the trajectories. Therefore, the density of nodes is uncontrollable, and it is highly relevant to history trajectories and may lead to great deviation. Moreover, it takes much time to compute the transfer probability between nodes.

3   MPR Inference Algorithm

In our work, the region is divided into disjoint grids to control the deviation, and then the MPR is discovered with ACO method. The grid size and the ant colony optimization parameters are adjustable to fulfil the requirements of the solution precision and the computation complexity. There are 3 steps in our method, to lattice the region, to discretize the trajectories and to determine the MPR with ACO. The details are discussed as follows.

3.1   Region Latticing

First of all, we divide the region into disjoint grids and index each grid with a unique code (for example, (11,11)). The accuracy of the most popular route we found will be influenced by the size of grids. The smaller the grids are, the more details the route shows, but the longer the time consumes.

We define the neighbor of a grid in Definition 1.

Definition 1: Neighbor. Given a grid with grid code (m, n), the grids with grid code $(m - 1, n - 1)$, $(m, n - 1)$, $(m + 1, n - 1)$, $(m - 1, n)$, $(m + 1, n)$, $(m - 1, n + 1)$, $(m, n + 1)$ and $(m + 1, n + 1)$ are the neighbors of grid (m, n). Noted that when the grid locates at the edge of the region, some of its neighbors may not exist.

In Fig. 1, the grids (1,1), (2,1), (3,1), (1,2), (3,2), (1,3), (2,3), (3,3) are neighbors of the grid (2,2).

3.2   Trajectory Discretizing

The second step in our approach is to discretize the trajectory. The process is shown in Fig. 2. For example, for a given history trajectory $q_1 \rightarrow q_2 \rightarrow q_3 \rightarrow q_4 \rightarrow q_5 \rightarrow q_6 \rightarrow q_6 \rightarrow q_7 \rightarrow q_8$, there are three kinds of situations for any two adjacent trajectory points.

1. Adjacent points lie in neighbor grids. We use the corresponding grids to represent the points respectively. For example, q_2 and q_3 will be discretized by (1,3) and (2,2).
2. Adjacent points both lie in the same grid. We use this grid to represent the two points. For example q_4 and q_5 will be discretized by (3,2), and the latter will be optionally omitted.
3. Adjacent points lie in neither neighbor grids nor the same grid, such as q_6 and q_7. We use the grids intersecting with the line from the former to the latter to represent this segment of the trajectory. As a result, $q_6 \rightarrow q_7$ is discretized by $(4, 3) \rightarrow (5, 3) \rightarrow (5, 4) \rightarrow (6, 4) \rightarrow (6, 5)$.

Thus the trajectory in Fig. 2 will be discretized to $(0, 3) \rightarrow (1, 3) \rightarrow (2, 2) \rightarrow (3, 2) \rightarrow (4, 3) \rightarrow (5, 3) \rightarrow (5, 4) \rightarrow (6, 4) \rightarrow (6, 5) \rightarrow (7, 5)$.

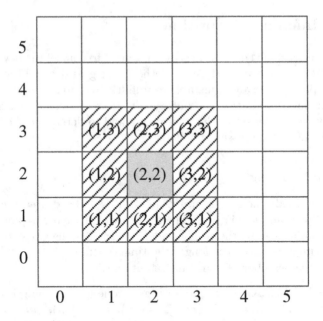

Fig. 1. Neighbors in the latticed region.

Definition 2: Transfer angle. Given a discretized trajectory trj_k be noted by $grid_1 \rightarrow grid_2 \rightarrow grid_3 \ldots \rightarrow grid_i$ and the destination grid $grid_d$, we define the moving direction of the trajectory in grid $grid_i$ as $\overrightarrow{grid_i\ grid_{i+1}}$ and the destination direction in $grid_i$ is $\overrightarrow{grid_i\ grid_d}$. The transfer angle of trj_k in $grid_i$ is the angle formed by the $\overrightarrow{grid_i\ grid_{i+1}}$ and $\overrightarrow{grid_i\ grid_d}$, denoted by $\theta_{i,(trj_k,d)}$. Obviously, for different trajectories, the transfer angle in the same grid may be different.

In Fig. 2, for example, the transfer angle of grid (3,2) in the discretized trajectory trj_k is tagged as $\theta_{(3,2),(trj_k,d)}$.

3.3 Route Discovering

We apply the ant colony optimization method to discover the most popular route. Suppose there are N route discovering iterations and k ants in each iteration. An ant can only move to the neighbor grids (except the grids which the ant has ever passed) of the current grid in the next step. For example in Fig. 3, when an ant is in the grid (2,2) now and it has passed the grid (1,1), the next step of this ant must be one of (2,1), (3,1), (1,2), (3,2), (1,3), (2,3) or (3,3).

When two adjacent grids $grid_i$ and $grid_j$ ($grid_i$ is the current grid and $grid_j$ is neighbor of $grid_i$) are given, the probability of objects moves to $grid_j$ from $grid_i$ in the next step according to the history data is

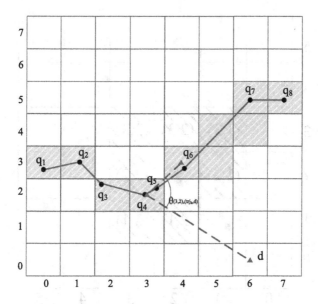

Fig. 2. Trajectory discretizing.

$$P(grid_i \rightarrow grid_j) = \frac{number\ of\ trajectories\ between\ grid_i\ and\ grid_j}{number\ of\ trajectories\ go\ through\ grid_i}$$

When we consider the probability of reaching destination d from $grid_i$ through $grid_j$, we adjust the formula to Definition 3.

Definition 3: Reachable Probability. Given two adjacent grids $grid_i$, $grid_j$ and destination d, the reachable probability of $grid_i \rightarrow grid_j$ with regard to d is defined as

$$\eta_{ij} = P_d(grid_i \rightarrow grid_j) = \frac{\sum_{\text{traj}(grid_i, grid_j)} likely(traj, d)}{\sum_{\text{traj}(grid_i)} likely(traj, d)} \tag{1}$$

It is also served as the attractiveness in the ACO method. The function $likely(traj, d)$ is to measure the possibility of a trajectory leading to d, defined as

$$likely(traj, d) = e^{(cos\theta_{i,(trj,d)})^\gamma} \tag{2}$$

where $\theta_{i,(trj,d)}$ is the transfer angle of trajectory trj in grid $grid_i$, and γ is a tendency factor which implies the importance of the direction to d. Since the moving direction of the trajectories and the direction of the destination are not always identical, we use γ to evaluate which direction is more important. This will constraint the ants' action and induce them to move toward the destination, we will discuss the setting of γ in the experiment section.

Now let us define the route from source s to destination d.

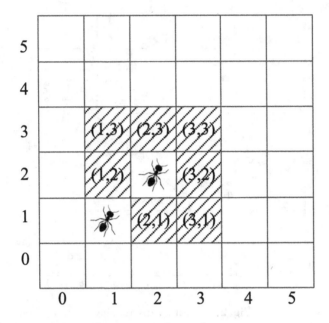

Fig. 3. Transfer mechanism.

Definition 4: Route. A route from the source s to destination d is indicated by a sequence of grids

$$s(grid_1) \rightarrow grid_2 \rightarrow grid_3 \rightarrow grid_4 \rightarrow \ldots grid_j \rightarrow d(grid_{j+1})$$

Definition 5: Route Reaching Probability. The reaching probability of a route $P_d(R)$ is the product of reachable probability of each step in the route. For a route $s(grid_1) \rightarrow grid_2 \rightarrow grid_3 \rightarrow grid_4 \rightarrow \ldots grid_j \rightarrow d(grid_{j+1})$,

$$P_d(R) = \prod_{i=1}^{j} P_d(grid_i \rightarrow grid_{i+1}) \tag{3}$$

When a route discovering iteration is finished, the pheromones are updated according to $\Delta\tau_{ij} = P_d(R)$. The probability of an ant moving from $grid_i$ to $grid_j$ in each iteration is

$$Prob(grid_i \rightarrow grid_j) = \frac{\tau_{ij}^{\alpha}\eta_{ij}^{\beta}}{\sum_{grid_k \in \text{all } grid_i's \text{ neighbors}} \tau_{ik}^{\alpha}\eta_{ik}^{\beta}} \tag{4}$$

The pheromone concentration τ_{ij} is updated by $(1-\rho)\tau_{ij} + \Delta\tau_{ij}$, where ρ is the pheromone evaporation coefficient.

The process to discover the most popular route is demonstrated in Algorithm 1.

Algorithm 1. MPR discovering algorithm

Input: A latticed region; A set of discretized history trajectories $trjset$; given source location and destination location s and d

Output: The most popular route R from s to d

1: $S \leftarrow grid\ code\ of\ s$;
2: $D \leftarrow grid\ code\ of\ d$;
3: $MPR \leftarrow null$;
4: $MPR.pro \leftarrow 0$;
5: $generation \leftarrow N$;
6: $n \leftarrow 1$;
7: **while** $n \leq N$ **do**
8:     $antset \leftarrow generate\ k\ ants$;
9:     **for** each ant $ant_i \in antset$ **do**
10:        $r_i \leftarrow path\ of\ ant_i\ from\ S\ to\ D$;
11:        $r_i.pro \leftarrow P_d(r_i)$;
12:    **end for**
13:    $best.pro \leftarrow maximum\ r.pro\ of\ all\ discovered\ r$;
14:    $best \leftarrow route\ of\ maximum\ pro$;
15:    **if** $best.pro \geq MPR.pro$ **then**
16:        $MPR \leftarrow best$;
17:        $MPR.pro \leftarrow best.pro$;
18:    **end if**
19:    $update\ the\ amount\ of\ pheromone$;
20:    $n \leftarrow n + 1$;
21: **end while**
22: **return** MPR;

In Algorithm 1, we first get the grid codes of s and d and initialize the parameters. In the while-loop, we check the reaching probability of all routes in this iteration. If the solution is better than the current solution, then the MPR is updated. After each route discovering iteration, the pheromones will be updated by the ants.

Obviously, the MPR is a sequence of grids, and we can connect the centers of these grids as the final route we derived. Our approach can give the top-k popular routes when necessary with trivial modification and will be discussed in Sect. 4.

4   Experiments and Discussion

In this section, we conduct experiments on vehicle trajectory dataset which were obtained from the mobility track logs of 27,000 participating Beijing taxis carrying GPS receivers and GPRS (General Packet Radio Service) modules during May 2010 [20]. In the experiments, there are 30 ants in each iteration and there are totally 50 iterations. The pheromone evaporation coefficient $\rho = 0.2$, and the parameters $\alpha = 1$, $\beta = 1$. We choose the area from 116.178° to 116.576° of east latitude and 39.747° to 40.053° of north longitude and partition the region into grids.

In all the following figures, we use translucent red lines to draw the trajectories of vehicles. Thus the deeper the colour is, the more trajectories pass the road segment. The source and the destination are drawn with black points and marked with *s* (116.364797 longtitude and 39.999452 latitude) and *d* (116.378832 longitude and 39.865127 latitude) in Figs. 4, 5 and 6, respectively. The MPR we found is denoted by lines with different colours.

Two different routes with $\gamma = 1$ and $\gamma = 3$, marked with the green line and the blue line respectively are shown in Fig. 4. We can see the route of $\gamma = 1$ is more inclined to move to *d* in each step than the route of $\gamma = 3$.

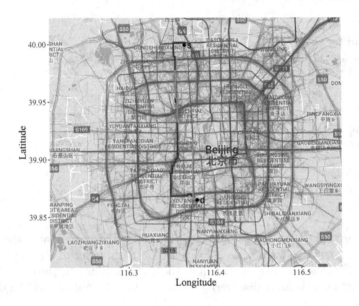

Fig. 4. MPR with grids 200 × 200. (Color figure online)

The MPR changes with the parameter of grid size. When we divide the region into 100 × 100 grids, the MPR is the green route in the Fig. 5. And the blue route is derived when the region is divided into 200 × 200 grids. The blue route contains more details than the green route.

Figure 6 gives the top-3 routes from *s* to *d*. The best route, the second route and the third route are represented by the blue line, the black line and the green line, respectively.

Figure 7 gives the most popular routes from *s* (116.31 longtitude, 39.89 latitude) to *d* (116.355 longtitude, 39.94 latitude) which are derived through our algorithm and the Maximum Probability Product algorithm in paper [6]. They are marked with the blue line and the green line, respectively. The MPR of our algorithm lies on the roads, while the other has deviation from the roads. It is

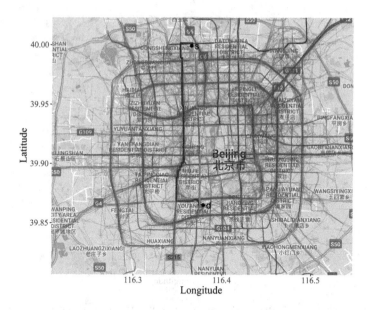

Fig. 5. MPR with $\gamma = 3$. (Color figure online)

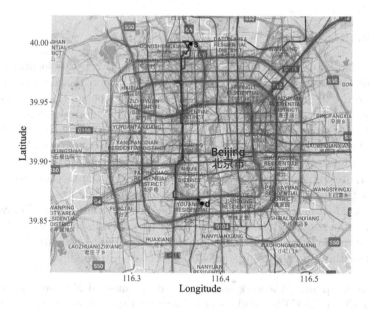

Fig. 6. Top-3 routes with $\gamma = 3$, grids 200×200. (Color figure online)

because the clusters in paper [6] is highly relevant to history trajectories and
may deviate from the roads.

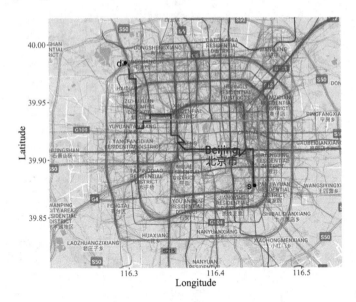

Fig. 7. Route comparing with Maximum Probability Product algorithm. (Color figure online)

5   Conclusions

An algorithm to discover the most popular route between two locations based on the history trajectory data is introduced in this paper. Based on the latticed region and the discretized history trajectories, we can control the error bound of the route to the size of the grids. Based on the ant colony optimization algorithm, we could make a tradeoff between the route precise and time consuming. We have evaluated our method in terms of effectiveness and practicality with real data. The experiments show that our method performs well in discovering the most popular route between two given locations. Moreover, the method can provide the top-k popular routes when necessary for alternative choices.

We provide a new method to discover the most popular route. However, the popularity of a route is difficult to verify. Thus we only displayed some results of our algorithm. Reasonable criterions should be proposed to evaluate the accuracy of the algorithm and the results should be discussed in detail in future.

Acknowledgement. This work was supported by National Natural Science Foundation of China (61370191) and the Fundamental Research Funds for the Central Universities (FRFBR-16-024a).

References

1. Banerjee, P., Ranu, S., Raghavan, S.: Inferring uncertain trajectories from partial observations. In: 2014 IEEE International Conference on Data Mining, pp. 30–39, December 2014

2. Liu, Y., Ester, M., Qian, Y., Hu, B., Cheung, D.W.: Microscopic and macroscopic spatio-temporal topic models for check-in data. IEEE Trans. Knowl. Data Eng. **29**(9), 1957–1970 (2017)
3. Aryal, A.M., Wang, S.: Discovery of patterns in spatio-temporal data using clustering techniques. In: 2017 2nd International Conference on Image, Vision and Computing (ICIVC), pp. 990–995, June 2017
4. Zheng, K., Zheng, Y., Xie, X., Zhou, X.: Reducing uncertainty of low-sampling-rate trajectories. In: 2012 IEEE 28th International Conference on Data Engineering, pp. 1144–1155, April 2012
5. Zheng, Y.: Trajectory data mining: an overview. ACM Trans. Intell. Syst. Technol. **6**(3), 29:1–29:41 (2015)
6. Chen, Z., Shen, H.T., Zhou, X.: Discovering popular routes from trajectories. In: 2011 IEEE 27th International Conference on Data Engineering, pp. 900–911, April 2011
7. Dorigo, M., Maniezzo, V., Colorni, A.: Ant system: optimization by a colony of cooperating agents. IEEE Trans. Syst. Man Cybern. Part B (Cybernetics) **26**(1), 29–41 (1996)
8. Zheng, Y., Zhou, X.: Computing With Spatial Trajectories. Springer, New York (2011). https://doi.org/10.1007/978-1-4614-1629-6
9. Lee, J.G., Han, J., Whang, K.Y.: Trajectory clustering: a partition-and-group framework. In: Proceedings of the 2007 ACM SIGMOD International Conference on Management of Data SIGMOD 2007, NY, USA, pp. 593–604. ACM, New York (2007)
10. Lee, J.G., Han, J., Li, X., Gonzalez, H.: Traclass: trajectory classification using hierarchical region-based and trajectory-based clustering. Proc. VLDB Endow. **1**(1), 1081–1094 (2008)
11. Yao, D., Zhang, C., Zhu, Z., Huang, J., Bi, J.: Trajectory clustering via deep representation learning. In: 2017 International Joint Conference on Neural Networks (IJCNN), pp. 3880–3887, May 2017
12. Monreale, A., Pinelli, F., Trasarti, R., Giannotti, F.: Wherenext: a location predictor on trajectory pattern mining. In: Proceedings of the 15th ACM SIGKDD International Conference on Knowledge Discovery and Data Mining KDD 2009, NY, USA, pp. 637–646. ACM, New York (2009)
13. Jeung, H., Liu, Q., Shen, H.T., Zhou, X.: A hybrid prediction model for moving objects. In: 2008 IEEE 24th International Conference on Data Engineering, pp. 70–79, April 2008
14. Tao, Y., Faloutsos, C., Papadias, D., Liu, B.: Prediction and indexing of moving objects with unknown motion patterns. In: Proceedings of the 2004 ACM SIGMOD International Conference on Management of Data, SIGMOD 2004, NY, USA, pp. 611–622. ACM, New York (2004)
15. Chen, C.C., Chiang, M.F.: Trajectory pattern mining: exploring semantic and time information. In: 2016 Conference on Technologies and Applications of Artificial Intelligence (TAAI), pp. 130–137, November 2016
16. Chen, C.C., Kuo, C.H., Peng, W.C.: Mining spatial-temporal semantic trajectory patterns from raw trajectories. In: 2015 IEEE International Conference on Data Mining Workshop (ICDMW), pp. 1019–1024 November 2015
17. Sacharidis, D., Patroumpas, K., Terrovitis, M., Kantere, V., Potamias, M., Mouratidis, K., Sellis, T.: On-line discovery of hot motion paths. In: Proceedings of the 11th International Conference on Extending Database Technology: Advances in Database Technology, EDBT 2008, NY, USA, pp. 392–403. ACM, New York (2008)

18. Li, X., Han, J., Lee, J.-G., Gonzalez, H.: Traffic density-based discovery of hot routes in road networks. In: Papadias, D., Zhang, D., Kollios, G. (eds.) SSTD 2007. LNCS, vol. 4605, pp. 441–459. Springer, Heidelberg (2007). https://doi.org/10.1007/978-3-540-73540-3_25
19. Wei, L.Y., Zheng, Y., Peng, W.C.: Constructing popular routes from uncertain trajectories. In: Proceedings of the 18th ACM SIGKDD International Conference on Knowledge Discovery and Data Mining, KDD 2012, NY, USA, pp. 195–203. ACM, New York (2012)
20. Li, Y., Jin, D., Hui, P., Su, L., Zeng, L.: Revealing contact interval patterns in large scale urban vehicular ad hoc networks. In: Proceedings of the ACM SIGCOMM 2012 Conference on Applications, Technologies, Architectures, and Protocols for Computer Communication, SIGCOMM 2012, NY, USA, pp. 299–300. ACM, New York (2012)

Trust Model Based Uncertainty Analysis Between Multi-path Routes in MANET Using Subjective Logic

Sohail Muhammad[1]([⊠])[iD], Liangmin Wang[1]([⊠]), and Bushra Yamin[2]

[1] School of Computer Science and Communicatoin Engineering,
Jiangsu University, Zhenjiang 212013, People's Republic of China
engrsohailaslam@yahoo.com, Wanglm@ujs.edu.cn
[2] School of Library and Archive management,
Jiangsu University, Zhenjiang 212013, People's Republic of China
bushrasohail@yahoo.com

Abstract. Mobile ad hoc networks (MANET's) are short range wireless devices. In these distributed networks secure communication is the key agenda. Recently incorporating the concept of trust into distributed networks bring significant challenges. Achieving nodes cooperation in ad hoc networks is not an easy task. In this article, we proposed a novel subjective logic (SL) trust model for handling ignorance between neighbor nodes in ad hoc network. Trust Model based on SL is applied on multi path routes in a distributed environment to know the uncertainty between random entities. In this work we also highlighted that SL is not enough to evaluate multi path trust, thus providing selection operator as an SL extension. By using subjective opinion nodes can easily make trust evaluation regarding first and second hand observation. Also, the trust information exchange mechanism reduces extra routing and computation overhead. The simulated results validate the scheme, so after calculating the results based on trust judging algorithm, the path having higher trust value is selected for communication.

Keywords: MANET · Subjective logics · Trust model · AOMDV

1 Introduction

MANET's are open and short-range wireless nodes and vulnerable to security threats. Providing security solution with trust, trust management, and trust based routing has changed the direction of research. "Trust" actually comes from social science and defined as the degree of subjective opinion about the behavior of an entity in particular context [1]. Blaze et al. in [2] also introduce trust management as "it provides a particular approach for interpreting security policies, credentials and relationship". Trust management can help in building cooperation between mobility nodes without any previous interaction to a desired level of trust.

© Springer Nature Singapore Pte Ltd. 2018
J. Li et al. (Eds.): CWSN 2017, CCIS 812, pp. 319–332, 2018.
https://doi.org/10.1007/978-981-10-8123-1_28

Ad hoc networks are still very hot research topic because it brings new challenges due to security and privacy need by leading future trends. In MANET nodes operate in the hop by hop fashion, mostly used in disaster scenarios. In previous literature authors mainly used cryptographic and key management systems for securing ad hoc networks by totally ignoring uncertainty as an important notion in these networks. The dynamic nature of MANET results in incompleteness and uncertain. Ad hoc networks due to its open and dynamic nature are vulnerable to many security threats. In MANET security and privacy is a key thing to handle. Many authors address this issue and try to present a solution using cryptographic and certificate exchange methods [4–7]. Also researcher despite providing complex solutions rarely counted uncertainty as an important element in distributed networks. Author in [8] described an algebraic logic for determining uncertain probabilities. Mobile nodes before joining the network are uncertain about neighbor nodes. Subjective logic marked promising results in finding uncertain values between random nodes. Venkat et al. in [9] also came up with the subjective logic idea for knowing uncertainty between neighbor nodes. Li et al. in [10] used subjective logic as an advantage for trust evaluation and showed trust as triplet metric using (SL). Autor in [11] used very important theory "DST Dempster Shafer Theory" produced by P. dempster and applied for evaluating the uncertainty between indirect observation, which also leads to the significant results. Tan et al. in [12] proposed trust-based routing using the OLSR-V2 protocol with fuzzy logic, which is also a class of binary logic and efficient in trust evaluation. Pirzada and McDonald in [13] also make use of the trust-based reactive routing with different protocols like AODV, TORA, and DSR and gained meaningful results.

MANET's are vulnerable to the interior and exterior security threats. Exterior attacks normally produced by outsider nodes by putting erroneous route message, invalid route message replying and so on. The interior attacks come from internal participants like black hole attacks, jellyfish and sybil attacks [14]. To overcome exterior attacks cryptographic solutions are needed to be deployed in advance, however, these solutions also increase computation overhead. In this article, we bring the idea of trust in multi path routes to evaluate uncertainty between random nodes using subjective logic. This new trust based routing has many featured advantage like (1) nodes perform trusted routing behavior and follow trusted paths. (2) Through trust-based routing, it is easy to detect malicious nodes due to its unnatural behavior during the routing process. (3) It also reduces computation overhead as nodes do not require certificate verification at each request. The rest of the paper sectioned as follow, Sect. 2 revealed some facts about trust metrics and properties, subjective logic. In Sect. 3, we mentioned AOMDV routing protocol. Sections 4 and 5, explored system operations and describe trust model for AOMDV. In Sect. 6, we introduced basic routing operations in T-AOMDV. In Sect. 7, trusted route discovery and judgement algorithms were explained. Finally, Sect. 8 was experimental setup and Sect. 9 was conclusions and future work.

2   Background

In this section, first we described some properties of trust and second part is about subjective logic fundamentals.

2.1   Trust Properties

Due to unique nature of MANET, it is necessary that some properties of trust must be carefully defined.

Trust is dynamic, not static; which mean trust establishment will take on temporarily bases over continues values because in MANET information changes very rapidly. Trust is subjective; a trustee may have different trust opinions about the same trustee due to different experiences by the mobility of nodes and placed in different context. Trust is not necessarily transitive i.e. if A trusts B and B trusts C it does not mean that A will trust C.

$$A = B, B = C, \quad then \quad C \neq A$$

Trust is asymmetric; if A trusts B at a certain level it does not mean that B trusts A at the same level. Trust as Composability; trust from the different paths can be combined into a single opinion value this property is called trust composability. Trust is context dependent i.e. if Bob trust Alice as car mechanic expert so, it does not mean that Bob will also have the same level of trust about driving a car for Alice.

2.2   Subjective Logic

Subjective logic is basically a class of algebraic logic, first proposed by A. Josong 1997. SL based on subjective opinions like in the real social world. Subjective logic can also be seen as an extension of binary logic and basic for probability calculus. Subjective logic is a kind of trust model which facilitates mobile nodes to explicitly represent their opinion about the neighbor node and to manage the uncertainty between the interacting nodes. Subjective logic uses triplet opinion about the trustworthiness of a node which is belief, disbelief and uncertainty over the continuous interval $[0, 1]$. Such that

$$(b, d, u) \in [0, 1], \quad (b + d + u + a_x) = 1$$

where a_x is called base rate, it is used in absence of evidence also called prior probability of an event but here we are just strict to other three values i.e. belief, disbelief, and uncertainty of said event.

3   AOMDV Routing Protocol

AOMDV is the most efficient reactive routing protocol for the MANET [19, 20]. In AOMDV routing discovery and route maintenance are two major characteristics. In AOMDV each route request packet contains broadcast id, source

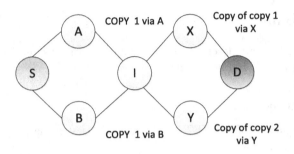

Fig. 1. The multi path ad hoc routing protocol for MANET.

sequence number, destination IP address, advertised hop counts and control flags, sequence number identifies the freshness of the routing packet and advertised hop count contains the distance between the source node and the current node. When source node S broadcasts RREQ packet in search of destination node each recipient of the RREQ packet looks up in its routing table. If receiving node doesn't contain any fresh information i.e. fresh sequence number it rebroadcast the same packet with incrementing the advertised hop count, these nodes are also reserve routes to the source node for certain time. After that if any intermediate node has fresher route information are sent to the destination, duplicate RREQ packet received at any node are discarded. A route reply packet is generated RREP back to the originator. Each RREP packet also contains id, IP addresses of source and destination, adv hop count and control flags. In creating a reverse path in AOMDV each intermediate route increases adv hop count to the source. This is called AOMDV routing thus path is established between the source and the destination and start data transmission. After this period the source searches for the new route information to the destination.

In AOMDV, there are multiple paths between source and destination, also this protocol has variety of loop freedom and link disjoint multiple path to the destination. Loop freedom is achieved by advertised hop count instead of hop count and link disjoint of multiple paths is achieved by flooding property [21]. Through AOMDV, we get the advantage of advertised hop count as;

- If Sequence number of two paths is same then path with lowest adv-hop count will be preferred.
- If two paths have same adv-hop-count then source look at sequence number or fresher route will be preferred to the destination.
- If the above two conditions are met then path with largest accumulated single hop trust will be given priority.

Route maintenance in AOMDV is maintained using route update packet (RUPD) and route Error packet (RERR). When there is a link failure detected by link layer feedback a RERR packet is sent using predecessor link to all sources and this packet is dropped and expired using the timer based technique in routing maintenance.

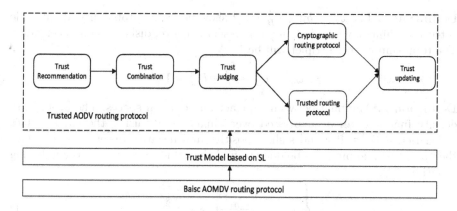

Fig. 2. Frame work of trusted multi-path routing.

4   Frame Work for Trusted AOMDV

Our framework includes three modules first is basic AOMDV routing protocol which is kind of reactive routing protocol. The Second module is trust model and the last step is to combine these two previous steps producing trust based multi path routing. In third module, these blocks are performed one by one i.e. trust establishment (direct, recommended), trust combination, trust judging, trusted routing protocol and trust update.

Let us consider the beginning stage when new nodes initiate communication with the network but they are uncertain about each other. Let A be an opinion about B which is (0, 0, 1) that is fully uncertain about B's behavior i.e. A is not sure about B's behavior so, A uses cryptographic algorithms or other routing discovery schemes.

After this initial activity having some successful or failed communication A can change its opinion about node B's behavior using trust update algorithm. Once the trust is established between neighboring nodes then node can used our trusted routing protocol for routing operation. As we have mentioned earlier trust is asymmetric so for this, each node uses a recommendation for other nodes from its neighbor nodes and finally combines into a single trust value.

5   Trust Model

Our trust model is extension of original subjective logic based trust model i.e. evaluation of node's trustworthiness is achieved by applying subjective logic.

5.1   Trust Representation

In our model, we have used trust as triplet metric i.e. $[b, d, u]$ over the continues range of $[0,1]$, where 0 is complete distrust and 1 showing full trust so,

Definition 1. Let $w_B^A = b_B^A + d_B^A + U_B^A$ show node A's probability about node B trustworthiness, where b, d and u represents believe, disbelief and uncertainty. The total sum of these triplet will be 1

$$w_B^A = b_B^A + d_B^A + U_B^A = 1$$

Definition 2. Mapping between evidence and opinion spaces. The probability density function can be expressed over binary events using the (α, β) values called Beta PDF's. If r and s show positive and negative observation opinions then bijective mapping can be done to find the values of α, β from the following equations.

$$\begin{cases} b_x = \frac{r}{(r+s+2)} \Rightarrow r = \frac{2b_x}{u_x} \\ d_x = \frac{n}{(r+s+2)} \Rightarrow s = \frac{2d_x}{u_x} \\ u_x = \frac{2}{(r+s+2)} \Rightarrow u_x \neq 0 \end{cases} \tag{1}$$

5.2 Trust Combination

A node can gather evidence from its neighbor and make relative judgment for the observed node. we have following definitions.

Discounting operator: Let A, B and C are three nodes $w_B^A = b_B^A + d_B^A + U_B^A$ shows A's opinion about B and $w_C^B = b_C^B + d_C^B + U_C^B$ shows B's opinion about C as triplet space now $w_C^{AB} = b_C^{AB} + d_C^{AB} + U_C^{AB}$ shows A's opinion about node C trustworthiness based on B's recommendation about C such that

$$b_C^{AB} = b_B^A b_C^B$$
$$d_C^{AB} = b_B^A d_C^B \tag{2}$$
$$U_B^A = d_B^A + u_B^A + b_B^A u_C^B$$

where w_C^{AB} shows opinion of A about C as discounting of node B. Discounting $\otimes$ increases uncertainty as it comes from recommendation of indirect opinion. It is easy to prove that discounting operation is associative but not commutative.

Consensus operator: Let, we have three nodes A, B and C $w_C^A = b_C^A + d_C^A + U_C^A$ and $w_C^B = b_C^B + d_C^B + U_C^B$ be the opinions that nodes A and B have about node C's trustworthiness such that by equations.

$$b_C^{A,B} = \frac{b_B^A u_C^B + b_C^B u_C^A}{U_C^A + U_C^B - U_C^A U_C^B}$$

$$d_C^{A,B} = \frac{d_C^A u_C^B + d_C^B u_C^A}{U_C^A + U_C^B - U_C^A U_C^B} \tag{3}$$

$$U_C^{A,B} = \frac{u_C^A u_C^B}{U_C^A + U_C^B - U_C^A U_C^B}$$

Then w_C^{AB} is called consensus between w_C^A and w_C^B representing node A and B opinions about C's trustworthiness by using the symbol, we can show in mathematical form $\oplus$ and $\omega_C^{AB} = \omega_C^A \oplus \omega_C^B$ is called consensus and can be extend up to multiple nodes opinion about the same node. It can be easily proved that concatenation operator is associative and commutative. Here point to remember $\oplus$ consensus decreases uncertainty and increase confidence as it mainly relies on both nodes direct opinion.

5.3   Selection Operator:$\circledS$

When we talk about multi path routing then consensus and discounting operators are not enough to describe this topology. In conventional topology, trust along each path is combined in between source to target using concatenation operator and then using aggregation operator beliefs from all paths are gathered into final value. But this technique fails to describe the phenomena refer to the Fig. 3, witness w_i report positive and negative experience using node B_1 and B_2. A should not use aggregation operator to combine these two report, since their beliefs originate at the same source, to describe this multi path topology we need some additional operators. Solution is proposed by Yonghong et al. in [22] introducing another operator called selection operator that selects most trusted path among multiple available paths.

let suppose, P_1 and P_2 are two paths from A to W_i. $T_1 = (b, d, u)$ and $T_2 = (b, d, u)$ concatenated along path P_1 and P_2. Then if $b_1 > b_2$ then $T_1 \circledS T_2 = T_1$ else $T_1 \circledS T_2 = T_2$. Consider Fig. 3, we have two path P_1 and P_2 from originating node to target node $Path_1 = A...B_1....W_i$ and $Path_2 = A...B_2....W_i$. Let A's trust in B_1 and B_2 be T_1 and T_2 similarly B_1 and B_2 trust in W_i be T_1' and T_2'. Let suppose that $T_1 \otimes T_1' = (0.6, 0.3, 0.1)$ and $T_2 \otimes T_2' = (0.5, 0.3, 0.2)$ by this evaluation we can easily chose most trusted available path from A to Wi. As $T_1 \otimes T_1' > T_2 \otimes T_2' = (0.6 > 0.5)$, so applying selection operator $(T_1 \otimes T_1')\circledS(T_2 \otimes T_2') = (T_1 \otimes T_1')$. $T_W \otimes T_1' \otimes T_1 = (0.6,0.3,0.1)$ trust concatenated along B_1 and $T_W \otimes T_2' \otimes T_2 = (0.5,0.25,0.25)$ trust concatenated along B_2, so applying

$$T_W \otimes T_1' \otimes T_1 \circledS T_W \otimes T_2' \otimes T_2 = T_W \otimes T_1' \otimes T_1 \tag{4}$$

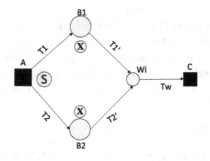

Fig. 3. Selection operator between two paths.

If we have multiple path let say $T_1, T_2, ...T_n$ then applying only discounting and consensus operator will lead to double counting problem and trust will be out of bounds.

6   Routing Operations in TAOMDV

6.1   Node Model Description

In our trust model, we have added trust fields to the conventional routing table, which take place between the neighboring nodes in particular time. By Positive event, we mean successful communication between nodes and trust repository counter is updated with increase trust value and vice versa (Table 1).

Table 1. Standard vs Trusted AOMDV routing table

AOMDV	Trusted AOMDV
Destination IP address	Destination IP address
Destination seq number	Destination seq number
...	...
Advertised hop count	Advertised hop count
...	...
Expiry time	Expiry time
...	+ve, -ve, opinion (trust field)
...	Trust update

6.2   Trust Judging Rules

If node A want to communicate with node B and if believe of A in B is $b_B^A >= 0.5$ then, A will trust B and start to route packet to node B.

If disbelieve of A in node B i.e. $d_B^A > 0.5$ then, A will not trust node B and will not route packet and ask for another route discovery.

If uncertainty of node A in node B is $u_B^A > 0.5$ then, A ask for digital signature for node B and waits for the verification. If A successfully verifies B's signature then A will start communication with B (Table 2).

6.3   Trust Update Rule

When we talk about trust aggregation then trust update is very important because it also counts good history of nodes and recommendation but, we keep updating our repository due to dynamic nature of ad hoc networks.

Table 2. Trust judging algorithms based on (b,d,u).

Belief	Disbelief	Uncertainty	Action
		≤0.5	Request and verify digital signature
	>0.5		Distrust node until next RREQ
>0.5			Trust a node and continue routing
≤0.5			Request and verify digital signature
		>0.5	Search for alternate route

1. If node A had successful interaction with node B, then it updates the counter by incrementing trust value in that node. By successful communication we mean normal packet forward or RREP with in the desired time interval.
2. If node A had failed communication with node B by number of means, then it degrades trust values by decrementing the update counter.

6.4 Trust Information Exchange

Many trust models do not consider trust information exchange in between the nodes. This feature help as trust recommendation for the neighboring nodes, three type of messages that can be exchange i.e. TREQ (Trusted Route Request) TREP (Trusted Route Reply) TWARN (Trusted Route Warning). When a node wants to check new route trustworthiness it will send TREQ message to its neighbors and waits for TREP and leaves the fields the Recommender, opinion and Expiry time. The type field is set to 0. Nodes which receive TREQ message will send TREP to the source nodes and type field is set to 1. When a route becomes uncertain and nodes behave maliciously then source will broadcast TWARN message with type field set to 2 and waits for expiry time and then search for new route discovery. Here it is assumed that during trust recommendation process nodes are protected from modification adversaries.

7 Trusted Routing Discovery

We illustrate our idea using multi paths on demand routing AOMDV using three cases.

7.1 Beginning of Routing Discovery

Suppose, we have two paths from source to destination, one is A-B-C and other is A-D-E-C. Now consider Fig. 4, A wants to discover a route to node C the process of node A, B and C are as A broadcast RREQ requesting route path to node C and waits for time t for RREP. B receive RREQ packet after that node B will check ω_A^B and ω_C^B because it is beginning of network so uncertainty will be high and currently no route to C. Node B authenticate both the neighbors to verify certificate if A passes the successful event it gets credit and the new opinion $\omega_A^B = (0.33, 0, 0.67)$ is made. B also authenticates C and revises the same process.

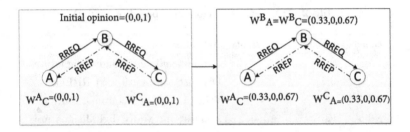

Fig. 4. Network initializing, at start uncertainty between entities is very high but after some interactions entities made opinions on each other behavior.

If node A fails the authentication the new opinion will be $\omega_A^B = (0, 0.33, 0.67)$. Node B will not forward the packet. If C has also been authorized then node C will also check ω_B^C node B's trustworthiness. If B passes authentication, C will generate an RREP packet to B and update its route table.

7.2   Alternate Route Having Low Uncertainty

Now Consider another scenario in Fig. 5(a), i.e. path A to C via node E and D here is the example of multi path routes as we described in system operation if second path has more trust value in the routing table after some interaction, so instead of having less number of hop counts the source will prefer this route because this route is more trustworthy or if link of one route has got failed so, we are still able to forward route packets. Now let's consider the Fig. 5(a), after initial stage. The node authentication and judgment in route discovery is done by Algorithms 1 and 2. For example in Fig. 5(b) a general trusted route discovery is explained, so path from node S to target node T is uncovered in which intermediate node N_2 plays important role between S and T. In Algorithm 1 trusted path discovery is described with intermediate node and in Algorithm 2 how N_2 is authenticate by neighbor nodes and finds trust path also described.

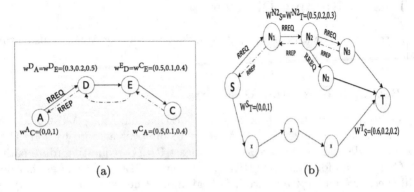

Fig. 5. (a) Alternate route having low uncertainty paths, (b) General route discovery and Node authentication by trust judging rules.

Algorithm 1. General behavior of Node N_2 in performing trusted route discovery

> *Receive an route request from node N_1*
> **if** *RREQ* (N_2, N_1)*==true* **then**
> **if** *RREQ* (N_2, S) *==true* **then**
> **if** *RREQ* (N_2, T) *==true* **then**
> *Update opinion* $\omega_{N_1}^{N_2}, \omega_T^{N_2}, \omega_S^{N_2}$
> *Update Route table of N_2*
> *Re-broadcast RREQ*
> **endif**
> **endif**
> **endif**
> *if every authentication fails* **then**
> *update opinion*
> *Do not forward RREQ*
>   *end if*

Algorithm 2. Authentication of Node N_2 to N_1.

Exchange opinions about N_1 with all the neighbors of N_2 using the trust information Exchange protocol.
Combine these opinions using subjective logic operators
/* Judge the next step using conditions set in table 1*/
    if uncertainty > 0.5 then
        Request and verify N_1's certificate
        else if disbelief > 0.5 then
        Distrust N_1 for an expiry time
      else If belief > 0.5 then
      Trust N_1 and rebroadcast RREQ/RREP
    else if uncertainty > 0.67 then
    Search for another route to target
end if

8   Experimental Setup

For the simulation we have used MATLAB 2015a due to its powerful capability to built probability models consider a random network topology, which is distributed over 800*800 meter area. At start of the network nodes are at 0 m/s and move up to maximum 10 m/s. The transmission range is 250 m with in the area. Based on the trust judging algorithms the neighbor nodes decide whether to forward the packet or not.

8.1   At Network Startup Uncertainty is Very High

In our trust model, we have considered that at network startup opinion space is $(b, d, u) = (0, 0, 1)$ in order to avoid any malicious effect from the new incoming nodes. After some interaction neighboring nodes decide the trustworthiness of that node. if it behaves well so, trust is updated with positive value if it act maliciously so it is mediately dropped. We can set the threshold level according to one's desired security level. This kind of environment also identify malicious nodes like Modification attacks, Black hole attacks as, they can not interpret the network until they have good interaction with existing nodes.

8.2   Uncertainty Reduce After t_1

After some interaction opinion metric changes and uncertainty is reduced $u < 0.5$ and believe tend to increase $b >= 0.5$ then, based on authentication algorithm it forwards the RREQ packet and updates the trust counter. Trust and distrust value is updated in the repository after every interaction that a node made with the neighboring nodes. After evaluating the final trust value decision is made. if at a certain level a good behaving node tries to act maliciously and disrupt the network communication, so trust level decreases and disbelieve increases if $d >= 0.5$, so according to the algorithm intermediate nodes do not forward the packet until its trust value increases up to the threshold level. The source node can also check another available route that is most trustworthy and having less uncertainty. This design also gives space to malicious nodes as by changing their behavior into good interaction and getting good recommendation they may join the system (Fig. 6).

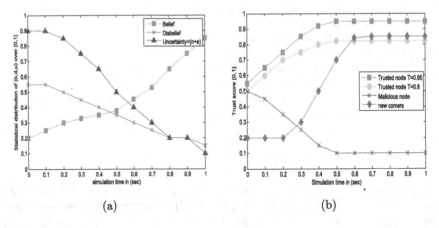

(a)   (b)

Fig. 6. (a) Nodes behavior with (b, d, n, e) at network initialization, (b) Trusted, malicious and new comers behavior after network initialization.

9   Conclusions

In this paper, we have proposed novel idea i.e. subjective logic based trust model to enhance the security solution of MANET. Trust and trust relationships among nodes can be represented, combined, evaluated using the term opinion.

Using subjective logic rules prediction methods to compute node's trust value for future decision, this makes our model more stable, robust, and enhances system security. In this article, we have used the notion of opinion, which uses cooperation among nodes and computational overhead is reduced without the need of requesting and verifying certificate at every route request. In short trust model based AOMDV routing using subjective logic is a lightweight solution for discovering trusted forward paths. Future work includes improvement in trust prediction model by introducing new trust decision factor. A comprehensive performance evaluation will be conducted to compare with other routing protocols. A trust model resilience will be checked by considering new malicious attacks over different parameters. An updated version of Subjective logic will be used to present our trust model [23, 24].

References

1. Cook, K.S., (eds.): Trust in Society, vol. 2, Russell Sage Foundation Series on Trust, New York, Feb 2003
2. Blaze, M., Feigenbaum, J., Lacy, J.: Decentralized trust management. In: Proceedings of the IEEE Symposium on Security and Privacy, 6–8 May, 1996, pp. 164–173 (1996)
3. Pirzada, A.A., McDonald, C.: Establishing trust in pure ad-hoc networks. In: Proceedings of the 27th Australasian Computer Science Conference (ACSC), vol. 26, Australian Computer Society, pp. 47–54 (2004)
4. Li, R., Li, J., Liu, P., Chen, H.H.: On demand public key management for mobile ad hoc networks. Wiley's Wirel. Commun. Mob. Comput. **6**(3), 295–306 (2006)
5. Chang, B.J., Kuo, S.L.: Markov chain trust model for trust value analysis and key management in distributed multicast MANETs. IEEE Trans. Veh. Technol. **58**(4), 1846–1863 (2009)
6. Hegland, A., Winjum, E., Mjolsnes, S.F., Rong, C., Kure, O., Spilling, P.: A survey of key management in ad hoc networks. IEEE Commun. Surv. Tutor. **8**(3), 48–66 (2006)
7. Jiang, T., Baras, J.S.: Ant-based adaptive trust evidence distribution in MANET. In: Proceedings of the 2nd International Conferecne on Mobile Distributed Computing Systems Workshops, Tokyo, Japan, 23–24 March 2004, pp. 588–593 (2004)
8. Josang, A.: A logic for uncertain probabilities. Int. J. Uncertain. Fuzziness Knowl. Based Syst. **9**(3), 279–311 (2001)
9. Balakrishnan, V., Varadharajan, V., Tupakula, U.: Subjective logic based trust model for mobile ad hoc networks. In: Proceedings of the 4th international conference on Security and privacy in communication networks. SecureComm 2008. ACM, New York, NY, USA (2008)
10. Li, X., Lyu, M.R., Liu, J.: A trust model based routing protocol for secure ad hoc networks. In: 2004 IEEE Aerospace Conference Proceedings (IEEE Cat. No. 04TH8720), Vol. 2, pp. 1286–1295 (2004)
11. Wei, Z., Tang, H., Yu, F.R., Wang, M., Mason, P.: Security enhancements for mobile ad hoc networks with trust management using uncertain reasoning. IEEE Trans. Veh. Technol. **63**(9), 4647–4658 (2014)
12. Tan, S., Li, X., Dong, Q.: Trust based routing mechanism for securing OSLR-based MANET. Ad Hoc Netw. **30**, 84–98 (2015). ISSN 1570-8705

13. Pirzada, A., McDonald, C., Datta, A.: Performance comparison of trust-based reactive routing protocols. IEEE Trans. Mob. Comput. **5**(6), 695–710 (2006)
14. Xia, H., Jia, Z., Ju, L., Li, X., Sha, E.H.-M.: Impact of trust model on on-demand multi-path routing in mobile ad hoc networks. Comput. Commun. **36**(9), 1078–1093 (2013). ISSN 0140-3664
15. Theodorakopoulos, G., Baras, J.S.: Trust evaluation in ad-hoc networks. In: The 3rd ACM workshop on Wireless security, WiSe 2004, pp. 1–10 (2004)
16. Jøsang, A.: An algebra for assessing trust in certification chains. In: The Network and Distributed Systems Security Symposium, NDSS 99 (1999)
17. Zouridaki, C., Mark, B.L., Hejmo, M., Thomas, R.K.: Robust cooperative trust establishment for MANETs. In: The fourth ACM workshop on security of ad hoc and sensor networks, pp. 23–34 (2006)
18. Wen, T., Jianbin, H., Zhong, C.: Research on a fuzzy logic-based subjective trust management model. J. Comput. Res. Dev. **42**(10), 1654–1659 (2005)
19. Li, X., Jia, Z., Zhang, P., Zhang, R., Wang, H.: Trust-based on-demand multipath routing in mobile ad hoc networks. IET Inf. Secur. **4**(4), 212–232 (2010)
20. Zhang, C., Zhu, X., Song, Y., Fang, Y.: A formal study of trust-based routing in wireless ad hoc networks. In: 2010 Proceedings of the IEEE INFOCOM, pp. 1–9 (2010)
21. Marina, M.K., Dass, R.: On-demand multipath distance vector routing for ad hoc networks. In: Proceedings of International Conference on Network Protocols, Riverside, CA, USA, pp. 11–14, Nov 2001
22. Hang, C-W., Wang, Y., Singh, M.P.: Operators for propagating trust and their evaluation in social networks. In: 8th International Conference on Autonomous Agents and Multiagent Systems, AAMAS 2009, 10-15 May, 2009 Budapest, Hungary (2009)
23. Liu, G., Yang, Q., Wang, H., Lin, X., Wittie, M.P.: Assessment of multi-hop interpersonal trust in social networks by Three-Valued Subjective Logic. In: IEEE INFOCOM 2014 - IEEE Conference on Computer Communications, Toronto, ON, pp. 1698–1706 (2014)
24. Liu, G., Chen, Q., Yang, Q., Wang, H., Zhu, B., Wang, W.: Opinionwalk: An efficient solution to massive trust assessment in online social networks. In: IEEE INFOCOM 2017 - IEEE Conference on Computer Communications (2017)

SA-Min: An Efficient Algorithm
for Minimizing the Spread of Influence
in a Social Network

Yong Liu[✉], Zhe Han, Shengshu Shi, Wei Zhang, and Ping Xuan

HeiLongJiang University, Harbin, HeiLongJiang Province, China
acliuyong@sina.com

Abstract. Minimizing the spread of influence is to find top-k links from a social network such that by blocking them the spread of influence is minimized. Kimura et al. first proposed the problem and presented a greedy algorithm to solve this problem. But the greedy algorithm is too expensive and cannot scale to large scale social networks. In this paper, we propose an efficient algorithm called SA-min based on Simulated Annealing (SA) for the problem. Experimental results on real networks show that our algorithm can outperform the greedy algorithm by more than an order of magnitude while achieving comparable influence spread minimization.

Keywords: Social networks · Influence spread · Simulated Annealing

1 Introduction

In recent years, many large-scale social networks, such as Facebook, Twitter, Friendster, Microblogs are becoming more and more popular. Social networks are playing a more and more important role in disseminating information. We usually regard a social network as a graph with nodes standing for persons and links standing for the connections between them [1]. Social networks can spread information and influence to a large number of people at a very fast speed. But social networks also allow viruses and other undesirable things to disseminate quickly. Thus, minimizing the spread of undesirable things through a social network is an important research problem in the data mining community.

In this paper, we focus on the problem of minimizing the propagation of undesirable things, such as computer viruses and malicious rumors, by removing a fixed number of edges in a social network. There are usually two means for preventing the spread of influence: (a) deleting vertices in a social network; (b) deleting edges in a social network. Previous works usually focus on deleting nodes from a network. They usually remove nodes by descending order of out-degree. Albert et al. [2], Callaway et al. [3] and Kimura et al. [4] show that when nodes are removed, links are also removed. But deleting edges is usually more effective than deleting vertices. Kimura et al. [4] propose a greedy algorithm by removing edges in a social network and show

© Springer Nature Singapore Pte Ltd. 2018
J. Li et al. (Eds.): CWSN 2017, CCIS 812, pp. 333–343, 2018.
https://doi.org/10.1007/978-981-10-8123-1_29

that the proposed methods are superior to the method which removes vertices. In their work, Kimura et al. [4] define the Contamination Minimization problem and greedily choose the edge that could minimize the average influence spread of the whole nodes in the graph. The time complexity of the algorithm is $O(k|E|n\delta)$, where k is the number of edges that we need to choose, $|E|$ is the number of edges in the graph, n stands for the number of nodes in the graph, and δ is the maximum time to calculate the average influence spread of each node. In order to accurately calculate the average influence spread of each node, the existing works usually use Monte Carlo (MC) simulation for many times. For example, 10000 times MC is applied in [5]. We call this greedy algorithm Greedy-min in the paper. When the size of the network is moderate, Greedy-min is still infeasible. In our experiments, Greedy-min cannot finish within 6 h in a graph with 100 nodes when 10000 MC is applied. It is accordingly desirable to develop an efficient algorithm for Contamination Minimization problem that scales to large networks.

In this paper, we propose a novel algorithm called SA-min for the Contamination Minimization problem. We apply the Simulated Annealing framework to the problem. The time complexity of SA-min is $O(Tn\delta)$, where T is the number of iterations, n stands for the number of nodes in the graph, and δ is the maximum time to compute the average influence spread of each node. The running time ratio between Greedy-min and SA-min is $\frac{k|E|}{T}$. Obviously, when k and $|E|$ become bigger, SA-min can run faster than Greedy-min by several orders of magnitude.

If we use MC simulation to compute the influence spread, the cost of SA-min is still expensive. To further improve the efficiency of SA-min, we propose an efficient heuristic algorithm ML_CS for computing the influence spread. ML_CS only computes the influence of a node v on nodes that are at most m hops far away from v. Therefore, when ML_CS is used to compute the influence spread for all nodes, the time complexity of ML_CS is $O(nd^m)$, where n stands for the number of nodes in the graph, d represents the average out-degree in the graph, and m is the number of hops. Because the average out-degree d in social networks is usually small, ML_CS is more efficient than the Monte Carlo (MC) simulation. When ML_CS is used in the framework of SA-min, the time complexity of SA-min is $O(Tnd^m)$.

Our results on real and synthetic networks show that SA-min can achieve almost matching results with Greedy-min and sometimes outperform Greedy-min. When ML_CS is applied in both SA-min and Greedy-min, SA-min is faster more than 30 times than Greedy-min on moderate networks. Furthermore, SA-min scales beyond networks with tens of thousands of nodes where Greedy-min becomes infeasible.

2 Related Work

Influence Maximizing is the dual problem to our problem. Kempe et al. [5] first formulated Influence Maximization problem as a discrete optimization problem. Given a directed graph G = (V, E), a positive integer k, we aim to find k influential users, so that by activating them, the expected number of users that are activated is maximized under a given propagation model. Kempe et al. [5] investigate Influence Maximization problem on two classical diffusion models. One model is the independent cascade (IC) model and another model is the linear threshold (LT) model. Kempe et al. [5] show the discrete optimization problem is NP-hard and propose a greedy approximation algorithm that guarantees a (1-1/e)-approximation. Since then, lots of works present various optimization strategies to improve the efficiency of the greedy algorithm. Leskovec et al. [6] develop an efficient algorithm called CELF which is up to 700 times faster than the navie greedy algorithm. W. Chen et al. [7] propose a heuristic algorithm called degree discount to solve Influence Maximization problem. Qingye Jiang et al. [8] proposed an efficient approach based on Simulated Annealing (SA) to solve this problem and show that SA method can run faster than greedy algorithm and also improve the accuracy of greedy algorithm. In addition to improve the efficiency, the influence maximization problem is also extended to multiple variants [9, 10].

Different from Influence Maximization problem, Contamination Minimization problem in social networks receives little attention although Contamination Minimization problem is an important research problem. In 2000, Albert et al. [2] and Barabasi et al. [3] prevent the spread of influence in social networks by deleting nodes in accordance with the order of descending out-degrees. Kimura et al. [4] define the Contamination Minimization problem and present the greedy algorithm in order to choose top-k links. However, existing methods cannot scale to large networks because a large number of Monte Carlo simulations are applied. In this paper, we propose an efficient algorithm based on Simulated Annealing for Contamination Minimization problem.

3 Preliminaries

In this paper, we need to compute the influence spread of a node under the independent cascade (IC) model. We first introduce influence propagation process on the IC model. Given a directed graph $G = (V, E)$, every edge is associated with a probability $P(u, v) : E \rightarrow [0, 1]$, where $P(u, v)$ denotes the probability that u actives v through the link between u and v after u is activated by its adjacent node. When a seed set $S \subseteq V$ is given, the IC model works as follows. We denote $S_t \subseteq V$ as the set of vertices which are activated at step $t \geq 0$. Initially we set $S_0 = S$. At $t + 1$ step, each node $u \in S_t$ only has one opportunity to activate his inactive out-neighbors $v \in V \setminus \bigcup_{0 \leq i \leq t} S_i$ with an independent probability $P(u, v)$. If u successfully activates v, then v will become active at $t + 1$ step and be put into S_{t+1}. If u fails to activate v, u cannot attempt to active v again in the following steps. The propagation process ends until $S_t = \phi$. The expected influence spread of S, denoted as $\delta(S; G)$, is the number of active nodes after the propagation process ends. Obviously, we have $\delta(S; G) = |\bigcup S_i|$.

We apply Simulated Annealing framework in our algorithm. We introduce the process of simulated annealing in this section. Metropolis et al. [11] proposed a new intelligent algorithm called Simulated Annealing in 1953. It is used to simulate the process of metal annealing. The purpose of the algorithm is to bring down the initial temperature of the system as possible as we can. We can use Simulated Annealing to optimize lots of NP-hard problems, such as Traveling Salesman Problem and other problems. Simulated Annealing works as follows. First, we construct an initial solution i and an initial system temperature $T = T_0$. Then the fitness function of the solution is computed, denoted by $f(i)$, which represents the initial energy of the system. Next, it seeks the neighbor solutions of the current solution and constructs a new solution j. If $\Delta f = f(j) - f(i)$ is negative, then the new solution is a better one and will replace the current one i; otherwise, the new solution j will replace the current one i with a probability $P(i,j) = \exp(-\Delta f / T_t)$, where T_t is the current system temperature. During the whole process, we need to minimize the energy state of the system. The initial temperature T_0 must be set large enough. After lots of iterations for neighbor solutions, we cut down the current temperature $T_t = T_t - \Delta T$. The whole process ends until the temperature reaches the termination temperature T_f.

In this paper, we use the same metric function as Kimura [4]. We use the contamination degree $c(G)$ of a graph G to represent the average influence spread of all the nodes in G, i.e., $c(G) = \frac{1}{|V|} \sum_{v \in V} \delta(v; G)$. Here, $|V|$ stands for the number of nodes in graph G. For any link $e \in E$, let $G(e)$ represents the graph $G(V, E \backslash \{e\})$, thus $G(e)$ is created by deleting e from graph G. In the same way, for any $D \subseteq E$, let $G(D)$ represents the graph $(V, E \backslash \{D\})$, thus $G(D)$ is created by deleting D from graph G. The contamination minimization problem on graph G is defined as follows. Given a positive integer k with $k < |E|$, find a subset D^* of E with $|D^*| = k$ such that $c(G(D^*)) \leq c(G(D))$ for any $D \subseteq E$ with $|D| = k$.

4   Algorithms

4.1   SA-Min Algorithm

In this section, we introduce SA-min algorithm based on Simulated Annealing. We define the fitness function of a solution $D \subseteq E$ as $c(G(D))$, which represents the average influence spread of all the nodes in graph $G(D)$ under IC model. In this case, we reduce the value of $c(G(D))$ as possible as we can. First, we create a neighbor solution D' of the current solution D. If $\Delta c = c(G(D')) - c(G(D))$ is negative, i.e., the neighbor solution D' is better, we replace the current solution D; otherwise, we generate a random number $\varepsilon \in (0, 1)$, if $\exp(-\Delta c / T_t) > \varepsilon$, then we replace the current one. When the number of inner iteration reaches q, we cut down the current temperature $T_t = T_t - \Delta T$, where T_t stands for the current temperature. When reaching the termination temperature T_f, the algorithm stops. The pseudo-code of SA-min is outlined in Algorithm 1.

Algorithm 1. SA-min: SA based mining Top-K links

Input: graph $G = (V, E)$, a positive number k, initial temperature T_0, termination temperature T_f, the amount to cut down the current temperature ΔT, the number of inner loop q

Output. the set of Top-K links

1: $T_t = T_0$, $count \leftarrow 0$;

2: Select an initial solution randomly $D \subseteq E$ such that $|D| = k$;

3: **while** $T_t > T_f$ do

4:      compute $c(G(D))$;

5:      $D' = N(D)$; //create a neighbor solution

6:      $count++$;

7:      compute the change of the fitness function $\Delta c = c(G(D')) - c(G(D))$;

8:      **if** $\Delta c < 0$ **then**

9:          $D \leftarrow D'$;

10:    **else**

11:        generate a random number $\varepsilon \in (0, 1)$

12:        if $\exp(-\Delta c / T_t) > \varepsilon$ **then**

13:            $D \leftarrow D'$;

14:    **if** $count > q$ **then**

15:        $T_t = T_t - \Delta T$, $count \leftarrow 0$;

16: **return** D;

Complexity Analysis: The time complexity of the SA-min algorithm is $O(Tn\delta)$, where $T = \frac{T_0 - T_f}{\Delta T} * q$ is the number of iterations, n stands for the number of nodes in the graph, and δ is the maximum time to compute the influence spread of each node. From the above analysis, we can see that SA-min can run $\frac{k|E|}{T}$ times faster than Greedy-min. When $|E|$ and k become bigger, SA-min outperforms Greedy-min significantly.

4.2 ML_CS Algorithm

To compute $c(G(D))$ for any $D \subseteq E$, the existing algorithm usually employs Monte-Carlo simulations. But this algorithm is computationally expensive. We propose an efficient algorithm ML_CS to compute $c(G(D))$ efficiently. When the propagation probability p is small, we estimate the influence spread of one node by only computing its influence on the m-hop area. That is to say, we can estimate average influence spread by computing the activated probability of each node by its j-hop neighbors. Specially, for each $v_i \in V$, let $h_{i,j}$ be the number of j-hop paths ($j \in (1, 2, \ldots, m)$) from some node to v_i. The probability that v_i will be activated is approximated by $1 - \prod_{1 \leq j \leq m} (1 - p^j)^{h_{i,j}}$.

In order to further illustrate the algorithm, we give an example as shown in Fig. 1. We want to compute the activated probability of node v_6. From the graph, we can see the 1-hop paths are $\{(v_1, v_6), (v_2, v_6), (v_3, v_6), (v_5, v_6)\}$, thus the number of $u_{6,1}$ is 4; the

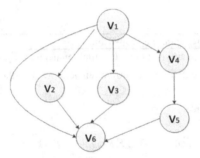

Fig. 1. An example for approximating activated probability

2-hop paths are $\{(v_1, v_2, v_6), (v_1, v_3, v_6), (v_4, v_5, v_6)\}$, thus the number of $u_{6,2}$ is 3; the 3-hop paths is (v_1, v_4, v_5, v_6) thus the number of $u_{6,3}$ is 1. The probability that v_6 will be activated is approximated by $1 - (1 - p)^4 (1 - p^2)^3 (1 - p^3)^1$. When the propagation probability p is small, this approximation is almost same as the real activated probability. The pseudo-code of ML_CS is outlined in Algorithm 2.

Algorithm 2. ML_CS: compute $c(G(D))$

Input: graph $G = (V, E)$, a positive number m, propagation probability p, the current solution $D \subseteq E$;

Output: the contamination degree $c(G(D))$ of the current solution $D \subseteq E$;

1. $Sum = 0$;
2. **for each** $e \in D$ **do**
3. $\quad E \leftarrow E - \{e\}$; // delete e in graph G
4. **end for**
5. **for** $i = 1$ to $|V|$ **do**
6. $\quad f = 1$;
7. $\quad$ **for** $j = 1$ to m **do**
8. $\quad\quad$ **for each** j-hop neighbor u of v_i **do**   // compute the number of j-hop to node v_i
9. $\quad\quad\quad h_{i,j} = h_{i,j} + 1$;
10. $\quad\quad$ **end for**
11. $\quad$ **end for**
12. $\quad$ **for** $j = 1$ to m **do**
13. $\quad\quad f = f * (1 - p^j)^{h_{i,j}}$ //probability that v_i is not activated by its j-hop neighbors.
14. $\quad$ **end for**
15. $\quad Sum = Sum + (1 - f)$; // add up the probability that v_i is activated
16. **end for**
17. $c(G(D)) = Sum / |V|$;
18. **return** $c(G(D))$;

Complexity Analysis: The time complexity of the ML_CS algorithm is $O(nd^m)$, where n is the number of nodes in the graph, d stands for the average out-degree of the network, and m is the number of hops. The time complexity of Monte-Carlo simulation algorithm for computing $c(G(D))$ is $O(nR|E|)$. ML_CS can provide $\frac{R|E|}{d^m}$ speed-up ratio.

5 Experimental Evaluation

We conduct extensive experiments on several real-life and synthetic networks. We compare our SA-min algorithm with two other algorithms from two aspects: (a) its scalability (b) its contamination degree. The first algorithm is Random method, which removes links uniformly at random; the second one is Greedy-min [4], which removes the edges that can minimize the contamination degree greedily.

5.1 Experimental Setup

The first network is obtained from Amazon website [13]. Products stand for nodes. If two products are purchased at the same time, the corresponding graph has a directed edge between them. The raw data contains $n = 262111$ nodes and $m = 1234877$ edges. We extract the first 5000 nodes and their relevant 19110 edges. We denote the subgraph as Amazon-5000. The second network is Who-trust-whom network of Epinions.com [14]. Users in the network can show their trust to other users. If user i trust user j, there is a directed edge in the corresponding graph. The raw data includes $n = 75879$ nodes and $m = 508837$ edges. We extract the first 100 nodes and 2172 edges that connected to the nodes. We denote the subgraph as Epinions-100. We compare our algorithm with Random and Greedy-min on these two networks. In order to compare the scalability of different algorithms, we also extract $n = 2000$ nodes, $m = 8145$ edges; $n = 5000$ nodes, $m = 20426$ edges; $n = 10000$ nodes, $m = 41760$ edges; $n = 20000$ nodes, $m = 85535$ edges on Amazon dataset.

We employ ML_CS algorithm to compute the influence spread in both SA-min and Greedy-min. This is because that if we use Monte-Carlo simulations in Greedy-min, the running time of Greedy-min exceeds 6 h even in a graph with 100 nodes. For SA-min algorithm, we set $T_0 = 100000$, $T_f = 10000$.

5.2 Experimental Results

(1) varying the propagation probability p

In Fig. 2, we compare the contamination degree when p changes. From the tendency of curve, we can see that when the propagation probability increases, the contamination degree increases as well. SA-min can provide the matching result with Greedy-min. When p is 0.25, the contamination degree of SA-min is about 8.25% smaller than that of Random.

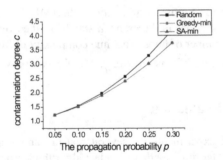

Fig. 2. Contamination degree of SA-min compared with Random and Greedy-min when k = 50 on Amazon-500.

(2) varying the value of k

In the following experiments, we conduct experiments on Amazon-500 and Epinions-100 respectively. We compare the contamination degree when blocking different number of links with $p = 0.3$ on two graphs. From Fig. 3(a) and (c), we can see that SA-min can run close to the result of Greedy-min in terms of contamination degree. In Fig. 3(a), when blocking 60 links, the contamination degree of SA-min is 4.0302, the result of Greedy-min is 4.0313. SA-min outperforms Greedy-min by 0.27%. In Fig. 3(a), when k is 70, the contamination degree of SA-min and Greedy-min is 3.9855 and 3.9864 respectively. SA-min outperforms Greedy-min by 0.23%. SA-min can exceed Random by about 9.3% when k is 70. Hence, we can conclude that SA-min is very effective. From Fig. 3(b) and (d), we can see that when the number of blocking edges becomes large, the running time of Greedy-min is linear growth. At the same time, the running time of SA-min decreases. In Fig. 3(b), when k is 70, SA-min runs 3.8 times faster than Greedy-min. Moreover, SA-min is more stable when removing more links compared with Greedy-min.

(3) varying the value of ΔT

In the following experiments, we compare the contamination degree when ΔT changes on Amazon-500 with $p = 0.3$, $k = 50$, as shown in Fig. 4. When ΔT becomes larger, the number of iteration decreases, so the contamination degree becomes bigger. When ΔT is 400, SA-min outperforms Greedy-min by 0.18% in terms of contamination degree. From the tendency of the graph, when the iteration number is large enough, SA-min can converge to the optimum.

(4) varying the number of nodes

We compare the contamination degree when the number of nodes increases with $p = 0.3$, $k = 50$. From Fig. 5(a), SA-min can achieve the matching result with Greedy-min in contamination degree. In Fig. 5(b), when n is 10000 and m is 41760, the running time of SA-min and Greedy-min is about 30 min and 12 h respectively. Thus SA-min runs 24 times faster than Greedy-min. We can see that SA-min is more scalable to large graph than Greedy-min.

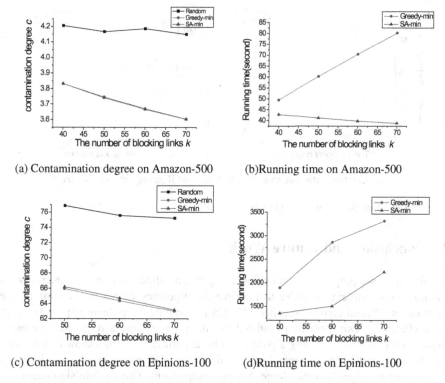

(a) Contamination degree on Amazon-500   (b)Running time on Amazon-500

(c) Contamination degree on Epinions-100   (d)Running time on Epinions-100

Fig. 3. SA-min vs. Random and Greedy-min with $p = 0.3$

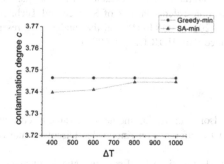

Fig. 4. Contamination degree of SA-min and Greedy-min with $p = 0.3$ and $k = 50$ on Amazon-500

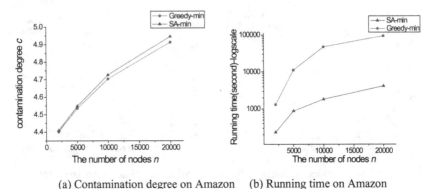

(a) Contamination degree on Amazon   (b) Running time on Amazon

Fig. 5. SA-min vs. Greedy-min with $p = 0.3$, $k = 50$ on Amazon

6   Conclusion and Future Work

In this paper, we propose a novel efficient algorithm called SA-min for contamination minimization problem. In order to improve the efficiency of SA-min algorithm, we propose an efficient algorithm called ML_CS to compute the influence spread of each node efficiently. Our algorithm both reduces the running time and the contamination degree compared with existing algorithms. Our experimental results show that SA-min can achieve a better performance both in efficiency and effectiveness. Especially when the number of edges becomes large, SA-min outperforms Greedy-min significantly.

Acknowledgments. This work was supported by the National Natural Science Foundation of China (No. 61602159), the Natural Science Foundation of Heilongjiang Province (No. F201430, No. F2015013), the Innovation Talents Project of Science and Technology Bureau of Harbin (No. 2017RAQXJ094, No. 2015RAQXJ004), and the fundamental research funds of universities in Heilongjiang Province (No. HDJCCX-201608).

References

1. Domingos, P., Richardson, M.: Mining the network value of customers. In: Proceedings of the 7th ACM SIGKDD Conference on Knowledge Discovery and Data Mining, pp. 57–66 (2001)
2. Albert, R., Jeong, H., Barabási, A.L.: Error and attack tolerance of complex networks. Nature **406**(6794), 378–382 (2000)
3. Callaway, D.S., Newman, M.E.J., Strogatz, S.H., et al.: Network robustness and fragility: percolation on random graphs. Phys. Rev. Lett. **85**(25), 5468 (2000)
4. Kimura, M., Saito, K., Motoda, H.: Minimizing the spread of contamination by blocking links in a network. In: Proceedings of the 23rd National Conference on Artificial Intelligence, pp. 1175–1180 (2008)
5. Kempe, D., Kleinberg, J.M., Tardos, É.: Maximizing the spread of influence through a social network. In: Proceedings of the 9th ACM SIGKDD Conference on Knowledge Discovery and Data Mining, pp. 137–146 (2003)

6. Leskovec, J., Krause, A., Guestrin, C., Faloutsos, C., VanBriesen, J., Glance, N.S.: Cost-effective outbreak detection in networks. In Proceedings of the 13th ACM SIGKDD Conference on Knowledge Discovery and Data Mining, pp. 420–429 (2007)

7. Chen, W., Wang, Y., Yang, S.: Efficient influence maximization in social networks. In: Proceedings of the 15th ACM SIGKDD Conference on Knowledge Discovery and Data Mining (2009)

8. Jiang, Q., Song, G., Cong, G., Wang, Y., Si, W., Xie, K.: Simulated Annealing based influence maximization in social networks. In: AAAI (2011)

9. Tang, Y., Xiao, X., Shi, Y.: Influence Maximization Near-Optimal Time Complexity Meets Practical Efficiency. In: Proceedings of the 2015 ACM SIGMOD/PODS Conference, pp. 796–805 (2014)

10. Lin, S.C., Lin, S.D., Chen, M.S.: A learning-based framework to handle multi-round multi-party influence maximization on social networks. In: Proceedings of the 21st ACM SIGKDD Conference on Knowledge Discovery and Data Mining, pp. 410–419 (2015)

11. Metropolis, N., Rosenbluth, A.W., Rosenbluth, M.N., et al.: Equation of state calculations by fast computing machines. J. Chem. Phys. **21**(6), 1087–1092 (1953)

12. Mitra, D.; Romeo, F.; Vincentelli, A.S.. Convergence and finite-time behavior of simulated Annealing. In: Proceeding of 24th Conference on Decision and Control, pp. 761–767 (1985)

13. Leskovec, J., Adamic, L., Adamic, B.: The dynamics of viral marketing. ACM Trans. Web **1** (1), 39 (2007)

Author Index

Bian, Yixiong   86

Cai, Qingsong   234
Cao, Shaozhong   3
Chen, Wenping   44
Chen, Zhikui   55
Cheng, En   201
Cheng, Zhen   127

Dang, Xiaochao   175
Dawei, Sun   211
Deng, Yu   201
Ding, Zhongxiang   3
Dong, Wenyong   155
Dong, Xueshi   155
Du, Junzhao   139

Feng, Guangsheng   296
Fengyun, Li   211

Guo, Zhongwen   165

Han, Yulong   67
Han, Zhe   333
Hao, Zhanjun   175
He, Wei   222
Hei, Yili   175
Hu, Shunren   222
Hu, Xiaoyan   307
Hu, Yueming   55
Huang, Hai-ping   86
Huangfu, Wei   307

Ji, Guangrong   22
Jiang, Xiaoxiao   222
Jing, Wei   22
Junchao, Xue   211

Kuang, Wenxin   247

Leng, Yonglin   55
Li, Deying   44
Li, Peng   55
Li, Qiucen   55

Li, Shuang   222
Li, Xian   67
Li, Ye   201
Li, Yinglong   33
Lin, Junyu   296
Lin, Yaguang   273, 285
Liu, Gang   262
Liu, Haoran   12
Liu, Hui   139
Liu, Jing   165
Liu, Jizhao   191
Liu, Shiyong   22, 165
Liu, Sicong   139
Liu, Wei   222
Liu, Yong   333
Lv, Hongwu   296
Lv, Mingqi   33

Ma, Qing   74
Muhammad, Sohail   319

Nan, Kaiming   139

Pan, Gen-mei   127
Pan, Heng   191
Pan, Mengjiao   234
Pengcheng, Wang   117

Qin, Peng   262
Qin, Xueyang   273
Qu, Guoliang   74

Sha, Dan   86
Shi, Jiahao   67
Shi, Shengshu   333
Song, Guozhi   74
Su, Dongdong   296
Sun, Zhongwei   165

Tang, Qiuling   67
Tang, Xiong   86
Tao, Lin   117
Tian, Ying   22

Wang, Huiqiang 296
Wang, Liang 273
Wang, Liangmin 319
Wang, Xi 22
Wang, Xiaoming 273, 285
Wang, Xin 139
Wang, Xinyan 285
Wang, Xupeng 165
Wang, Yufeng 155
Wei, Yuheng 139
Wu, Min 86

Xia, Fumin 296
Xu, Xing-Ze 127
Xu, Yinhan 12
Xu, Zhenqiang 262
Xuan, Ping 333

Yamin, Bushra 319
Yanfang, Gao 211
Yang, Weidong 262

Yang, Yanhong 3
Yi, Jinwang 201
Yin, Rongrong 12
Yin, Xueliang 12
Yu, Bin 103
Yuan, Chi 44
Yuan, Fei 201
Yuan, Li-yong 127

Zhang, Hong 307
Zhang, Junbao 191
Zhang, Lichen 273, 285
Zhang, Qian 191
Zhang, Wei 333
Zhang, Xin 74
Zhao, Ming 247
Zhao, Ruonan 285
Zheng, Qiusheng 191
Zhou, Weiwei 103
Zhu, Yi-hua 127

Printed in the United States
By Bookmasters